Robert Gordon Univer:
University Library

Functional Representation and Democracy in the EU

The European Commission and Social NGOs

Corinna Wolff

WITHDRAWN FROM
THE ROBERT GORDON UNIVERSITY
LIBRARIES

THE ROBERT GORDON UNIVERSITY

0060033520

© Corinna Wolff 2013

First published by the ECPR Press in 2013

The ECPR Press is the publishing imprint of the European Consortium for Political Research
(ECPR), a scholarly association, which supports and encourages the training, research and
cross-national co-operation of political scientists in institutions throughout Europe and beyond.

ECPR Press
University of Essex
Wivenhoe Park
Colchester
CO4 3SQ
UK

All rights reserved. No part of this book may be reprinted or reproduced or utilised in any form
or by any electronic, mechanical, or other means, now known or hereafter invented, including
photocopying and recording, or in any information storage or retrieval system, without
permission in writing from the publishers.

Typeset by Anvi

Printed and bound by Lightning Source

British Library Cataloguing in Publication Data

A catalogue record for this book is available from the British Library

ISBN: 978-1-907-301-65-0

www.ecpr.eu/ecprpress

ECPR – Monographs
Series Editors:
Dario Castiglione (University of Exeter)
Peter Kennealy (European University Institute)
Alexandra Segerberg (Stockholm University)
Peter Triantafillou (Roskilde University)

Other books available in this series
Agents or Bosses? (ISBN: 9781907301261) Ozge Kemahlioglu
Causes of War: The Struggle for Recognition (ISBN: 9781907301018)
Thomas Lindemann

Citizenship: The History of an Idea (ISBN: 9780954796655) Paul Magnette

*Coercing, Constraining and Signalling: Explaining UN and EU Sanctions After
the Cold War* (ISBN: 9781907301209) Francesco Giumelli

Constraints On Party Policy Change (ISBN: 9781907301490) Thomas M.
Meyer

Contesting Europe. Exploring Euroscepticism in Online Media Coverage (ISBN:
9781907301513) Pieter de Wilde, Asimina Michailidou and Hans-Jörg Trenz

*Deliberation Behind Closed Doors: Transparency and Lobbying in the European
Union* (ISBN: 9780955248849) Daniel Naurin

Democratic Institutions and Authoritarian Rule in Southeast Europe
(ISBN: 9781907301438) Danijela Dolenec

*Economic Knowledge in Regulation: The Use of Expertise by Independent
Agencies* (ISBN: 9781907301452) Lorna S. Schrefler

*European Integration and its Limits: Intergovernmental Conflicts and their
Domestic Origins* (ISBN: 9780955820373) Daniel Finke

Gender and Vote in Britain: Beyond the Gender Gap? (ISBN: 9780954796693)
Rosie Campbell

Greece in the Euro: Economic Delinquency or System Failure?
(ISBN: 9781907301537) Eleni Panagiotarea

Globalisation: An Overview (ISBN: 9780955248825) Danilo Zolo

*Joining Political Organisations: Institutions, Mobilisation and Participation in
Western Democracies* (ISBN: 9780955248894) Laura Morales

Paying for Democracy: Political Finance and State Funding for Parties
(ISBN: 9780954796631) Kevin Casas-Zamora

*Policy Making In Multilevel Systems: Federalism, Decentralisation, and
Performance in the OECD Countries* (ISBN: 9781907301339) Jan Biela, Annika
Hennl and Andre Kaiser

*Political Conflict and Political Preferences: Communicative Interaction Between
Facts, Norms and Interests* (ISBN: 9780955820304) Claudia Landwehr

Political Parties and Interest Groups in Norway (ISBN: 9780955820366)
Elin Haugsgjerd Allern

Regulation in Practice: The de facto Independence of Regulatory Agencies
(ISBN: 9781907301285) Martino Maggetti

Representing Women?: Female Legislators in West European Parliaments
(ISBN: 9780954796648) Mercedes Mateo Diaz

The Nordic Voter: Myths of Exceptionalism (ISBN: 9781907301506) Åsa
Bengtsson, Kasper M. Hansen, Ólafur Þ. Harðarson, Hanne Marthe Narud and
Henrik Oscarsson

The Personalisation of Politics: A Study of Parliamentary Democracies
(ISBN: 9781907301032) Lauri Karvonen

The Politics of Income Taxation: A Comparative Analysis
(ISBN: 9780954796686) Steffen Ganghof

*The Return of the State of War: A Theoretical Analysis of Operation Iraqi
Freedom* (ISBN: 9780955248856) Dario Battistella

*Transnational Policy Innovation: The role of the OECD in the Diffusion of
Regulatory Impact Analysis* (ISBN:9781907301254) Fabrizio De Francesco

*Urban Foreign Policy and Domestic Dilemmas: Insights from Swiss and EU
City-regions* (ISBN: 9781907301070) Nico van der Heiden

*Why Aren't They There? The Political Representation of Women, Ethnic Groups
and Issue Positions In Legislatures* (ISBN: 9780955820397) Didier Ruedin

*Widen the Market, Narrow the Competition: Banker Interests and the Making of
a European Capital Market* (ISBN: 9781907301087) Daniel Mügge

Please visit www.ecpr.eu/ecprpress for information about new publications.

Contents

List of Figures and Tables

Acknowledgements

This is an enquiry into functional representation in the European Union, into how it is hoped to make European governance more democratic, and what kind of democracy results from the ways in which the involvement of functional representatives is conceptualised by those organising it in practice. The book grew out of my frustration with the apparent difficulty of producing justified, precise, and generalisable criteria to determine whose participation would render policy making more democratic in a given case, how exactly it would do so, and how this could be evaluated in any concrete situation. Functional representation helps in establishing such criteria by connecting the sphere of 'participation' to the formal decision-making system and, especially, by connecting the participants to the constituents of the polity. It is therefore particularly useful for making sense of the messy tangle of governance and democracy in the EU's multi-level system.[1]

I am grateful to my interviewees at the European Commission and the European Anti-Poverty Network for giving me their time and their thoughts. The criticism presented in this book is not addressed to any individuals, but to their institution and to the structures that incentivise it to act in particular ways.

Professor Heikki Paloheimo at the University of Tampere, Finland, acted as my supervisor in writing the Ph.D. thesis upon which this book is based; I would like to thank him for his support and professional guidance as well as for the privilege to benefit from his robust academic experience. I extend my thanks to Professor Tapio Raunio for suggesting that new modes of governance were worth looking at if one was interested in EU governance and democracy. He also provided me with informed and extremely to-the-point advice along the way. For constructive and helpful comments and discussions at different stages of my work I am grateful to the participants of the 9th and 10th meetings of the European Civil Society Ph.D. Network in Leuven and Heidelberg, respectively; of the Political Science Research Seminar at the University of Tampere; and of several seminars organised by the Finnish National Graduate School of Political Studies, Politu. I would also like to thank all my colleagues at the University of Tampere for their fellowship and support. Finally, I feel greatly indebted to Helena Rytövuori-Apunen and Osmo Apunen for their support and friendship over the years. It has been very reassuring to be able to rely on their experience of academic life.

Professor Susana Borrás and Professor Martin Rhodes pre-examined my Ph.D. manuscript and approved it for the public defence; their comments helped me to clear my thoughts in the finalising stage. I am especially indebted to Professor Rhodes for acting as my discussant in the defence.

---

1. For easier reading, I have referenced most of the numerous primary sources as footnotes. These are mainly Internet documents that are only referred to once and that in most cases are no longer available online. Printed primary sources and those that are cited several times are referenced in the Bibliography.

On the technical side, I am grateful to Riitta Lehtimäki for her friendly handling of all administrative matters, to the Tampere University Library for buying all the books I asked for over the years, and to Virginia Mattila for taking a look at my English. Special thanks go to Dario Castiglione and Laura Pugh and everyone at the ECPR Press for the pleasant collaboration.

This research was funded by Politu, the Finnish National Graduate School of Political Studies. I highly appreciate the privilege of having been able to concentrate on my research, to study and think through one thing properly.

For having had the energy to do so, I deeply thank all the special people in my life. I am grateful to my friends for being there, each in their own individual way, and for all the things we have been sharing. Especially heartfelt thanks go to my parents for their moral and practical support over the years as well as their imperturbable trust that everything would work out.

Finally, very special thanks to Georges de Brito for accompanying me through the ups and downs of the entire work process and for taking me to altitudes where even mountainous reliefs become just part of the landscape on the way to entirely different destinations.

Corinna Wolff
Norderstedt, Germany – October 2013

Chapter One

Introduction

The idea that policy-making processes are more democratic if civil society or those especially affected by a decision are involved in the process is a familiar one. Yet, the closer one looks at the issue, the more questions arise: Who exactly should be involved and who ought to make this choice, on the basis of which criteria? In what processes should the concerned actors be involved, and to do what? What should the relationship be like between those who participate and those who do not? Who should be accountable for which parts of the process, to whom, and by what procedures? In which sense exactly can this involvement be democratic, if many of the actors are unelected officers from civil society organisations (CSOs) or business agents? How do we assess the legitimacy of participants speaking for informal movements or EU-level umbrella organisations without individual supporters? There is no single or obvious answer to these questions, and hence no certainty that any specific way of involving affected citizens necessarily makes the political process in question more democratic.

This book tackles these questions in two ways. First, it develops a conceptual framework to analyse issues of participation and democracy in a systematic way by conceptualising participation as functional representation, i.e. the representation of functional groups. So far, it has been difficult to find reliable theoretical foundations to examine the roles of third actors (non-governmental organisations (NGOs), social partners, interest groups, experts, movements, etc.) in governance from the perspective of democratic legitimacy. The legitimacy of different kinds of unelected or informal participants has been particularly challenging to evaluate. However, recently, theories of representation have advanced remarkably and now provide powerful tools to deal with such processes. Understanding the involvement of affected actors as representation does not as such answer questions such as those above, but it provides the concepts to analyse them on the basis of reliable theoretical starting points and with little a priori assumptions about the actors in question. It also helps in integrating examinations of 'participation' and of territorial representation into a view of the democratic process as a whole. The first part of the book introduces the relevant developments in theories of representation and shows how they can be applied to evaluate the democratic legitimacy of complex governance settings involving representatives who may be unelected or who may speak for ill-defined constituencies.

Second, this approach is applied to a concrete case – EU social policy – in order to tackle some of the real-life issues involved in making governance more democratic through functional representation. This part of the book starts from the notion that it is political actors who introduce and design processes of functional representation on the basis of their ideas, ideals, world views, and – not least – interests. Looking at their concepts can therefore explain or at least illuminate how these processes work in practice. Put differently, how the involvement of affected groups is meant to function in the perspective of those who organise it determines to an important extent what may be expected of this involvement in terms of democratic legitimacy. Hence, the case study in the latter part of this book introduces the political dimension by examining a concrete process in the light of institutional interests and political strategy. It analyses the European Commission's model of involving affected groups in European social policies, with the help of theories of functional representation, and evaluates the democratic credentials of this model, including the questions posed above.

EU social policies are implemented through the Open Method of Coordination (OMC) in social protection and social inclusion (the so-called social OMC). The social OMC is a case of new modes of governance (NMGs), which are typically meant to work through the inclusion of civil society (i.e. the affected), a multi-level structure, decentralisation, a deliberative policy-making style, soft law, and the aim to learn from each other (Scott and Trubek 2002: 5–6; Radaelli 2003: 24–6). As such, it is still a rather young institutional environment, for which it is not yet very clear how democracy should be realised. However, involving the affected is generally seen as the most important way in which the OMC can be made democratic. The practices of such involvement are significantly shaped by the Commission's Directorate General (DG) Employment, which coordinates the process. Hence, I enquire into precisely how they envisage the role of the affected in the social OMC. How is their involvement seen to generate legitimacy, and what kind of legitimacy? What concept of democracy is informing these notions? The model they lay out in their public text is their presentation of how the inclusion of third actors should be conceptualised and carried out in order to contribute to the legitimacy of the policy-making process; i.e. the DG advances here a certain set of values that governance in the OMC should be based on. Such a vision by a pivotal institution can be expected to influence the further evolution of the social OMC, all the more so as DG Employment also strongly controls the access of third parties to the OMC in practice.

Moreover, the DG's vision should also be seen from a strategic point of view. For the Commission, the OMC is also an instrument to Europeanise social policies, which in turn means that they have an interest in establishing a concept of legitimate policy making that supports their own role in the process. In the absence of a mandate to impose policies and of any strong parliamentary legitimation, the involvement of the affected is the most promising basis on which to claim legitimacy for political initiatives. The notion that 'civil society participation' makes policy making more legitimate is widely accepted and has not least been promoted by the Commission itself, but there is no clear model for how it should be organised in the OMC. Hence, the DG has an incentive to build on this existing general acceptance to advance a concept of democratic legitimacy that is strongly built on involving those especially affected in the policy-making process *in such a way* as suits the DG's needs. Put differently, DG Employment justifies their initiatives with the argument that in preparing them, especially affected groups have been involved; this implies arguing that involving such-and-such groups in such-and-such ways generates legitimacy, i.e. promoting a particular model of democratic participation. Such normative concepts shaped by political actors with institutional interests deserve careful analysis on the basis of normative democratic theory in order to hold up the authority of the latter 'to defend ambitious notions of democratic legitimacy' (Borrás and Conzelmann 2007: 546; cf. e.g. Kröger 2009) against an increasing tendency of 'democratic pragmatism' (Usui 2007: 628, using a term from Dryzek 1997: 84–101). Publicly promoted notions about how legitimate governance should be organised influence not only evolving practices, but also how democratic governance in general is understood in a society.

However, despite recognition of the central role that political discourse plays in the OMC, despite awareness of problems with democratic legitimacy in the OMC, despite the huge potential seen in the involvement of the affected in tackling these problems, and despite the fact that the Commission is known to be the hub of this involvement at EU level, the Commission's vision of how this should be done has so far not been examined in detail. Therefore, this study provides a close, material-rich rhetorical analysis of the model the Commission presents for the role that the especially affected should play in the OMC's EU-level policy making. Drawing on the texts published by DG Employment during the period of 2000–10, I analyse how the involvement of the affected should in their view be organised, how exactly democratic legitimacy is meant to follow from this, and more precisely what kind of legitimacy this is thought to be.

This chapter introduces the main concepts and issues the book builds on, *viz.* functional representation, a working definition of democracy, EU governance and so-called new modes of governance, such as the Open Method of Coordination, as well as the rationale of analysing political actors' publicly advanced ideas about legitimate governance.

Functional representation

The concept of functional representation is based on the dichotomy of functional and territorial representation. While in the latter, citizens are represented according to the territorial constituency they live in (a city, region, state, etc.), functional representation means the representation of groups that share a functional characteristic. For example, trade unions represent employees, child protection agencies represent children, and associations of every sort and kind represent people owning dogs, riding bikes, suffering from a specific disease, or concerned by the pollution of the oceans, for example. To somewhat simplify this variety for the purposes of this study, I use the shorthand definition of functional constituencies as those especially *affected* by some issues or policies. Involving representatives of such groups – i.e. functional representatives – in policy making thus rests on the recognition that out of everyone living within a political system, some are more affected than others by a particular piece of legislation, and should thus be given additional, specific representation.

Most polities rest on both territorial and functional representation. Territory defines national states,[1] their subunits, and associations such as the EU, and the territorial representative system is the backbone of their political systems. However, citizens have always been represented functionally as well, mostly in less institutionalised and formal structures. Together, these modes of representation form two pillars of one system of 'composite representation' (Benz 1998, quoted by Hüller and Kohler-Koch 2008: 168; cf. Schmitter 2007: 20–1 (n. xvii); Saward 2009: 7–8; Lord and Pollak 2010) that are both needed for democratic governance and that both need each other.

The territorial system of representation for its part is above all based on elections, which are rather 'information-poor' (Warren 2009: 6), unspecific, and designed to represent mainly territorial constituencies (Urbinati and Warren 2008: 402–4). Moreover, legislatures lack not only expertise about many of the issues they decide on, but also increasingly the capacities to represent more and more diverse societies on their own (Warren 2009: 6–7; Smismans 2004: 12–16; Urbinati and Warren 2008: 390). In the particular case of the European Commission, the necessity for functional representation is amplified even more by the lack of parliamentary control in certain policy fields (such as the social OMC), low administrative resources, and the strategic needs of their position *vis-à-vis* the European Parliament and the Member States. At the same time, people organise less in political parties and more in functional associations and ad hoc organisations or movements, and demand to be heard through these structures as well (Rosanvallon 2008: 25; Warren 2009: 7; Schmitter 2001). One just needs to imagine a parliament deliberating exclusively within itself and adopting legislation without consulting any societal groups to realise how essentially practices of functional representation are part and parcel of today's political cultures and perceptions of what is legitimate policy making.[2] Nevertheless, it is worth noting that functional representation is not automatically democratic representation. Democratic theory is only at the beginning of finding ways to conceptualise and assess the contributions to democracy that different forms of functional representation can make (Urbinati and Warren 2008: 404).

Conversely, functional representation cannot function without territorial foundations either. For one thing, it is impossible to use the functional principle as the primary means of delineating constituencies. Not only is it in most cases very difficult to define the affected unambiguously (cf. Hilson 2006: 64, 71; Abromeit 1998: 113), but this would also mean changing constituencies for every decision, thus changing the rights of individual persons from one decision to the next. Hence, in a purely functional system, citizenship itself would be unstable. This conflicts with the guarantee of democratic rights, which should belong equally

---

1. *See* Ruggie 1993 for the development of the modern territorial state.
2. This is true even for societies in which practices of consultation and cooperation are not strong parts of democratic traditions. Regarding the example of France, *see* Saurugger 2007, and Schmidt 2006.

and permanently to all citizens. 'The protection of democratic rights', Michael Saward concludes, 'depends on secure and equal membership in a given unit. Membership is only secure, because the grounds of citizenship and rightful political participation can only be clear, in a territorial entity' (Saward 2000: 38). On top of that, defining the proper constituency for an issue is itself a decision that has to be taken.[3] Applying the functional principle to this meta-decision leads us to a 'regression from which no procedural escape is possible' (Whelan 1983: 19), and which therefore forces us back to a geographically bounded territory.[4] In addition to this negative reasoning, territorial representation is also necessary because territory defines the scope of the validity of political rules, including those arrived at through functional representation. Hence, ultimately, all those living under the rules are affected by them, at least potentially or in the sense that the rules shape the society they live in. The logic of different degrees of affectedness can therefore only be an addition to territorial citizenship, not an alternative. Lastly, it is only the territorial representatives who can coordinate the functional sectors, determine the overall direction of politics, and set down the rules of the game. It is the territorial tier of representation that can create and shape a common world to live in (Rosanvallon 2008: 27–9)[5] (*see* Chapter Two and the Conclusions section of Chapter Four). This is why, although the involvement of functional actors has increased enormously, it is in most cases still the parliaments that take the final, formal decision, and are also accountable for the processes leading up to that decision, including the role of functional representatives. The problem is that, in practice, parliamentarians often have no means to effectively control the processes they are formally accountable for.

Hence, the question is not which of the two modes of representation is 'better', but how both should be combined to best complement each other. While territorial representation forms the basis of legitimate representation, adequately using functional representation can increase the legitimacy of the territorial tier and therefore the polity at large (Saward 2000: 45). In some cases, such as the EU's Treaty of Lisbon,[6] the consultation of the affected is in fact prescribed by constitutional law. It is also important to keep in mind that political representation is much more than elections – important though these are. As Chris Hilson points out, beyond voting and other formal mechanisms of the territorial tier of

---

3. Moreover, the delimitation of functional constituencies depends decisively on the definition of the issue itself. It is thus an inherently political decision and should therefore be nested in a system of equal representation.

4. Of course, the question of how to define territorial borders democratically equally leads to impasses (Whelan 1983: 22–4; Dahl 1989: 193–209). Because, in this study, I deal with functional representation in the EU, I take its territory as given.

5. Cf. Immergut 1995: 202; Andersen and Burns 1996: 243–9. *See also* F. R. Ankersmit's criticism of 'brainless networks' (Ankersmit 2002: 184–6).

6. 'The European Commission shall carry out broad consultations with parties concerned in order to ensure that the Union's actions are coherent and transparent' (Treaty on European Union, Article 11(3) (under 'Provisions on democratic principles')).

representation, there are vital parts of the democratic process in which active citizens can play a key part (Hilson 2006: 66; cf. Ch. 2).

There is a vast literature about functional representation under the names of, amongst others, (civil society) participation, interest representation, and lobbying. However, the concept of functional representation is fitter, in particular for normative analyses from the perspective of democracy. First of all, the practices referred to are de facto instances of representation. The individuals involved in governance processes are not involved qua individuals, but because they speak for a group that is meant to be involved. Their legitimacy as political actors is based on them speaking for others, not for themselves. Moreover, when the intention is to involve a particular group, those speaking in the name of that group need not themselves be its members, and often they are indeed not. An association of the blind can be represented by a seeing person, and the representative of an association of small and medium enterprises (SMEs) need not own or work for an enterprise herself. Yet, even if she does, while she sits at the table of some governance arrangement that 'involves SMEs', she speaks for a larger group of people who are not present themselves. This group can only be said to be 'involved' or to 'participate' by being represented.

Secondly, as an analytical concept, functional representation has advantages over other more frequently used notions, such as 'participation', 'civil society', or 'lobbying'.

'Participation' is a tricky concept because of its application to both individuals and groups.[7] Its use frequently evokes the participation of individual citizens in a kind of grassroots democracy, when the actual case under discussion is in fact about group participation (cf. Smismans 2003: 494; Scharpf 1999: 7), i.e. the representation of groups, where the vast majority of group members mostly do not participate actively (Warren 2009: 10; Kohler-Koch 2007: 265). More to the point, the concept of 'participation' does not contain tools to answer the question of who should participate in what way in a given process, and what should be the relation between those who participate and those who do not.

Those involved in governance processes are also often referred to as actors from the 'civil society'. This concept has indeed considerable common ground with functional representation. However, there are two crucial differences. For one thing, civil society is usually defined as comprising actors outside both the state (the political sphere) and the economic sphere. A functional group, by contrast, is defined by being affected by a specific issue under consideration, which includes no formal criteria about what functions might or might not be included. Functional representatives can thus also represent economic or public actors like local administrations, i.e. the scope of possible participants is much wider. For another thing, civil society is mostly assumed to be 'civil' in the sense of non-

---

7. Michael T. Greven (2007) traces the recent conceptual history of 'participation' and illustrates the shift from the level of the individual citizen and the meanings of emancipation and politicisation in the 1960s and 1970s, to today's application to the group level.

violence and tolerance, to differentiate between desired and illegitimate structures such as mafia organisations (Thiery 2005: 1175; Ehrenberg 1999; Keane 2003: 9–10, 12–13). In the same vein, the notion of 'civil society' frequently implies a distinction between 'good' civil society and 'bad' producers or lobbyists. Both 'participation' and 'civil society' are often supposed to be democratic as such. 'Functional representation' makes no such assumption. By taking affectedness as the starting point, it does not require actors to act in the public interest, nor does it imply that certain types of actors were doing so or otherwise by definition (cf. Richardson 2007: 272; Smismans 2006: 16). Instead, it is compatible with many different conceptualisations of democracy and takes the realisation of democratic legitimacy as an empirical question. Furthermore, because of the positive connotations implied in 'civil society' and 'participation', official governance discourses are often built on these concepts. Since this study analyses one such discourse, the more neutral concept of functional representation also helps to avoid taking over the official language and the ideas transported by it.

Finally, the involvement of third actors in policy making is often analysed as 'lobbying', which tends to evoke 'very broad, opaque, and largely unregulated' activities (Smismans 2004: 39), as opposed to more formal and more legitimate forms of representation. However, lobbying can also be done via institutionalised structures. If lobbying is defined as the organised promotion of the interests of an organisation or group, in which the lobbyist takes the initiative in contacting the officials,[8] this does not restrict the forums through which that activity might be exercised. If the intention is to involve the affected in policy making, being affected will in most cases mean having an interest in the matter at hand, which is indeed one important reason for being included. Governance actors are thus expected both by their constituencies and by officials to articulate those interests in the respective forum. The borderline with more informal (and maybe illegitimate) attempts to influence other members of that forum on the fringes of their official activities is fluid. Consequently, whether an activity is described as 'lobbying' often depends on the attitude of the speaker, although there are signs that the pejorative connotations of 'lobbying' might be decreasing. Writers inclined to see a positive role for functional representatives within a larger frame of democratic governance tend to use the term synonymously with 'interest group participation', 'interest representation', and 'functional representation', thus referring to one aspect among others of the policy-making process's input side.[9]

In contrast to all these concepts, functional representation puts the focus on the relationship between those concretely participating in policy-making processes and those they speak for. It therefore opens up more possibilities to analyse governance systematically from a normative-democratic perspective. Recently,

---

8. I thank Heikki Paloheimo for providing me with this definition.

9. *See*, for example, Ruzza 2004: 6–7. Goodin (2003a: 384–6) defines lobbying as an essential function within democratic political systems. Andersen and Burns (1996: 234–5) equate lobbying and the 'principle that directly affected parties have a right to participate in and influence policy- and law-making'. For a perspective with a focus on political representation, *see* Whelan 1983: 20.

this has been increasingly realised,[10] in particular in the context of the European Union, where some have observed a 'representative turn' (Bellamy and Kröger 2011: 1). Yet, so far this literature has not engaged too much in detailed empirical studies (cf. Kröger and Friedrich 2012: 4).

Notwithstanding, functional representation is not a new concept, and in spite of its conceptual openness as such, there exist different models, which are informed by different concepts of democracy and representation. Out of the several branches of its conceptual history,[11] it is worth taking a short look at its intellectual roots in early British pluralism[12] (cf. Navari 1995), particularly at G. D. H. Cole's guild socialism and David Mitrany's functionalism. The starting points of these theories continue to be relevant for many of today's conceptualisations of governance; moreover, they are especially pertinent to the present study since both start from a concern for democratic representation and deep doubts about the capacities of (territorial) parliaments to meaningfully and democratically represent increasingly diverse and complex societies.

For George Douglas Howard Cole (1889–1959), representation based on 'mere numbers of people' cannot be democratic because of its abstraction (Cole 1950: 93; Cole (no date), cited in Houseman 1979: 61). Since every individual has a unique variety of interests, associations, and specific preferences related to her particular fields of life, it is not only impossible for a parliament to represent the electorate in all its aspects, but the representation of anyone *as a person* is impossible, because no MP or party can ever be representative of her views on each single issue (Cole 1920: 103–6; 1950: 99). 'All true and democratic representation is therefore *functional* representation' (Cole [1920] 1980: 33), in such a way that every citizen is represented by a different functional representative in relation to each of the areas she is engaged in. Moreover, since humans naturally form functional associations (Cole 1950: esp. 95, 101) and are by nature adapted to live in small communities, where they have 'the chance to count as an individual and to do something that is distinctively [their] own' (Cole 1950: 99), real democracy takes place in such small functional units whose members know each other personally. It is a 'fundamental exercise [...] of free creative activity' (Cole 1950: 97) and means deciding collectively on things related to one's own experience. It is not simple majoritarianism, but close and constant consultation and working together for a shared purpose that gives everybody the chance (and expects everybody) to play an active part. All spheres of society should therefore be decentralised

---

10. *See* Smismans 2003, 2004; Saward 2005, 2006, 2010; Castiglione and Warren 2006; Saurugger 2006; Kröger 2007; Hüller and Kohler-Koch 2008; Trenz 2009; Warren 2009; Kohler-Koch 2010a; Lord and Pollak 2010; Bellamy and Castiglione 2011; Bellamy *et al.* 2011; the contributions in *Journal of European Integration* 33(4); Kröger and Friedrich (eds) 2012.

11. Other traditions of thoughts informing concepts of functional representation are Catholic thought (cf. Leo XIII: 1891; Pius XI: 1931), the cooperative movement within Catholic labour movements (cf. Gide 1904), and economic representation (the history of economic parliaments, such as the (never implemented) *Reichswirtschaftsrat* of the Weimar Republic; corporatism; pluralism).

12. Not to be confused with the post-war theory of pluralism developed in America.

down to the level of workshops and neighbourhoods, upon which the higher levels of organisation rely (Cole 1950: esp. Ch. VI, VII, X). For his theory, Cole took inspiration from the medieval guilds (cf. von Gierke 1990: esp. Ch. III and V). In short, functional representation is here based on political anthropology as well as a concern for human self-determination, and conceptualised as participation.[13] More recent accounts of 'associative democracy' are essentially based on this tradition of thought (cf. Hirst 1994; Cohen and Rogers 1995).

As with Cole, David Mitrany (1888–1975) also heavily criticises the democratic qualities of large-scale electoral, territorial representation (Mitrany 1966a: 121, 126). For him, the increasing size and functional scope of political systems means that the 'mass of the voters find themselves with a lessening influence on parliament, and parliament in turn with less influence on government' (Mitrany 1966a: 122). This not only leads to a democratic deficit, but also compromises the quality of political outputs, since 'even in parliament, only a few members find time to pay attention to any particular proposal, and even fewer can understand it' (Mitrany 1966a: 123). Due to this parliamentary incapacity, tasks are increasingly delegated to autonomous boards and agencies, which have more expertise, but are outside democratic initiative and control. For Mitrany, this shows how the traditional representative system is not compatible with the functional requirements of government in the 'new social state' (Mitrany 1966a: 124). His solution 'to check on a cankerous executive centralisation' (Mitrany 1975a: 32) and restore true democratic control is functional representation. Contrarily to parliaments, functional associations are specialists in their field and can therefore meaningfully shape particular policies as well as represent clear and informed opinions (Mitrany 1966a: 126). Referring to the examples of the International Labour Organization (ILO) and the European Coal and Steel Community (ECSC), Mitrany proposes creating for each functional agency its 'own little functional parliament' made up, in addition to expert officials, of relevant non-governmental experts

> who really know what the scope of the legislation in that particular field should be, and who also have the knowledge and the direct interest to watch, on behalf of the political community at large, how policy is carried out in that field (Mitrany 1966a: 125; cf. Mitrany 1966b: 206).

---

13. The political system Cole depicts is a functional council democracy. In seeking to avoid any centralised authority ruling from above, he abolishes the state and decentralises power as much as possible, aiming at a functional grassroots democracy. However, notwithstanding his aversion to large-scale representation, Cole concedes that modern societies need a representative body of government to coordinate different functions and to deal with issues of a national scale. Thus, he in fact rebuilds central authority in the form of national levels of the many local guilds and councils, and ultimately in the form of a central coordinating body, the Commune. Consequently, he faces great difficulties in bringing his model of the polity in line with his theory of representation. That said, the compatibility problems of Cole's guild-socialist political system with his reasoning about functional representation also mean that the latter does not imply guild socialism, but has theoretical relevance beyond this. For more on G. D. H. Cole's theory of guild socialism, *see* Cole 1917; 1920; 1950; [1920] 1980; Carpenter 1973; Houseman 1979; Hirst 1993.

The proper 'experts' for Mitrany are representatives of NGOs. He points out that this role also implies responsibilities and requirements for the involved organisations. Firstly, they will have to 'display a sense of restraint and responsibility in their views and claims' (Mitrany 1966a: 127–8). Secondly, they have to act as two-way communicative channels:

> It is as important for them to bring back to the general public [and to their constituents (Mitrany 1975a: 31)] information on what their particular specialized agency is doing, and make clear the reasons for it, as to act as the voice of that public opinion at the seat of power (Mitrany 1966a: 127–8).

For Mitrany also, people naturally organise functionally. This principle should be extended to organise and govern societies, and beyond national borders too, in order 'to build a world community' (Mitrany 1975b: 265) and sustain peace in the long run through practical functional entangling (Mitrany 1966c: 92 and cf. 95). In brief, Mitrany's reasoning is based on three concerns. Firstly, he seeks to re-establish proper democratic initiative and control in view of increasing tendencies towards 'that "administrative state" which was the instrument of benevolent autocracy' (Mitrany 1966a: 123). Secondly, he aims to ensure the quality of political outputs to satisfy the people's needs, which is why for him functional representation is chiefly based on expertise.[14] Finally, based on the transnational nature of most of these needs, he envisages international representation as a means to further peace and welfare. The reception of his ideas has mainly delved into the latter two aspects, and much of today's governance literature has a lot in common with this approach.

It is worth recalling these theories when enquiring into different concepts of functional representation, because many of Cole's and Mitrany's ideas are basic building blocks of other conceptualisations, including current visions, about why functional representation ought to be used, in what ways it makes government more democratic, and how it should be organised.

However, the concept of functional representation only shifts our attention to the kinds of constituencies that can possibly be represented; it is not as such concerned with how representation itself works – a question that poses itself all the more as the variety of representatives and represented increases. Given the plurality of actors involved in governance processes, it is crucial to consider how we can know who represents whom and in what ways, if we want to analyse the democratic legitimacy of these processes. For example, in what sense and with what kind of legitimacy does an NGO represent people living in poverty,

---

14. Mitrany's rationalistic ideas have been criticised for seeing the role of autonomous agencies as unpolitical (Claude 1965; cf. Mitrany 1966a: 125–6). He also perceives them as unproblematic with regard to different actors' interests, i.e. pathologies related to institutional self-interest (cf. Barnett and Finnemore 1999), as well as – in the case of international agencies – potential conflicts between the constituent Member States. Moreover, his approach has a technocratic bias. However, the reception of Mitrany's model has generally concentrated on his ideas about the output-driven functional entangling of national states, while his concepts of functional representation have received much less attention. About functional representation in Mitrany, see Navari 1995; Imber 1984: 114–18; Taylor 1990.

most of whom have never heard about that organisation? The way these questions are answered is an essential part of any concept of how functional representation produces democratic legitimacy. I return to them in Chapters Two to Four.

A working model of democracy

In order to analyse and evaluate the democratic credentials of political practices, one needs a working definition of democratic legitimacy. This study is mainly about democratic legitimacy in the sense of normative legitimacy, concerning 'whether the rules and practices satisfy certain standards of legitimacy' (Føllesdal 2011: 85), as opposed to social legitimacy (Smismans 2004: 74), i.e. the empirical question of how far citizens perceive institutions and policies as legitimate. In other words, the Commission's claims to legitimacy, and the concepts of democracy underlying these claims, are assessed on the basis of normative concepts derived from democratic theory. Notwithstanding, normative and social legitimacy are of course linked. Democratic theory is not an isolated science, but is rooted in society's values and believes; hence the criteria used here are not separate from those used by citizens when they evaluate political practices. At the same time, political actors have an interest in being perceived as legitimate,[15] and therefore seek to rhetorically shape the norms applied in their environment. Thus, they aim at legitimising their position and activities by justifying why and in what sense it is legitimate, and thereby promote particular concepts of legitimacy. I come back to this in the subsequent section.

If normative legitimacy is about whether institutions and policies meet 'certain standards', in Europe these standards are above all those of democracy. Policies are legitimate if they are democratic. I understand democracy as 'any set of arrangements that instantiates the principle that all affected by collective decisions should have an [equal] opportunity to influence the outcome' (Urbinati and Warren 2008: 395).[16] This is an ideal definition, one that is hardly ever fulfilled. Yet, normative approaches to democracy need ideal, prescriptive definitions. As Giovanni Sartori explains, real-life democracies 'are as they are because they embody ideals', i.e. they are established 'as a result of deontological pressures' that are based on ideals (Sartori 1987: 7–8). Hence, our imperfect democracies owe their existence to their ideals, and what they are cannot be separated from what they should be (Sartori 1987: 7–8). It follows from this that idealistic criteria of democracy also help maintain – or improve – the level of democracy reached in a polity, because they help 'to keep ever before us the ideal – what democracy *ought to be*' (Sartori 1987: 8). They provide standards to evaluate actual political systems, they can serve as guides for their (re)shaping and development, and they

---

15. Cf. Seymour Martin Lipset's definition of legitimacy as 'the capacity of the system to engender and maintain the *belief* that the existing political institutions are the most appropriate ones for the society' (Lipset 1960: 77; emphasis added).

16. In addition to the sources mentioned by Urbinati and Warren, cf. also Saward 2000: 33; Hilson 2006: 56. For a critical view of this 'all-affected principle', *see* above and Whelan 1983: 16.

generate relevant questions for scholars studying these issues (Dahl 2000: 42). Starting from an ideal definition does not mean ending up concluding simply that all existing political systems are undemocratic, but the ideal constitutes one end of a continuum, on which actual cases can be placed. Doing this does not mean, either, that there were no means to distinguish democratic and undemocratic cases. As Sartori puts it, '[t]hat day and night gradually shade into one another does not entail that their difference is only of degree or (still worse) that light and darkness are inseparable' (Sartori 1987: 8).

In order to make such distinctions, and to analyse and evaluate actual cases, one needs to break down the above definition into more concrete tools to work with. For this purpose, I start out from the conception that on the basis of this general understanding, democracy can be defined as comprising the three elements of input legitimacy, output legitimacy, and political accountability. All three are abstract criteria that can be realised in different ways (e.g. also in non-electoral institutions), and combined and weighted in various manners, resulting in different models of democracy.

The distinction of political inputs and outputs goes back to David Easton's system-theory view. In his simplified model of a political system, he pictures the governmental institutions as a black box receiving inputs (demands and support) from its environment, and producing outputs (decisions and actions) that influence this environment. Reactions to the outputs are transformed into new inputs via a feedback loop (Easton 1965: 29–33). Fritz W. Scharpf applied this distinction to normative theories of democracy and coined the concepts input and output legitimacy (Scharpf [1970] 1975: esp. 21). Although he developed these notions to categorise different theories according to their respective emphases, they have subsequently mostly been used to analyse political institutions and processes, and been fleshed out for this purpose. In line with this understanding, *input legitimacy* means that '[p]olitical choices are legitimate if and because they reflect the "will of the people" – that is, if they can be derived from the authentic preferences of the members of a community' (Scharpf 1999: 6). The inputs to the political process are the articulated interests (Scharpf 1975: 21) of the governed, who must have equal chances to participate in this articulation (Scharpf 1975: 25) and to have their views taken into account. *Output legitimacy* in turn means that 'political choices are legitimate if and because they effectively promote the common welfare of the constituency in question' (Scharpf 1999: 6).

The gist of analysing democracy through the concepts of input and output legitimacy is that both are necessary to make a process democratic. What is more, neither makes sense on its own, without the other. Inputs are of little worth if no acceptable outputs follow, and outputs are legitimate only if they are endorsed by the governed (Christiansen *et al.* 2003: 13). Although output legitimacy is defined as effectively promoting common welfare – i.e. legitimate outputs are by definition acceptable ones – there remains a lot to be determined about how exactly this welfare should be understood and realised, and these choices should be based on democratic inputs. Their relationship to *equality* also shows the close link between input and output legitimacy. Scharpf defines input legitimacy as based on the equal participation of all, and output legitimacy as promoting the constituency's common welfare, i.e. equally furthering the wellbeing of all. In other words, legitimacy is not created by inputs and outputs as such, but these have to treat all citizens with equal consideration.[17] Importantly, equal or fair inputs are causally linked to equal or fair outputs: 'Expanding the franchise is quintessentially a matter of giving everybody an input; but doing so helps to give everyone equal power over the bottom line as well' (Goodin 2003a: 163).[18]

Both input and output legitimacy are thus necessary for democracy; nonetheless, they are not sufficient, but need to be complemented with *political accountability*. Only accountability gives the governed effective tools to ensure that policy makers do in fact take their preferences into account and promote their welfare (cf. Føllesdal 2011: 99). It therefore makes the citizens the ultimate authority of the polity. In addition, accountability furthers the communication between represented and representing by giving the former the opportunity to hear justifications for political choices and to express their views on them (Benz and Papadopoulos 2006: 5). I avail myself of Mark Bovens' definition, according to which accountability is 'a relationship between an actor and a forum, in which the actor has an obligation to explain and to justify his or her conduct, the forum can pose questions and pass judgement, and the actor may face consequences' (Bovens 2007: 450). This can be realised in different arrangements, which need not be electoral. One of the key prerequisites for any such arrangement is *transparency and clarity* of the policy-making process, so that the governed can at reasonable cost find out who has taken which decision in what circumstances. Accountability creates a clear distinction between account holders and account givers: it is the accountability '*of* some agent *to* some other agent *for* some state of affairs' (Goodin 2003b: 361). This makes it the pivot of theories of political representation, which are about the relationship between represented and representing. At the same time, accountability is the most difficult of the three elements of democracy with respect to governance processes and their non-electoral and informal forms of representation. I use this working model of democracy (input legitimacy, output legitimacy, and accountability) throughout this study to conceptualise how different forms of representation relate to democracy, and to analyse the Commission's concepts of representation and democracy in the social OMC.

EU governance and the Open Method of Coordination

Governance can be defined as a process of defining collective goals and sustaining coordination and coherence by bringing together a large variety of different actors relevant to the issue at hand, in order to utilise the resources of these actors (Pierre 2000a: 3–4; Peters and Pierre 2004: 77–8; 2006: 29). It is typically characterised

---

17. Equality does not necessarily mean equal treatment, but should rather be understood as referring to equal consideration and fair treatment of all (Phillips 1995: 37–8; cf. Williams 1998: 197, 19–20). *See* Chapter Three.

18. Cf. Mill 1991: 246; Phillips 1995: Ch. 2; Weale 2011: 62. For a problematisation of this link, *see* Chapter Three.

by informality; a plurality of policy-making centres with functional and fluid boundaries and without clear hierarchies; a variety of different modes of policy making; and elected as well as unelected participants from political institutions, the economic sector, expert organisations, CSOs, and other arenas (Benz and Papadopoulos 2006: 2–3).[19]

For a long time, the governance literature centred on the extent to which the state, or other societal actors, are steering these processes, and how the performance of the system as a whole is influenced by the ways governance is organised. Against the background of the debates on 'overloaded government' and the 'ungovernability' of society (Peters and Pierre 2006), policy output was given primacy (Peters and Pierre 2004: 84), and the roles of various actors were analysed with respect to the potential of different arrangements to deliver public goods. Democratic control, by contrast, was not a major concern (Peters and Pierre 2004: 85; Papadopoulos 2007: 469–70; Kröger 2009; cf. Hirst 2000).[20] However, since around the turn of the century, attention has increasingly shifted to also include questions of democratic legitimacy beyond output legitimacy. In particular, scholars have increasingly addressed issues concerning political accountability, unequal possibilities to participate and exert influence, power relations, and the informality and intransparency of governance processes, all of which have been found to be highly problematic.

Looking at governance from the perspective of input legitimacy and political accountability introduces a category that remains in the background of distinctly output-orientated approaches, *viz.* constituencies with their different interests and preferences. Hence, when addressing democratic aspects of governance, processes are often analysed in terms of political representation (*see* e.g. Halpin 2001; 2006; Benz and Papadopoulos 2006: 8–11; Greenwood 2007a). Yet, this is usually done implicitly and by drawing on some particular understanding of representation, without taking into account that governance has, if not changed the very ways in which representation takes place, at least immensely diversified the range of modes of representation in policy making. Most participants are unelected, some of them seem to have no relation to the represented at all, constituencies are often fluid, and it is not always possible to determine unambiguously who is representing whom. Therefore, this study takes political representation itself as one of the objects of enquiry. I define the involvement of various actors in governance processes as functional representation (*see* below), and one central research question is how DG Employment conceptualises representation as working here.

---

19. For an overview of different definitions and uses of the term 'governance', *see* the contributions in Pierre (ed.) 2000, especially Hirst 2000 and Rhodes 2000.

20. In CONNEX's GOVDATA database of 1,700 scientific research projects on EU governance in thirty European countries between 1994 and 2005, only 292 projects (17.2 per cent) address questions of legitimacy and/or democracy, 242 of which do so under the subject of political science (GOVDATA 2013). *See also* Kohler-Koch 2006 for an overview of insights gained from the database.

'*New modes of governance*' are 'new' in the sense that they rely on soft (non-binding) law and aim at collective learning through experimentalism or comparing different actors' achievements. They are thus marked by deliberative or discursive policy-making styles. From the perspective of European integration, they overcome the dichotomies of European vs. national (Palier 2008: 54), positive vs. negative integration (Ferrera *et al.* 2002: 230), law vs. governance (Dawson 2009: 3) (or formal vs. informal policy making), and soft vs. hard governance (Trubeck and Trubeck 2005). New modes of governance like the Open Method of Coordination (OMC) have shown that integration can be deepened without delegating legal competences to the Union, but also that such an outcome is conditional on other factors. Nonetheless, the difference between 'old' and 'new' governance is one of degree (Trubeck and Trubeck 2005).

In the EU, the OMC is the most important instance of such processes, although there are differences among the various OMCs (*see* Laffan and Shaw 2005).[21] After the OMC had been introduced by the 2000 Lisbon European Council,[22] a large number of scholars embraced the new method and its promises of learning, participation, and deliberation (e.g. Scott and Trubek 2002). Again, many followed the official EU discourse and its output-orientation, including its terminology of problem solving, learning, and depoliticised cooperation for shared goals across different types of social actors, rather than addressing questions of democratic legitimacy (e.g. Eberlein and Kerwer 2002; Radaelli 2003: 59; Zeitlin *et al.* 2005; Sabel and Zeitlin 2008; cf. the criticism in Kröger 2007: 567). However, with the growth of empirical experience, criticism increased. Today, participation and deliberation are still seen as potentials of the OMC, but evidence of their realisation has been sobering. In contrast to 'old' governance, assessing democratic legitimacy in the OMC has required scholars to justify why a political process without binding rules needs its own democratic legitimacy in the first place. It has been argued that through its discursive policy making in networks, the OMC has a subtle impact on national politics (which, after all, is its *raison d'être*). In particular, through the OMC, political goal setting has been transferred to the EU level (Borrás and Jacobsson 2004: 197), so that policies can be framed before they are debated nationally (Borrás and Conzelmann 2007: 532–7; cf. Armstrong 2003; Büchs 2008: 767; Kröger 2007: 568; 2009). The Commission for its part can guide Member States by means of its coordinating and mediating role, and has thus expanded its area of influence (Borrás and Jacobsson 2004: 198). Scholars have also challenged the Commission's managerial discourse to the effect that 'these new governance instruments are as much political devices as the "old" more conventional instruments, and as such, they will be equally subject to

---

21. For literature overviews about the OMC, *see also* Kröger 2008: 13–16; Kröger 2009.

22. The Lisbon European Council introduced the name 'Open Method of Coordination', defined the OMC's main elements, and announced the launching of OMCs for various areas (Lisbon European Council, 23 and 24 March 2000, Presidency Conclusions). Afterwards, a (varying) range of political processes already existing prior to Lisbon have been classified as OMCs as well. *See* Laffan and Shaw 2005 for an overview.

considerations about their democratic credentials and legitimacy features' (Borrás 2008: 101; cf. Borrás and Conzelmann 2007: 534–5; Büchs 2008: 767). Also, non-binding processes are 'purposive action [that] entails a political process of choice, selection and interpretation of specific norms and values' (Borrás and Conzelmann 2007: 532; cf. Kröger 2009). Hence, Sandra Kröger notes straightforwardly that 'if there is EU action, and as long as the EU is made up of democracies, this action needs to be legitimate and legitimated through the consent of the peoples of the EU' (Kröger 2007: 567). Analyses of the OMC's democratic credentials have been concordant and rather deflating. The OMC is criticised as being opaque, closed, technocratic, based on unequal and informal participation, excluding parliaments, lacking public debate and accountability, establishing a pseudo-technical political discourse, and framing policies in closed arenas before public debate even has a chance to start (Bellamy and Castiglione 2011; Borrás and Conzelmann 2007: 542; Borrás and Greve 2004: 333–4; Borrás and Jacobsson 2004: 199–200; Büchs 2008: 775–8; Dawson 2009; Føllesdal 2011: 94–5; Kröger 2007: 572–3, 578; Pfister 2009; de la Porte and Nanz 2004; de la Porte and Pochet 2005: 376; Radulova 2007; Smismans 2006: 18–19; Usui 2007).

Despite this increasing criticism, a look at the OMC literature also shows that it is challenging to find a stable ground on which to evaluate democracy in the OMC and to apply established normative yardsticks in a context of discursive, informal, multi-level governance. With this research, I aim to show that the perspective of political representation provides a reliable starting point for enquiries into democratic legitimacy also in complex and new settings. It allows the analysis of different kinds of political actors (in the present case, particularly representatives of especially affected functional groups) and provides the tools to deal systematically with the relations of policy makers and the people.

The social OMC offers itself as a case to study the involvement of functional representatives for two main reasons. Firstly, it is located at DG Employment, the DG with the longest tradition of involving 'stakeholders' and a distinct self-perception as an organisation cooperating with a wide range of external actors (Kröger 2008: 13; cf. Cram 1997; Greenwood 1997; 2003). At the same time, DG Employment is also 'one of the most expansionist-orientated services of the European Commission' (Greenwood 2007a: 181), which makes more visible the strategic aspect of their concepts about how functional representation relates to democratic legitimacy. Secondly, the social OMC is interesting from a theoretical point of view. For one thing, it is a case where functional representation is the executive's only representational structure, without a parallel pillar of territorial (parliamentary) representation. For another thing, those most affected by social policies are exactly the people who are structurally most disadvantaged with regard to getting involved in policy making. People living in or at risk of poverty have rather diffuse interests and lack resources to organise and influence politics (cf. Olson 1965). Moreover, they tend to be socially marginalised and overlooked by elites. It is therefore interesting to study a case where the poor are the most important group to be involved in policy making, because, on the one hand, governance processes often have a tendency to aggravate existing social inequalities (since participation does not rest on any equivalent to the formal one-person-one-vote principle), but on the other hand, they are also often seen as a means to improve the inclusiveness of the policy-making process by opening the door to different kinds of actors. The social OMC, the Commission's position, and the role of functional representation in it are introduced in Chapter Five.

Analysing political argumentation

There is no shortage of research about the OMC. Most of the literature dealing with democracy in the OMC starts from a set of abstract criteria derived from normative theory in order to test their realisation in the OMC (*see* e.g. de la Porte and Nanz 2004; Borrás and Conzelmann 2007; Kröger 2007; Büchs 2008). In general, these studies reveal deficits in the OMC's democratic legitimacy. However, it is often difficult to determine empirical facts about OMC processes, and even more difficult to establish causal relationships with outcomes on the national level. Hence, in contrast to this extensive empirical research, I concentrate less on what the Commission does, and more on what they *say*, i.e. their published text, and enquire into what *concepts* of democracy are underlying this text. One of the Commission's main lines of reasoning is that functional representation generates democratic legitimacy for their political initiatives, or more generally for their position as the coordinator of the process. The purpose here is to examine more closely how they envisage this link to work, i.e. how exactly and in what sense legitimacy is supposed to come about through functional representation. These notions are then assessed against the normative standards laid out in Chapters Two to Four.

To study the concepts of democracy underlying the Commission's text, I take this text as *argumentation* claiming: 'What we do is legitimate, and you should heed our propositions, because we involve functional representatives'. This claim, itself not fully explicit, draws on mostly implicit norms, values, principles, ideas, accepted facts, ways of thinking, etc., which support the argument by establishing *why* and *how* functional representation leads to *what kind* of legitimacy. These topoi are analysed by examining the single arguments at the micro level of the text in order to find paradigmatic lines of argumentation. Importantly, the Commission's discourse is analysed in its political context. I thus do not take the text as a treatise in democratic theory, but as strategic, political text that is guided by institutional interests and is meant to have an influence on how functional representation works in the social OMC.

But why does it matter what the European Commission says about democracy? In a nutshell, it matters because what they say about functional representation and democratic legitimacy is part of the OMC's essentially discursive political process, in which not only policies are developed, but also concepts are shaped about what constitutes sound policy making and who are legitimate participants. The Commission not only plays a pivotal role in this discursive process, but also acts as a key gatekeeper for functional representatives seeking access to the OMC. At the same time, it has vested institutional interests to promote particular concepts of legitimate policy making that support its own position *vis-à-vis* other actors. The model they advocate influences the ways in which the organisation of functional representation in the OMC evolves.

As stated at the beginning, the notion that functional representation can enhance democracy is widely accepted, but how exactly the link between the two could work remains unclear (cf. Kohler-Koch 2008: 9–11; Saurugger 2008: 176). The brief look at some strands of conceptual history has demonstrated that very different models are possible. This lack of clarity applies also and especially to the OMC, which is still a rather young institutional setting. From the outset, there have been high expectations that functional representation in particular would contribute to the democratic legitimacy of the method, but the precise way in which this should happen is not obvious. Ideas about this, as well as practices informed by them, are developed as part of the ongoing political process. The shaping of concepts about what functional representatives' role should be does thus not take place separately from shaping policies, but within the same arena and as part of the same discourses.

Policy making in the OMC is an inherently *discursive* process (*see* Chapter Five) that works via 'the development of common discourses, establishing certain key concepts as well as policy principles and understandings of causal linkages' (Borrás and Jacobsson 2004: 196; cf. Jacobsson 2004; Pfister 2009). In other words, OMCs are instrumental in establishing common ways of talking about issues and policies, including a shared vocabulary carrying particular meanings. They influence national policies subtly by constructing seemingly 'uncontroversial definitions of sound policies and the common good' (Borrás and Conzelmann 2007: 535) in deliberative processes and spreading these ideas in informal and discursive ways (Borrás and Conzelmann 2007: 534; Kröger 2007: 568). Political orientations and initiatives are established on the agenda and implemented if they are 'packaged' (Radulova 2009)[23] so as to fit a successful master discourse (Usui 2007: 626; cf. Radulova 2009) that frames a broader range of issues in a particular way in order to create consistency. For example, the dominant way of conceptualising social inclusion and social protection policies has been that of economic growth. Adopting such a discourse means taking over certain ideas about what the goals of social policies should be and what constitutes good social policy (cf. Büchs 2009). This means that the use of *language* – talking and writing – is the central way of acting and exerting influence within this setting. Hence, the texts published by the Commission in the social OMC (official documents, speeches, etc.) have to be understood as political *tools* influencing the political process (Palola 2007: 38, 43–4). In the absence of formal authority to impose measures, the Commission – just as with the other actors – can only seek to guide processes in desired directions by arguing, persuading, and convincing.[24] Their saying and doing are thus not separate actions.

---

23. The saying *'emballage et remballage'* ('packaging and repackaging') is also used within the Commission.

24. *See* Chapter Five for the discursive ways of policy making characteristic of the social OMC.

The discursive dynamics of policy making within the OMC have been increasingly recognised. However, less attention has been paid to the fact that the same dynamics are also at work when it comes to determining how the political *process* itself should be organised, for example concerning the question of who are legitimate participants.[25] Just as ideas about social policy contents are shaped in collective and deliberative ways, concepts about how policy making in the OMC should take place are also shaped discursively. The evolution of such norms about what constitutes good or appropriate modes of policy making influences the development of institutions, especially in settings such as the EU, whose political system is in flux, and which has discovered new modes of governance relatively recently (cf. Kohler-Koch 2000: 514–15; Borrás and Jacobsson 2004: 197; Heidenreich and Bischoff 2008: 505–6). This is all the more true in the OMC, where governance relies to an important extent on informal processes.

The *Commission* is a pivotal actor in this. Although it has little formal power, it has a strong discursive position, based on its role as the coordinator of the OMC. This role not only gives it the central position of a mediator between the Member States, but also that of a gatekeeper *vis-à-vis* other actors – notably functional representatives – and that of the OMC's informational centre where knowledge is collected, processed, and disseminated (Jacobsson 2004; Borrás 2007; Sbragia 2000: 228–31). This location provides it with privileged possibilities to influence the political process (Borrás and Jacobsson 2004: 198). However, in order to do so, the Commission needs to legitimise its own position, i.e. argue why others should accept its influence and follow its propositions. One central argument used in this is its involvement of functional representatives. In other words, the Commission backs up its political propositions with the argument that functional representatives have been involved in drawing them up. This implies the conception that such involvement makes proposals more legitimate. The Commission thus has an incentive to support the existing notion that functional representation leads to legitimacy, and, what is more, to promote a *particular model* of legitimate functional representation that suits its own position and interests.[26] This concerns, for instance, the kinds of organisations that are presented as legitimate participants in the OMC, the criteria that are offered to assess the legitimacy of individual associations, or the roles assigned to them in the governance process. In promoting its views on these matters, the Commission participates from a privileged position in shaping the norms guiding functional representation in the social OMC, as well as in EU-level (new modes of) governance more generally. The social OMC is no isolated arena in this respect, but DG Employment's discourse here is part of the wider Commission discourse about functional representation in the EU and builds on years of conceptual work, the culmination of which has so far been the White

---

25. An exception is Borrás and Conzelmann 2007: 535, 546.

26. *See* Smismans 2003 for an analysis of how the Commission, the Economic and Social Committee (EESC), and the European Parliament (EP) shape concepts of 'civil society' according to their respective institutional interests. Cf. Chapter Five, and Skinner 2002: Ch. 8.

Paper on European governance.[27] No single actor has animated discourses about EU governance as the Commission has.

Such norms promoted by political actors always deserve careful scrutiny (cf. Borrás and Conzelmann 2007: 546). Not only is the combination of power and shaping democratic norms a delicate one, but seen from a wider perspective, public discourses about democracy and the concepts of democracy used by political actors are themselves part of how democratically a political system works (cf. Buchstein and Jörke 2007: 193–5). Democracy is 'an ongoing human artefact that hinges on the set of ideas and ideals that make it, uphold it (in its makings), and that (if misunderstood and mismanaged) will also unmake it' (Sartori 1987: 18). When the OMC was introduced it was widely embraced as a promise of more participation and a new quality of democracy in EU governance. This optimism was largely based on official discourses. Only later has it been asked what 'civil society participation' actually means in practice and how it is implemented. However, the literature has for the most part concentrated on analysing practices in the OMC, which are opaque and difficult to get a hold of. Much less attention has been paid to the concepts used to justify these practices, although it is these concepts on the basis of which practices (and, through this, institutions) evolve. What is more, publicly advanced notions about legitimate policy making participate in the shaping of what we understand by 'democratic decision-making'.[28] Since these notions are not only motivated by concerns about democracy, but also by interests, institutional configurations, and structural circumstances, we should be sensitive to the concepts advocated by political actors.

Since the 'new' modes of governance in the OMC have met with such a huge amount of scholarly interest, and since the importance of discourse within the OMC in particular is widely recognised, it is astonishing that when such discourses have been analysed at all, this has mainly been done with respect to their role in policy development, but not concerning the ways governance is organised. On the contrary, the Commission's 'civil society participation' discourse has usually either been embraced as a potential way to tackle the EU's democratic deficit, or dismissed on the grounds that actual practices do not live up to expectations of more democratic legitimacy through 'civil society participation'. Only rarely have scholars taken the time to examine in detail what is actually being said. As well as that, it has seldom been asked what democratic improvements can realistically be expected on the basis of how political actors conceptualise and design practices, i.e. whether shortcomings in actual practices are already inbuilt in the way the Commission conceptualises 'civil society' and 'participation', and what the widespread adoption of their discourse means in terms of democracy. The present study not only fills this gap, but also shows how governance and 'civil society participation' can be analysed in a systematic manner from the perspective of democratic norms by conceptualising it as functional representation.

---

27. COM(2001)428 of 25 July 2001.

28. In the absence of any authoritative definition, what we understand by democracy is shaped by the way the concept is used (Sartori 1987: 3–4, cf. Ch. 1; Buchstein and Jörke 2007: 190).

Chapter overview

The book consists of three parts. Chapters Two to Four explore theories of representation and develop them into a tool to analyse the democratic legitimacy of governance processes. Chapters Five to Nine demonstrate the use of this instrument. They present the social OMC and examine in detail the Commission's arguments for the participation of functional representatives. Chapters Ten to Twelve synthesise the results of this analysis with regard to the concepts of representation and democracy underlying the Commission's argumentation, and reflect on their implications for democratic governance in the EU more broadly.

Chapter Two

What Does it Mean to Represent?

Representation as such need not be political nor democratic. Following Hanna Pitkin's classical definition of representation as 'the making present *in some sense* of something which is nevertheless *not* present literally or in fact' (Pitkin 1967: 8–9; emphases in original),[1] we can speak of *political representation* when a participant in the political process (widely understood) is participating by virtue of also giving political presence to actors other than herself. Such representation is *democratic* if it ensures input and output legitimacy as well as accountability in relation to the represented. These criteria are most familiar to us in the context of elected parliaments and governments. Yet, the political stage is also filled with unelected actors perceived or claiming to represent various functional constituencies. How are we to evaluate the assertion that the European Anti-Poverty Network (EAPN) represents socially excluded Europeans, given that their staff is not elected by their supposed constituents, nor is their organisation even known to most of them? Intuitively, many will still recognise them as representing the poor *in some way*. At the same time, it is obvious that the EAPN represents excluded people in a different way than a Member of Parliament represents either her constituency or the nation as a whole, and that EAPN's representing also differs from that of an equally unelected monarch. So how does it work? The question is a fundamental one, because the intended democratic value of involving such actors in governance processes rests first and foremost 'on the extent to which they legitimately represent [...] some group or larger set of social interests' (Saward 2005: 179). In a democracy, those taking part in governance processes do not in general participate on their own behalf, but speak for a larger group of citizens. Representation is thus the key to studying the democratic credentials of the involvement of functional organisations like EAPN in democratic policy making. Scrutinising representation is the prerequisite to dealing with questions of democracy, such as, for example, should and can functional actors be accountable, and if yes, in what way and to whom?

These issues are discussed in the following chapters. In the present chapter I consider the question of how we know if someone represents a given constituency. I look at different theories of representation and the concepts and criteria they use, to assess if and in what kinds of ways unelected actors on the political stage in particular can legitimately be said to represent a certain functional constituency.

---

1. Plotke (1997: 27–30) criticises Pitkin for linking representation with *absence* and argues that 'it is plausible to say that in a given context, someone is present politically but not physically' (Plotke 1997: 30). Although I am not entirely convinced by his reading of Pitkin in this case, I find this latter distinction clarifying and helpful.

Chapter Three looks at the special case of the descriptive representation of disadvantaged groups, i.e. their representation by people who themselves belong to these groups. Descriptive representation has become an important issue for many enquiries in democratic representation, because the question of whether and in what sense a representative should resemble the represented, and what difference this makes for representation, goes to the core of what representation itself is about. What is more, descriptive representation is one mode of functional representation that is used in the social OMC. Chapter Four changes the angle of observation to address the question of in what ways functional representation can make governance processes more democratic. It works out the main issues and difficulties we encounter when analysing governance from the perspective of democratic legitimacy, and looks at the ways in which the different theories of representation relate to these issues.

Actors who are representing functional constituencies are in most cases not elected by the represented. How, then, can we tell whether someone is legitimately representing a certain group of people? 'Legitimate' in this context does not necessarily mean democratic legitimacy; it merely refers to whether an actor is accepted as a representative of a particular constituency. Different criteria are possible for determining this. In the following, I present three perspectives, each of which interprets in different ways what it means to represent. The first notion is based on a simple principal–agent model. The second view builds on this, but widens it with deliberative concepts of democracy, and emphasises the role of ongoing communication between the representing and the represented. Thirdly, the theory of the representative claim challenges the fundamental assumptions of the former two perspectives and proposes a new view of what representation is about, while at the same time providing the concepts to integrate all three theories into one framework.

Simple principal–agent models[2]

Simple principal–agent models are a theory of delegation.[3] Because the people cannot govern themselves, they delegate this task to agents. At the same time, however, the people remain the sovereign, i.e. the principal who is in control of her agents.[4] The agent needs to be *authorised* by the principal, but, mainly for

---

2. I speak of 'simple' principal–agent models because the application of these models is here restricted to their core elements that are relevant for the purpose of the study. Principal–agent theories serve here as an analytical framework to understand how political representation in general comes about, rather than being meant as an accurate description or prescription of how political systems function in practice. For more complex accounts, *see* for example the contributions in Przeworski *et al.* 1999.

3. In this sense, the terms 'principal' and 'agent' were first used by Alexander Hamilton in *The Federalist*, synonymously with those of 'master' and 'servant' (Hamilton 1788: 379–80). For the historical context, *see* Grimm 2009: 38–9.

4. From a different angle, principal–agent theory can also be seen as originating in the self-government vs. rule dichotomy, i.e. the question of whether representation is democratic at all. In this interpretation, self-government is equated with direct democracy, referring to the Athenian roots

practical necessities (Dunn 1999: 342–3), she has a free mandate. Therefore, a central role is given to political *accountability*. Thus, we can say that someone legitimately represents a given constituency if that constituency has chosen and authorised her to act in their interest (Manin *et al.* 1999: 2–3, referring to Pitkin 1967; Przeworski 1999: 32), and if she is accountable to them.

In realising these principles, the key role is usually given to *elections*. Since they are recurrent, they merge the act of authorisation and the exercise of accountability together, thus providing, simultaneously, an incentive for the agents to be responsive to the preferences of their constituents, and an instrument of control for the principals. At the same time, elections create an abstract equality among the people (one person, one vote) and thus also function to establish procedural fairness. In order for elections to fulfil their role, they need to be supplemented with other procedural norms, such as the freedom of information (Dunn 1999: 339–41), of opinion, and of expression (Manin 1997: 174–5, 237). Transparency in particular is an important prerequisite for principals to be able to make enlightened choices and effectively control their agents.

As long as the two core criteria of authorisation and accountability are met, it is irrelevant who does the representing, because any representative will be induced by elections to act in the interest of the represented, and can be replaced if they perceive her to have failed to do so. Consequently, the main issue is not who the representatives are, but what they do,[5] and the former is not expected to have any decisive impact on the latter (Williams 1998: 138–9).

This does not mean, though, that every participant in the political process has to be elected by the people. The legitimacy of functional representatives rests on two pillars: the internal legitimacy of their organisation and external legitimacy via the democratic chain of delegation.

Internal legitimacy means that the functional representative legitimately represents her constituency, i.e. she is authorised by and accountable to them. Consequently, functional representatives can usually legitimately represent only membership-based organisations with formal structures. They can hardly be said to speak for those who are not organised, and can therefore mostly not legitimately represent an entire functional constituency, defined as all those affected.

External legitimacy refers to whether it is legitimate to involve a functional representative in a political process, for which she has not been authorised by the principals of that process. In other words, under what conditions is she legitimately

---

of democracy. Representation, on the other hand, is interpreted as separating the governed from the governing; it is thus not self-government, but mainly a substitute for direct democracy, which has become impossible in large-scale societies. Representative democracy, then, is not genuine self-government but *rule*, which is intrinsically humiliating and potentially harmful (Dunn 1999: 342). The classical question in this paradigm is 'what makes this rule legitimate?' and the answer is: choosing the rulers, who through this become agents of the people. In other words, representative democracy is an oligarchy with elected rulers (Manin *et al.* 1999: 4–5; Sartori 1987: 111).

5. Cf. Pitkin 1997: 90; and cf. Phillips (1995: 4–5), who has termed this 'the politics of ideas', as opposed to 'the politics of presence' (*see* Chapter Three).

Figure 2.1: A chain of delegation

participating in the preparation of, for example, national legislation, which has been delegated to the national parliament? This participation is legitimate if the parliament has delegated a particular part of this task to her; that is, she occupies a proper place in the chain of delegation.

The chain of delegation is the basis for any legitimate action in the political process. To put it in a simplified way, voters delegate decision making to legislators, legislators delegate certain tasks to executives, and executives to their bureaucracy. Every delegator is a principal, and the one carrying out the delegated tasks is her agent. In other words, authorisation moves down a line, where agents become principals to their own agents by authorising them to take certain decisions. At the same time, every agent is accountable to her principal, and this accountability includes responsibility for the actions of one's 'own' agents.

In the same way, the actors of this chain are accountable for their interactions with unelected functional representatives, who are not themselves responsible to the citizenry at large. For example, legislators meet the representatives of associations, but because these do not take political decisions, it is the legislators who are accountable to their principals (the voters) for the contacts they have and the decisions they take. These contacts are thus part of the preparation of legislation; they are regulated by law and have to be transparent so that elected representatives can be made accountable for them. It is via this accountability of elected representatives for the role they give to unelected actors that the latter are ultimately within the sphere of public accountability, in the sense that the citizens have some influence on whose involvement in policy making they accept. Otherwise, the functional representative herself is internally accountable to the organisation that has authorised her to act in its name.

Simple principal–agent models are thus focussed on the *formal* structures of authority. Representation comes about – i.e. we can say that someone legitimately represents a given constituency – if the actor who formally takes a decision is chosen by and responsible to those formally bound by that decision. This perspective stresses the importance of hard mechanisms of control over representatives, as well as the ultimate responsibility of all political actors, via the chain of delegation, to the sovereign people – the citizenry at large.

Simple principal–agent models are associated with *modernity*. At the time, the relative homogeneity of constituencies facilitated the treatment of numerical majorities as expressions of a general will (Rosanvallon 2010: 9–12). Furthermore, societies were organised in more pyramidical, centralised, corporatist ways (Rosanvallon 2010: 132), so that political activities were channelled through formal, membership-based organisations, notably political parties. These structures underpinned the position of elections as the central legitimating method. Because elections took place within a predictable, structured environment with clear cleavages, they were not perceived in merely procedural terms, but the voting decision was seen to include substantial political choices. Hence, elections could generate a robust mandate to govern relatively freely (Rosanvallon 2010: 14, 54), and representativity was primarily established by the formal status of being elected (cf. p. 328). In the same vein, it was expected that universal suffrage would lead, as it were, automatically to the satisfaction of the greatest number of citizens (p. 54). These notions were closely related to that of a hierarchical, neutral administration implementing political choices (pp. 12–13, 59–99; cf. Smismans 2004: 21–6). By the end of the 1980s, social structures had changed and the concepts of legitimate representation changed accordingly.

With increasing complexity, social fragmentation, and heterogeneity, society came to be perceived as made up of a multitude of particularities and minorities (Rosanvallon 2010: 14). Together with individualisation and social emancipation, this led to a change in the citizens' agency. The notions of a general will and of evident or objective truths lost their meaning, traditional authorities diminished, and people took on a more active role *vis-à-vis* the governing, demanding more transparency, more responsiveness to different arguments, and above all more openness and dialogue between represented and representing (Rosanvallon 2010: 15, 101–2, 132). Public administration is no longer seen as a neutral service, acting in the public interest, and elections are no longer an a priori legitimation of future policies, but merely a method of choosing the governing (pp. 14–15). Legitimate representation in postmodernity depends primarily on the continual interaction between constituents and representatives, based on the exchange of arguments and the justification of decisions. This means that legitimacy is established anew with each issue and that the distance between the governing and the governed has decreased considerably.[6] Their relationship has become stronger, denser, and more diverse, taking place through a multitude of different forums and organisations, including increasingly informal ones (Rosanvallon 2010: 328–31). Citizens 'assume power neither by "taking" it, nor by "commanding" it, but by redefining it, by making it function differently' (p. 331; author translation). The key concepts of this understanding of representation are discourse and deliberation.

Deliberative representation

Deliberative representation is the understanding of representation that underlies theories of deliberative democracy. Although these theories do not often deal with the nature of representation expressly or in detail, deliberative democracy is clearly based on a distinct notion of representation that is essentially meant to develop the principal–agent concept further. Although most of these authors remain within

---

6. Paradoxically, at the same time as the *hierarchical* distance between governing and governed has decreased, the *psychological* distance (in terms of their life-worlds) has increased to the point of an alarming alienation of large parts of the population from political life. Cf. Bussemer 2011.

the sphere of electoral representation, the concepts they have developed to deal with those dimensions of representation that go beyond elections can directly be adapted to study non-electoral forms of representation. In particular, deliberative representation has established new ideas about how legitimate representation can be conceptualised (i.e. how we know whether someone really represents those she speaks for), and about what should be understood as the sphere of political representation. In this section I work out these concepts and show what they contribute to the understanding of unelected functional representation.

Deliberative representation builds on the principal–agent model, i.e. it understands representation as a relation of principals and agents. However, it maintains that, notwithstanding the *necessity* of formal authorisation and accountability as well as procedural equality, these are not *sufficient* to make representation fully legitimate. For one thing, mere elections do not allow the represented to control the representing efficiently. The duration of mandates, the incapacity of the vote to differentiate between various actions of a representative, and the lack of publicity given to most acts of most representatives mean that elections alone do not ensure that political decisions take the views of the represented into account (Gargarella 1998: 272). For another thing, these views are themselves conceptualised differently. Political preferences are not meant to be simply aggregated, but they are seen as evolving and changing in interaction (Manin 1985: 93). Moreover, people not only form their views in exchanges with others, but it is also desirable for them to do so, because deliberation can lead to more enlightened (better reasoned) choices. For example, it can induce people to take the preferences of minorities into account and aim at solutions based on principles that are acceptable for everyone (Setälä 2003: 131). Although deliberation can be followed by a vote, in the perspective of deliberative representation, simple numeric majorities as such do not make a decision fully legitimate, but minorities deserve special consideration. Hence, *legitimate representation* means here, in addition to principal–agent structures (such as elections), functioning two-way communication between the representing and the represented, as well as substantial fairness. This communication should be of high quality, i.e. characterised by argumentation and justification (Rosanvallon 2010: 329–30); it should be ongoing and public. Based on its double function – on the one hand, mediating preferences to the representing, and on the other, providing the means to arrive at fair results – being represented essentially means taking part in this communication, either directly or indirectly, and being taken into account in the debate.

This leads to a focus on the *relationship* between the representatives and the representees (as well as the representees with each other, which has received much more attention in the literature on deliberative democracy), and it is denied that this could be described exclusively as dyadic relations between individual voters and candidates (Urbinati 2006: 9, 15). Instead, it becomes reflexive and diffuse. This diffuseness concerns, on the one hand, the locus of the relationship; represented and representing communicate through a plurality of media and forums, including the press, opinion polls, internet campaigns, associations, prominent personalities, etc. On the other hand, the modus of their relation is also diffuse, including such forms as networking, informal campaigning support (e.g. by visiting or contributing to internet platforms, or by spreading information about them), donations, participating in ad hoc events, etc. Overall, representation is thus taken to more varied and more informal arenas. Elections are still the fundaments of this universe, but, importantly, not all instances of representation that occur in the public sphere need to be electoral.

A central problem for representation to be legitimate in this sense, then, lies in the fact that the capacity to take part in public debates and have one's views considered by others is unevenly distributed. Deliberation is biased towards the more educated parts of society. Although it is possible for gifted members of disadvantaged groups to become popular advocates of their peers (Gutmann and Thompson 2004: 50), the structural lack of power that characterises the most marginalised groups often prevents them from participating effectively in public debate. James Bohman (2000: 125) calls this inability to place a group's concerns on a more general agenda 'political poverty'. Being politically impoverished essentially means not being represented because of not being able to communicate one's views to an appropriate representative or to the public. From this perspective, it becomes problematic to interpret silence as tacit consent, since disadvantaged sections of society may not have the capacity to make their objections heard (Bohman 2000: 125–6). They may thus need assistance from more privileged actors in order to get their views considered. In other words, for deliberative representation, procedural equality (the equal *right* to take part in public debate) is not sufficient to ensure legitimate representation, but one also needs to foster substantial fairness in order to establish social conditions that allow as many citizens as possible to make use of their rights. It is thus not enough that some deliberation takes place – attention has to be paid to who deliberates (Gargarella 1998: 274). One way of dealing with this problem will be the subject of the following chapter.

Part of the reason why deliberative representation is attuned to this question is its demand that for a political process to be legitimate, all *relevant* views should be considered (Gargarella 1998: 271; Bohman 2000: 27, 139–40). There is thus something wrong with representation if significantly *affected* actors have not been heard in the deliberation leading to a decision. Looking at relevance rather than formal institutions opens the perspective not only to silenced people within a representative's formal constituency, but also to affected people outside these borders, and, what is more, to different arenas and ways of representation. For example, Amy Gutmann and Dennis Thompson point out that those most affected by a national government's decision may be citizens of other countries, who should thus be included in the deliberation about such decisions (Gutmann and Thompson 2004: 37–8). More important for the present case, the focus on public deliberation by all those affected also leads to the recognition of arenas of political representation other than the electoral system. Hence, *functional representation* is seen as one important way for citizens to become represented in the political process. On the one hand, it is part of a functioning public sphere; on the other hand, it is also a potential way to make up for deficits in parliamentary representation, such as the impossibility of representing each perspective in parliament, or systematic biases in electoral representation (Bohman 2000: 132; Gargarella 1998: 273; cf. Cohen and Rogers 1995: 43). This again leads to a more systemic view of representation in general, i.e. an awareness that multiple forums of political representation together form, as it were, the infrastructure of a functioning democratic life. Accordingly, '[d]emocracy can also be strengthened by pluralizing the modes and sites of representation' (Young 2000: 133). This includes non-electoral representation.

Most scholars addressing these issues have concentrated more on different modes of representation than on the various sites where these can take place. However, as will be shown, both have implications for each other. Perhaps the most influential contribution to the exploration of different ways in which representation can and does take place is Jane Mansbridge's seminal article 'Rethinking representation' (Mansbridge 2003), in which she demonstrates how a deliberative perspective on representation leads to the recognition of multiple modes of representation, and on this basis advocates a shift to more plural, deliberative, and systemic criteria of legitimate representation, although she remains herself within the realm of formal, parliamentary representation. In the following, I show how the modes of representation she describes can be applied to unelected, functional representation, and how this increases the understanding of how such forms of representation can work in legitimate ways.

Mansbridge singles out four major modes of representation: promissory, anticipative, gyroscopic, and surrogate representation. The first, *promissory representation*, is one aspect of what I have called simple principal–agent models: built on electoral authorisation and accountability, candidates make promises to the voters, who in the next elections reward or punish the representatives for keeping their promises or otherwise. 'Although promissory representation has never described actual representation fully, it has been and remains today one of the most important ways in which citizens influence political outcomes through their representatives' (Mansbridge 2003: 516).

The second mode, *anticipatory representation* (Mansbridge 2003: 516–20), starts from the assumption that preferences can change and voters are educable – or, therefore, manipulable. The representative who seeks re-election thus has an incentive to anticipate the preferences of the voters at the time of the next elections. She will therefore be attentive to information about the citizens' evolving interests and opinions as well as their potential reactions to specific decisions. What is more, representation becomes an ongoing deliberative process of mutual education, where not only citizens communicate their views (via the public sphere, media, opinion polls, functional associations, consultations, etc.), but the representing seek to *influence* the preferences of voters, e.g. by continually justifying their political choices (cf. Young 2000: 131; Trenz 2009: 41) to gain approval for them. There is thus ongoing interaction and mutual adjustment (Benz and Papadopoulos 2006: 6) between representatives and representees.

This means that *accountability* does not take place solely through elections, but also in a deliberative way. Representatives continually give accounts of their actions – they justify and explain (Rosanvallon 2010: 329) – and the reactions of the accounters can follow immediately, so that the representatives may face consequences of their actions instantly, and will again react promptly (cf. Williams 1998: 231–2). Hence, the quality of this deliberation and the realisation of *deliberative accountability* become central to the normative evaluation of representation. At the same time, accountability is understood to include the entire process of communication and all its actors, such as political parties, associations, the media, etc.[7] In the context of electoral representation, deliberative accountability fills the spaces between elections, which in turn structure deliberation, the shadow of which makes deliberative accountability work. Mansbridge's concern is to develop normative criteria for modes of representation that have been empirically established as occurring in the US parliamentary system. Here, anticipatory representation is something on top of the fundaments of electoral representation. In the same vein, Gutmann and Thompson (2004: 62) argue that 'publicity' should fill the gap if there is a lack of electoral accountability. However, elections are not always requisite for deliberative accountability to work. For example, an association advocating the interests of single parents will typically have very little or no electoral accountability to single parents in their society. In order to be viewed as their legitimate functional representative in spite of this, it needs to make its activities and positions public and justify them, thus seeking support in the form of membership, donations, public acclamation, etc. This support can in turn increase its legitimacy and political weight, and thus its influence as an interlocutor of other political actors. At the same time, the reactions on the part of the public may also prompt it to adjust its activities. An association can thus be accountable at least to attentive sub-publics in a deliberative way, and the extent to which this is the case can serve as one criterion to evaluate their legitimacy as representatives.

Deliberative accountability, in different forms, is also essential for Mansbridge's remaining two modes of representation. The third mode of representation, *gyroscopic representation*[8] (Mansbridge 2003: 520–2), refers to the common practice of voters selecting a candidate 'with similar policy preferences, who is relatively honest and principled (hard to buy off), and who is skilled' (Fearon 1999: 68). They expect the representative to stay committed to her internally determined principles and thus to act in a predictable way. As the represented share their basic values with the representing, they *trust* her to act at her discretion, so that no ongoing communication is needed. Deliberation of a good quality is necessary only at election times, to enable the voter to evaluate the candidates and select a 'good type'. In other words, trust is more important than

---

7. Hirst (2000: 27) speaks of 'organised publics' who 'conduct a dialogue with government and thus hold it to account'. Cf. Young 2000: 132.

8. A gyroscope is a fast-spinning wheel, mounted in such a way that its axis is free to move in any direction. In this way, the influence of external forces is minimised, so that the orientation of the wheel can stay in a plane that is fixed in relation to the stars, independently of the earth's rotation and of other influences.

scrutiny of the representatives' actions, and political change is not brought about by influencing the representatives' behaviour but by changing the representatives (also Mansbridge 1999: 644).

The same mechanism can be observed in the ways citizens support unelected functional representatives. Associations are often chosen on the basis of the values or objectives they profess to advocate, but supporters seldom closely follow their activities or engage in their internal processes (Warleigh 2001: 634; Maloney 2008: 75–7). The difference to Mansbridge's account is that here, in the absence of periodic elections, unelected gyroscopic representatives need to seek support and thus engage in public deliberation continually. What results, however, is that once they have gained the support of a particular person, engagement in regular deliberation with this person will then not be necessary any more. People may arrange, for example, for a monthly donation to be automatically transferred from their bank account to Greenpeace, and subsequently trust that organisation to advocate environmental concerns independently.

How does this trust come about? To evaluate whether a representative can be relied upon to follow a certain direction when decisions are left at her own discretion, the representees need some hints. This can be the publicly built identity of the organisation and their representatives, which to some extent restricts their activities so that they remain credible. For example, Greenpeace can be expected to adhere to a general orientation towards environmental protection. If one shares this value and has no particularly specific preferences about single issues within this frame, there is no need for constant communication. In the case of not-for-profit organisations, this trust is often underpinned by the expectation of a 'motivational distinctiveness' (Goodin 2003b: 372–3), i.e. strong personal commitment of their personnel to their 'cause' that does not easily change. Another possible hint is the visible belonging of a representative to the particular social group she represents. For example, the above-mentioned association advocating the interests of single parents may gain confidence and support among their constituency if their representatives appearing in public are single parents themselves. Representees may infer that if these persons share a relevant aspect of their life situation, they can be expected to advocate the interests common to others in the same situation out of their own inner motivation (cf. Mansbridge 2003: 522).

In any event, gyroscopic representation acknowledges that in order to be represented, citizens do not need to be continually politically active. Rather, the focus is shifted towards *feeling* represented. Passivity and tacit support are legitimate as long as the represented has the possibilities to become active and exert influence at any moment she chooses to.

Finally, *surrogate representation* (Mansbridge 2003: 522–5) is a relation of citizens to a representative from a different (formal, territorial) constituency, i.e. a person they cannot vote for. This occurs when those concerned by a certain matter support a member of the representative assembly who is advocating their views on this specific matter. Mansbridge distinguishes two types of surrogate representation: 'monetary surrogacy' means the material support of a representative, which entails the danger of inequality due to the citizens' unequal possibilities to exert influence in this way. The other type is based on the responsibility a representative feels for a particular cause. Often, this personal commitment rests on a shared identity or experience between the representative and those whose concerns she defends.

Surrogate representation is thus as such a form of functional representation and could also be described as virtual representation (Burke [1972] 1999).[9] Importantly, it comes about not primarily by a functional constituency approaching a member of the representative assembly to represent them, but rather by the representatives choosing their represented by committing themselves to a particular cause. The functional constituents have no relation of electoral accountability with the representative, but they have the option to give or withdraw their support (money, voluntary work, information, networking, etc.), and can thus exercise deliberative accountability. Clearly, the concept of surrogate representation can be directly applied to unelected functional representation:[10] people choose to support someone who represents their views on a given matter in a relevant political arena. Furthermore, surrogate representation entails the notion that different representatives can represent different aspects of the same person, such as her area of residence – represented by her constituency's MP – and her concern for the rights of homosexuals, for example, represented by an MP from a different territorial constituency who actively promotes these concerns. Being represented well can thus be interpreted as finding a representative for each issue that is important to oneself (cf. Cole 1920: 103–6). Finally, surrogate representation departs the furthest of Mansbridge's four modes of representation from formal relationships between represented and representing. In order to be represented by someone, one does not need to be a *member* of an organisation (be it a territorial constituency or a functional association), as the represented can also be informal *supporters* (cf. Halpin 2006).

Taken together, the concepts developed here considerably recast the notions of what it means to represent. However, this becomes much clearer when applying them to non-electoral representation, which the writers of this literature do not do themselves.

9.　Burke defines virtual representation as follows:
> Virtual representation is that in which there is a communion of interests, and a sympathy in feelings and desires between those who act in the name of any description of people, and the people in whose name they act, though the trustees are not actually chosen by them. This is virtual representation. Such a representation I think to be, in many cases, even better than the actual. It possesses most of its advantages, and is free from many of its inconveniences: it corrects the irregularities in the literal representation, when the shifting current of human affairs, or the acting of public interests in different ways, carry it obliquely from its first line of direction. The people may err in their choice; but common interest and common sentiment are rarely mistaken (Burke [1792] 1999).

It is often overlooked that 'sympathy in feelings and desires' is an essential characteristic of virtual representation. It can thus not take place merely through institutional arrangements.

10.　Michael Saward has criticised the term 'surrogacy' for implying that 'real' representation always remains the electoral variant, even though the concept as such lends itself directly to non-electoral representation (Saward 2005: 183; 2009: 2). I do not contest this, but retain Mansbridge's established terminology to avoid confusion.

First of all, deliberative representation applies a more *systemic* view of representation. We cannot tell whether representation works well by looking exclusively at elections; we need to take into account the whole political process, including the public sphere, the media, the communication between representing and represented (as well as within both of these groups), associational life, questions of justice and fairness, social relations of domination and exclusion, governance processes, and many other things. Non-electoral, functional representation is an indispensable part of this. Viewed from the perspective of deliberative representation, it can be conceptualised as an essential part of the representative system, one that is necessary for other parts to function well, and that itself needs those other parts, particularly the fundaments of electoral, territorial representation. Deliberative representation thus evokes a conception where an electoral frame based on the principal–agent model is necessary, but not sufficient, for legitimate representation, and where within that frame, individual instances of legitimate representation may or may not be electoral. Representation is thus recognised to work in many different modes and styles, which are not alternatives but overlapping and parallel, i.e. different dimensions of representation rather than opposing interpretations. This insight makes it possible to analyse governance and participation as political representation.

The work on *deliberation* and *communication* can shed light on how non-electoral representation functions in practice, i.e. what the relationships between representatives and representees can be like. It fits well with the notion of different degrees of affectedness, or different intensities of preferences, which underlies an understanding of functional representation as the representation of the affected. By the same token, it helps to deal with cases in which preferences are oppressed and thus not articulated. The concept of *deliberative accountability* is particularly valuable in this respect, because it allows tackling the question of how functional representation can have democratic legitimacy of its own, even though it does not have electoral legitimacy in the traditional principal–agent sense (cf. Chapter Four).

How, then, do we evaluate the *legitimacy* of unelected functional representatives from the perspective of deliberative representation? Briefly, someone can be seen as a legitimate representative of a given constituency if she has a communicative relationship with that constituency that is strong enough to commit her to heeding their views, be it because of the shadow of elections, her own inner convictions, or pressure emanating from public debate. More precisely, the criteria hinge on the quality of communication between (would-be) representatives and representees, as well as on the functional representatives' role in public deliberation. An association can be considered a legitimate representative of a functional constituency if it is in ongoing communication with a significant number of people from that constituency; in other words, they have a real relationship where information flows in both directions, and there is sufficient observable support among those represented. In this way, the representing and the represented develop and shape a common understanding of what the association is representing about the individuals associated with it, so that the represented *feel* represented by it in this respect. In addition, if an association seeks to influence public policy, it needs to engage in open public deliberation, i.e. at least make public their activities, organisation, financing, etc., and justify their choices, thus making themselves accountable to the public as well. Although they are representing only a part of the citizenry at large, it is ultimately the whole political community that decides who to accept as an interlocutor in shaping the rules of that community. In both of these arenas – the general public as well as the communication with the constituency – the legitimacy of the functional representative is built dialogically from either side. The most important indicator of legitimacy is the support received, from representees (acclamation, donations, membership) and in the form of wider public acceptance.

Despite the obvious differences of this view to simple principal–agent models, the two share a number of basic starting points. Both perspectives focus their attention on the representation of a constituency to an elected legislature, and both assume that this constituency is logically prior to their representation. Although proponents of the deliberative view maintain that preferences can change in interaction, while simple principal–agent models see a more aggregative process, in either case there first exists an original preference before this can be represented or possibly enter into an interaction with other preferences. It is unambiguously the represented who constitute the representing (Trenz 2009: 39)[11] and therefore are their principals. Hence, what ultimately makes representation legitimate is representativeness, defined as acting in the interest of the represented.

However, albeit building on the principles of principal–agent models, deliberative representation goes well beyond these models, which can especially be seen when applying its concepts to non-electoral forms of representation. The very recent theory of the representative claim takes up these concepts and separates them from the principal–agent framework.

The representative claim

In contrast to the former two perspectives, the theory of the representative claim is not primarily a theory of democratic representation, but is mainly concerned with the essence of representation as a social phenomenon, i.e. it addresses the questions of what representation is and how it comes about.[12] Representation is here seen as a two-way dynamic relationship. It is not a fact established through institutions (such as elections), but something imagined (in the sense of Benedict Anderson (1991)), created, constructed, constituted rhetorically, and therefore changing. Crucially, there is no constituency prior to representation, as the represented is 'constituted and defined and understood *within* the process of

---

11. Cf. Sieyès' distinction between '*pouvoir constitué*' (constituted power) and '*pouvoir constituent*' (constituting power) (Sieyès 1789: 76).

12. My account of the theory of the representative claim is essentially based on Michael Saward (2005; 2006; 2009; 2010), who coined the term 'representative claim'. *See also* Seitz 1995 and Ankersmit 1996.

political representation itself, and not somehow apart from or prior to it' (Saward 2005: 181). Michael Saward has pinned down the process in the concept of the *claim* that the (would-be) representative makes:

> [T]he represented play a role in choosing representatives, and representatives 'choose' their constituents in the sense of portraying them or framing them in particular, contestable ways. If I allege that you, a potential constituent of mine, possess key characteristic X, and if I can get you to accept this, I can then present myself as possessing capacity or attribute Y that enables me to represent you – by virtue of a certain resonance between X and Y. In other words, would-be political representatives, in this process of portrayal or representation of constituencies, *make claims* about themselves and their constituents and the links between the two; they argue or imply that they are the best representatives of the constituency *so understood*. (Saward 2006: 301–2)

This claim can be implicit or explicit, and it can be about oneself or about a third actor. Representation is a creative, performative, and essentially rhetorical activity. The representing constitute constituencies by creating and offering descriptions and images of them (making representations of them), in order to present themselves as their representatives (Saward 2006: 300–1).

For example, the European Commissioner for Employment and Social Affairs, Anna Diamantopoulou, speaking to the General Assembly of the Greek National Confederation of Disabled People, addresses her audience: 'Civil society, NGO volunteers, like yourselves, play your full role. Making the voices of people with disabilities heard' (European Commission 2003a). This is a representative claim about the organisation she addresses, evoking 'people with disabilities' as a constituency that can be represented, and claiming that 'civil society' and 'NGO volunteers' are appropriate representatives of this constituency. In other words, 'disability' is here constructed as a characteristic that demarcates a certain group of individuals, who thus become a constituency identified with this characteristic. At the same time, NGOs are constructed as political actors with a certain role, by virtue of representing this constituency.

Representation comes into being – i.e. a claim is successful – if, when, and as long as the audience *accepts* the claim, i.e. recognises both the described group in the portrait drawn and the proposed representative of that group. To say that the initiative lies with the potential representative to make an offer does thus not mean that the constituents are passive, nor that representatives could define constituencies arbitrarily. Instead, conceptualising representation as a claim for acceptance addressed to an audience makes it a dialogical process of 'mutual constitution' (Young 2000: 130n13) between representing and represented. Making a claim that is accepted, and receiving claims that one can accept, requires that the claimant knows her would-be constituency and reacts to the impulses coming from them. Representation is thus a 'two-way street' (Saward 2006: 301). Therefore, a claim has to connect to something that already exists. Representation does not create reality, as F. R. Ankersmit (1996: 48) stresses: 'The insight is better captured by considering what takes place when we encircle a certain territory on the map and call it "France" or "Germany"'. If such a claim is not perceived to correspond to something existing at least latently, it will not be recognised.

Crucially, however, although people with certain characteristics are already there (cf. Seitz 1995: 6), it is only through representation that they are invested with meaning and become a group (Saward 2005: 185; 2010: 51; cf. Rosanvallon 2008: 313). Put differently, although the claims-maker refers to something existing, she does not simply 'read off' (Saward 2006: 312) or discover constituency wants and needs as they are, because 'there will not be a clear "want", but rather a mixed and shifting set of preferences, half-preferences and apathy that a would-be representative must shape, mould, quite possibly "create" and try to sell back to the relevant constituency' (Saward 2005: 189). In Linda Alcoff's words, the representative tells the represented '*who they are*' by 'representing them *as* such and such' (Alcoff 1991: 9). Without representation, the represented do not exist *as such and such*, and therefore there is no constituency, no group with a shared identity.[13] Hence, constituencies and, therefore, '[s]ocieties exist through the practice of their own representation' (Trenz 2007, cited in Kohler-Koch 2010a: 106). The essence of representation is therefore not about mediating views: '[R]epresentation *is* mediation' (Coleman 2009).

Ultimately, then, representation is inherently *rhetorical*. The potential representative puts forward premises about the representees and herself, out of which she deduces the conclusion that she is their ideal representative. In order to persuade her audience, she has to build this argumentation on familiar, accepted styles and topoi, such as, for example, 'I am one of you'. The art of representing can therefore be described as the skill to pick certain elements out of the stream of amorphous reality and present them in such an integrated way that the whole proposition appeals to the audience as true. In Ankersmit's words, representation 'proposes that we see the world from a certain perspective and that we arrange what can be seen in a specific way' (Ankersmit 1996: 39).

Describing a group of people *as* such and such means choosing the characteristics out of which to construct their identity. To say 'you are like this' is to single out particular parts of reality and designate them the status of defining a group (a constituency). Representative claims are thus always selective and partial, alleging to represent the addressed people with respect to certain *aspects* of them. They can never claim to represent any individual in all her individuality (Ankersmit 1996: 25, 39; Cole 1950: 99). This means, firstly, that representation always means simplifying (Young 1997, cited in Pollak *et al.* 2009: 13 (as 'Young 1986')). Secondly, it makes the constituencies so created *fluid* and *overlapping*, because nobody is ever described once and for all. Different portrayals of me – a potential representee – can resonate with different parts of my identity, and

---

13. Trenz (2009: 40) calls this the 'integrative mechanism' of representation, as opposed to the 'aggregative mechanism' associated with principal–agent models. Cf. Seitz 1995: 5; Sørensen 2002: 706; Rosanvallon 2010: 224. Concerning the level of the individual, *see* Palonen 2009: 148.

I may subscribe to different claims in different circumstances. The theory of the representative claim thus fits with a conception of identities as constructed, multiple, and non-essentialist.

The interplay between claims-making and reactions to claims means that *power* resides with both the representing and the represented. Obviously, constituting constituencies is a form of power, which can be compared to the power of framing issues and defining problems.[14] Yet, as noted above, representatives cannot create any kind of constituencies, as they are restricted by what exists in reality and may resonate with their claim. As well as that, to make their claim compelling they have to formulate it in terms of cultural codes and connect it to familiar contextual frameworks, which are given and thus limit their choices (Saward 2006: 303, 311–12).[15] What is more, any representative claim can be contested and rejected, and the represented can choose what claims to subscribe to. This means that the power of the represented is essentially reactive and negative (Urbinati 2006: 28–9; cf. Rosanvallon 2008; Manin 1997: 222–6, 230).[16] Ankersmit (1996: 53) therefore concludes straightforwardly that 'the idea of popular sovereignty will have to be rejected'. In his interpretation, because representation comes into being in the interaction between represented and representing, power originates in the space between them. It is thus not possessed by either of them, but can only be used. The represented entrust the use of power to their representatives, and the use of this power is legitimate as long as it can just as easily be taken away again (Ankersmit 1996: 50, 54).

Saward, Ankersmit, and Seitz present their accounts of representation as descriptions which come closer to reality than others starting from the logical priority of the represented over the representing. However, Ankersmit explicitly stresses that the priority of the representing is nothing lamentable, because representation is vitally necessary in exactly this way. As it interprets and thus creates reality, representation organises knowledge, and therefore enables us to 'orient ourselves in reality and entertain a meaningful relationship with it' (Ankersmit 1996: 40; *see also* Rosanvallon 2008: 313).

Notwithstanding, representation can also be used as an instrument of power to silence the allegedly represented:

---

14. Claude Lefort has put it this way: 'Power belongs to the individual[s] [...] who speak in the name of the people and give them their name' (Lefort 1988: 109–10).

15. I do of course not mean that cultural codes and frames are 'given' like natural laws that cannot be changed. My point here is that a single actor (an individual or an organisation) cannot change or choose cultural paradigms at her convenience, but has to act within the paradigm she finds herself in. Cf. Kangas 2007: 29.

16. The same may of course be said within the paradigms of simple principal–agent models and deliberative representation. However, these theories start from the ideal of *self*-government and seek to stress elements of the positive power of the represented. They thus regret the primacy of negative power (e.g. Dunn 1999: 343), while the representative claim acknowledges it as an empirical fact and makes this the starting point of its analysis.

Claims can by their nature silence the constituencies or people or groups which they constitute by evoking; reinforce, or bring about or claim the necessity of the absence of the represented from the political arena; appropriate the voice of the represented by the very process of evoking into being a represented with a voice; and become privileged weapons in the hands of elite minorities with privileged access to technologies and institutions of claim-making. (Saward 2006: 304)

Representative claims-making does thus not automatically empower the represented. However, the instrument of claims-making cannot be monopolised by anyone. Even if the intention of the maker is to silence the group she evokes, she inevitably gives them an identity by claiming to represent them, thus calling them into existence as an addressable entity (Trenz 2009: 41). This can be the starting point for the addressed to object to the claim, which can empower them (Saward 2006: 304).

The process of creating constituencies can also be used for social engineering from above. In this vein, Hans-Jörg Trenz argues that the civil society discourses of the European Commission and other EU institutional bodies, 'instead of reading off civil society's objective interests or expressing its inherent identity, constitute [...] civil society by representing it' (Trenz 2009: 40). At the same time, these European actors define what counts as 'civil society' and constitute themselves as the appropriate representatives of 'civil society'. The outcomes of this process also demonstrate that representation is a two-way relationship that is not established just by someone claiming so, and that also may take time to come about.

The theory of the representative claim looks at representation from a wide angle and takes into account very different kinds of representatives, constituencies, and styles of representation. This first of all means that it does not make a categorical distinction between *electoral and non-electoral representation*. Instead, elections are part of the cultural institutions conditioning the styles of representative claims and establishing norms of what is accepted as legitimate in a particular context (Saward 2006: 311). For example, when it comes to voting on legislation or signing international treaties, we would expect the actor to be elected according to specific procedures. If she is, we would accept the resulting rules as legitimate, even if we had not voted for her ourselves, or if we disagreed with her action. In addition, elections structure and enhance public deliberation (Saward 2009: 22; cf. Urbinati and Warren 2008: 402). This function, and the established status that elections have, means that electoral representation is not just any kind of representation among all the others, but it is – and rightly remains – at the core of political representation. There is nothing wrong with electoral representation, but representation also takes place in a multitude of non-electoral settings (Saward 2005: 183). In most cases, electoral representation will be territorial, and non-electoral representation functional, representing those affected by a particular matter. Saward stresses that the democratic value of these two modes of representation is positive-sum, because elected territorial representatives' possible styles of representation are very limited, and unelected functional representatives can represent people in ways that elected

Table 2.1: Possible grounds for representative claims

Cognition	Contact	External conditions
Descriptive similarity	Authorisation and	Authorisation by an
Empathy	accountability	external authority
Expertise, knowledge, or	Being in touch	Hypothetical consent
experience	'Closeness'	Tradition or history
Independence from	Demonstration of support	Traditional belief systems
electoral politics	of the street	(e.g. religion)
Impartiality	Networking	
Reflexivity		
Shared identity		
Speaking for the excluded		

Source: Based on Saward 2009; O'Neill 2001: 489–90, 496; Rosanvallon 2010; Coleman 2005: 199–200.

politicians cannot. Functional representation is much more flexible with respect to interests that transcend territorial borders; partial, evolving, or temporary interests; and new patterns of representation (Saward 2009: 21, 4–9; cf. Urbinati and Warren 2008: 403–4). One key argument in making claims to represent such constituencies is their right to be involved on the grounds of their *affectedness*, in some way, by the matter at hand. The claim-maker will then present herself as their ideal representative by virtue of her special expertise; of being authorised by a relevant, appropriate actor; of giving voice to those who would otherwise remain unheard; of being herself a member of that constituency (descriptive representation); or other reasons that tap into established topoi of representation (cf. Saward 2009: 10–15).

Representative claims can be based on many different grounds. They can roughly be categorised in three groups: *cognitive claims* are based on the claimant's knowledge or attitude, claims based on *contact* draw on a communicative connection between the representative and the represented, and claims based on *external conditions* refer to some independent third authority or circumstance. These categories are not exclusive, but individual claims can quite obviously combine several elements, e.g. to maintain that because of a communicative relation a representative knows the represented especially well. Yet, given the plurality of claims, this systematisation can make the field clearer.

As the examples in Table 2.1 show, representative claims can be based on principal–agent or deliberative logics, but also on other arguments.

Symbolic representation[17] becomes a central element of what representation is about. First of all, this is because depicting what is to be represented is an

---

17. Cf. Pitkin 1967: Ch. 5. In Pitkin's definition, symbolic representation means that someone represents to the extent that a relevant constituency accepts her as symbolising them, regardless of the constituency's reasons for doing so (1967: 102–4).

inherently symbolic activity (Saward 2006: 301). For instance, parliamentary buildings usually symbolise the unity of the nation – the key constituency for many national politicians, who actively utilise symbols and images like this in order to back up their claim to represent this entity. At the same time, the constituency is constructed and kept up by the continual re-application of the same symbols. Seen from the side of the represented, symbolic representation is not least about the *feeling* of being represented, which is an essential factor of what makes people accept representative claims. As with the proponents of deliberative representation, the theory of the representative claim refuses to oppose symbolic to substantial representation (in the sense of 'acting for'[18]), but it does so on different grounds. Whereas the former rehabilitates symbolic representation because it has substantive consequences (*see* Chapter Three), it is here seen as an indispensable *element* of substantive 'acting for' that cannot be ignored (Saward 2006: 301). In the same vein, Pierre Rosanvallon (2008: 313–17) has stressed the role of the lack of collective symbols in the increasing estrangement of the people from the political process.[19] Contrary to the formalistic approach of simple principal–agent models, whereby representation is a fact established through elections, it is in this perspective a precarious state of affairs that is kept up essentially by its *visibility* to the represented. Because representation is an abstract entity, it has to be symbolised in order to be perceptible. Hence, the media shows us pictures of representatives climbing out of their limousines, waiting for a meeting to begin, or inaugurating bridges, because these acts and their mediation are part of representing. Representative claims have to be communicated, thus put into some language, which is symbolic by definition. If we do not see, hear, or read about our representatives representing – i.e. making (implicit) claims to be our representatives – we cannot relate to these claims, and there is therefore no representation.

Consequently, a *functioning public sphere* is a key prerequisite for representation to take place, and to take place legitimately. It conveys representative claims and their reactions, and therefore it is the environment that conditions whether and how different claims and reactions are heard. It offers the instruments to manipulate representations as well as to expose manipulations.

How, then, do we evaluate the *legitimacy* of representation in this perspective? That is, how do we know whether someone's claim to represent a constituency is justified? The theory of the representative claim shifts the focus to the legitimacy of the *claim*. Put simply, if a claim to represent a particular constituency is accepted by the relevant *audience* to which it is addressed, the claim is legitimate and with this, representation comes about (Rehfeld 2006; Saward 2006; 2009). Importantly, this does not necessarily mean that an instance of representation is democratic, only that there is representation at all. The audience is defined by Andrew Rehfeld as 'the relevant group of people who must recognize a

---

18. *See* Saward's criticism of Pitkin (Saward 2006: 300–1; 2005: 180–1).

19. Cf. Trenz's (2009: 40) concept of the integrative function of representation.

claimant as representative, and the relevance of the group will always depend on the particular Function of a case of representation' (Rehfeld 2006: 5; emphasis omitted). Saward specifies that

> the audience for a given claim is that group which receives (listens to, sees, or is aware of) the claim. The audience for a given representative claim might, in principle, be coterminous with, overlap with, or even be wholly different from (including larger or smaller than) the would-be constituency. [...] However, in many cases audience and constituency will overlap considerably. (Saward 2009: 3–10)

Rehfeld's illustrative example is a clear one: the relevant audience for the person claiming to represent Libya at the WTO is the WTO General Council (Rehfeld 2006: 1, 19–20), not the people of Libya or Human Rights Watch. In most situations, and especially in cases of functional representation, it is more difficult to determine the audience, and there will mostly be several relevant parties involved. What is clear, however, is that in *democratic* contexts the audience cannot be completely separate from the constituency (see below).

Following this reasoning, the key to evaluating the legitimacy of any particular claim is the criteria applied by the audience. The crux of the matter is that most claims have several relevant audiences, and different audiences apply different criteria in different situations. The above example of Libya, used by Rehfeld in 2006, also shows that criteria and the ways of applying them can change, and such changes have consequences. Luckily, what at first seems to complicate things is in fact the key to integrating the perspectives of simple principle–agent models, deliberative representation, and the representative claim into one picture: the norms of the first two theories are two possible sets of criteria that audiences can apply to determine whether they accept someone as representative of a given constituency. In some situations, some audiences require electoral authorisation by a relevant body, and others accept representatives who have significant deliberative support within a relevant forum. However, different criteria are possible as well. Conversely, would-be representatives can build their claims on principal–agent or deliberative grounds, or on other considerations.

For example, a functional representative taking part in a governance arrangement needs to be accepted as a legitimate representative of her constituency by three main audiences: the constituency, the general public, and her governance peers (elected politicians, executives, other functional representatives, etc.). These three audiences can apply different criteria. The rules constituencies apply obviously vary a lot from one constituency to another and depend a lot on the nature of the functional association or movement. They can in principle be based on any of the grounds for representative claims listed in Table 2.1. The general public may apply different criteria, and they may also see the constituency differently from the picture given by the representative. Finally, peers may have different criteria than citizens, because they are not spectators but colleagues. Thus, in addition to criteria concerning the relationship of a representative with her constitution, they may require those wanting to participate to have an agenda compatible with the governance network's mainstream thinking, and to act according to a certain professional culture (Papadopoulos 2007: 481). Crucially, the criteria these different audiences apply need not be compatible, so that representatives may have to find ways to retain legitimacy in the perception of all three audiences without losing credibility (Halpin 2001).

In brief, what the theory of the representative claim does is to open the concept of what it means to represent to whatever relevant groups of people may endorse as representation. In this sense it is a descriptive theory. However, the approach has normative implications by conceptualising possible new styles and modes of governance as political representation. This should make it easier to analyse their potential to be integrated in the democratic system, and develop criteria and procedures to make them meet democratic standards, instead of seeing them as parallel structures more prone to undermining or sidelining democracy (cf. Saward 2006: 298–9).

So how is *democracy* conceptualised in the perspective of the representative claim? Obviously, for democratic representation, the key reference point is the *constituency*. First, a claim can be evaluated on the grounds of whether it refers at all to any specifiable constituency that might in principle react to it. An important criterion here is the extent to which the would-be constituency is part of the audience. Next, the reaction of this constituency will show whether the claim can be considered democratically legitimate. If there is no immediate positive response, the absence of opposition to a claim repeatedly expressed in public can also preliminarily be interpreted as acceptance, while a more definitive evaluation is shifted to a later point in time. This criterion thus builds on deliberative principles whereby the acceptance or otherwise of a claim will be the outcome of public consideration (Saward 2009: 18; cf. Saward 2010: 143–54). If, after a reasonable period of time, there is no positive response from a substantive number of constituents, the claim cannot be seen as democratic (Saward 2010: 157–8). Conversely, 'evidence of sufficient acceptance by appropriate constituencies over time under reasonable conditions of judgement' (Saward 2011: 10) confirms a claim as democratic. Importantly, acceptance once given is no final verdict but is provisional, since the level of support, and thereby the democratic legitimacy of a representative, can change at any time. Again, this matches with deliberative accountability.

Clearly, such benchmarks leave a lot of room for interpretation. While they take account of new forms of representation as potentially democratic, it also becomes much more difficult to make definite judgements as to the democratic credentials of any particular instance. One additional problem is that for representation to work democratically according to these standards, it already needs a sufficiently democratic infrastructure. Would-be constituencies can only reasonably relate to representative claims in an open society 'where the freedom to support and to criticise political figures, claims, and proposals is of paramount value, and [...] where pluralism of ideas and values is widely accepted and practiced' (Saward 2010: 154) in a functioning public sphere. When it comes to more closed societies, it may be impossible to present claims at all or to reach potential constituencies; responses may be suppressed, and the actual support that a claim has may be impossible to evaluate. Another concern is the role of (alleged) tacit consent, especially in cases where the claimed constituency is made up of socially marginalised and therefore 'politically impoverished' (Bohman 2000: 125) people, who do not have the social and political resources to engage with more powerful political actors (Bohman 2000: 125–6). Arguably, it may still be desirable, precisely in the name of democracy, that these constituencies be represented in the political process (I come back to this issue in the following chapter). In any case, from simple principal–agent models and deliberative representation to the representative claim, the importance of political and social skills as well as education for democratic representation becomes recognised as one of the key factors. In other words, social equality is a cardinal prerequisite for democratic representation.

Although the theory of the representative claim renders democracy more slippery, it does preserve its conceptual core: that it is still the *constituency* that decides. The precise mode of decision varies with the style of representation. For example, in territorial representation constituents choose (elect) representatives, but they cannot choose whether they want to be represented by elected representatives. In functional representation people can mostly not choose associations' representatives, but they can choose what kinds of organisation to support, and through this have a choice of the mode of representation they prefer in a given area (Saward 2009: 9). It is a moot point whether the constituents are still sovereign in this conception; certainly, they are not the 'constituting power' in Emmanuel-Joseph Sieyès's sense (1789: 76). Notwithstanding, although the sovereignty of the people may be a fiction, the fact that the people is *recognised* as the source of all power has real consequences that distinguish a regime from others (Grimm 2009: 75). This recognition is part of the cultural conventions that influence what kinds of representative claims are accepted as legitimate in a society. This also means that rather than formal institutions (such as periodic elections or a free press), what is decisive for democracy is a society's day-to-day political culture (cf. Buchstein and Jörke 2007: 193–5).

In the following chapter, I take a brief look at a particular issue of political representation, namely the question of what difference it makes if people are represented by someone who is similar to them, such as the representation of women by women or of ethnical minorities by people from the same group. *Descriptive representation* in particular has been dealt with as a possible solution to the problems touched on above concerning the representation of socially marginalised groups. Furthermore, it is one form of functional representation practised in the social OMC. After that, Chapter Four changes the perspective to look at the democratic legitimacy of involving functional representatives in governance processes. For such involvement to be democratic, the question of whether the representatives are legitimately and democratically speaking for their constituencies is one key criterion. However, other issues also have to be taken into account.

Chapter Three

Descriptive Representation

Representation does not *per se* imply anything about the characteristics of the representative; very different concepts and practices are possible concerning what a good representative should be like. One of these, descriptive representation,[1] means that the representing *resemble* the represented in certain important aspects. Theorists of this perspective argue that, under certain conditions, women are better represented by women, and black people by black people, for example. Therefore, measures should be introduced to deliberately increase the share of women and black people in legislative assemblies.[2] This chapter gives an overview of the main arguments supporting this mode of representation, which are interesting for theoretical as well as practical reasons. First of all, in order to deal with the issue of whether, why, and in what sense, for example, women may be better represented by women than by men, the scholars of this orientation have had to give thought to what representation fundamentally is, and when it can be considered as legitimate and democratic. The concepts they develop in this regard add to the insights of the previous chapter. Secondly, descriptive representation is especially relevant for functional representation, where it takes place much more than in territorial representation. In the latter, the possibilities to represent social groups by their members are very restricted, mainly due to the necessarily limited number of representatives. By contrast, the sphere of functional representation accommodates any kind of representatives that find support among some constituency. Finally, descriptive representation is also important in the case of this study. One way in which functional representation is applied in the social OMC is the descriptive representation of poor people by poor representatives. The literature about this mode of representation offers important concepts to analyse this practice; however, the case of people living in poverty also emerges as a challenging one, because the concepts developed for descriptive representation are generally applied only to women and ethnic minorities.

---

1.   I use this term because it has become the most common one since it was used by Pitkin (1967). Notwithstanding, it is worth noting that Pitkin makes no clear distinction between mimetic or 'mirror' representation and descriptive representation as it is understood today, i.e. the purposeful resemblance of representatives and represented regarding certain chosen characteristics. As well as that, her use of the term 'descriptive' leads interpretations in the direction of the map metaphor and thus to a view of representation as mere 'giving information about' the represented, which is not intended here (Pitkin 1967: 84; cf. Saward 2006: 300–1).

2.   The proposed measures include party list quotas, caucuses, racial districting, and proportional representation (Dovi 2002: 729). Particularly gender quotas for parties' candidate lists have been increasing around the world. See 'Global database of quotas for women' (Quota Project, 2013).

To begin, it is important to distinguish descriptive representation from the concept of mimetic or 'mirror' representation.[3] The idea that the representative body should be a 'mirror' of the represented is an ideal that is commonly captured by quoting John Adams, the second president of the USA, who stated that the 'representative assembly should be an exact portrait, in miniature, of the people at large, [...] it should think, feel, reason, and act like them' (Adams 1851: 205).[4] Such mimetic representation is not only implausible but also undesirable, because a certain difference between the represented and the representing is precisely the essence of representation itself. If an exact mirror representation were possible, it would become unnecessary, since producing such an accurate copy would imply that every possible characteristic and view of the people were known and readily accessible, and that people actually had a view ready on all issues. Instead, representation offers us ways and perspectives to see the world, thereby making this world accessible to us. Relating to the world presupposes a certain distance (Ankersmit 1996: 39–40; cf. 21–56).[5]

Descriptive representation, by contrast, does not mean that the representative should be descriptive of the represented in every aspect, but concerning particular, chosen attributes.[6] If the representative body cannot and should not be a perfect miniature of the represented in all their characteristics, it is necessary to pick out those characteristics that ought to be represented. In fact, most theorists of political representation would argue that representatives should have something in common with the represented. The choice of these shared characteristics will be guided by normative values (cf. O'Neill 2001: 486) and by the purpose of the representative body. Thus, the representatives could be descriptive of the represented in terms of their interests, preferences, values, identities (O'Neill 2001: 489), area of residence, social class, gender, ethnic background, mother tongue, religion, etc. For example, most parliaments are meant to be descriptive regarding nationality, area of residence, and political party affiliation. This is a normative choice based on the belief that it is these characteristics that are most relevant with respect to the main purposes of parliaments. Other characteristics, such as profession, are considered less relevant. The gist of the literature arguing for descriptive representation is that representative bodies should be *more* descriptive with respect to certain social characteristics whose representation is now systematically skewed, but which

---

3.   Much of the criticism that has been put forward against descriptive representation has in fact addressed mirror representation, which, however, is rarely advocated by anyone. *See* Williams 1998: 28, 241–2; Mansbridge 1999: 629–30.

4.   It should be noted, though, that in the same paragraph Adams also describes the representatives as 'a few of the most wise and virtuous' (Adams 1851). In fact, he speaks about the exact representation of *interests* rather than about a real mirror of the represented in all their characteristics. *See also* Manin 1997: Ch. 3.

5.   The term 'mimetic representation' is Ankersmit's. Cf. Borges 1998: 422–36; Pitkin 1967: Ch. 4.

6.   Cf. the question Pitkin insists upon: Descriptive with respect to what? (Pitkin 1967: 87). In Pitkin, this question functions above all to demonstrate the implausibility of mirror representation and the map metaphor; she does not enter a discussion about what characteristics of the represented actually could or should be represented in a descriptive way.

are politically relevant. These writers mostly point to the under-representation of women and visible minorities, and much more seldom to that of the poor.

Mainly in the 1990s, a number of feminist, multiculturalist theorists advanced and conceptually developed descriptive representation within a framework of deliberative (electoral) representation (Young 1990; 2000; Phillips 1995; 1998; 2004; Williams 1998; Mansbridge 1999; Dovi 2002). In the following, I present their ideas, before I deal with how these ideas relate to the other two theoretical frameworks, *viz.* simple principal–agent models and the representative claim.

As pointed out in the previous chapter, in the perspective of deliberative representation the key to legitimate representation is the *communication* between represented and representing. This communication hinges decisively on the quality of public deliberation, and therefore includes a great variety of arenas, such as the media, committee hearings, consultations, civil society associations and interest groups, opinion polls, political parties, etc. Gaining representation means participating in this deliberation, and, accordingly, equal representation comes down to the equal possibility to do so. Furthermore, political equality is here understood as requiring *substantive equality* in addition to procedural (one-person-one-vote) equality. It is not enough that everybody has a formally equal share of power over political decisions (the right to vote, to express, and to advocate their views), but there also needs to be a solid level of equality in outcomes. This involves treating everybody fairly and with equal concern and attending to structural obstacles that result in de facto inequalities of opportunity (Phillips 1995: 37–8; 2004). The point, then, is that groups with a history of marginalisation have structurally unequal possibilities to gain representation and influence policy making, including being elected, putting their concerns on the political agenda, or gaining public visibility (cf. also Sanders 1997). This inequality can be reduced by deliberately increasing the share of representatives who are members of these groups; i.e. deliberate differences (less equality) on the formal, procedural input side can result in fewer differences (more equality) in the outcomes.

> In some circumstances equality means differential treatment; in other circumstances it means treating people the same – there is no logical or political requirement to stand by just one of these two options. [...] [W]e cannot deduce what is politically fair from abstract principles of political equality: we have to draw on empirical judgements of what is likely to happen as well as what seems in principle to be fair. (Phillips 1995: 37–8; cf. Williams 1998: 19–20, 197)

Descriptive representation is thus tied to a distinct *telos*: the transformation of society to become fairer, i.e. more equal in a substantial sense.

Since descriptive representation is representation 'with a purpose' (Phillips 1995: 47), this overall objective of transforming society guides the *choice* of groups to be given additional descriptive representation. Melissa Williams (1998: 176–7) proposes two criteria to choose the groups that need stronger descriptive representation: contemporary inequality, and a history of discrimination and oppression, i.e. historically marginalised groups that are still underrepresented in politics today. The process of choosing should be two-sided and deliberative. Decisions are left neither to the potential descriptive groups, nor to those dominating politics, but both of these are needed. The 'subjective' side of this process, i.e. a group's claim to be represented as a group, is necessary to ensure that the measure is applied only to groups having a sense of a shared identity – really existing groups, as it were (Williams 1998: 196). The 'objective' side is needed to establish the criteria of what constitutes a valid claim (p. 241). However, neither Williams nor her collaborators deal with the question of how to delimitate the chosen constituencies and determine who their members are. This may be because their starting point is the representation of women, but all of them extend their discussion to ethnic minorities, in which case it may quickly become difficult to determine whether a given person should be considered as a descriptive representative.

Now, how is such representation supposed to reduce the social disadvantages that some groups face? One very straightforward way is by improving the *communication* between represented and representing. As was shown in the previous chapter, in the perspective of deliberative representation, being represented means taking part in public deliberation and having one's view taken into account; the relationship between representing and represented is an ongoing, mediated, two-way communication. In the case of groups with a long experience of social exclusion, this communication can be severely impaired. The majority may have attitudes of inattention or even arrogance towards these groups, while the minority may have deep distrust of the majority and the political process. In this case, 'the shared experience imperfectly captured by descriptive representation facilitates vertical communication between representatives and constituents' (Mansbridge 1999: 641; cf. Williams 1998: Ch. 5). Descriptive representatives may be more attentive to the views of the social group they come from, and for members of that group the threshold to engage with representatives who share important parts of their background may be lower.

However, representation is much more than direct, dyadic relations between individual citizens and representatives, and descriptive representation in particular is essentially about group representation. Especially in this regard, scholars advocating descriptive representation have needed to differentiate themselves from essentialism, i.e. the 'assumption that members of certain groups have an essential identity that all members of that group share and of which no others can partake' (Mansbridge 1999: 637) so that it is impossible to represent members of social groups other than one's own (cf. Phillips 1995: 157; Williams 1998: 6). Iris Marion Young solves this difficulty by starting from the question of what exactly is supposed to be represented in descriptive representation. Because representation is not about substituting one person with another but a mediated relation (Young 2000: 126–7), 'systems of political representation cannot make individuals present in their individuality, but rather should represent *aspects* of a person's life experience, identity, beliefs, or activity where she or he has affinity with others' (Young 2000: 133; similarly, Williams 1998: 141). Young pinpoints interest, opinion, and perspective as possible aspects of the individual that can be represented, out of which *perspective* is the one relevant for the argument supporting the descriptive self-representation of socially marginalised groups. Young defines social groups in a relational way: individuals are positioned in social structures rather than having their identity determined by them. Crucially,

> differently positioned people have different experience, history, and social knowledge derived from that positioning. I call this social perspective. Because of their social locations, people are attuned to particular kinds of social meanings and relationships to which others are less attuned. Sometimes others are not positioned to be aware of them at all. (Young 2000: 136; emphasis omitted)

The latter being the case in instances of histories of marginalisation, it is therefore in these particular situations where perspectives are very difficult to represent for those who do not immediately hold them. Young stresses that social perspective does not contain a specific content: 'Representing an interest or an opinion usually entails promoting certain specific outcomes in the decision-making process. Representing a perspective, on the other hand, usually means promoting certain starting points for discussion' (Young 2000: 140). When perspectives differ considerably between different social groups, a body of representatives can only be said to be *representative* if it reflects these differences, and sometimes this may necessitate descriptive representation (Phillips 2004: 9). In view of the special purpose of descriptive representation, Suzanne Dovi (2002: 737) maintains that part of the perspective to be represented should be the shared aim or vision to 'improv[e] [...] the social, economic, and political status' of the group in question, as a broad direction of politics.

Representing a particular social perspective, based on the representative's own experience, raises the question of how this relates to political *accountability*. All theorists of descriptive representation apply their ideas to electoral settings, notably parliamentary representation, i.e. they operate on the fundaments of electoral accountability. At the same time, they subscribe to a deliberative view of representation, where electoral accountability is not sufficient to make representatives genuinely accountable, but needs to be complemented with deliberative accountability. Crucially, sometimes descriptive representation may be necessary to make deliberative accountability work (Dovi 2002: 730, referring to Sapiro 1981), by introducing representatives who are able to mediate marginalised views into the political process and establish communicative relationships with the excluded. Importantly though, resemblance is no alternative to political accountability. Quite to the contrary, for descriptive representation too, accountability is necessary to be legitimate, since descriptive representatives do not automatically represent the self-identified interests of a group (Williams 1998: 131),[7] and the choice of individuals to represent any given group matters

---

7. Cf. Williams' discussion of accountability and her criticism of Phillips' way of conceptualising the issue (Williams 1998: 228–31; Phillips 1995: Ch. 6).

(Dovi 2002). In addition, deliberative accountability ensures that descriptive representatives perceive themselves and are perceived by their descriptive constituency as belonging to the same group (Dovi 2002: 735), and strong mutual relationships prevent representatives from becoming co-opted by dominant social groups.

Overall, the assumption underlying these arguments is that who the representatives are influences what they do, such that policy *outcomes* will be different depending on the social composition of a representative body. For one thing, this is because through different representatives, different inputs are mediated into the process. In the case of representatives coming from socially disadvantaged groups, the overall impact of their inputs is expected to transform society to become more equal in terms of substantial fairness:

> Because of their social positioning, members of structurally differentiated groups often have different understandings of the causes of the problems and conflicts and the possible effects of proposed solutions. [...] If only a few of those understandings influence discussion and decision-making, political actors are likely to perpetuate injustice or take imprudent action. (Young 2000: 144–5; cf. Williams 1998: 139; Mansbridge 1999–654)

Moreover, descriptive representatives may also be more motivated than their colleagues from more privileged backgrounds to advance such outcomes and actively push for them (cf. Gargarella 1998: 262). Therefore, Dovi (2002: 738) argues that preferable descriptive representatives should 'share [with their descriptive constituency] a political vision aimed at relieving the plight of their communities' and be 'perceived by members of a historically disadvantaged group as improving their linked fate'. Clearly, descriptive representation is theorised around a very distinct purpose and is not meant as a value as such; it is not a compensation for past discrimination (Williams 1998: 197), or designed for different groups to 'express their culture in public discussion or be recognised in their distinctiveness' (Young 2000: 146; cf. Mansbridge 1999: 651; Taylor 1992). What is more, the intended effects of descriptive representation are not only meant to come about through mediating preferences of marginalised groups 'as they are'. Rather, preferences are also endogenous, i.e. formed in relation to a context (Sunstein 1991: esp. 5, 10), such that people adapt their demands to the conditions and norms they are used to. Consequently, disadvantaged people may not be able to formulate and push issues on the political agenda or challenge dominant conventions unless their peers are more consistently present in the process of developing political alternatives (Phillips 1995: 44–5).

This means that descriptive representation closely links *symbolic* and *substantive* representation. The dichotomy of these modes of representation goes back to Pitkin, who defines symbolic representation as someone representing to the extent that a relevant constituency believes in her or accepts her as symbolising them, regardless of their reasons for doing so (Pitkin 1967: 102–4). Pitkin dismisses symbolic representation because the concept is indifferent to what the representative does (i.e. the substantial dimension of representation). Theories of descriptive representation do not construct such an opposition. Although descriptive representation is meant to have a strong symbolic dimension, this is not valued as such but because of its substantial consequences. Already, the visibility of people from marginalised groups on the political stage may empower others from the same groups to participate and engage themselves, thus integrating them in society (Young 2000: 144). Such visibility also has an effect on how a group is perceived by the majority. Phillips speaks of the 'infantilization' of those parts of the citizenry who are not present in the political process and thus remain 'to be cared for by those who know best' (Phillips 1995: 39; cf. pp. 43–4). The resulting notion is that these groups cannot govern or are not suitable to govern (Mansbridge 1999: 649). Jane Mansbridge therefore argues that 'symbolic' and 'substantive' representation should not be contrasted (pp. 650–2).

Concerning other modes of representation, descriptive representation obviously has strong affinities to *gyroscopic* (cf. Phillips 1995: 41–3, 159; Mansbridge 1999: 643–6; Dovi 2002: 738) and *surrogate* (cf. Mansbridge 1999: 642–3) representation (see Chapter Two). Sharing a particular background with a representative can be a reason to support her and to trust her, and without closely following her political activities.

The theory of descriptive representation in cases of social marginalisation is firmly built on the fundaments of deliberative representation. What does it look like from the perspective of the other two theories of representation, simple principle–agent models and the representative claim?

Simple principal–agent models are mainly what theorists of descriptive representation argue against. In this perspective, a major role is given to procedural fairness and formal equality, built on the idea that universal suffrage would lead to the consideration of all preferences. Issues such as structural inequalities and processes of silencing – preventing people from expressing their preferences and becoming aware of ways to advance them – are not part of this paradigm, neither are cognitive barriers to understanding between different social groups (Williams 1998: 138–9). However, all theorists of descriptive representation develop their ideas for a context of electoral representation, notably parliaments. Also, in their view, formal authorisation and accountability are necessary to make descriptive representation legitimate, although they do not see it as sufficient. Thus, as with deliberative representation more generally, these theorists also develop principal–agent models further, rather than questioning their basic assumptions.

For the theory of the *representative claim*, descriptive representation is one possible ground for making and accepting claims to represent a constituency. This can be done on the basis of different (often complementary) logics, all of which are also discussed by the scholars cited above:

> [F]or example, one could claim to represent women by virtue of descriptive similarity (being a woman), substantive capability and orientation (knowing women's interests and being motivated to act upon them), claiming to be mandated by women to act in a certain capacity, or claiming to be a trustee for the interests of women possibly regardless of what many women may think of as constituting their interests. (Saward 2010: 73)

Many insights developed by theorists of descriptive representation, if taken one step further, correspond to central ideas of the representative claim. For example, when Dovi (2002: 735) maintains that descriptive representatives and their constituencies should 'mutually recognize each other' in an 'interactive relationship' and share common aims or visions, this is not far from saying that these two parties mutually constitute each other. Similarly, when Young differentiates between different aspects to be represented (interest, opinion, and perspective), this corresponds to the insight that nobody can ever be represented in her full individuality, and that we are thus always represented *as* somebody. Hence, different aspects of individuals can be represented by different representatives. Someone can be represented in her national parliament as a national of her country, as a resident of a particular region, and as an affiliate of a given party; by Greenpeace as a person concerned about the environment; by an informal Internet-based movement as an opponent of right-wing extremism; by a trade union as an employee in a particular sector, and so on. The possibilities are as unlimited as is the universality of individuals, and therefore new claimants can always attempt to construct new constituencies based on some characteristic they find relevant in some context. In the perspective of the representative claim, it is not as such surprising that some claims may be based on descriptive similarity; rather, one would examine how precisely these are justified and how they are successful in some cases and not in others.

None of the theorists of descriptive representation apply their ideas to *functional representation*, which also has to do with the specific ends they aim at. Arguably, legislatives are a major arena for transforming societies. Notwithstanding, they are not the only ones, and it is obvious that in the sphere of functional representation there is much more room for descriptive representation than in the territorial domain. Elected assemblies have a limited number of members and can therefore never be made to describe or symbolise every aspect of the represented that may be found relevant. Electoral systems also tend to be rather inflexible and inert, for good reasons. Functional representation, as a complement of territorially organised legislative assemblies, can be an almost unlimited means of flexibly making representation more descriptive of whatever characteristic is seen to be relevant for some matter. Descriptive representation is thus one possible mode in which functional representation can work. Alternatively, of course, functional representatives can also speak for those affected by some issue, without being affected themselves. Either way, functional representation is often supported with the argument that it makes representation as a whole more 'fine-grained' (Cohen and Rogers 1995: 43; Urbinati and Warren 2008: 403). 'Fine-grained' means, for one thing, the possibility to represent more aspects of the represented individuals – i.e. more different perspectives, preferences, etc. – than would be possible through territorial representation alone (cf. Smismans 2004: 47). For another thing, 'fine-grained' also refers to the possibility to register the intensity of different views through functional representation, a dimension difficult to realise in parliament. Another way in which the literature on descriptive representation is relevant for functional representation is its discussions about how descriptive constituencies are to be chosen for enhanced representation, and according to what criteria some descriptive representatives may be preferable to others (Dovi 2002), although the literature does not go very far here. Yet, its writers stress that choices should be guided by some general principle or objective and be made in a dialogical process involving the constituency and its representatives, as well as the social majority.

Functional representation – in associations, spontaneous movements, executive committees, independent agencies – can thus be a way to introduce more descriptive representation, if this is found desirable in a given context. In the social OMC this is mainly done through the annual European Meetings of People Experiencing Poverty, a yearly conference of poor citizens from all Member States and of European decision makers. However, theorists of descriptive representation deal primarily with gender and ethnic minorities. Anne Phillips critically examines this preference in view of the fact that 'the most persistent structure of political exclusion is surely that associated with inequalities of social class' (Phillips 1995: 171). She attributes the absence of poverty from her own work in part to the particular agenda underlying theories of descriptive representation in general, namely the concern with transforming the political agenda by articulating and introducing previously unheard voices (pp. 175–6). Unlike gender or skin colour, social class has long been a central principle for defining political options and organising the political spectrum (p. 173). Moreover, it has usually been perceived in terms of objective class interests that could also be understood, identified with, and defended by members of other classes (pp. 174–6). However, Phillips admits that this way of dealing with 'working class interests', for instance, does leave out many important considerations and perspectives of which representatives located in more privileged situations are not aware. She concedes that '[t]here is no real substitute for being there [being represented descriptively] when policies are being developed', and notes that the general absence of the poor's descriptive representation from political debate may also be due to the fact that,

> however controversial the guaranteed representation of women or ethnic minorities is proving, it is in many ways less threatening to current practices of democracy than guaranteed representation by social class. Most of those who benefit from gender quotas, for example, will resemble the current incumbents of political office in their occupational or class characteristics, and this makes it easier to include them as new members of the political family. (Philips 1995: 177–8)

Hence, it will be interesting to examine how the deliberate descriptive representation of the poor practised and promoted by the European Commission is conceptualised, and how this argumentation relates to the arguments developed for the case of women or visual minorities. This is dealt with in Chapter Nine.

Chapter Four

Functional Representation and Democracy

One of the main difficulties in dealing with the democratic aspects of governance processes is that settings tend to be complicated. They involve a variety of different actors on different levels, and the functional representatives among these are often unelected and represent fluid constituencies of mostly not formally organised citizens. In Chapter Two I have worked out the tools representation theories provide us with to deal with such complex contexts. Theories of representation are especially equipped to deal systematically with the relations between the different actors involved – in particular, functional representatives, the members of their organisations, their wider functional constituencies (the affected), and the citizenry of the polity. They offer conceptual tools to tackle the question of who should be accountable to whom, and they lay down the constitutive role of the represented as the basic principle of democratic representation. Concerning the ways to realise this principle, they emphasise different aspects. Principal–agent models stress the possibility of effective sanctioning ('throwing the rascals out') as well as the procedural equality of the represented. Deliberative representation adds substantial fairness and the quality of deliberation between representatives and representees. The representative claim shifts the focus to how representation is built in rhetorical ways. It opens the concept of representation up to also accommodate new, evolving forms and understandings, while confirming the recognition by the constituency as the key benchmark for democratic representation. In other words, each perspective is based on slightly different concepts of what makes political representation democratic. The purpose of this study is not to test any of these theories, but to use them as analytic tools in studying the concepts underlying the Commission's argumentation.

In this chapter, I use the tools of these representation theories to elaborate on in what ways governance processes involving functional representatives can be democratic, and what the critical issues are in this regard. I do this by analysing functional representation in policy making through the three dimensions of my working model of democracy, i.e. input legitimacy, output legitimacy, and political accountability (cf. Chapter One). Democratic legitimacy in governance is looked at from two perspectives: firstly, the democratic legitimacy of the whole political process, insofar as this depends on the functional representatives involved (i.e. legitimacy gained through functional representation); and secondly, the internal legitimacy of these representatives *vis-à-vis* their constituencies (i.e. legitimacy of functional representatives), which is of course an important part of the former aspect. Together with the previous two chapters, this provides the fundaments to analyse practices of functional representation as well as the concepts used to shape them.

Output legitimacy

Output legitimacy is usually seen as the key strength of governance, in comparison to traditional government.[1] It has also been a primary perspective of the governance literature. The basic assumption in analysing functional representation from this viewpoint is that the choice of participants in policy making has an impact on the outcomes. Against the background of the debates on 'overloaded government' and the 'ungovernability' of society (Peters and Pierre 2006: 31–7), the roles of various actors have been analysed with respect to the potency of different arrangements to deliver public goods or steer society. Output legitimacy in this context means better quality of political decisions as well as reaching them more efficiently.

Output legitimacy is seen as a characteristic of the political process and the choice of participants, rather than being associated with the internal organisation of the involved actors. There are two main arguments for the enhanced output legitimacy of involving functional representatives. Firstly, functional actors control resources that are needed in policy-making processes and that governmental actors lack, such as information, technical expertise, and the capacity to ease implementation and improve compliance by communicating decisions to their constituencies. It would therefore be wrong to start from the premise that policy makers were struggling to resist functional organisations that are vigorously knocking on their door (Maloney *et al.* 1994: 19–22). On the contrary, executive administrations need functional representatives for their own success. The second main factor to which output legitimacy is attributed is based more on the reasoning of deliberative democracy and on the main mode of policy making in governance, i.e. negotiation. As the study of Sonja Wälti *et al.* has shown, negotiation in networks has a '(potential) ability to mediate and overcome particularistic interests and enhance solidarity and community-building, and, on the other hand, to provide forums of exchange and mutual learning' (Wälti *et al.* 2004: 107). Output legitimacy can thus also include fairer outcomes.

Recently, the optimism concerning the potentials of governance in terms of output has been criticised for its underlying rationalistic problem-solving orientation, which tends to render other democratic values instrumental to the production of rational outcomes (Buchstein and Jörke 2007: 186–9; Greven 2007). It has been stressed that output legitimacy is not 'just performing well' (Schmitter 2002: 57). In particular, it not only implies delivering results that citizens endorse, but also means that the represented support – or at least accept – the goals that are pursued (Christiansen *et al.* 2003: 13; Kohler-Koch and Rittberger 2006: 41; Bellamy 2010; cf. Wälti *et al.* 2004: 104). Hence, instead of simply equating

---

1.   It is worth noting that it is somewhat questionable to compare the output legitimacy of these two regime types. Given the differences in historical context, including changes in the expectations towards public authorities and in the ways of conceptualising democratic legitimacy, it becomes problematical what criteria to apply. I seek to avoid such comparisons here and restrict my analysis to evaluations from a present-day perspective.

output legitimacy with efficiency, attention has to be given to how the goals, which are then realised as outputs, have been defined, and more generally, who has had a chance to influence the process leading to particular outputs (cf. Føllesdal and Hix 2006: 544–6; Bellamy 2010). Such a stronger definition links output legitimacy tightly to input legitimacy:

> While the democratic idea of the political process depends on the contingent articulation of the preferences of equal citizens – or their representatives – which inherently and incrementally leads to the construction of political problems and a possible agenda, the new approach of participatory governance rests on the very traditional premises of technocratic politics. In this framework, problems are given or defined by governance agencies and framed before the problem-solving process has even started. (Greven 2007: 242)

Furthermore, there are also trade-offs between output legitimacy on the one hand and input legitimacy and accountability on the other hand. This is especially the case if output is conceptualised mainly in terms of efficiency, because 'broad access to group negotiation may conflict with the effectiveness of these negotiations' (Immergut 1995: 204; cf. Dahl 1994). B. Guy Peters and Jon Pierre therefore speak of a 'Faustian bargain' in the sense that core values of democratic government could be 'traded for accommodation, consensus and the purported increased efficiency in governance' (Peters and Pierre 2004: 85; cf. Peters and Pierre 2006: 37). Hence, when analysing the output equality of a process, attention has to be paid to the definition of the concept and its balance with the other two dimensions of democracy, including particularly how participants are chosen and how the process is carried through (e.g. publicity, openness to alternatives).[2]

Closely related to this, the above-mentioned accommodation and consensus is another alleged virtue of governance that has come under criticism. As such, there is no reason to assume that the affected parties' views should be compatible. Rather, being affected presumably entails having an interest in the matter, which may well be opposed to the interests of other actors involved. If the main goal is reaching a consensus efficiently, there is a danger that actors outside the main players' mainstream thinking are excluded from governance networks (Wälti et al. 2004: 101–7; Wälti and Kübler 2003; Papadopoulos 2007: 481). In other words, accommodation is not an inherent system characteristic, but something that has to

---

2. The relation of output legitimacy with other democratic values has been a prominent topic of discussion in the debate around the democratic legitimacy of the EU. The father of the concepts of input and output legitimacy, Fritz W. Scharpf, argues that the legitimacy of the Union can be founded primarily on output legitimacy as long as it deals only with uncontroversial issues that do not require zero-sum redistribution (Scharpf 1999: 22–3; for a related argument, see Majone 1998). More recently, the notion that a lack of input legitimacy (and accountability – see Føllesdal 2011) can be compensated for by output legitimacy has come increasingly under fire. In parallel, the argumentation for a balance of input and output legitimacy has been turning to conceptualising the issue more from a perspective of representation. See, for example, Føllesdal and Hix 2006; Bellamy and Castiglione 2011.

be worked for,[3] and that can be arrived at in different ways, for example through inclusive deliberation aimed at learning and mutual understanding, or through restricting access. Such different strategies affect the outcomes of the process. In particular, there is a risk that the interests of those excluded from policy making are not taken into account, or, worse, that negative externalities of decisions are primarily imposed on those groups who are not involved.[4] This leads us to the concept of *outcome equality*, i.e. the idea that not only should everybody have the possibility of equal input, but also the outputs should treat everybody with equal concern (cf. Phillips 2004). Put differently, when looking at the output legitimacy of a process, one should also ask whom the outputs benefit.

All this suggests that the output legitimacy of functional representation is conditional on a number of factors, such as pluralistic enough governance networks (Wälti *et al.* 2004: 105, 107; Benz and Papadopoulos 2006: 10) with cooperative participants holding the required resources. These conditions can be compatible with each other and with other norms of democratic legitimacy, but they do not need to be. Trade-offs can also affect the involved associations' internal organisation. For example, if participants are mainly chosen on the grounds of efficiency as perceived by executive officers, this tends to favour highly professionalised organisations with only thin supporter participation and control (cf. Maloney 2008; Saurugger 2006; Sudbery 2003). By adapting themselves to such expectations, functional associations can increase their influence, yet at the cost of their input legitimacy and accountability. At the same time, less professional and more participative organisations are disadvantaged.

In view of this criticism of overly output-oriented perspectives, one should, however, be careful to avoid the other extreme and neglect the significance of output legitimacy for democracy. Besides the obvious fact that listening to citizens and being accountable to them does not amount to much if no approved outputs are produced, output legitimacy is also essential for the legitimacy of political rule and the system as a whole. As well as that, high levels of welfare for broad parts of the population reinforce and sustain attitudes necessary for democracy (Greven 1993: 404–7).

In sum, when looking at arguments building on the output legitimacy of functional representation, it is important to examine first of all how output legitimacy is conceptualised in relation to the represented (for example, efficiently achieving conditions deemed beneficial for them or pursuing such policies as the represented wish). Secondly, we have to ask in what relation this stands to the

---

3. In view of the predominantly optimistic governance literature, in particular with respect to the expected harmoniousness of processes, Pierre (2000b: 245) suggests that conflict management and resolution in governance, as well as governance failure, should be studied more.

4. The contributions in *Government and Opposition* 46(1) therefore argue that functional representation should be tightly controlled by a system of territorial representation, in order to make sure that the public interest and unrepresented interests are taken into account (Bellamy and Castiglione 2011; Føllesdal 2011; Héritier and Lehmkuhl 2011; Weale 2011). *See also* Bellamy 2010; Papadopoulos 2010: 1040.

other two dimensions of democracy: input legitimacy and political accountability; for instance, whether the three are seen to reinforce or compensate each other. As will be shown in the following sections, it is the analysis of these other two dimensions where theories of representation are of most help.

Input legitimacy

Functional representation has the potential to enhance democracy by increasing both the quality and the quantity of input. Regarding quantity, functional associations are channels relating citizens' views, in addition to political parties,[5] polls, the media, etc. While only a limited number of issues can be taken on board through the territorial party-based system of representation, any kind of view can be represented functionally. Additional channels also provide the individual citizen with a larger choice of representatives and representational styles that they may want to support, so that for the individual there is a greater potential to find actors by whom she feels herself represented. More to the point, many issues and interests are nonterritorial or difficult to organise territorially and can better be mediated by functional representatives (Cohen and Rogers 1995: 43). All this means that the input directed at the policy-making process is more and more diverse; the range of actors claiming to speak for functional groups has been mushrooming, as has the variety of functional constituencies (cf. Urbinati and Warren 2008: 389–90).

In terms of quality, the main advantage seen in this diversity is the possibility to provide policy making with issue-relevant input. Now of course 'relevance' can be defined in different ways and assessed according to different criteria. Firstly, relevance can mean technical knowledge of the matters under discussion. This is the traditional functionalist argument, according to which utilising the expertise of functional representatives (and academic experts) will improve the quality of the policy output. Secondly, seen from a strategic angle, the specific input sought includes information about potential reactions 'on the ground' to particular decisions. Functional representatives are here negotiation partners and 'warning indicators' (Ruzza 2006: 172), involved with the aim to ensure an efficient implementation of the ultimate decision as well as the support of their constituencies. This interaction between policy makers and the affected is thus a form of anticipatory representation. In a third view, input can also be relevant in the sense of being sensitive to the intensity of different groups' preferences. Functional representation specifically registers intensity, by contrast to pure territorial representation, which mainly regards numerical quantity (cf. Cohen

---

5.   To some extent, functional associations and movements have been taking over some of the functions of political parties. While party membership and voting have been decreasing, political activity has been changing its forms and has been moving to functional associations and spontaneous movements. Cf. e.g. Hay 2007; Hintikka 2009; Rosanvallon 2008; Schwarzmantel 2008.

and Rogers 1995: 43).[6] Hence, it may also be more sensitive to the concerns of minorities. This criterion of relevance thus builds on deliberative concepts whereas substantial fairness is an important prerequisite of legitimate representation (see Chapter Three). Finally, functional representation responds to new issues much more flexibly than the territorial system (Urbinati and Warren 2008: 402).

If these arguments are comparatively straightforward and uncontroversial, the realisation of these potentials raises more complex questions, mainly clustering around the *choice of actors* to involve. Since policy goals, problem definitions, and even what counts as scientific expertise are controversial, the legitimacy of functional input hinges on the question of whose input is taken into account, and how it is mediated into the governance process (cf. Borrás and Conzelmann 2007: 535). Since Mancur Olson's *Logic of Collective Action* (1965), the social and economic inequalities inherent in functional representation have dampened the optimism about its democratic potentials. At the same time, the internal structures of many functional organisations have given rise to enquiries about intraorganisational democracy.

Given the enormous variety of functional representatives, the key question concerning the governance process as a whole clearly is which of them should be involved in a given governance arrangement, and according to what criteria that choice should be made. Since there is rarely a clear-cut answer, choices can be challenged and discussed, and therefore need to be justified. Although the criteria of choice are crucial for the input legitimacy of the process, this does not mean that the criteria applied in practice are necessarily designed to increase input legitimacy. The following discussion looks at the choice of participants from the perspective of input legitimacy, but as could be seen in the previous section, who gets involved can also depend on other considerations.

To begin with, it is not always obvious who those 'affected' by an issue are. Among other things, the definition of the affected also depends on how the issue itself is defined. Yet, even on the basis of an issue definition, it often remains difficult to delineate the functional constituencies in intension as well as extension, i.e. to determine the characteristics that demarcate them, and to determine which individuals they include. Ideally, this should be a deliberative process involving those professing to be affected, the authorities, and the general public. Defining the affected in a deliberative way can avoid biases towards well-organised and privileged groups or towards those groups whose participation is opportune for the involved executives. However, the condition for this is high-quality public deliberation that makes it more likely that all relevant perspectives are heard (Bohman 2000: 27; Cohen and Rogers 1995: 65) and gives potential actors the possibility to claim involvement. The blurry limits of functional constituencies and their contingency on the matter under discussion accentuate the discursive

---

6. Philippe Schmitter (2007: 20–1 (n. xvii)) rightly notes that 'real existing democracies' maintain a range of institutions that reflect intensities of preferences. Purely numerical democracy is a theoretical abstraction for heuristic purposes.

construction of constituencies; the downside of this is that no one can claim a formal right to be considered a legitimate 'stakeholder' (cf. Papadopoulos 2010: 1043).

Fuzziness continues when it comes to deciding which actor should represent a particular functional constituency. Most functional groups will be organised in several, perhaps partly overlapping or rivalling associations, and often not all of them can be involved. Who, then, could be a legitimate representative of the whole constituency?[7] Here, the associations' internal organisation comes into play. As I have shown in Chapter Two, there are several ways to look at this.

Maybe the most obvious criterion of choice is *inclusive membership*. This favours large associations or umbrella organisations and networks. Inclusiveness as a criterion has the disadvantage that the views of smaller subconstituencies may not be heard (Immergut 1995: 205); although, on the other hand, participating in a larger organisation may be their only possibility to get involved at all, considering that small marginal associations often have little chance to take part in policy-making processes. Also, more generally, the internal input-flow from the level of individual members to the umbrella level may be weak. In the EU, this is aggravated by the (spatial and psychological) distance between local and national organisations and Brussels offices. Inclusive membership is a criterion depending on principal–agent reasoning: the representative should be authorised by and accountable to a majority of constituents. However, an increasing number of functional associations do not follow this logic any more and are based on more informal forms of support than membership. This kind of support is difficult to measure, and takes different forms in different types of associations. In such cases, the concepts of deliberative representation and the representative claim are more useful. Instead of formal membership, they look at the level of support an organisation has in the wider constituency for which they are to speak. These perspectives also help to deal with associations where the represented and the supporters are not identical, as is the case with charities and social NGOs working for and claiming to speak for disadvantaged people. Here, criteria based on membership and formal authorisation miss the point, so that the legitimacy of representation has to be considered with more deliberative tools. This is also necessary given that involving a limited number of associations rests on the expectation that these will then speak for the whole functional constituency, i.e. represent people beyond their own members or supporters. Hence, a helpful criterion of choice may be an organisation's networks in the field, i.e. their contacts

---

7. Castiglione and Warren (2006: 18) point out that the *universality of inclusion* is unproblematic in territorial representation, where 'an elected representative is charged with representing those within the [territorial] constituency, whether in fact he does so or not'. Notwithstanding, as we have seen in the previous chapter, the more deliberative viewpoints are added to this formal picture, the less straightforward the universality of *any* representation becomes. Functional representatives can rarely build their representative claims on long-standing institutions and therefore have to do more argumentative work to establish a claim to legitimately represent a certain constituency.

with other associations and representatives. Well-networked associations may mediate views from a larger number of actors, and they are more easily accepted as proxies by other organisations. However, privileging such networks can also disadvantage associations that dissent from the sector's mainstream. In any case, it is clear that for such deliberative criteria it is impossible to establish definite benchmarks. Solutions can be found through deliberation, but they are rarely obvious.

An additional criterion of choice, as well as an important element of the input legitimacy of the whole process, is the *internal democracy* of the associations to be involved. In the case of membership-based organisations, the de facto functioning of formal democratic institutions is often found to be weak. On the one hand, this has to do with conflicts of goals at the leadership level. When representatives of functional associations participate in governance networks, strong participative structures in their organisation can conflict with the prerequisites of gaining influence on the political process (Halpin 2001; cf. Kohler-Koch 2010b: 1129; Schmitter and Streeck 1999), so that they have to find a compromise between membership input and political strategies. On the other hand, many functional organisations pursue different styles of representation rather than a pure principal–agent mode. Often, members or supporters do not want to engage actively, but prefer chequebook organisations; giving ideal, informal support; and more gyroscopic modes of representation (Warleigh 2001: 633–4; Sudbery 2003: 89–90; Clarence *et al.* 2005; Kohler-Koch 2007: 265; Maloney 2008: 75–7; concerning local organisations, *see also* van Deth and Maloney 2008; van Deth 2008: 335–7). The question, then, is whether and in which sense such representation can be democratic.

An interesting case in this regard is associations without members, or speaking for others apart from members. In their case, the meaningfulness of the traditional aggregative input model as such has been questioned. Darren Halpin argues that the purpose of such groups is not to aggregate their supporters' views but to advocate a certain cause, which is a different thing: 'For example, if the affiliates of WWF Scotland were to decide lobbying positions, would that actually contribute to representing the environment?' (Halpin 2006: 938). In other words, cases like this do not sit well with the principal–agent logic of representation, so that intraconstituency input legitimacy has to be conceptualised differently:

> The size of what social movement scholars term a group's 'attentive public' [...] is perhaps more important than its supporter base [formal members or donators]. It is the resonance of the group's views with an attentive public, as opposed to the affiliated supporters, that provides groups with political power. (Halpin 2006: 927)

This concept can also be applied to other informally organised groups. Associations put forward a claim to represent a particular constituency, and that claim is accepted by those who feel their views represented by it. The constituency's support is largely deliberative, and the resulting political power is based on the group's mobilisation capacity, reputation, moral authority, and their potential influence on elections. Democratic input is here not the aggregation of constituents' views, but a dialogical process in which the representatives pick up sentiments from their attentive public, and the represented react to the representatives' statements. The representing cannot normally be voted out, but to keep their position and influence they are dependent on the resonance with a sufficient constituency (cf. Maloney 2008: 80–1). Although this model works for associations defending the interests of their supporters, as well as for charities, caution is necessary in cases of organisations representing adult constituencies who could in principle make their views known, but do not have the resources to do so, such as people living in poverty for example. Although these often depend on 'advocacy by proxy' by more privileged people concerned about their cause in order to gain representation (Maloney 2008: 82), such representation cannot be regarded as democratic unless the representatives are recognised by their constituents. Their mutual relationships and communication thus have to be examined.

All this has great significance for organisations with membership and formal aggregative-democratic structures, too. Firstly, if they speak for a functional constituency which is not congruent with their membership, deliberative and claims-based concepts are needed to evaluate their representative legitimacy among non-members. Secondly, as mentioned above, intraorganisational input through formal structures is often low, because members are often inclined towards more deliberative and flexible styles of representation.

Hence, for the question of how to choose functional associations for the participation in governance processes, criteria based on simple principal–agent models are of less and less help, because people increasingly organise and act in different ways. Theories of representation have developed concepts to deal with this situation, but their use in concrete cases leaves much more room for different interpretations. There is no one-size-fits-all pattern, much less one that would lead to unambiguous choices; rather, solutions depend on the individual setting, the kinds of actors present, the ways in which they are organised, their interests and goals in the process, the issues dealt with, the resonance they receive in different parts of the public, etc. This also means that choices are open to discussion and have to be justified. All in all, requirements for legitimate representation have become much more deliberative.

Apart from the question of which association(s) best represent a given functional group, a central concern for functional input legitimacy is the *unequal capacities* of different functional groups to organise and represent themselves. This means that in a market-like situation, input legitimacy would be impaired because groups advocating very specific issues and well-resourced groups would be systematically overrepresented compared to groups with general concerns and groups with little financial means and weak 'social capital'.[8]

---

8. It is worth noting that although this central finding of Olson (1965) is generally valid, the degree of functional pluralism varies a lot between different policy fields. One important independent

To balance these inequalities, functional associations representing weaker constituencies often receive public funding, frequently coupled with privileged access to governmental actors. This, however, increases the risk that the funded organisations get colonised by the public actors they depend on; that is, in the competition for funding, organisations converge towards the paradigm set by public officials rather than functioning as authentic input channels (Wälti and Kübler 2003: 509–11). The result can be a detachment of the governance process from the constituencies that are supposed to be represented, and an aggravated divide into insider and outsider groups. One way to prevent such dependencies could be an arrangement where funding decisions are taken by institutions other than those that the respective functional representatives are directly involved with in governance processes.

The public support for the representation of weak groups shows that decisions concerning who should be involved in governance processes can be the result of public deliberation, societal consensus, or established practice. In other words, weak groups rely not only on support from more privileged ones, but also on the political culture. This in turn leads to strong demands concerning the democratic principles held up in a society.

In all such issues, formal institutions of authorisation and accountability do not lead very far; notwithstanding, the basic principle–agent reasoning still holds: for democratic representation, the decisive actor remains the constituency. Yet, there are less and less concrete and unambiguous benchmarks to determine what the relevant constituencies are, who belongs to them, and who should represent them. Instead, we are referred to the communication between constituencies, representatives, executive officers, and the general public, and to public deliberation on individual cases, which entails claims for involvement, justification, and possible challenges to choices. These perspectives take real-life complexity into account, but do not provide easy solutions. What is more, the criteria they use rely to a great extent on the democratic culture of a society.

Finally, when dealing with the input legitimacy of governance processes, it should be kept in mind that in the usual case, functional representatives do not decide on policies. The ultimate decision rests with territorial representatives, who are in principle free to deal with the received input at their discretion. Nevertheless, considerations of input legitimacy are crucial for functional representation too, because those involved in governance processes have a privileged chance to influence policies. Having said that, functional input legitimacy cannot *substitute for* input legitimacy generated through territorial representation, because the outcomes are binding on all citizens. Thus, attention has to be paid to how functional representation is linked to the territorial chain of delegation, such as

---

variable in this respect is the interests of the public institutions involved. Thus, apart from the 'supply side' of functional representation, attention has to be paid to the 'demand side' as well. A case in point is the European Commission, which in many cases actively supports the organisation of 'weak' functional interests. Hence, Justin Greenwood (2003: 275) finds that, taken as a whole, the 'business rules OK' thesis is not valid for the EU.

the setting of political priorities by the executive, and legislative control. Strong fundaments of territorial representation enhance the role of the polity's citizenry as the ultimate constituency, and they can also strengthen public deliberation and thereby increase not only democratic input but also the accountability of the governance actors (Wälti *et al.* 2004: 96–8; Føllesdal 2011). This is also important with respect to the question of what ultimately happens to the inputs provided by functional representatives. For example, consultations are often open to all interested actors, but it is up to executives which contributions are taken into account. Hence, attention has to be paid to their accountability and their rationales for dealing with functional representation.

Accountability

Political accountability is notoriously the key problem of functional representation, empirically as well as conceptually.[9] Because the term is sometimes used to denote a broad range of things – such as transparency, responsiveness, responsible and efficient administrative or financial conduct, 'good governance', and the like (cf. Bovens *et al.* 2008: 226–7; Bovens 2007: 449–50) – it is worth recalling Mark Bovens' narrower definition used in this study: 'Accountability is a relationship between an actor and a forum, in which the actor has an obligation to explain and to justify his or her conduct, the forum can pose questions and pass judgement, and the actor may face consequences' (Bovens 2007: 450–2; cf. Ch. 1 of this publication). While conceptually narrow, this definition is open with regards to how accountability is implemented institutionally. For example, it does not require formal arrangements. Accountability so defined can be analysed according to four elements: it is accountability *of* some agent *to* another agent *by* some process *for* some state of affairs (cf. Goodin 2003b: 361). What makes this difficult in functional representation is that all these four elements are uncertain, i.e. it is mostly unclear who should be accountable to whom, for what, by what process, and also how the functioning of accountability could be assessed. Theories of representation are well developed to deal with the 'who to whom' question, but how this should work efficiently in practice is still a puzzling question. It is therefore worth briefly introducing some major kinds of accountability, *viz.* democratic, electoral, deliberative, peer/horizontal/network, and internal accountability.

Democratic accountability means that a representative is held to account by the represented, at least in the last instance, at the end of a chain of delegation. The traditional way to do this is through *electoral accountability*, which recently has been increasingly seen as complemented by *deliberative accountability*. The latter means that representatives publicly give accounts of their positions (and changes thereof) (Urbinati and Warren 2008: 399) as well as explain and justify

9. Recently, accountability has become a prominent subject in the literature about democracy in governance. See the special issues of the *European Law Journal* 13(4) and of *West European Politics* 33(5).

their political choices (e.g. Gutmann and Thompson 1996: 128–9; cf. Ch. 2 of this publication). Because this reason-giving takes place in public, representatives are compelled to justify their actions with arguments based on the common good or other generally accepted values,[10] which at least makes it difficult to act in a too-contradictory way afterwards. Citizens react to these accounts, which may lead to consequences for the representatives (e.g. Bovens 2007: 452). Deliberative accountability is 'soft', working more along a logic of appropriateness than a logic of 'hard' consequentiality (Papadopoulos 2007: 472). It rests on an ongoing communication between representing and represented, which to work well is not only dependent on the individual behaviour of the participants, but also on systemic factors, such as the functioning of political parties, functional organisations, parliament, opinion polls, and particularly the media (Mansbridge 2003).[11] The quality of this communication – and thus of deliberative accountability – can be assessed with criteria such as transparency, plurality of voices, continuity, density, openness and equal opportunities of access, factual accuracy of statements, the absence of coercion and manipulation, and the effect of inducing reflection and mutual education (Mansbridge 2003: 519, 525–6; Dryzek 2000: 2). Deliberative accountability has been conceptualised as a complement to improve electoral representation; hence, the shadow of elections often plays an important role in theories of deliberative democracy (cf. e.g. Urbinati and Warren 2008: 402). Elections structure and animate public deliberation, and it is not least because they anticipate the next elections that representatives have an incentive to take the feedback of the represented into account (Mansbridge 2003: 518–19; cf. Føllesdal 2011: 92–3). Applying deliberative accountability to non-electoral forms of representation therefore raises the question of whether and how it can work democratically without these fundaments. Notwithstanding, the realisation of deliberative accountability even within electoral structures is often dubious as well, mainly because mechanisms that oblige representatives to justify actions, answer questions, and face consequences are often missing, and because citizens' resources to take part in public deliberation are unequal (*see* Kohler-Koch 2010b). Moreover, it is questionable how the public support of a particular view could be measured in a fair and reliable way while minimising the possibilities for manipulation.

Horizontal, peer, or *network accountability* refers to accountability to forums made up of other representatives or political actors, rather than the represented. It is therefore not democratic accountability; however, it can have considerable influence. Governance is a collective undertaking and therefore based on a minimum of mutual trust and cooperation, so that participants are answerable to each other for their comportment. A stronger form of horizontal accountability results when those participating in governance processes – elected politicians, executive officers, or functional representatives – form informal epistemic

---

10. Elster (1988: 111) speaks of the 'civilizing force of hypocrisy'.

11. For a critical analysis of the media's role, *see* Bussemer 2011.

communities (Haas 1989; 1992) with shared outlooks and values. Particularly if these are densely networked, their members effectively hold each other to account for their actions informally within the joint policy sphere, based on interdependencies and resulting blackmailing capacities, as well as on the central role of mutual trust and reputation for their cooperation (Goodin 2003b: 385–6; Papadopoulos 2007: 480–1; 2010: 1039–40). It is worth noting that network and democratic accountability have direct trade-offs, in that peers' relationships are marked by mutual dependencies and confidentiality, which make cooperation possible, but which are diametrically opposed to the requirement of transparency. Moreover, the account holders are by definition only those participating in the process, which need not be as inclusive as one might wish from a democratic perspective.[12] Mutual monitoring in governance networks therefore needs to be nested in public accountability, i.e. linked to a wider forum of account holders.

Finally, one can also be *internally accountable*, meaning personal answerability to one's own consciousness (March and Olsen 1995: 167; Mansbridge 2003: 522). This form of accountability is of course not democratic either, but can have substantial weight. Internal accountability also makes other mechanisms of accountability more effective if the internalised norms of the representative's consciousness are identical to those of the account holders. Concerning democracy, this means that the internalisation of democratic norms considerably strengthens other democratic mechanisms.[13]

In governance processes, there are two sets of actors who should be accountable: executive officers and functional representatives. The former are of course accountable to their hierarchy, a chain ultimately leading to the citizens.[14] For my purposes their accountability is relevant insofar as the involvement of functional representatives is sometimes seen as a means to improve the accountability of executives. Functional representatives are thus here the account holders. There are two ways in which this may take place. First, public administrators can be subject to peer accountability within a governance network. Importantly, in their capacity as peers, participants in such networks may have quite different expectations of their partners than their respective (functional) constituencies do.[15] Thus, they do not necessarily relate their constituencies' preferences to the networks' policy-making processes, but can also use the information gap between the two strategically. As stated above, network accountability is not democratic accountability, but has to be nested in other, democratic mechanisms of control.

---

12. For a critical assessment of peer accountability in governance networks, see Papadopoulos 2007: 480–3.

13. On these grounds, Andersen and Burns (1996: 247) conclude that there is 'hope' for democracy in the EU.

14. On administrative accountability, *see* Page 2010.

15. Schmidt (2006: 32) relates the illustrative example of NGO representatives sitting together with European Commission officials on a plane scheduled to take off to take them to the Cancun WTO meeting, while members of their own organisation were protesting outside the plane and preventing it from leaving.

The second way in which public officials can be held to account through functional associations is deliberatively through the public sphere. The momentum that this kind of accountability can have stems from functional representatives' capacity to relate issues further to their constituencies or the public at large and to mobilise support, or pressure those held to account (cf. Kohler-Koch 2010b). This is a central element of political accountability not only for governance processes, and may in fact work better with those functional actors not directly participating in political processes. Functional representatives are here one of the most important groups of actors making up the public sphere, i.e. part of a wider system of deliberative accountability that also works through opinion polls, the media, etc. The role they can play in holding policy makers to account thus depends not only on their own internal structures, but also on the functioning of this system as a whole, including the general relationships between policy makers and the public sphere in general, transparency legislation, dominant practices in the media, traditions of organised civil society, etc. I come back to these issues later in this section.

A more difficult question than the accountability of executives is that of the functional representatives participating in governance processes. Yet, considering that in nearly all cases they do not take binding decisions, why is their democratic accountability important in the first place?

Traditionally, based on principal–agent reasoning, representatives should be accountable for the binding decisions they take, to those who have authorised them to take that decision and are bound by it. According to this logic, what is crucial is the accountability of the actors of the territorial system, i.e. executive officers, the political executive, and the legislative. As Stijn Smismans points out, this model of parliamentary control implies a 'hierarchical and neutral bureaucracy' working as a 'transmission-belt' to implement the will of the people, which finds its sole expression in parliament (Smismans 2004: 7, 12–16). It is obvious that this model does not fit multilevel-governance policy making in the European Union. Firstly, it assumes that political sovereignty, the capacity to steer society as well as to control the complete chain of delegation, and the answerableness for political rule all lie in the hands of clearly identifiable, democratically authorised centres of political power. Secondly, the assumption of a neutral administrative process suggests that it is sufficient that decision makers be mainly accountable for the outcomes. However, the governance processes leading to the final outcomes are anything but neutral. Nevertheless, due to the complexity and intransparency of governance arrangements, parliaments have difficulties holding executives to account for the whole policy-making process, or even controlling other parts of the chain of delegation. Hence, the functional representatives participating in policy making also need an accountability of their own.

Furthermore, the principal–agent model assumes that representatives are accountable to their own immediate principals. For functional representatives this means responsibility to their organisations. Yet, as noted earlier, functional representatives are generally involved in order to speak for wider parts of the functional constituency than those organised in their respective association, and through their involvement they have privileged influence on policies binding on the whole citizenry. In other words, they exert political power over broader parts of the population than those who may have had a share in authorising them. As the possibilities for the indirect accountability of this power via parliaments are feeble, there also needs to be some form of more direct accountability of functional representatives to their wider constituencies and to the general public. This does not replace the formal accountability to their organisation, but is a necessary addition. In a nutshell, functional representatives ought to be politically accountable to three forums: their own organisation, the functional constituency, and the public.

As to the question of what functional representatives should be accountable *for*, one has to take into consideration the characteristics of the kinds of processes that they participate in. Typically, there are multiple actors involved and causalities are complex, such that it is difficult or impossible to assign clear responsibilities for single outcomes (March and Olson 1995: 157–8).[16] Moreover, the role of functional representatives in the process is usually consultative, and the decision about what to do with their input, as well as the formal adoption of the final decision, lies with public officials who are accountable for these choices to territorial constituencies. Functional representatives can therefore not be made accountable for the ultimate outcomes. Even so, they can have substantial influence on these outcomes. Hence, they should be accountable for the positions they hold, the goals they advocate, and the ways in which they pursue them.

How, then, should this accountability to their three forums work? The accountability to the representatives' *own organisation* remains important in spite of the requirement that functional representatives be accountable to wider groups as well. When functional representatives participate in a governance process, it is generally an association that is selected and then appoints its representatives. Accountability to this association is thus meant to ensure that the individual representative really conveys the views of the organisation in the name of which she is speaking, and whose resources (supporters, networks, expertise, money, reputation, etc.) make her representing possible. As mentioned in the previous section, the formal democratic structures of functional associations are frequently weak, because their representational styles often do not work according to the principal–agent logic. Yet, this does not mean that their representatives are not accountable. Instead, their accountability tends to work in more deliberative ways, for example in networks and via the media.

This trend towards deliberative accountability blurs the boundaries between members and non-members, since membership is not a prerequisite to support or engage in communication with an association. Deliberative accountability thus involves a *continuum* of people, from formal members or supporters to the wider functional constituency and the general public. Out of these, the *functional*

---

16. This has been called the 'problem of many hands' by Thompson 1980 (cf. Bovens 2007: 457–8; Benz 2007: 508). Accordingly, output legitimacy is often assigned to governance *processes* rather than to single actors.

constituency is the key forum of accountability, because functional representatives generally (claim to) speak for affected groups beyond their formal membership, and in the case of organisations advocating the case of disadvantaged groups, those to be represented are usually not members at all. Instead of drawing a line between formal members and non-members, it therefore makes more sense to distinguish between more and less actively participating parts of the functional constituency.

The deliberative accountability of functional representatives to the most actively participating parts of their constituencies can be conceptualised as a kind of network accountability (e.g. Goodin 2003b). The relevant networks consist of organisations and individuals who are active in the sector through supporting their functional representatives and communicating with them and among each other. They exist through the relationships and communication of their members, which can be more or less dense, and their boundaries are fluid (cf. Saward 2009: 17). Entering such a network is voluntary,[17] and exit is possible at any time. In some functional constituencies there is a fairly dense network around the central organisations, which generates a strong sense of community among its members. This strengthens deliberative accountability because of the dense communication (also enhancing input legitimacy), and because a spirit of community leads to the internalisation of the social norms guiding the network (cf. Goodin 2003b: 373–9; Ruzza 2004: 7), thus also bringing about internal accountability.

Many people prefer a more gyroscopic style of representation and do not seek to actively engage in an association or have an influence on its representatives (Maloney 2008: 75–7). If they join an organisation, they become so-called chequebook members, but gyroscopic representation can also work in non-material ways, such as silent acceptance of the organisation's public statements, or referring to these statements as authoritative information in private discussions. Being accountable to these constituents means transparent information about the goals and ways of working of the organisation, and keeping those interested up to date, for example through a regular newsletter and through making information easily available on the association's internet pages. The communication with these less active supporters also takes place via the public sphere. If they do not feel themselves represented any more, they can vote with their feet and exit (i.e. stop supporting the association) (cf. Saward 2011: 14). In order to prevent this, functional representatives tend to anticipate their supporters' views in the actions they take (Maloney 2008: 81). They are thus accountable also in the sense that they heed the messages they receive from the ground and either adapt their activities to the wishes of the represented or attempt to gain their endorsement by explaining and justifying their choices.

Those constituents who have a (more or less tight) relationship with a functional representative are thus those out of the arguably affected who see themselves as belonging to such and such a functional group *and* feel themselves represented by certain actors. Put differently, functional representatives constitute their

---

17. Cf. Mansbridge's surrogate representation (2003: 522–5).

constituency in a certain way by claiming to represent it, and by accepting such a claim one enters into a relationship with the representative. It is also possible to recognise one's belonging to the evoked functional group without accepting the claimant as one's representative, thus 'reading back' the claim (Saward 2006: 303–4). In this case, the relation of accountability can be compared to that of an elected politician with those not having voted for her. If the number of these people becomes too great, the claimant can no longer legitimately act as a representative of the entire functional constituency.

The need to establish functional constituencies means that in order to represent such a group, the claimant's message has to reach the people potentially belonging to it. The claim thus has to be made to a wider audience, from out of which the representees are recruited or self-select themselves. Hence, the deliberative space in which functional representatives act goes beyond that of their constituency and out to the general public sphere. In many respects, the deliberation within the constituency of course differs from that with the general public, but the borders are blurred.

Deliberative accountability to the *general public* is mainly what Thorsten Benner *et al.* have termed 'public reputational accountability', i.e. functional representatives 'are accountable to the public for their actions and face reputational costs or can reap reputational benefits' (Benner *et al.* 2004: 199), manifested, for example, in the form of access to and influence on policy making. That is to say, those outside the functional constituency can only indirectly induce consequences for functional representatives for their actions, while the represented have the options of loyalty and exit (and sometimes voice). Both affect the resources that functional representatives need in order to gain influence on policy making.

Deliberative accountability to the wider constituency and the citizenry at large via the public sphere hinges on two key factors, *viz.* openness and the media. Concerning the former, Thorsten Hüller and Beate Kohler-Koch make a useful distinction between transparency and *publicity* in a stronger sense (Hüller and Kohler-Koch 2008: 153–4; cf. Trenz 2009: 42). While the former means the accessibility of information and documents at low cost, the latter means that an issue enters public debate and general awareness. Because deliberative accountability works through publicity, transparency alone is thus not accountability but its precondition. Not everything in the political process has to be public in this stronger sense; indeed most parts of it never need to be (cf. Papadopoulos 2010: 1032–3). However, the entire political process has to operate in the 'shadow of publicity' (Hüller and Kohler-Koch 2008: 154), i.e. in principle any part of it can be brought to public discussion. To ensure an effective shadow there have to be institutionalised mechanisms maintaining a strong potential of publicity, so that whether or not an issue becomes subject to public debate cannot be determined by the accountees, and does not depend on the resources of the concerned groups. Contrarily to the territorial sphere of representation with its government–opposition arrangement and periodic electoral campaigns, for functional representation it is difficult to establish legal mechanisms, beyond transparency regulations, to ensure a credible shadow of publicity. Rather, it often depends on the potential for controversy inherent in particular policies and in the way governance is organised, as well as on the ability of functional associations to mobilise their constituencies around an issue (cf. Kohler-Koch 2010b: 1121–2, 1133). Furthermore, publicity is affected by policy-making styles. Yannis Papadopoulos argues that multilevel governance is detrimental to political accountability because it reduces visibility, is uncoupled from the territorial system of representation (notably parliaments), and because the represented are situated on one level while the representatives move and cooperate across levels (Papadopoulos 2010; 2007: 478–80). In EU governance in particular, this is aggravated by the high complexity of policy making, especially the sheer amount of different processes and actors, making it difficult for the average citizen to follow. In Pierre Rosanvallon's terms, the legibility (*lisibilité*) of governance processes is low (Rosanvallon 2008: 313), which also leads to the detachment of the citizens and decreases the credibility of the shadow of publicity. If citizens can no longer understand who is responsible for what and how they can engage with the political process, they decreasingly perceive themselves as the authors of legislation and the owners of the system as a whole (Pollak *et al.* 2009: 25). As a result, the attentive publics around European governance processes, as well as the networks participating in them, are usually highly elitist. Certainly, these elite actors often represent socially disadvantaged functional groups, but the democratic legitimacy of this representation remains a question mark as long as processes are by their very nature incomprehensible, if not invisible, to the represented.

Much depends, therefore, on the second key factor of public deliberative accountability: the media. The working of the media is the single most important determinant of the quality of public discourse, and in practice the only channel of communication between functional representatives and the general public. Moreover, the media also have an important structuring function, contextualising bits of information and rendering the political process comprehensible. However, they also pursue agendas other than this, which can have repercussions for the quality of public deliberation and should be taken into consideration when the media are given the central role in public accountability.

To sum up, also for functional representation the principal–agent logic remains the decisive guideline to determine who should be accountable to whom in a democratic regime. Representatives must be accountable to those they represent, and the last authority over public policy making is with the citizens of the polity. Yet, this logic is less and less realised through formal institutions, such as elections, and more through deliberative accountability. This means that a number of different, overlapping and complementary mechanisms are possible, which can be designed and weighed differently in individual cases (cf. Saward 2000: 41–2).

The problems with this are, empirically, that the functioning of deliberative accountability is contingent on a number of circumstances, which can be given in some cases but not in others; and theoretically, that the concept of deliberative accountability is not yet developed enough for normative purposes. The empirical realisation of deliberative accountability is precarious because of its inherent 'softness', as opposed to 'hard' mechanisms. The effect it can have depends on the political context, the resources of the affected groups, the functioning of the public sphere, the quality of the media, the internal organisation of functional associations, the organisation and participants of a political process, issue salience, etc. What is more, the represented cannot enforce sanctions or compel representatives to justify choices (Bovens 2007: 457). Of course, the quality of accountability and democracy in general always depends on the political culture of a society, which can undermine even 'hard' electoral mechanisms. Yet, deliberative accountability offers representatives many more possibilities to circumvent democratic control than formal arrangements do. In the theoretical perspective, the key weakness of the concept of deliberative accountability is the difficulty to pin down clear criteria and unambiguous evaluations (cf. Papadopoulos 2010: 1037). The literature describes processes that arguably take place, but has difficulties prescribing normative requirements. This is not least because for a long time, functional representation has primarily been conceptualised as 'civil society participation', so that accountability was no issue (cf. Kohler-Koch 2010b: 1136), and also because of the positive connotations of both 'civil society' and 'participation', associated with the public good. In addition, governance was for a long time analysed mainly in terms of efficiency and output legitimacy, combined with a very optimistic attitude concerning its potential for cooperation and learning. Specifically concerning the EU, the participation perspective has made it possible to depart from methodological nationalism (Beck and Grande 2004; cf. Trenz 2009: 37) and the no-demos impasse (Smismans 2003: 474), which had dominated EU studies until the late 1990s. Democracy in the EU could thus be treated in a more optimistic manner. It is also worth noting that the civil society participation paradigm has been actively promoted particularly by the European Commission (cf. Trenz 2009: 37; Smismans 2003).

Conclusions

Concerning all three dimensions of democracy as well as political representation, the tendency is clearly towards *public deliberation*. Many modes of representation rest more on different forms of deliberation than, for example, on elections. When functional representatives are involved in policy making, the outcomes aimed at should be determined in deliberative processes, deliberation should be used when selecting participants, and accountability is increasingly seen as a deliberative process. In short, deliberation is more and more offered as an answer when hard principal–agent mechanisms do not seem to work any more or appear insufficient. However, this has not yet led to the formulation of a theory that could provide a clear road map to analyse individual instances of functional representation systematically in terms of democracy (Warren 2009: 11). Political equality has been emerging as a key benchmark and an important weak point, yet it is difficult to see what kinds of institutions this should be realised through and 'why elites would want to adopt them' (Warren 2009: 10). As well as that, it has become apparent that the potential of public deliberation to strengthen the democratic legitimacy of governance is limited. In particular, governance processes often work through a strategy of depoliticisation, are too many to be duly deliberated in public, and are often too informal to provide strong democratic safeguards.

Governance processes involving functional representatives are often based on negotiations and avoiding confrontation, i.e. they aim at finding solutions in a pragmatic, depoliticised manner. Accordingly, their participants may have no interest in discussing political choices in public. This 'post-political thrust' (Hirst 2000: 33) is increasingly perceived as a problem, because it means that the prospects for more open controversy and opposition (cf. Kohler-Koch 2010b: 1121–2) are low. Although single issues may well become mediatised, politicised, and debated in public, governance often prevents this structurally by depoliticising choices and therefore making them uninteresting for the public, so that deliberation is unlikely to occur beyond a small insider circle.

Public deliberation also has internal limits: out of the myriads of ongoing governance processes, not everything can possibly be deliberated about in public, and many things do not need to be. The challenges, then, are how to make sure that the more important issues enter the public sphere, how to establish what is an important issue, and how to ensure the democratic control of the less important issues. Sectoral sub-publics around functional representatives can function as whistle-blowers, but there are no structural safeguards to make sure this works, and functional groups have unequal resources to participate in this way.

In brief, relying on public deliberation means that democratic legitimacy becomes *precarious*. Deliberation is for the most part informal and categories are blurred conceptually as well as in practice; for instance, functional constituencies cannot be clearly delimited. This increases political inequality as well as the possibilities for manipulation. Furthermore, considering the multitude of different and constantly evolving processes, it is not only difficult to establish in any given case whether democratic norms have been sufficiently fulfilled, but the situation can also be very different in the next case. Democracy needs to be built anew for each new process, much more than, for example, in the working of parliamentary legislatives, which rely on established, formal institutions, a government–opposition arrangement, publicity, and regular general elections.

It is therefore not surprising that the governance literature concerned with democratic legitimacy has recently tended to stress the role of the *state* as the guarantor of democracy (e.g. Pierre 2000b: 242–4; Peters and Pierre 2004: 78, 88; Wälti *et al.* 2004: 108; Benz and Papadopoulos 2006: 2; Papadopoulos 2007; Føllesdal 2011; Héritier and Lehmkuhl 2011).[18] In this view, processes involving functional representation should be firmly nested in the territorial system, which is to coordinate political processes, ensure basic normative principles, and function as

---

18. In parallel, governance has also been conceptualised less in terms of replacing the state or crowding out traditional government, and rather as changing or shifting the state's role (e.g. Peters and Pierre 2006: 30; 2004: 78; Benz and Papadopoulos 2006: 2; Kooiman 2000: 139). To be sure, the thesis of shrinking government was also to a large part based on the illusion of a state with a monopoly of capacities (Hirst 2000: 22).

the highest authority. For one thing, this means emphasising the role of the polity's citizenry at large as the ultimate constituency, which is justified on the grounds that governance outcomes are binding on all. Even if not everybody is directly affected by each regulation, each regulation has an impact on the allocation of tax revenues and shapes the rules the society lives by. Therefore, according to the principal–agent logic, all chains of delegation should ultimately trace back to the people as the sovereign. What is more, strengthening the control of territorial representatives also means ensuring a reliable minimum level of formal (procedural) equality of the citizens (Pollak *et al.* 2009: 15). It is worth noting that voting is the most equitable form of political participation, and also the one with the lowest threshold for citizens (Klatt 2010).

For another thing, strengthening the role of the state also means providing a stronger framework for the multiplicity of different forms and processes of representation going on. If all these different modes of representation are to complement each other to make the political system as a whole more representative, they not only need stable foundations to ensure democratic legitimacy and to oversee what kinds of representation are appropriate for what political process, but they should also be given a clear place within a whole. By taking a higher profile in this role, the state could make the complex governance field more intelligible, which could in turn improve the possibilities for public deliberation to generate legitimacy. One problem of governance processes is their lack of perceptibility and comprehensibility, making it difficult for citizens to feel represented, i.e. perceiving themselves as the prime movers of political choices. Crucially, in a democracy, it is not enough to factually *be* represented (in the sense that at least one of the participants in a governance processes advocates my views), but the decisive thing is *feeling* represented. Only if people are aware of their representation, do they have the chance to cast an informed vote, communicate with their representatives, and react to the claims the representatives make. Public awareness is the precondition for taking all affected groups into account, for ensuring that the goals pursued and the outputs produced are endorsed by the represented, for holding policy makers to account, and for engaging in meaningful deliberation and exerting meaningful influence. Pierre Rosanvallon proposes enhancing the symbolic elements of political representation in order to make politics more legible and provide the citizens with tools to interpret processes, orient themselves, and react in meaningful ways. He warns of symbolising government by returning to historical images of national glory or by evoking fears of new threats. Instead, he envisages a reflexive symbolisation by constantly calling to mind the central task of constituting a community together (Rosanvallon 2008: 312–17). Thus, the state could return to the very basic issues of political life (How do we want to live? Where do we want to go?), and take a strong, visible lead on such fundamental choices. Together with a stronger grip on governance processes, this could reinforce the democratic legitimacy of the political system as a whole. However, this would also require changes in the relationships between politics and the media.

Now it is an obvious question, what 'the state' should mean in the different domains of the EU. Particularly in new modes of governance without a clear centre of authority, such as the OMC, this role has to be taken on by each of the Member States, but also, in addition, by the Commission, which is coordinating and guiding the process. However, considering the Commission in this perspective requires reflecting on its own democratic legitimacy as well as addressing its strategic position *vis-à-vis* the Member States. When (national) territorial legislatives and executives are demanded to ensure democratic standards, this is based on strong democratic safeguards – such as their governance–opposition arrangement generating controversy and bringing out possible problems – and the citizens' possibilities for control. All this is much more dubious on the European level. The Commission's ways of dealing with functional representation therefore deserve attention also in view of the question of how their practices affect the chances for democratic legitimacy in European governance.

Chapter Five

The Use of Functional Representation in EU Social Policy

So far, I have worked out the central questions that functional representation poses from a theoretical point of view. I have shown that there are different conceptions of what political representation is and who counts as a representative of what constituency. Notions also differ concerning issues of fairness and social equality in the representation of different groups in society. Concerning the democratic legitimacy of functional representation, it has turned out that it is difficult to balance input legitimacy, output legitimacy, and accountability, which gives room for different accentuations but also makes the democratic quality of overall processes somewhat dubious. Taken together, this diversity of ideas about functional representation as such, as well as about its realisation in democratic ways, means that there is no single or obvious way in which functional representation should be organised and in which it could contribute to the democratic legitimacy of political processes.

In the second part of this book, these issues are studied through a specific case, *viz.* the involvement of functional representatives by the European Commission in EU social policies. Rather than trying to resolve any of the questions raised, I take them as the starting point to examine a political process – the Open Method of Coordination (OMC) in social protection and social inclusion (the social OMC) – where functional representation is often presented, or hoped, to be a key solution to make European governance more democratic. Since it is the Commission that organises functional representation in this area, I enquire into how they present their own practices, and what the concepts of representation and democracy underlying their argumentation are.

I begin by introducing the social OMC, the Commission's role, and the part functional representation plays in this setting. The social OMC is in many respects a stimulating case for studying functional representation at the European level, given its multilevel intergovernmental character, the discursiveness of its policy-making processes, and the symbiotic relationships between functional organisations and DG Employment. What is more, the democratic qualities of new modes of governance have so far not been analysed systematically from the point of view of (functional) representation. The latter part of the chapter unfolds the rationale for examining the Commission's text as argumentation and working out the underlying concepts and ideas.

The OMC in social inclusion was initiated by the Lisbon European Council in March 2000.[1] In this Council meeting, the heads of state and government set

---

1.   The Lisbon Council also introduced OMCs in various other policy areas: better regulation, training and education, enterprise policy, information society, and research and development. Since

the goal for the Union 'to become the most competitive and dynamic knowledge-based economy in the world, capable of sustainable economic growth with more and better jobs and greater social cohesion'[2] within the following decade. Part of the strategy to achieve this goal was 'modernising the European social model, investing in people and combating social exclusion',[3] and the OMC was introduced as the instrument to implement this strategy. The new method was meant 'as the means of spreading best practice and achieving greater convergence towards the main EU goals'.[4] Its features were outlined as including guidelines and timetables to achieve agreed goals, translating these European guidelines into national and subnational policies, establishing indicators and benchmarks to promote 'best practice', and periodic monitoring, evaluation, and peer reviews to induce mutual learning.[5] Later, additional OMCs were set up for pensions (2002) and health and long-term care (2006), and in 2006 these three policy areas were integrated into what is today known as the 'social OMC'.[6] Since 2010, the social inclusion section has been realised through the Europe 2020 strategy (the successor to the Lisbon Strategy (2000–10)).

The social OMC is part of a wider development towards so-called new modes of governance (NMGs), which have typically been introduced for policy areas where the Member States' governments perceive the need for some coordination, but do not want to transfer authority to the European level (Schäfer 2006). Ideally, OMCs are meant to work through the coordination of national policies (as opposed to shifting legal competences to the EU), soft law, exchange of experience aimed at learning, the involvement of various types of actors from different levels of government, and a deliberative style of policy making (Scott and Trubeck 2002: 5–6; Radaelli 2003: 24–6; Kohler-Koch and Rittberger 2006: 36–7). While the name 'Open Method of Coordination' was established by the Lisbon Council, a number of structurally similar processes had already been launched in the 1990s, which are now sometimes referred to as OMCs too. The main forerunners and inspirers of the OMC have been the macro-economic policy coordination (1992), the European Employment Strategy (EES) (1997) and the Stability and Growth Pact (1999). However, although there is now a range of OMCs, this does not mean that those processes all work in the same way. OMCs differ in their degree of institutionalisation (treaty base, political bodies involved), their repertoire of policy instruments (e.g. common objectives, indicators, peer reviews, policy

---

Lisbon, OMCs have been launched in pensions, health and long-term care, sustainable development (environmental policy), youth, and tourism.

2.   European Council (2000) 'Lisbon European Council, 23 and 24 March 2000: presidency conclusions'. The European Council's decision is based on Articles 136, 137, and 140 of the Treaty of Amsterdam.

3.   *ibid.*

4.   *ibid.*

5.   *ibid.*

6.   Cf. European Commission Communication COM(2005)706 of 22 December 2005.

recommendations), and the balance of power between the European and the national level.[7]

The social OMC's main institutional features are as follows. There are *common objectives* establishing broad policy goals, such as to 'ensur[e] [...] the active social inclusion of all, both by promoting participation in the labour market and by fighting poverty and exclusion'.[8] These objectives are drafted by DG Employment, accepted by the Employment and Social Policy Council and adopted by the European Council. Member States submit bi-annual National Reports on Strategies for Social Protection and Social Inclusion (National Reports hereafter) in which they lay out their strategies and policies to attain these objectives. On the basis of these reports, DG Employment drafts an annual Joint Report, which is adopted by the Council of the European Union (the Council hereafter). The Joint Reports assess progress made, identify good practice, and name priorities and issues to work on. Since the start of the Europe 2020 strategy, the Commission can also issue policy recommendations and warnings to Member States. Candidate countries can participate in the process by signing a Joint Inclusion Memorandum together with the Commission, which forms the basis of a process meant to prepare the country for accession to the EU as concerns social policy. The European Parliament (EP) has become somewhat more involved following the ratification of the Lisbon Treaty; however, given that the OMC is an intergovernmental process of coordination, the EP's role remains weak.[9] An important hub of the OMC process (in addition to DG Employment) is the Social Protection Committee (SPC), a treaty-based body[10] consisting of two representatives of each Member State and two Commission representatives. Its secretariat is provided by DG Employment. The SPC's task is to strengthen cooperation between the Member States; monitor developments in social policy in the Member States and the Community; promote the exchange of information, experience, and 'good practice'; and prepare the annual Joint Report (drafted by DG Employment). It has contacts with the corresponding committee in the EES, the Employment Committee (EMCO), with the Economic Policy Committee (EPC) coordinating economic and monetary policies under the Economic and Monetary Affairs Council, as well as with social partners and social NGOs.[11] The SPC has set up an Indicators' Sub-Group (ISG) to draw up and develop the common indicators used to measure and compare

---

7. For an overview of all OMCs and comparable processes, *see* Laffan and Shaw 2005: esp. 13–14.

8. Council of the European Union, 7243/06 of 23 March 2006: 5 (Draft Minutes of the 2714th meeting of the Council of the European Union (Employment, Social Policy, Health and Consumer Affairs), held in Brussels on 10 March 2006) and 5070/06 of 4 January 2006: 5 (COM(2005)706 of 22 December 2005).

9. Treaty on the Functioning of the European Union, Articles 153 and 161. However, the Lisbon Treaty has increased the EP's budgetary powers. For the EP's role in the Lisbon strategy, *see* Tsakatika 2007.

10. Treaty on the Functioning of the European Union, Article 160 (formerly 144).

11. Council Decision 2000/436/EC of 29 June 2000 and Council Decision 2004/689/EC of 4 October 2004.

Member States' progress. This *statistical data* is collected nationally according to harmonised methodologies and reported to Eurostat, which produces comparative overviews.[12] The idea is on the one hand to inform policy making with comparable information about all European countries, and on the other hand to spur Member States to increase their efforts by inducing competition among them. Another mechanism of exchange in the social OMC is *peer reviews*, which have been organised seven to ten times per year in different Member States since 2004. In facilitated discussions, Member States present national policies with perceived potential for dissemination, or alternatively policy reform plans under preparation, to typically five to ten interested Member States. Participants in the sessions include senior national officials, Commission officials, independent experts, representatives of two European NGOs and possibly also of national NGOs, as well as consultants managing the project.[13] Peer reviews are funded by the Community Programme for Employment and Social Solidarity (Progress). This programme (2007–13) is a financial instrument to support the achievement of the Lisbon goals; it integrates the previous separate funding programmes of the areas of social inclusion and protection (the social OMC),[14] employment (the EES), working conditions, and antidiscrimination and gender equality. Concerning social protection and social inclusion, Progress funds policy analysis and studies; the development of statistics and common indicators; monitoring and evaluation; the exchange of experience; awareness raising, information disseminating, and promotion of public debate about the policy issues concerning the OMC; a microfinance facility (since 2010); and the running costs of EU-level networks of social NGOs to develop 'the capacity of key European level networks to support and further develop Community policy goals and strategies on social protection and inclusion'.[15]

---

12. This happens particularly through the framework of EU-SILC (European Union Statistics on Income and Living Conditions). *See* Regulation (EC) No 1177/2003 of the European Parliament and of the Council of 16 June 2003.

13. *See* European Commission (no date) 'Peer review programme'. Online. Available http://ec.europa.eu/social/main.jsp?catId=1023&langId=en, accessed 7 March 2013.

14. Progress was preceded by the Community Action Programme to Combat Social Exclusion (the Social Exclusion Programme (SEP), 2002–2006), which was similar in content, but restricted to the OMC in social inclusion (*see* Decision 50/2002/EC of the European Parliament and of the Council of 7 December 2001).

    Participating countries in Progress (and, therefore, in the peer reviews) include, in addition to the EU Member States, the EFTA/EEA countries (Norway, Iceland, and Liechtenstein), the candidate countries (Turkey, Croatia, Macedonia), and the western Balkan countries included in the stabilisation and association process (Albania, Bosnia and Herzegovina, Serbia and Montenegro, Kosovo) (Decision No 1672/2006/EC of the European Parliament and of the Council of 24 October 2006).

15. Decision 1672/2006/EC of the European Parliament and of the Council of 24 October 2006; amendment of this Decision by Decision 284/2010/EU of the European Parliament and of the Council of 25 March 2010.

This core funding of European networks of social NGOs brings me to an aspect that makes the role played by functional representatives in the social OMC stand out. Not only is there more functional representation than in most other OMCs, but promoting functional representation is *as such* part of the common objectives. The common objectives of 2006 (confirmed in 2008) include good 'governance, transparency and the involvement of stakeholders in the design, implementation and monitoring of policy' for the social OMC as a whole, and one of the three specific objectives for the social inclusion strand is to ensure 'that social inclusion policies are well-coordinated and involve all levels of government and relevant actors, including people experiencing poverty'.[16] The previous common objectives for social inclusion (2000 and 2002) contained the objective 'to mobilise all relevant bodies' and stressed especially 'the participation and self-expression of people suffering exclusion, in particular in regard to their situation and the policies and measures that affect them'. As well as that, they prescribed the promotion of

dialogue and partnership between all relevant bodies, public and private, for example: by involving the social partners, NGOs and social service providers, according to their respective area of competence, in the fight against the various forms of exclusion [...].[17]

However, this relative openness towards functional representatives applies only to the social OMC's social inclusion strand. In health care and pensions, the involvement of functional representatives is neither mentioned in the specific objectives, nor does it take place in a stronger way.[18] Functional representation is also not a significant part of the policy discourses in these areas. This is certainly not surprising considering the sensitivity of these policy areas as well as their functional representation sectors. Yet, it means that most of the research materials used for the present study are necessarily related to the social inclusion strand, so that the results also pertain mainly to this oldest part of the OMC. Social inclusion differs from health care and pensions not only with respect to functional representation; it is also more institutionalised, and therefore policy coordination is denser. One the one hand, this is due to its older age (Laffan and Shaw 2005: 15–17), and on the other hand, social inclusion policies have also been easier for the Member States to open to European coordination, especially when they have been framed in terms of increasing employment rates. As regards the Commission, the stronger Europeanisation of these policy areas means greater room for manoeuvre *vis-à-vis* the Member States, as compared to health care and pensions.

---

16. Council of the European Union, 7243/06 of 23 March 2006: 5 (Draft Minutes of the 2714th meeting of the Council of the European Union (Employment, Social Policy, Health and Consumer Affairs), held in Brussels on 10 March 2006), and 5070/06 of 4 January 2006: 5–6 (COM(2005)706 of 22 December 2005).

17. Council of the European Union (Employment and Social Policy): 14110/00 of 30 November 2000: 9–10; 14164/02 of 15 November 2002: 12–13.

18. Concerning pensions, *see* de la Porte and Nanz 2004: 276, 281.

In the following two sections, I look at the social OMC as DG Employment's *strategic environment* for social policies. 'Strategic environment' refers here to the specific configuration resulting from the Commission's institutional interests, the OMC's institutional set-up and ways of functioning, as well as the positions of other involved actors. I work on the assumption that it is the institutional interest of the Commission (a) to extend the range of issues on which it has a say (cf. Cram 1997: 156), and (b) that the kind of policies it advocates are adopted, either on the European level or nationally. In other words, the Commission aims at extending and intensifying the Europeanisation of policy areas. In this endeavour, it acts as a 'purposeful opportunist', i.e. it is 'an organisation which has a notion of its overall objectives and aims but is quite flexible as to the means of achieving them' (Cram 1997: 186–7; the term 'purposeful opportunist' was coined by Klein and O'Higgins 1985: 227). It will make strategic use of those means that are likely to lead to success in a given situation (although not necessarily in the short term), which means that its choice of instruments will be directed by two main conditions: the attitudes of the Member States' governments and the institutional environment. Both factors condition the range of strategies that could be promising in a given situation; they open some opportunities and close others.

DG Employment has been called 'one of the most expansionist-orientated services of the European Commission' (Greenwood 2007a: 181). However, social policy and the OMC are environments that differ from many areas where integration has been deepened by delegating legal competences to the EU. Such a delegation of substantive powers has always been rather improbable in welfare policies. However, saying that the Commission endeavours to extend the *range* of issues on which it has a say does not mean that it is necessarily aiming at full legal authority, but that it systematically attempts to gain some kind of influence on a growing number of matters. The means to do this have to be adapted to the political environment. Soft coordination such as in the OMC is one way to Europeanise a policy field, and the Commission's position as the mediator of this process allows it 'to take initiatives and to expand cooperation to new areas belonging to the legal competencies of the Member States; hence, it has been able to bypass the subsidiary principle. It is thus not obvious that the OMC has weakened the Commission' (Borrás and Jacobsson 2004: 198). This applies even though the OMC 'has strengthened the role of the European Council, particularly after the Lisbon summit, where this EU institution was granted clear political leadership in its co-ordinating and guiding role' (Borrás and Jacobsson 2004: 198.).

The Commission's strategic action within soft coordination regimes can be seen both in the history of European social policies and within the social OMC. The subsequent section provides a brief overview of the historical development of EU social policies and the creation of the OMC through this perspective of the Commission's seeking to Europeanise the policy field. After that, I turn to the ways of policy making that characterise the OMC's architecture and the use DG Employment makes of them to promote their goals.

A short history of social Europe

Originally, the Community's competences in the area of social policies were restricted to issues closely related to the single market, such as labour law, regulations connected to the free movement of workers, health and safety at the work place, and non-discrimination. However, the Commission has always showed ambitions to expand its sphere of activity into more traditional welfare policies. One strategy in this endeavour has been to take advantage of the national governments' vague declarations about the significance of the social dimension. The first instances of this were already Articles 117 and 118 of the Treaty of Rome (1957),[19] the content of which is rather indeterminate, and about the interpretation of which there was no consensus among the Member States. Nevertheless, the Commission referred to these provisions to underpin its claim to responsibilities in social matters, and on these grounds organised conferences and issued official documents. This brought them into direct opposition with the Social Affairs Council, which eventually boycotted the Commission by not meeting between October 1964 and December 1966. Finally, the issue was resolved with a clear victory of the Council, putting a halt to the Commission's activism (Cram 1997: 31–3).

Subsequently, the Commission changed its approach and concentrated on the gradual establishment of European forums to deal with social issues from a European perspective without explicitly advocating specific policy outcomes

---

19. Treaty establishing the European Economic Community. The articles read:

    'Article 117

    Member States hereby agree upon the necessity to promote improvement of the living and working conditions of labour so as to permit the equalisation of such conditions in an upward direction.

    They consider that such a development will result not only from the functioning of the Common Market which will favour the harmonisation of social systems, but also from the procedures provided for under this Treaty and from the approximation of legislative and administrative provisions.

    Article 118

    Without prejudice to the other provisions of this Treaty and in conformity with its general objectives, it shall be the aim of the Commission to promote close collaboration between Member States in the social field, particularly in matters relating to:

    – employment,

    – labour legislation and working conditions,

    – occupational and continuation training,

    – social security,

    – protection against occupational accidents and diseases,

    – industrial hygiene,

    – the law as to trade unions, and collective bargaining between employers and workers.

    For this purpose, the Commission shall act in close contact with Member States by means of studies, the issuing of opinions, and the organising of consultations both on problems arising at the national level and on those of concern to international organisations.

    Before issuing the opinions provided for under this Article, the Commission shall consult the Economic and Social Committee'.

or directly claiming competencies. In this way, social policies were placed on the European agenda, but adverseness *vis-à-vis* the Member States was avoided. From the 1970s onwards, Commission activities in the field were characterised by two strategies. Firstly, it started adapting its rhetoric to the discourse of the national governments. In practice, this meant framing social issues in economic terms and stressing the close relation of social and economic policies (Cram 1997: 34). With the Economic and Monetary Union (EMU) this discourse has been further reinforced. Today, it is an outstanding feature of the OMC language. Secondly, the Commission engaged in 'softening up' the policy field, i.e. the gradual building of a *European* discourse on social policy and of resources enabling the Commission to deal with the policy field. Laura Cram sees this as a long-term strategy of preparing the ground for a possible extension of its scope of competence, should a policy window open up (1997.: 38). However, it would be too narrow a perspective to conceptualise these activities merely as paving the way for something else. Rather, DG Employment's social policy activities in the 1970s and 1980s form a direct continuum with the 'soft' policy making in the OMC. They show how dealing with an issue in the first place can as such bring about change, even though there is no agreement on policy goals (cf. Lascoumes and Le Galès 2007: 16).

The main instruments in this were the Social Action Programme (1974–76) and especially three subsequent Poverty Programmes (1975–80, 1985–8, 1989–94), managed by the Commission.[20] The Poverty Programmes funded extensive research on poverty, analysis of national social policies, and the collection and exchange of data and knowledge. In 1989, the Council approved the setting up of the Observatory on National Policies to Combat Social Exclusion, which institutionalised these activities (Hantrais 2000: 170–2). At the same time, the Poverty Programmes' funds also served to build up a network of social NGOs on the European level with close relations to DG Employment (EAPN 2005: 9). Through these activities, poverty was conceptualised as a *European* issue by working out its specific characteristics (common to the European countries) in policy analysis, by inserting it in an economic context (crisis) allegedly shared by all Member States, and by pointing to the interdependence of the national policies.[21] On the basis of this problem definition, it was justified to work on *European* policy responses (cf. Bauer 2002: 385–8). In its interim report on the Poverty II programme, the Commission concludes that the programme's

> European dimension has operated on three levels. Firstly it has transferred new ideas and approaches to some Member States and to traditional charitable organizations in older Member States. Secondly it has created a European Community of practitioners and researchers dedicated to work with the poor

---

20. The Social Exclusion Programme (2002–6) and Progress (2007–13) mentioned above are the successors of these programmes.

21. *See* European Commission report COM(80)666 of 4 November 1980: esp. 3–4, 17.

and on the problems of the poor and begun to form a European Community if not yet of the poor, at least for the poor. Thirdly, it has developed the exchange of experience of specific problems. Most important of all it has helped to create an awareness that the problem of poverty, like the problems of agricultural and industrial policy, economic development, the environment and social security, is not merely a national concern but one which must be seen and acted upon in the context of the Community as a whole.[22]

At the same time, the Poverty Programmes built the necessary resources (information, policy networks) for DG Employment to do so.

New momentum, and thus the opportunity to use these resources, came with the 1990s. Two developments led to the emergence of a stronger political will on the side of the national governments to coordinate their social policies. For one thing, the completion of the single market, the Economic and Monetary Union (EMU), and the continuing integration of further policy areas had impacts on the welfare state and national social policies. In particular, the Stability and Growth Pact with its restrictions on national budgets led to reform pressures on the welfare systems. In this situation, European coordination was perceived as necessary to balance macro-economic policies with national welfare regimes (Palier 2008; Borrás and Jacobsson 2004: 186). For another thing, the reactions to the Maastricht Treaty (1992) and the crisis of the Santer Commission (1998/9) led to a more general legitimacy crisis of the Union. Among other consequences, this created pressures on the EU to address the social consequences of its economic policies. At the same time, however, it also made it difficult to transfer substantial competences in sensitive areas to the European level. Thus, despite recognition by the predominantly social-democratic national governments that common responses were necessary to preserve their social models in the new economic environment, they were reluctant to shift authority on these issues to the EU. In other words, the traditional mode of integration by transferring competencies upwards was not perceived as the right way to deal with the situation. In addition, the prospect of upcoming eastern enlargements and thereby growing intra-EU diversity led to a search for new balances between community and flexibility. The Commission-led discourse about governance and new governance is part of this same context (Borrás and Jacobsson 2004: 186–7).

In this situation, the Commission proposed a further institutionalisation of the soft coordination of social policies based on the notion that Member States faced similar – European – problems and needed to coordinate their responses. This approach directly continued the practices shaped in the 1970s and 1980s; it deepened the cooperation and strengthened the coordinative role of the Commission, but did not touch on the formal division of powers. This scheme was accepted by the governments, and in 1992 the Council adopted two Commission Recommendations, originally intended as Directives, about 'common criteria

---

22. European Commission report COM(88)621 of 28 November 1988: 36.

concerning sufficient resources and social assistance in social protection systems' and 'the convergence of social protection objectives and policies', respectively.[23] Together, these two Recommendations already represent an embryonic OMC (Ferrera *et al.* 2002: 228–9). They recognise 'social exclusion' as a problem in Europe; lay down a range of principles according to which Member States are recommended to organise their social policies; and ask the Commission to study and evaluate these policies, develop criteria for assessment, and encourage and organise exchange of information and experience, as well as report on these issues to the Council. These ideas were then included in the Treaty of Amsterdam (1997), which recognised 'the combating of exclusion' as one of the objectives of the Community. To this end, it created the possibility for the Council to

> adopt measures designed to encourage cooperation between Member States through initiatives aimed at improving knowledge, developing exchanges of information and best practices, promoting innovative approaches and evaluating experiences in order to combat social exclusion. (Treaty of Amsterdam, Article 137)

Additionally, the old Article 118 (now Articles 138–40) was strengthened and now requested the Commission to 'encourage cooperation between the Member States and facilitate the coordination of their action in all social policy fields under this chapter', including social security (Article 140). The Commission thus now had the juridical fundaments for requesting the Council to create 'a concerted strategy for modernising social protection'.[24] In a Communication with this title, it outlined how the cooperation in social protection and inclusion should be organised, thus in practice asking the governments to establish what then half a year later was baptised 'Open Method of Coordination' by the Lisbon Council.[25] The Communication included all three strands of the future social OMC, of which social inclusion was launched by the Nice Council, while pensions and health care followed only later. The forerunner of the SPC, the High-Level Working Party, was established by the Council in 1999.

The European social dimension thus finally took on a very different form from what might have been imagined in the 1950s or 1960s. Social policies have been Europeanised, while formal legal competencies have remained with the Member States. Notwithstanding, the OMC architecture gives a central role to the Commission by making it the focal mediator that shapes the agenda and controls important information. Most importantly, through the OMC it is acknowledged that social policies have a European dimension and that the Commission has a say concerning them. One can thus say that it has overall been successful in getting a toehold in social affairs. This has been possible firstly by prioritising the 'if' over the 'how' and the 'what exactly', i.e. being flexible concerning specific

---

23. Council Recommendations 92/441/EEC of 24 June 1992, and 92/442/EEC of 27 July 1992.

24. Commission Communication COM(1999)347 of 14 July 1999.

25. *ibid.*

policy outcomes and the institutional settings of the policy field on the European level. Secondly, success has been based on adapting strategies to the political environment, which in this case has meant persuasion rather than confrontation and framing issues in ways that serve the DG's overall goals. Both strategies continue in DG Employment's manner of policy making within the OMC.

Policy making in the social OMC: steering by persuasion

I now turn to how the Commission acts within the OMC in order to extend the scope of issues dealt with on the European level and to further the adoption of the kinds of policies it advocates. The social OMC is in this regard a specific environment, which opens certain possibilities of political action and closes others. It is essentially a European-level process of structured communication, while decisions are taken nationally or subnationally. The instruments available to the Commission in this setting are not specifically tailored for or restricted to the Open Method of Coordination, but together they make up a specific combination that is characteristic of the social OMC.

The fundamental idea of the OMC is *cognitive transformation*, i.e. 'learning' from each other. Processes aimed at 'learning' have, as such, an inbuilt tendency to lead to isomorphism, i.e. to national policies becoming more similar to each other. The harmonisation of policies thus does not presuppose authoritative enactments to take place, but can also come about informally through mimesis and normative pressures (DiMaggio and Powell 1991).[26] Mimesis, i.e. copying others, is a strategy of policy makers to cope with complexity and uncertainty by adopting models that have proven successful elsewhere. As well as that, policy networks can socialise the participants into certain ways of thinking, which generates normative pressures. Policy forums where policy makers meet regularly can develop a common paradigm of conceptualising issues, including problem definitions, categorisations, possible solutions, and norms of what counts as good policy making (cf. Radaelli 2000: 16–19). Once such a paradigm becomes strong enough, this creates pressure to join in. Hence, also in the absence of coercion, cognitive convergence, and subsequently a harmonisation of policies, can occur through forums of regular exchange. This is explicitly intended in the social OMC:

> Achieving a positive change in understanding of EU objectives and priorities among key EU and national policy/decision-makers and other stakeholders will facilitate the convergence of national policies with EU objectives and priorities. (European Commission 2008a)

'EU objectives' mainly refers to the OMC's common objectives, but also to consensus reached on smaller goals, such as tackling 'financial exclusion' or putting a special focus on child poverty.

---

26. Cf. Peter M. Haas's concept of epistemic communities (Haas 1989).

For policy outcomes, causalities are difficult to establish; yet, although the national welfare systems remain very different across the EU, recent reforms have been strikingly similar in their general orientation, and in national reform discourses it has become much more legitimate to draw on comparisons with other countries. Social policies have generally been subordinate to and framed in terms of economics.[27] The European single market and the Maastricht criteria significantly changed the economic environment and created pressures on national welfare systems, so that the idea of necessary reform developed in the context of economics, hand in hand with European integration, while solutions for the issue were increasingly looked for on the EU level (Palier 2008: 45). Welfare policies have been marked by a shift from social rights to conditional support, based on the notion that the causes of poverty lie on the individual level rather than in social or economic circumstances. Hence, measures are mainly aimed at inducing people to return to work (Büchs 2009; Palier 2008: 44–5). Concerning pensions, the trend is towards introducing multi-pillar systems combining both PAYGO and funded schemes, while in health care systems increasing competition has been a spreading strategy. More generally, welfare is no longer seen to depend only on public intervention, but private actors are expected to contribute as well (Palier 2008: 44–5). The social OMC provides the discourses promoting and justifying such policies,[28] while political ideas aiming in the opposing direction have no place in this framework. It can thus be said that the OMC encourages 'learning' mainly in particular directions.

Now, while the OMC's structure provides the prerequisites and incentives for convergence to occur, the Commission's interest is that this indeed takes place. If Member States agree on a problem definition and deal with an issue together in a European framework, this means that the matter has got a European dimension (i.e. basic conceptualisations are also developed in Brussels) and that the Commission has some role in and influence on it. More often than not, the Commission will also have some preference as to the particular direction in which it wishes national policies to converge. To succeed in this endeavour, it uses a range of discursive instruments that are based on exploiting its position as the key mediator in the OMC processes.

The OMC is a method of *discursive policy making*, i.e. it works mainly through language.[29] Finding a common way to speak about things is the first prerequisite for a process meant to coordinate different national policies (Palola 2007: 51). At the same time, language is not a neutral tool. Discourses carry meanings and

---

27. For some, the social OMC (as well as the EES) is a distinctly neoliberal tool used to dismantle institutions of market correction and capitalism regulation. E.g. Offe 2003; Nicol 2010: 125–6. Cf. Kröger 2009.

28. The arguments disseminated through the OMC, as well as the existence of the OMC as such, are also used by national politicians to justify policy reform. *See* e.g. Erhel *et al.* 2005; Büchs 2009.

29. Kerstin Jacobsson speaks of 'discursive regulatory mechanisms […], that is mechanisms related to language-use and knowledge making and thus fundamentally to meaning making' (Jacobsson 2004: 356; emphasis omitted).

ideologies; they make sense of the world in a certain way, which is never the only one possible. Adopting a discourse therefore means taking over a paradigm of thinking (Jacobsson 2004: 360–1, 366–7). The OMC is based on the creation of a common discourse about social policy, which makes it possible to define common goals and to search for solutions together. For example, conferences organised about specific topics are also meant to 'act as a first step towards a European consensus on diagnosis of the problems, the challenges to be met, and the action to be taken'.[30] In the same vein, one of the tasks of the Progress programme is to 'promot[e] shared understanding and ownership of EU objectives among national policy- and decision-makers and other stakeholders' (European Commission 2010a: 10).

The key mechanism of influencing such processes is *discourse framing*, i.e. working to establish a particular conceptualisation of an issue, including problem definitions, categorisations, ideas about facts and causalities, possible solutions, practices to tackle the issue, and desirable outcomes.[31] In short, by managing to frame the discourse about a matter, an actor shapes the meaning things are given – the terms under which something is discussed. Once such a paradigm becomes dominant, it becomes very difficult for individual actors to challenge it and discuss things from a different perspective (Usui 2007). As the mediator of the OMC, DG Employment is particularly well positioned to engage in framing discourses. Room for this is also created by the fact that the common objectives are very general and leave space for interpretation and different definitions. This gives the DG possibilities to influence the emergence of interpretations; it also means that such influence takes place to an important extent in informal ways.

One instrument in discourse framing is the choice of terminology used to present things. Common concepts are not only the prerequisite for a common policy process such as the OMC, but concepts also contain particular perspectives on the referent and therefore also affect the way the matter is dealt with. The enormous textual output of DG Employment, which is disseminated to the actors in the field, significantly affects the terminology used by those actors. Moreover, the DG structures the communicative exchanges within the OMC, for example by issuing guidance notes for the preparation of the National Reports, by conducting consultations, by drafting policy documents, and by organising conferences. This means that other actors' texts are in most cases reactions or responses to DG texts, and therefore tend to adopt their terminology.

---

30. European Commission press release SPEECH/05/432 of 11 June 2005.

31. Martin Rein and Donald Schön define framing as 'a way of selecting, organising, interpreting, and making sense of a complex reality so as to provide guideposts for knowing, analysing, persuading, and acting. A frame is a perspective from which an amorphous, ill-defined problematic situation can be made sense of and acted upon' (Rein and Schön 1991: 263, cited in Kohler-Koch 2000: 515). Cf. also Baumgartner and Jones 1991: 1045. For discourse framing in the OMC, *see* Bauer 2002: 386–8; Radaelli 2000: 18–19; Palola 2007; Armstrong 2003: 172; Borrás and Jacobsson 2004: 196. Cf. also Ruzza 2002; Kohler-Koch 2000.

The concept of 'social exclusion' (as well as its counterpart, 'inclusion') is a case in point. The Commission introduced the term – of French origin – into European discourse in the 1980s; during the 1990s, 'exclusion' became the key concept in the EU discourse about social problems. One reason for using the term was that it was more acceptable to national governments than 'poverty' to be applied to phenomena in their societies (Vleminckx and Berghman 2001: 28–9).[32] In other words, the issue was redefined as something where EU activities were easier to accept. However, 'social exclusion' also implies a specific conceptualisation of the matter in question; it suggests that poverty in Europe has particular characteristics and that it needs to be dealt with by involving a wide range of policy fields. 'Social exclusion' refers to the multidimensionality of social problems, i.e. 'poverty is not just a matter of money or of opening up access to traditional services',[33] but also involves people's housing conditions, health, social contacts, family relations, education, and behaviour, which 'cannot be considered in isolation'.[34] Through this concept, poverty in the EU could be reconceptualised as 'new poverty', which is '[q]uantitatively and qualitatively [...] different'.[35] On this basis, the Commission could justify a European approach to poverty. The imprecision of the term made it easier for the national governments to accept this, because 'social exclusion' allows different actors to emphasise different aspects which match their own perspective, and it is compatible with different social models. Despite different national situations, most actors can agree that 'social exclusion' is an area worthy of attention and action (Mayes 2001: 4–5; Matsaganis and Tsakloglou 2001: 188–9). At the same time, however, this ambiguity also gives the DG more room to manoeuvre (cf. Radaelli and Schmidt 2004: 367–8). Framing the problem as 'social exclusion' means that in order to tackle the issue effectively, its different dimensions have to be addressed. European action is thus no longer concerned exclusively with 'poverty' (however defined), but covers a whole range of somehow related social matters. In parallel, the information and analysis gathered and distributed by DG Employment continually provides knowledge about connections between poverty and associated phenomena, and can thus serve as justification for attending to specific issues. Accordingly, the scope of subjects discussed within the OMC has increased continually, mainly by drawing attention to more and more aspects of 'social exclusion' that need to be dealt with, such as housing, 'financial exclusion', or especially affected groups of people, such as children, the elderly, or minorities. In short, the 'social exclusion' frame widens the range of possible problem definitions and of issues that can be raised on the agenda (cf. Radaelli and Schmidt 2004: 369). Moreover, 'exclusion' has a capability for stretching

---

32. Cf. European Commission report COM(88)621 of 28 November 1988: 6.

33. European Commission report COM(88)621 of 28 November 1988: 34.

34. European Commission report COM(80)666 of 4 November 1980: 2–3.

35. European Commission report COM(88)621 of 28 November 1988: 6. Cf. European Commission report COM(80)666 of 4 November 1980: 4.

that allows the linking of different policy areas. For example, 'active inclusion' provides the link between social and employment policies.

As the mediator in the OMC, DG Employment is also the hub of an extensive exchange of *information*. Data about the Member States flows through a variety of channels to the Commission, which therefore has privileged access to encompassing and, importantly, comparative as well as increasingly comparable information (cf. Sbragia 2000: 228–31). The Progress programme in particular is used to generate and gather information, e.g. through commissioning studies and funding the establishment of statistical indicators. Through ordering studies, the DG can choose topics to be analysed and define the perspective from which this is done, or pick policy alternatives to be compared.

One way to utilise this advantage is to couple the generation of information with the carrying out of policy analysis, and disseminate the results as material to inform policy making. Policy analysis carried out or commissioned by an involved actor with vested interests is intended to persuade rather than being scientific enquiry to find optimal solutions (Cram 1997: 38). It is one instrument to direct discussions in certain directions by cooperating with experts who present scientific evidence and support for preferred policy orientations. References to policy analysis give the DG's propositions a neutral impression and thereby hide their political character (Palola 2007: 36–7). However, the analyses and assessments it presents generally identify policy priorities that the DG is also promoting through other forums (e.g. by organising thematic conferences or funding projects), and support the case that more European action and 'mutual learning' is needed.

The promotion of 'mutual learning' and 'best practice', a key element of the OMC, is another way to capitalise on privileged information. DG Employment has significant control over which policy instruments are presented as models worth copying. It orders and collects information about national practices, including studies and projects looking for 'best practice' and national actors' own proposals for 'good practice'. Subsequently, it drafts the documents presenting this information, and preselects potential policies for peer reviews. The OMC is thus a process of 'directed mimesis', as it were (cf. Lasoumes and Le Galès 2007: 14; Jacobsson 2004: 363).

Through all these practices, DG Employment has supreme possibilities to influence the *agenda* of the process. It drafts all central OMC documents and thus pre-frames their key messages and the perspective they take on issues. The DG also structures and schedules many deliberations; for example, by choosing topics for policy analysis and by organising thematic conferences, attention can be drawn to particular topics. Studies rarely end without pointing out that their topic is important and deserves to be followed, and European conferences about specific social problems invariably end with at least some joint statement to the effect that action is needed to tackle the issue, to which the Commission can then refer when presenting follow-up initiatives. This is of course also due to the participants that tend to be invited to and interested in such conferences.

A good example of a new issue put on the OMC agenda by DG Employment is the so-called 'financial exclusion', i.e.

A process whereby people encounter difficulties accessing and/or using financial services and products in the mainstream market that are appropriate to their needs and enable them to lead a normal social life in the society in which they belong.[36]

Financial exclusion is not (yet) mentioned in the common objectives. In 2006, the DG noted a particular need to better comprehend and monitor 'the prevention and tackling of over-indebtedness and financial exclusion' and included the issue in the matters to be covered by the NGO networks that it finances,[37] as well as commissioned a study on the topic, which was published in 2008.[38] Subsequently, the DG launched a public consultation 'to reflect on how to ensure that, by a certain date, nobody is denied access to a basic bank account',[39] and had the issue discussed at several European Meetings of People Experiencing Poverty and at conventional conferences with functional representatives. Finally, in 2010, its 'Poverty and Social Exclusion' Internet page stated that 'EU action has helped to create a consensus about the following key challenges: [...] to tackle financial exclusion and overindebtedness'.[40] The OMC is thus not a mere coordinating of issues adopted by the national governments, but a dynamic process that provides the DG with instruments to shape policy agendas.

Finally, DG Employment is the focal point of the OMC's *governance network*, having contacts with a host of governmental, non-governmental, European, national, and subnational actors. This network has been built up over time with the help of financing from the Poverty Programmes and subsequent funds. It not only helps gathering information, but also functions as a communicative channel in the opposite direction. Maintaining a wide network also means that for most if not all DG initiatives, supporters will be found. Last but not least, working in and with a network opens numerous options for strategic action. Functional representatives play a key part in the OMC governance network. Their relations with DG Employment, including their use as a steering instrument, are the topic of the following section.

---

36. European Commission 2008: *Financial Services Provision and Prevention of Financial Exclusion*: 9. Online. Available http://ec.europa.eu/social/BlobServlet?docId=760&langId=en, accessed 7 March 2013.

37. European Commission call for proposals VP/2006/009 (no date). Online. Available http://ec.europa.eu/social/main.jsp?catId=631&langId=en&callId=30&furtherCalls=yes, accessed 7 March 2013.

38. Specifications of European Commission call for tender VT/2006/017 (no date). Online. Available http://ec.europa.eu/social/BlobServlet?docId=854&langId=en, accessed 7 March 2013. Cf. European Commission press release IP/08/805 of 28 May 2008.

39. European Commission press release IP/09/224 of 5 February 2009; European Commission (2009) 'Financial inclusion: Commission launches public consultation on ensuring access to a basic bank account'. Online. Available http://ec.europa.eu/social/main.jsp?catId=437&langId=en&newsId=452&furtherNews=yes, accessed 14 September 2010.

40. European Commission (no date) 'Poverty and social exclusion'. Online. Available http://ec.europa.eu/social/main.jsp?langId=en&catId=751, accessed 9 September 2010. Emphases omitted.

In conclusion, the possibilities that the OMC architecture offers DG Employment to steer processes in certain directions are based on 'soft' discursive means. Since the method's rationale is 'learning' and voluntary action on the national level, it works above all through interlocution. This means that policy making in the OMC is inherently rhetorical, and influence is mainly possible through the argumentative use of language. As the coordinator of the process, the Commission is in a supreme position to exploit language as a political instrument. Through framing policy discourses, it shapes the common language used, and thereby possibly evolving common visions of social policies. It influences the perspective from which things are dealt with, because the concepts used to talk about them carry particular ways of thinking that cannot be separated from the language used. For example, the talk of especially 'vulnerable groups' with respect to social exclusion legitimates differentiated approaches for different parts of the population and special support for some of them. In this way, policy orientations are influenced gradually and subtly, and their harmonisation comes through the back door.

Legitimacy and functional representation in the OMC

All this means that the Commission needs democratic legitimacy for its activities within the social OMC. Coordinating social policies is not a politically neutral process, but such coordination presupposes common conceptualisations. The OMC is first and foremost an 'arena where a new common discourse has emerged […]. This discourse involves a specific language but also specific epistemic assumptions (e.g. about causal relationships) and normative evaluations' (Pfister 2009; cf. Radaelli 2003: 27–8). The norms and values entailed in this discourse gradually influence ways of policy making and policies affecting the citizens' living conditions, including the distribution of risks and costs. In other words, the OMC is no less political than more traditional ways of policy making, and therefore has to be democratically legitimated (Borrás 2008: 101; Borrás and Conzelmann 2007: 534–5; Büchs 2008: 767; Kröger 2007: 567; 2009). Since the Commission is playing an active role in this process, it thus needs democratic legitimacy for its activities. This requirement holds for all public policy, irrespective of the formal distribution of legal competence: '[I]f there is EU action, and as long as the EU is made up of democracies, this action needs to be legitimate and legitimated through the consent of the peoples of the EU' (Kröger 2007: 567).

Analyses of how this requirement is realised invariably conclude that the social OMC falls short of democratic norms, including those professed in the OMC discourse (Bellamy and Castiglione 2011; Borrás and Greve 2004: 333–4; Borrás and Jacobsson 2004: 199–200; Borrás and Conzelmann 2007: 542; Büchs 2008: 775–8; Dawson 2009; Føllesdal 2011: 94–5; Kröger 2007: 572–3, 578; Pfister 2009; de la Porte and Nanz 2004; de la Porte and Pochet 2005: 376; Radulova 2007; Smismans 2006: 18–19; Usui 2007; cf. Radaelli 2003: 49–50). Most of the problems are inbuilt in the OMC's discursive mechanisms. Output legitimacy is difficult to evaluate, because concrete outcomes are 'indistinguishable' (Borrás and Greve 2004: 334) and unambiguous causalities are impossible to establish.

Input legitimacy is insufficient because there is too little input and too few input channels. Public debate about the OMC is virtually non-existent, also due to its intransparent and 'clandestine character' (Kröger 2007: 578), and parliamentary debate is up to the single Member States, where the legislative's impact is generally very weak (Raunio 2007: 167–72). Despite DG Employment's emphasis on 'participation', the circle of associations involved in OMC processes is in practice limited to EU-level umbrella organisations. Moreover, there is a lack of openness and participation is highly selective. The OMC discourse is rationalistic, recasting redistributive matters 'as essentially technical or organisational matters to be decided on the basis of scientific and technical expertise' (Kröger 2009). In this way, political choices seem uncontroversial and without alternative. Views that do not agree with the hegemonic interpretation are left outside the governance forums and find it difficult to make their voices heard (Kröger 2009; Kröger and Conzelmann 2007: 545–6; Pfister 2009; Dawson 2009; cf. Usui 2007). In short, the general orientation of social policies evolves in relatively closed governance networks and not in public deliberation. Finally, accountability is elusive, since there are no clear relations of responsibility. National policies are still decided by answerable actors, but the rationales underlying them are developed in transnational and largely informal discourses among executive bureaucracies and experts.[41]

What is striking about this analysis is that the problems of democratic legitimacy in the OMC are inherent in the ways the method works, and is meant to work. It is difficult to conceive how a coordinative process of sensitive national policies could be organised in an open and accountable way at the European level. In other words, it is a puzzle whether and how NMGs like this can be democratic in any stronger sense at all.

In this study, I look at how DG Employment's discourse relates to this puzzle, i.e. how they present and justify the legitimacy of their activities. I analyse the ways in which they use functional representation argumentatively to legitimise their policies, in order to show what concepts of representation and democracy the DG proposes for the specific environment of the social OMC.

Any actor seeking to influence others has to legitimise her activities. The basis of legitimacy depends on the agent, her activities, and her relationships with other agents. In public policy, there are in many cases well-established traditions concerning what makes a given activity by a given actor legitimate. In Europe, most of these traditions are based on some concept of democracy. The social OMC is a case where it is not so obvious what legitimacy the Commission has to influence national policies and how democracy could be realised in the instance of an agent whose impact on the outcomes works mainly through informal mechanisms. This lack of an established model of strong legitimacy makes it all the more necessary for the DG to actively legitimise its role and activities in the OMC. Accordingly, the discourse promoted by the DG is not only about policy substance, but also about what is legitimate policy making (cf. Borrás and Conzelmann 2007: 546).

---

41. Regarding the accountability problems of discursive modes of policy making, *see* Usui 2007.

Generally, and not only in the social OMC, the Commission seeks to legitimise its activities in a parallel fashion in three main ways: (1) Through a persuasive 'manager discourse', which defines common challenges facing the Union as a whole and shows how European solutions need to be developed in order to cope with them. In this discourse, the Commission presents itself as the manager of the European project that has supreme knowledge, threats are described as facts, and the presented solutions are without alternative (Palola 2006: 379–80). (2) Through identity building. The Commission seeks to strengthen citizens' European identity, the idea being that feeling increasingly European entails identifying with the EU as a political actor, and thus also perceiving the Commission as one's legitimate representative. This is also based on the treaties mandating the Commission to represent the European interest, which gives it some room to interpret what this interest is (Bellamy and Castiglione 2011: 109–10). (3) By involving functional representatives. Political initiatives are legitimised by referring to consultations with and support of the *affected*, i.e. the Commission is not imposing 'the will of Brussels', but proposing policy that is based on the will of the people concerned. This is especially important in sensitive policy areas such as social policy, where the Commission's mandate is weak, and where the people as a whole are not represented directly at the European level, because the EP is not involved. The present study concentrates on this latter strategy of legitimisation.

The Commission's relationships with functional representatives and their strategic reasons to cooperate with them are well researched.[42] Firstly, involving functional associations provides policy preparation with valuable information both about technical aspects and about the interests of the concerned groups. Policies that take these into account are easier to implement and more likely to lead to the desired outcomes. Secondly, it creates 'local' legitimacy issue by issue, as opposed to the 'global' legitimacy created, for example, through electoral representation. This specific legitimacy becomes more important as the complexity of policy issues no longer matches the organisation of territorial constituencies, and in postmodern societies people no longer subscribe to stable political identities and groups (Warren 2009: 6–8). Moreover, in the EU, the Commission's proposals always have to be legitimised issue by issue *vis-à-vis* the Member States. This means, thirdly, that the information and legitimacy that functional representation can provide or generate also have a strategic dimension. Involving third parties is also about building coalitions to advance particular policies and influence other actors, most notably the Member States. The Commission thus has an interest not only in involving functional representatives but also in promoting the notion that such involvement constitutes good and legitimate policy making. In European normative standards, 'good and legitimate policy making' means it has to be democratic in some way. In other words, upholding the proposition that functional representation increases one's legitimacy as a political agent, or the legitimacy of one's actions, means simultaneously upholding a particular concept

---

42. For an overview, *see* Greenwood 2003.

of democracy that supports this proposition. It means choosing and interpreting particular norms and values for a particular context. As was shown in the previous chapter, the link between functional representation and democratic legitimacy is not straightforward or unconditional. It is the specific concept of democracy put forward by the Commission in the social OMC that this study is exploring.

The social OMC is a stimulating case for this undertaking, and not only because of the uncertainty of how democratic norms should be realised, the lack of legitimacy through territorial representation, and the extensive involvement of functional representatives on the European level. On top of this, there are two specific features that stand out in DG Employment's cooperation with functional representatives in the social OMC: the 'special relationships' between the DG and some European networks (*see* Chapter Eight), and the role of the poor as a functional constituency (*see* Chapter Nine).

Many forms of involving functional associations in the social OMC are open to all interested actors, such as consultations and various conferences. However, the core funding provided to some European-level networks (so-called 'Key Networks') via the Progress programme[43] gives these organisations a special position. Most of the associations that have received this funding are European umbrella organisations of national (umbrella organisations of) social NGOs, but they also include associations of public actors, such as Eurocities. These Key Networks have especially close contacts with and privileged access to DG Employment. Their funding through policy programmes and projects was initially based on Declaration 23 in the Maastricht Treaty, which stresses

> the importance, in pursuing the objectives of Article 117 of the Treaty establishing the European Community [*see* above], of cooperation between the latter and charitable associations and foundations as institutions responsible for social welfare establishments and services. (Treaty on European Union, 'Declaration on cooperation with charitable associations')

Despite this treaty basis, funding in the 1990s was incoherent and lacked an overall strategy. Moreover, in 1998 the European Court of Justice (ECJ) found that the Commission had been wrongfully funding social NGOs without a legal basis since 1996.[44] The case showed that the supported associations were dependent on the EU funds to the point that their existence was threatened when the Commission was not allowed to pay them. The following protest campaign by the NGOs

---

43. In 2011 it was up to 83 per cent of their running costs, and previously up to 90 per cent.

44. This situation followed the reluctance of the Council (particularly Germany and Denmark) to approve a fourth Poverty Programme in 1994. The Commission (and the EP) then continued funding the beneficiaries of the previous programmes on the basis of their discretionary budgetary powers. The British Conservative government, supported by Germany, Denmark, and the Council, took legal action against this, and the practice was ruled illegal by the ECJ (Geyer 2001: 483–4; European Court of Justice: Case C-106/96, Judgment of the Court of 12 May 1998).

Table 5.1: Organisations working in the social policy sector which have received support for their running costs through OMC funding programmes managed by DG Employment during 2002–13

ASB Schuldnerberatungen	2007
Caritas Europe	2005–13
Confederation of Family Organisations in the European Union (COFACE)	2008–13
Council of Europe	2007
Dynamo International	2011–13
Eurochild (until 2003: European Forum for Child Welfare (EFCW))	2002–13
Eurocities	2008–13
Eurodiaconia	2008–13
EuroHealthNet	2011–13
European Anti-Poverty Network (EAPN)	2002–13
European Confederation of Workers' Cooperatives, Social Cooperatives and Social and Participative Enterprises (CECOP)	2008–10
European Federation of National Organisations Working with the Homeless (FEANTSA)	2002–13
European Foundation for Street Children	2008–10
European Microfinance Network	2007–13
European Network of Social Integration Enterprises	2011–13
European Public Social Platform (EPSP)	2002–05
European Social Network	2006–13
Mental Health Europe	2007–13
Transnational European Network on Social Inclusion (RETIS)	2002–07

Source: Author's compilation

concerned – and the Commission (Bauer 2002: 392–3; Greenwood 2003: 184)[45] – not only successfully pressured the Council to continue their financial support, but also worked as a catalyst for their cooperation and mobilisation at EU level (Geyer 2001: 484). Eventually, it was the OMC's financial programmes (the Social Exclusion Programme, and Progress) that stabilised and regularised funding for functional network organisations in the social sector, from 2002 onwards. Table 5.1 lists the organisations that were provided with financial support for their running costs during the period 2002–13 in programme cycles of one to three years.

The formation of several of these organisations was initially sparked off by DG Employment at times when EU competences in the field were still very

---

45. In addition to the Commission, the EP also supported the case of the NGOs.

small. Contrary to the general trend in many sectors of interest representation, in social policy there is thus no evidence of functional groups going to Brussels in reaction to growing EU powers and with the goal of influencing EU policies (Cram 1997: 123–39; Greenwood 2003: 209–29, 259–64). For example, EAPN and FEANTSA, two of the most prominent anti-poverty NGOs on the European level, were both created with support from the DG. EAPN, the main functional association in the social OMC, arose from the networking activities within the Poverty Programmes, and its founding in 1990 was actively encouraged and supported by DG Employment as well as the Commission at the top level (cf. Farrell 2008: 128).[46] Although it is a network of national networks of social NGOs, it was not built from below, but from above. National networks did not exist when EAPN was set up, and constituting them was in many cases difficult because of different national traditions and structures, or a lack of interest in action at the European level (Cram 1997: 126, 127, 131, 135; Johansson 2012: 81). FEANTSA, in turn, originates in a Commission-funded conference on homelessness and housing provision in 1989. Offered initial funding from the DG, the assembled organisations founded a European network, which has since run the European Observatory on Homelessness, providing the DG with information on homelessness in Europe (Cram 1997: 129; Greenwood 2003: 216, 260). For both organisations, EU funds have been the decisive resource, enabling them to come into being and subsist.

Through this 'midwife' activity, for which DG Employment has a 'particular record' (Greenwood 2007b: 344), it makes strategic use of the legitimising role that functional representation plays. By supporting European functional organisations advocating similar political goals as those the DG would like to pursue on the EU level, the DG nurtures political allies, since both the Commission and Brussels-based advocacy associations have an institutional interest in promoting a stronger European dimension in social policies. The DG thus capitalises on these groups' 'legitimacy capital' to indirectly influence Member State governments. Michael W. Bauer has termed this cushion-shot strategy 'lobby sponsorship' (Bauer 2002: 388–9). The difference from other instances of cooperation between public actors and functional representatives is that here constituencies for *particular* policy projects are *created* rather than mobilised (Bauer 2002: 388-9). The DG and its chosen collaborators form a tight network (cf. Geyer 2001: 479, 491n2) that shares a common discourse about European social exclusion. Via the federated structure of the supported networks, policy concepts are transported into the Member States, bypassing the governmental level (Palola 2007: 43), while in the opposite direction this structure at the same time serves as important information channels for the DG. EU funding is too little to have any substantial impact on poverty itself; its purpose is rather to induce continual public advocacy for the social exclusion issue on the EU level. Bauer quotes a Commission official saying that EAPN's task was to 'put pressure on the system' to keep the fight against social exclusion on the

---

46. Fintan Farrell is the Director of EAPN Europe. Cf. Johansson 2012: 78–9.

public agenda (Bauer 2002: 389). To do this, functional associations are a supreme 'public relations platform' (p. 389) thanks to their specific moral authority based on their not-for-profit character and their reliance on dedicated, often voluntary work (cf. Goodin 2003b; cf. Heinelt and Meinke-Brandmeier 2006: 212).

In addition to keeping issues on the agenda and lobbying decision makers, functional associations also help the DG to frame discourses. In the calls for proposals on the basis of which organisations apply for funding, and through the networking activities in which they are subsequently involved (conferences, consultations, meetings, peer reviews, reports, informal contacts, etc.), the DG frames things in a certain way. Participating in this network (and thus becoming financially dependent) entails working in this paradigm (cf. Kohler-Koch 1999: 28–9), so that ultimately the funded organisations' public discourses promote the DG's framework. They thus form an 'axis' campaigning for similar policy orientations. Importantly, by supporting *European*-level networks of NGOs, parts of the NGO sector's energies are redirected to campaign for these policy orientations specifically on a European level. Since the *raison d'être* of social advocacy NGOs is to promote policies to reduce poverty, and the *raison d'être* of their Brussels-based associations is influencing EU institutions, the latter almost inherently call for stronger EU efforts to tackle poverty. In other words, funding European functional networks creates 'demand constituencies' for further integration in the area of social policies (Greenwood 2003: 214, 261). It also ensures that the functional sector has the resources to engage in efficient lobbying, and enables the DG to choose what kinds of organisation it wishes to see having these resources. Justin Greenwood and Michael W. Bauer describe how at strategic moments the DG and European NGO networks coordinate their campaigns *vis-à-vis* the Council (Greenwood 2003: 263–4, 215; Bauer 2002: 390). If they manage to capture the definition of issues and to embed them in an 'irresistible discourse' (Greenwood 2003: 264) (such as 'the fight against social exclusion'), it can become very difficult for national governments to resist this combined persuasive power, especially if they had made some rhetorical statements about the importance of decreasing poverty earlier (cf. Schimmelfennig 2001; Radaelli and Schmidt 2004: 368–9). The establishment of the social OMC is one case of the success of this strategy (*see* Chapter Eight). In brief, when analysing the DG's legitimising discourse drawing on the role of functional representation in the OMC, it is important to keep in mind that not only is this discourse also guided by institutional self-interest (cf. Smismans 2003), but what is more, the functional input into DG policies is not entirely independent. It will therefore be interesting to see how the DG's text deals with this dilemma between funding and legitimacy through representation.

The second special feature of functional representation in the social OMC is the fact that the primary functional constituency of these policies is poor citizens, and that their descriptive representation is explicitly part of the OMC's common objectives concerning social inclusion. Descriptive representation is here not justified with the general under-representation of certain groups, but functionally, with the affectedness of the poor by the policies in question. In the common objectives, they are subsumed under 'all relevant actors', who should be involved in policy making. However, these goals concern mainly the national policies. The DG regularly stresses the importance of involving people experiencing poverty in social policy making – for example, in their guidance notes for the National Reports – and also funds national projects to further this through the Progress programme. Evidence about the actual participation of descriptive representatives of the poor in national policies is mixed, owing to different national traditions (*see* de la Porte and Pochet 2005: 376–81). On the European level, the main events in this respect are the annual European Meetings of People Experiencing Poverty in Brussels. These meetings are co-organised by the rotating Council Presidency, DG Employment, and EAPN, and funded through the Progress programme. They assemble people experiencing poverty, recruited through and prepared by the national EAPN networks, and policy makers, such as Commission and Ministry officials, the Commissioner, and MEPs. In contrast to usual conferences, the people experiencing poverty are here 'delegates' and decision makers are 'guests', and the emphasis is on their interaction in facilitated workshops. Delegates from these Meetings also attend the major European social policy conference of politicians, civil servants, and functional representatives – the annual Round Table on Poverty and Social Exclusion, which is also organised by the Presidency while being funded and organisationally supported by the Commission. Involving descriptive representatives of the poor on the European level is a remarkable venture, considering their lack of social and financial resources, low organisation, and widespread estrangement from the political elites and their language, not to mention European Union politics. At the same time, this also entails a radical potential with respect to policy substance, which should not be underestimated and which contrasts with the general primacy of economics in social policies. Whether and how this potential is realised in practice, and what roles and meanings are given to this special mode of representation are among the questions this study seeks to answer (*see* especially Chapter Nine).

Hence, there are a number of features that make the social OMC a challenging and fascinating case to study functional representation. As a new mode of governance, it is as yet unclear whether democratic legitimacy can be realised in this setting at all, and what it might look like. Its discursive policy-making style sits uneasily with conventional means of democratic control, because NMGs follow a different logic than that of authorisation-cum-accountability. Not least, the Commission has offered functional representation as a solution to this dilemma, and in the OMC's social inclusion strand relies strongly on legitimacy based on this. The EP being weak, functional representation is here the only form of popular representation at EU level. Yet, it is not obvious that and how functional representation can provide democratic legitimacy. Additional interest and challenge comes from the symbiotic relationships between DG Employment and some European networks of functional representatives and from the role of the poor as a descriptive functional constituency.

Analysing political discourse as argumentation

Since the Commission's means of policy making as well as of legitimising their activities within the social OMC are essentially discursive, the present analysis of DG Employment's use of functional representation in this setting puts the focus on their argumentative use of language. The study is based on an inclusive corpus of Commission texts from 2000 to 2010 mentioning functional representation (in any form) in relation to the social OMC, including official documents, speeches, Internet pages, press releases, and printed publications, and adding up to 544 single pieces of text (*see* the Annex for a breakdown of the sources). In addition, I conducted six semi-structured interviews at DG Employment between November 2009 and February 2010 with officials working within the social OMC. All interviews were conducted in English. They comprise all but one of the Policy Officers who at the time personally dealt with functional representatives in the frame of the social inclusion stream of the OMC. Together with two interviews with EAPN officers from January 2009 and October 2010, respectively, these are used to complement the analysis.

The rhetorical analysis of this material starts from the notion that referring to the DG's specific ways of involving functional representatives is making representative claims about the latter, i.e. *arguing* that they represent a relevant constituency and that they therefore add to the legitimacy of the policy in question. In this way, DG Employment proposes a model of how governance in the OMC should be organised. These arguments and their justifications are examined in detail in order to analyse the underlying concept of democracy promoted by the Commission.

Arguing essentially means reason-giving for a proposition. Since the 1990s, social sciences have often dichotomised arguing and bargaining, often associating the former with communicative action à la Habermas and the latter with rational-choice-style strategic action (Holzinger 2004: 196). By concentrating on arguing, I do not wish to imply that bargaining does not take place in the social OMC, but rather that, notwithstanding whatever bargaining there may be (and presumably is), arguing plays an important role. I agree with Katharina Holzinger that '[a]lthough arguing and bargaining are analytically distinct forms of verbal conflict resolution, this does not mean that they are alternatives or semantic opposites. They are not substitutes for each other; rather, they complement each other' (2004: 198). Even when an actor's position is based on her interests (as assumed for bargaining), powerful social norms require her to *justify* her position as soon as it conflicts with that of another actor, and this justification cannot be 'because I want to', but has to draw on generally accepted norms or values – in other words, she has to argue in order to legitimise her position (p. 198; cf. Radaelli and Schmidt 2004: 374; Skinner 2002: Ch. 8; Elster 1998: 101; Schimmelfennig 2001: 62–3). Moreover, political communication tends to be complex, and is mostly about interests, values, norms, and facts at the same time, so that both bargaining and arguing occurs in the same discourse (Holzinger 2004: 199–200). Arguing can also precede bargaining, because participants first have to determine the rules of the game and the paradigm within which to deal with issues, such as the facts and values that are accepted as relevant (Radaelli and Schmidt 2004: 374). Put differently, framing issues is an argumentative activity. In short, arguing is a significant part of political communication.

Following Vivian A. Schmidt and Claudio M. Radaelli (Schmidt and Radaelli 2002: 7, 14–15; 2004: 184, 193, 197; Radaelli and Schmidt 2004: 364–5; Schmidt 2008: 305, 309–10; cf. also Schmidt 2006), I take *political discourse* as comprising an ideational and an interactive dimension. In other words, it is both content (ideas) and an interactive process, in which these ideas are generated, conveyed, shaped, and legitimated. This interactional dimension of discourse is a resource for policy makers to legitimise choices and influence political processes, while the ideational dimension means a cognitive and normative structure containing concepts that make sense of reality, such as information about the political environment and judgements based on norms and values. Taking both together, discourse can be defined as 'a specific ensemble of ideas, concepts, and categorizations that are produced, reproduced, and transformed in a particular set of practices and through which meaning is given to physical and social realities' (Hajer 1995: 44).

The reason for Schmidt and Radaelli calling their approach 'discursive institutionalism' is their insistence on dealing with discourses in their institutional context (Schmidt and Radaelli 2002: 6, 8–10; 2004: 193, 197; Schmidt 2008), i.e. the rules they are framed by in different political settings. As well as that, discourse has to be considered in terms of other factors influencing policy development, such as existing policy problems, policy legacies and their fit with particular solutions, actors' preferences, and institutional capacities to act (Schmidt and Radaelli 2004: 186–9). Furthermore, one has to take account of the position of the actor speaking, her ideas and interests, and the function of what she says (Fouilleux 2004: 236).

> Discourse is not just ideas or 'text' (what is said) but also context (where, when, how, and why it was said). The term refers not only to structure (what is said, or where and how) but also to agency (who said what to whom). (Schmidt 2008: 305)

Discourse is one factor among others influencing political change, and is itself influenced by other factors. Heeding its relevant contexts of institutions, culture, interests, and economic conditions prevents one from taking discourse for the whole reality, and, for example, improves the awareness of cases where discourse in fact conceals substance instead of reflecting it (Schmidt and Radaelli 2004: 193).

The other way around, institutions are themselves 'embedded in normative orders or structures of meaning' (Jachtenfuchs *et al.* 1998: 411; emphasis omitted) – including beliefs on legitimacy (Radaelli 2000: 9) – manifested in discourse. Discourses condition the environment of political actors in many ways; they give meaning to events, develop political identities, frame discussions and interests, determine choices among several possibilities, and transform ideas and values (Schmidt and Radaelli 2004: 202–3; cf. 2002: 15–19). The most important dimension for my purpose is the capacity of discourse to provide or deny *legitimacy* to actors and their activities. Institutional interest is therefore a powerful incentive for political actors to aim at shaping the concepts of legitimacy affecting their environment (cf. Smismans 2003).

Quentin Skinner has developed a useful apparatus to analyse such activities on the basis of J. L. Austin's speech act theory. Austin's central thesis is that by uttering something, we not only describe reality, but there are 'some cases and senses (only some, Heaven help us!) in which to *say* something is to *do* something; or in which *by* saying or *in* saying something we are doing something' (Austin 1975: 12; emphasis in original).[47] He calls such acts 'illocutionary acts' (1975: 98–9). Skinner uses the following example to illustrate this idea. A policeman sees a skater on a pond and says to him 'The ice over there is very thin'. The policeman not only describes a state of affairs, but in addition performs the illocutionary act of warning the skater (Skinner 2002: 104–5). Skinner builds on this insight to analyse political discourse by maintaining that utterances in a political context (widely understood) 'can never be viewed simply as strings of propositions; they must always be viewed at the same time as *arguments*' (2002: 115; emphasis added). Political actors not only or primarily aim at giving an accurate description of reality, but at the same time argue that we should see reality in this way. Arguing, again, means defending or criticising some point of view against that presented by someone else in discussion, i.e. it is an act of communication that has to be understood in its context. Skinner emphasises that the relevant context for an argument need not necessarily be its immediate environment, such as what the previous speaker just said. Rather, the appropriate context for understanding the point of an utterance is whatever context enables us to understand the illocutionary act performed by it (2002: 116).

Now, what does it mean in practice to understand the Commission's utterances about functional representation in the OMC as (implicit or explicit) arguments? I work on the central premise that by referring to its relations with functional representatives, the Commission seeks to *legitimise* its own position and activities within the OMC; it thus *argues* that its proposals are legitimate and should be taken into account because functional representatives have been involved in developing them, and that the Commission itself is a legitimate actor with a certain authority because it involves functional representatives.[48] This implies making representative claims about the involved functional representatives and the Commission itself. On a more general plane, the Commission argues that things should be seen (framed) in the way they present them. These arguments are addressed to three main audiences: the general public, national political actors, and the OMC governance network with its national representatives – MEPs, NGOs, the

---

47. Cf. Wittgenstein's famous statement, 'words are also deeds' (Wittgenstein 2001: 124, para. 546).

48. For the role of arguing for legitimising social behaviour, *see* Skinner 2002. Cf. also Schimmelfennig 2001: 62.

Commission's contractors, etc.[49] Now, the argument that functional representation enhances democratic legitimacy is as such widely held, but on a closer look the exact mechanism is not obvious or automatic. Functional representation can be conceptualised and organised in many different ways, leading to different kinds of legitimacy, or little democratic legitimacy at all. The fundamental question, then, is what *kind* of legitimacy the Commission claims, and how precisely this is supposed to be generated; in other words, what types of representative claims they make and what these are based on. For this, the structure of the (implicit) arguments put forward has to be analysed in detail in order to elaborate what the (perhaps unstated) premises are, and with the help of what kinds of concepts the propositions are developed from them.

Legitimising behaviour or an institution is an inherently *rhetorical* task that mainly consists of convincing the audience that the behaviour in question matches relevant social norms or principles. Agents seeking to legitimise what they do thus have to refer to *existing* norms, notions, and terms. Hence, when analysing representation as the making of claims presented to an audience (*see* Chapter Two), these 'representative claims need to be built out of "ready-mades", even if they are re-interpreted and re-presented in new ways; ready-made tropes like "I am one of you" [...] tap into existing understandings' of what is legitimate representation in a given context (Saward 2006: 311; cf. Ruzza 2002: 99). Showing that one's activities conform to a number of important social norms or principles thus means arguing, and involves, on the one hand, interpreting the activity in question so as to appear compatible with the norms referred to, and on the other hand, interpreting those norms in such a way that they accommodate the activities they are applied to. The general structure of arguments consists of the following elements: a *proposition* or claim (the statement which is sought to be legitimised) and one or several *premises* justifying this proposition (cf. Aristotle 1991: 75–7 (1356b–1357a), 195 (1395b–1396a)). These premises draw on facts, values, norms, principles, or widely held assumptions (topoi), which the argument relates to the proposition (cf. 1991: 79 (1358a), 195–7 (1395b–1396b); Perelman and Olbrechts-Tyteca 1969: 65–85; Perelman 1982: 21).

In our case, the Commission argues that their activities within the social OMC are legitimate (proposition), and one central justification they put forward for this is their involvement of functional representatives (premise). It is easy to see that there are certain reasons for them to choose this kind of justification rather than, for example, referring to some intrinsic superior knowledge held by them. Importantly, making such an argument involves drawing upon such concepts of legitimacy that link functional representation to legitimate behaviour. In other words, one can only argue that involving functional representatives generates legitimacy if this

---

49. Schmidt and Radaelli assign the Commission's discourse more generally with three main functions: reassure the public about the impartiality and transparency of the policy process, appeal to national publics and thereby exert pressure on national leaders, and, mainly, coordinate the governance networks involved in policy construction at the EU level (Schmidt and Radaelli 2004: 199).

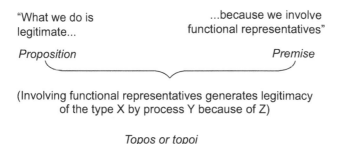

Figure 5.1: Concepts of democracy underlying the Commission's argumentation

is based on a norm which says that and how functional representation relates to legitimacy (topos). This is what I call the *underlying concepts of democracy* in the Commission's text – underlying because they are not spelt out explicitly, but they necessarily inform the surface argumentation by making it plausible to present such arguments by giving meaning to them, and by making them accessible to the audience. Put differently, if there were no topos available that in some way links functional representation to legitimacy, it would make no sense for the Commission to draw on functional representation.

But when the Commission says or implies that what they do is democratic, can we take this at face value? Is it not more realistic to assume that they are principally motivated by their interest to extend the scope of their influence, and that justifications drawing on democratic legitimacy are mere ex post rationalisations? It is important to note at this point that this study is not about whether the Commission actually 'means' what they say, but works on the assumption that irrespective of what they 'actually believe', what they say *matters*, because it is part of a discourse that influences and is influenced by political institutions and practices, power relations, different actors' interests, etc., and therefore has consequences for the extratextual world. I thus do not enquire about whether DG Employment's text is *true*, but treat it as argumentation seeking to convince others of DG Employment's truth or vision of the world. I take discourse as part of a dynamic process of constructing an intersubjective reality by building a convincing picture or narrative from various elements. In political communication, it can occur that the truth of facts is contested, but more often what is at issue is the (re)interpretation of facts, i.e. the meaning they are assigned (Radaelli and Schmidt 2004: 366). Studying the concepts of democracy underlying such discourse is thus to enquire into the *meaning* certain practices are *given*, and by the same token into the meaning 'democracy' itself is given in this context.

Disregarding the question of whether 'they really mean what they say' does not amount to maintaining that discourse would float free from reality. On the contrary, extratextual reality is not only influenced by the Commission's discourse, but it also influences this discourse, and through this, the Commission's actions.

The latter is mainly due to social norms that cannot be ignored if one wishes to successfully participate in policy making in the future too. This concerns firstly the arguments available for justifying political action. The range of reasons that it makes sense to use to vindicate proposals or actions depends on what reasons the audience is likely to accept. Therefore, not only do the terms and norms available to legitimise behaviour exist independently of the agent, but their application cannot plausibly be stretched indefinitely either, because not all interpretations will be accepted. For example, 'participation' is a concept that in Europe is widely accepted as a legitimate justification for political choices, while 'divine revelation' is not, and is therefore less likely to be used in argumentation by the Commission, irrespective of whether or not they perceive their policies to stem from it. Furthermore, arguments drawing on 'participation' cannot be applied to just any practice, but only have a chance to be acceded to if they are supported by reference to some non-Commission actors who have some relationship to the citizens and who took part in the process in question. If the Commissioner went to the mountain and returned with inspiration for a policy proposal, this would be much more difficult to legitimise with 'participation' arguments than if she met with a range of functional or territorial representatives. In view of these restrictions, she is therefore more likely to involve representatives, even if she preferred waiting for revelation. Hence, the range of activities that can be legitimised is restricted by the prevailing norms of a society, which are manifested in the language available to justify things (Skinner 2002: 156).

The second way in which extratextual reality influences discourse is the possibility of rhetorical entrapment (Schimmelfennig 2001). As shown above, political choices need to be legitimised by drawing on the relevant community's norms and values. Once an actor has justified her position with such arguments, the courses of action open to her will in part be determined by the notions she has used to legitimise her activities. This is because if she acted in ways contradicting the norms she had professed, or if she professed conflicting norms on different occasions, she would risk being exposed by other actors as inconsistent and cynical with respect to shared values (Schimmelfennig 2001: 64–5; Skinner 2002: 155; Elster 1998: 104). Such a loss of reputation and credibility can have serious consequences for her authority, especially where this is only weakly backed up by formal institutions. Political actors will thus be committed to act in ways compatible with their arguments, regardless of whether they sincerely believe in these arguments. However, this mechanism is restricted by intransparency and ambiguities concerning norms as well as particular activities' interpretation. The less visible activities are, the less interested different actors are in overseeing each other, the less media exposure there is, the less clearly actual activities can be classified as either fulfilling particular norms or not, and the less commitment will result from using normative arguments. Yet, shaming is a serious way of taking political influence. For example, Bauer quotes a German civil servant expressing his frustration about the negotiation situation when his federal government opposed the adoption of a fourth Poverty Programme: '[T]he situation became very tough for us [...] in Brussels. Everybody pointed the finger at us, complaining, "they're the ones who don't want to fight poverty"" (Bauer 2002: 390). Hence, social norms and rhetorical strategies drawing on them *influence* behaviour irrespective of whether agents really believe in the values they profess.[50]

Conversely, the Commission's discourse also impacts on reality by influencing the ways legitimate governance is conceptualised and organised in the EU in general and in the social OMC in particular. Arguing that functional representation adds to the democratic legitimacy of the Commission as an actor or of their specific activities means at the same time promoting the view that this interpretation of democratic norms is valid in general: functional representation makes institutions and their policies legitimate, and *therefore* the Commission's initiatives are legitimate, because they involve functional representatives. In other words, by using normative arguments, one also advances the norms drawn on and one's particular interpretation of them. Since norms are (re)shaped and evolve in discourse, such argumentation can influence their constant development. This is especially relevant in the social OMC, considering that it is still a puzzle how new modes of governance could be organised in properly democratic ways. As the Commission is a central actor in this type of European governance process, and among others controls which functional representatives are involved, and in which ways, the concepts they promote are significant for the evolving structures. Thus, the concepts of democracy advocated by the Commission are *relevant* irrespective of whether they represent 'genuinely' held convictions; they are not intrinsically important, but important because of their influence on the world outside themselves.

---

50. Leaving the question of political actors' true motives aside is a pragmatic solution for this study: whether or not the Commission believes in the values they profess is of little importance to the issue under investigation. However, I would not want to subscribe to the view that since actors' behaviour can be satisfyingly explained on the basis of their interests, norms and values play no causal role. Firstly, if all arguments drawing on generally accepted norms were mere ex post rationalisations, we would presumably know that they were, and they would therefore lose their persuasive force, so that it would not make sense to use them (Elster 1998: 104). Secondly, the theory of cognitive dissonance tells us that humans seek to maintain a coherent, positive self-image. It would thus be difficult to proclaim values known to be widely accepted and at the same time regard them as mere talk (cf. Skinner 2002: 147–8). Finally, I do not particularly like the view that political actors by definition, as it were, as part of their profession, never 'really' believe in any norms or values. Although for political scientists it is often easy – and justified – to show that interpretations of democratic legitimacy employed by practitioners do not fulfil the requirements of ambitious democratic theory, we cannot conclude from this that the use of such interpretations are just talk. It is perfectly possible that the same politicians 'really believe' that what they say and do is very democratic indeed. Whether this is the case we cannot know, and neither do we need to share their interpretation. Nevertheless, it is wrong to conclude from this that it is not important to study what kinds of norms and values political actors profess and promote.

Chapter Six

What Makes One a Stakeholder of the Commission?

When DG Employment speaks about involving representatives of functional groups in policy making in general terms, the ideal they depict is that of many different kinds of actors participating on all territorial levels and in all phases of the process: 'Business, workers and civil society must be involved at every stage – from formulation to implementation and delivery. And at every level: European, national, regional and local'.[1] Commission President Romano Prodi has called the ideal result of doing this a 'Network Europe' with 'all [territorial and functional] levels of governance shaping, proposing, implementing and monitoring policy together.'[2] Functional representation, as seen by DG Employment, can thus be characterised along three dimensions, namely the types of actors involved, the territorial level of their involvement, and the phase of the policy cycle they are involved in.

In this chapter, I deal with the horizontal axis of Figure 6.1, i.e. with the types of functional groups DG Employment involves or wants to involve in OMC policy making. I begin by looking at the criteria the DG uses to single out which groups or organisations are what they call their 'stakeholders'. Who and what exactly is meant by this? And what is it that constitutes stakeholding in the social OMC for the DG? Since out of the numerous actors categorised as 'stakeholders' in the DG's text by far the most prominent position is given to NGOs, I then examine their role as representatives in detail, analysing whom they are claimed to represent, and on what this claim is based.

When DG Employment speaks about involving representatives of functional groups in policy making, they use a wide range of terms to refer to many different kinds of agents, such as 'concerned actors', 'key actors', 'relevant actors', 'all who feel concerned', 'everyone working against social exclusion', 'interested groups', 'involved parties', 'partners', and 'key players'. By far the single most used expression is '*stakeholder*'. This term is used to refer to all specific agents that might be meant in a given context, such as social partners, civil society organisations, or city administrations. In general, any actor from outside the Commission services who participates in one way or another in a policy process administered by the DG is called a 'stakeholder'. This terminology of course does not originate in the Commission. The semantic widening that the term has

---

1. European Commission press release SPEECH/01/173 of 22 March 2001.
2. European Commission press release SPEECH/00/157 of 28 April 2000.

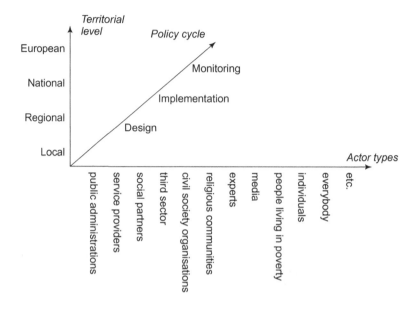

Figure 6.1: The three-dimensional space of functional representation in the social OMC

experienced over time has made the limits of its applicability fuzzy, such that there is no unambiguous definition that would make it possible to draw a clear line between who could be a stakeholder in a given situation and who could not. Originally, 'stake' designated '[t]hat which is placed at hazard; esp. a sum of money or other valuable commodity deposited or guaranteed, to be taken by the winner of a game, race, contest, etc.'.[3] Later, the notion was also used figuratively in the sense of 'to have something to gain or lose by the turn of events, to have an interest in'.[4] This widened concept was then taken up by business management theories to conceptualise the whole range of actors or institutions that are in some way directly or indirectly affected by the decisions of an enterprise. It is from here that the 'stakeholder' entered politics, in parallel to the rise of the 'governance' concept, with which it formed a perfect match. In the framework of mainstream governance discourses, 'involving stakeholders' is an essential virtue of policy-making processes. Because the semantic stretching of the term has included increasingly abstract senses of the 'stake', it is now essentially a matter of definition and perspective who is a stakeholder of what. Hence, the concept gives

---

3. *Oxford English Dictionary Online*, 'stake, n²', accessed 29 September 2010, http://www.oed.com/view/Entry/37160?redirectedFrom=commit#eid. Cf. 'stakeholder, n.', *ibid.* (draft revision September 2004), accessed 1 October 2010, http://www.oed.com/view/Entry/246856?redirectedFrom=stakeholder#eid.

4. *ibid.*

policy makers some degree of freedom to deal with those agents they prefer under the heading of 'stakeholders'. Accordingly, the 'stakeholders' of the social OMC can and do include groups whose stakeholding is based on different grounds. However, this does not mean the DG is completely free to define the term for itself, as there are limits of plausibility. 'Stakeholder' still has a core meaning that DG Employment also has to start from in order to be understood. I next take a look at what they make out of this, i.e. how they use 'stakeholders' and what interpretation they give to the term.

What makes one a stakeholder of the social OMC?

In order to figure out what it is that makes someone a 'stakeholder' of the social OMC for DG Employment, the term can be looked at from two different sides: the term itself, and the meaning it is given in use.

The choice of terminology tells something about the general approach to the issue. The concept originates in financial contexts and suggests that the agents involved in policy making are those organisations that have something to win or lose, depending on the decision taken. In other words, the implemented policy affects their own activities or wellbeing, which gives them an interest (a stake) in what that policy is going to be. The implication is that this stake *justifies* a claim to be represented in the policy-making process; i.e. 'good governance' means involving the more directly affected. Hence, the term that is used makes a difference in the sense that it frames practices in a specific way and establishes a particular rationale for involving functional agents. Publicly speaking about the DG's use of functional representation as 'involving stakeholders' thus means promoting such a normative concept of legitimate governance.

If the question of who gets involved in the social OMC were scrutinised and debated in public, the use of the term 'stakeholder' could also be utilised by the DG to justify why one agent is involved and not another (because of their stakes or otherwise), or by would-be participants to claim involvement by drawing on their having a stake. Such a debate could then lead to some clarification of what kinds of stakes entitle an agent to be involved in the social OMC's policy-making processes. Yet, this not being the case, the DG's application of the term 'stakeholder' is hardly challenged. It thus has considerable freedom to use the concept at its discretion. Therefore, in order to elaborate what it is that makes one a stakeholder in the social OMC, one needs to look at the *use* of the term, i.e. at the examples or lists given in the text of who is involved, or meant to be involved. Figure 6.2 compiles the functional constituencies mentioned in the DG's text and the rationales given or implied for involving each of these agents.

The characteristics that make agents stakeholders (agency, direct affectedness, expertise, potential impact) are not exclusive, i.e. an agent can be a stakeholder on the grounds of two or more different characteristics, and many of these are causally linked. For example, agency and direct affectedness both entail expertise, and most of those being active in the field have the potential to influence outcomes or other agents. The purpose of Figure 6.2 is therefore not to classify different

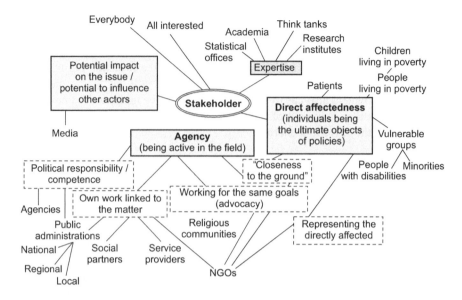

Figure 6.2: What makes one a stakeholder?

functional constituencies in unambiguous categories, but to work out which categories are used by DG Employment to define their stakeholders.

The chart shows first of all that those seen as 'stakeholders' of the social OMC by DG Employment are not limited to constituencies with a stake, in the sense that these agents' situation would be particularly linked to social policies. There are two groups of agents who are not stakeholders on the grounds of being directly affected by the policies in question: those with a potential to influence social policies, and experts.

The potential to exert an impact on social policies is of course in most cases connected to being active in social policy (agency); yet the DG has also made efforts to involve the media in the process and considers them as stakeholders, because they influence the public perception of poverty and can thus indirectly influence how the public as well as politicians conceptualise the problem and those affected by it (Interview no. 8).[5] In the same vein, expertise can be a consequence of agency or direct experience of poverty. However, among the experts named in the DG's text, there are many whose expertise does not derive from the practitioner's experience, such as think tanks, academia and research institutes, or statistical offices. Both these experts and the media play minor roles in the DG's text.

---

5.   For example, the DG has organised a conference, Poverty Between Reality and Perceptions: The Communication Challenge, directed at journalists (Brussels, 29 October 2009), and the 2010 European Year for Combating Poverty and Social Exclusion included a journalist award for reports about poverty in the EU.

A third peculiar group of stakeholders is 'everybody', meaning all citizens as individuals. This is mainly based on the idea that in order to considerably decrease poverty, one needs wide public support for this goal as well as for the measures taken, i.e. a 'shared understanding of and consensus on the EU's objectives' (European Commission 2008a). From this it follows that a major occupation of the DG is to 'raise awareness' among the public at large of the problem of poverty and of the European process dealing with the issue.[6] Yet, *awareness* is also the first step to make people realise 'the *responsibility* of everyone in society to tackle poverty',[7] and subsequently to become *mobilised* to make a contribution themselves, according to their possibilities and their specific functional position in society. For example, with respect to especially vulnerable groups: 'At home and at school we must teach children about diversity and difference. To foster respect and to raise awareness of disability issues from an early age'.[8] Altogether, the objective is 'public ownership', i.e. a wide-ranging commitment among the citizens to the common European social policy goals, and their engagement in processes furthering these goals.[9] Thus, 'everybody' is a *potential* stakeholder, who is supposed to be awakened to realise their 'stake'. Remarkably, the link between becoming aware and supporting is depicted as almost automatic. I come back to this automaticity in the following chapter.

On the other hand, 'in the broadest sense, we're all stakeholders. Now, obviously to different degrees' (Interview no. 4). Not only the direct beneficiaries of social policies, but '[l]astly, every EU citizen, as a taxpayer, a worker, a volunteer or whatever, also contributes to social policy in Europe'.[10] The same could of course be said about all policies; however, in social policy this general affectedness is perhaps more easily felt than in, say, fisheries or competition. Now, general affectedness on the grounds of living within a certain jurisdiction is the basis for territorial representation and thus follows a different logic than that underlying the concept of stakeholding. In the social OMC, representing the population at large belongs to the Member States, which are represented in the Social Protection Committee (SPC) and legally fully in charge of the social policies implemented on their territory. Accordingly, although the Commission occasionally refers to views held by the citizenry at large on the basis of Eurobarometer surveys,[11] this

---

6. E.g. European Commission press release SPEECH/10/30 of 18 February 2010.

7. European Commission (2008) 'Eradicating poverty: the 2010 European Year'. Online. Available http://ec.europa.eu/social/main.jsp?catId=437&langId=en&newsId=407&furtherNews=yes, accessed 14 September 2010. Emphasis added.

8. European Commission press release SPEECH/03/92 of 21 February 2003.

9. European Commission staff working document SEC(2007)1662 of 12 December 2007.

10. DG Employment document EMPL 123–2009. Online. Accessed 8 June 2009. No longer available.

11. E.g. European Commission press release IP/09/1585 of 27 October 2009, referring to the Special Eurobarometer 321 report about poverty and social exclusion, commissioned by DG Employment, according to which '[o]n average, 89% of Europeans say that urgent action is needed by their national government to tackle poverty. Across Europe, 53% feel that their national governments

argumentation is not a major part of their discourse. The notion that 'everybody' has a stake in the social OMC therefore mostly has to be understood in the sense that all citizens are *potential* stakeholders in the sense that anyone can get engaged in activities aimed at reducing poverty, for example in a civil society organisation. By contrast, the idea that we are all potential stakeholders because we might all depend on social redistributions one day does not appear in the DG's text.

In any case, the range of 'stakeholders' in the DG's text is clearly wider than the range of agents who are especially *affected* by social policies. Rather than affectedness in a stricter sense, the characteristic all of them share (from the DG's point of view) is *relevance*. This is maybe not surprising, considering that from its creation onwards, the mobilisation of 'all relevant bodies' and promoting 'dialogue and partnership between all relevant bodies, public and private'[12] have been among the objectives of the OMC. Within the OMC, it has been the DG that has most emphatically advanced the 'involvement of all relevant actors'.[13] But what does it mean to be relevant? Above all, relevance is defined with respect to the declared policy goals of the social OMC: the DG 'involves [...] the principal actors who can contribute to attaining the strategic objective of the Union'[14] (here referring to the Lisbon objectives). This is based on the notion that '[b]y working *together* we will achieve our aims'.[15] The roles of the various stakeholders then differ according to the specific *contribution* each of them is able to make. Relevant contributions are either essential information or the capacity to move social policies towards the desired goal, and this is why what makes one a stakeholder are the four above-mentioned characteristics, i.e. agency, direct affectedness, potential impact and expertise. Different stakeholders can contribute different things. For instance, Member States have the legal responsibility and can share their experience about the effects of different sorts of legislation. NGOs

---

are primarily responsible for combating poverty. Even if Europeans do not regard the European Union as primarily responsible for combating poverty, its role is nonetheless seen as important by many (28% see it as "very important", and 46% "somewhat important")'. Commissioner Špidla concluded that 'These results show that Europeans are strongly aware of the problems of poverty and social exclusion in today's society and want to see more action to tackle them [...] While most people see their national government as primarily responsible, three quarters also expect the EU to play an important role. Next year's European Year gives us the perfect opportunity to put the fight against poverty centre stage across the EU'. Cf. also European Commission press release IP/10/36 of 20 January 2010. Similar Eurobarometer surveys have been conducted regularly. They are funded through the Progress programme and are thus part of the social OMC.

12. Council of the European Union (Employment and Social Policy): 14110/00 of 30 November 2000.

13. European Commission (2008) 'The process: the open method of coordination'. Online. Available http://ec.europa.eu/employment_social/spsi/the_process_en.htm, accessed 21 November 2008.

14. DG Employment and Social Affairs (2002) *Annual Management Plan 2002*. Author translation.

15. European Commission (2003) Commissioner Diamantopoulou's address at the General Assembly of the National Confederation of Disabled People, Athens, 14 February 2003. Online. Available http://ec.europa.eu/employment_social/speeches/2003/ad140203_en.pdf, accessed 8 October 2008. Emphasis in the original.

provide information in the form of 'policy advice, research and analysis', as well as 'reports aimed at identifying good practice' (European Commission 2010a), which is meant to 'influence policy in the European Union and in the Member states [*sic*]' (European Commission 2010b). Service providers contribute their 'concrete experience' in the work that is regulated by social policies, so that policy makers better understand the phenomena they deal with.[16] Local administrations know about the implementation of policies and social services. 'In addition, local government is often best placed to relate directly to people experiencing social exclusion and to identify new ways of tackling problems'.[17] Finally, people living in poverty have unique knowledge about 'what [it] is like to be poor', which it is necessary for policy makers to understand in order to 'be able to develop policies, programmes and practices to combat poverty'.[18] Importantly, to be relevant for policy making, an actor needs not only resources that help in the attainment of political goals, but must also be able to provide those resources efficiently, i.e. have the capacity to manoeuvre professionally in the OMC and its logic and speak the language of its discourses (*see* the following two chapters).

The construction of problems and policy goals as common issues that 'we all' face together, for which reason it 'is [...] essential that we all join in a common project',[19] gives a particular twist to the 'stake' of those meant to participate in this common effort. It means that not only is success in reaching the common goal dependent on every relevant contribution, but also that all agents somehow related to the issues in question are dependent on each other, because they all face the same challenges and cannot overcome them alone. Within this narrative, any agent with some relation to social policies has a stake in them, i.e. something to win or to lose, because they all collectively face the same problems.

This output-orientated perspective illuminates the talk about 'key actors' and 'key players': depending on the issue, different groups are more or less important to achieve the defined policy goals, and some agents are essential ('key') to achieve anything at all. Accordingly, who is seen as a 'stakeholder' also depends on the individual policy issue. Generally, a 'stakeholder' can be any agent who 'can really be part of the solution to the problem' (Interview no. 5), anyone 'whose opinion

---

16. European Commission (2008) speech by Commissioner Špidla, 17 March 2008. Online. Available http://ec.europa.eu/employment_social/spsi/docs/social_situation/spidla_opening_fr.pdf, accessed 17 July 2008. Author translation.

17. European Commission (2006) background paper for workshop 2c at the conference Learning Together: Lessons Drawn from the Community Action Programme to Combat Social Exclusion, Brussels, 29–30 March 2006. Online. Available http://ec.europa.eu/socialBlobServlet?docId=361 &landed=en, accessed 19 December 2008.

18. Deputy Director-General Lenia Samuel, quoted in Austrian Presidency of the European Union 2006: 5th *European Meeting of People Experiencing Poverty – How do we cope with every day* [*sic*] *life?* conference report. Online. Available http://ec.europa.eu/employment_social/spsi/docs/ social_inclusion/2006/pep-report_en.pdf, accessed 25 September 2008.

19. European Commission press release SPEECH/08/223 of 5 May 2008. Cf. Palola 2006: 383–4; Palola 2007: 44.

or whose experience can help us to better define our policies and better define our actions and our programmes' (Interview no. 1). Policy output thus depends among other things on having 'all relevant actors'[20] on board.

To be relevant in this sense does not necessarily mean representing affected groups in society, although this is often the case. In most cases, holding important information or capacities in view of the policy goals directly *results* from being affected, and it is these resources, rather than affectedness *as such*, that are the primary rationale for involving these agents. 'Stakeholders' are therefore a wider group than functional constituencies in the stricter sense of affected groups. Having said this, most of the agents described as 'stakeholders' by DG Employment, including the most important ones, are organisations representing constituencies especially affected by OMC policies. This affectedness either results from their functional role (agency) or from their personal situation, which makes them addressees of these policies (direct affectedness). Most of the OMC 'stakeholders' are thus what I call 'functional constituencies'.

The dominance of the output perspective in determining who the 'stakeholders' of the social OMC are explains in part why the DG uses the term in such an all-embracing and imprecise way. Addressing 'all interested' aims at reaching all relevant among those eventually coming forward. Since the question of who is relevant also depends on the issue under consideration, it makes sense for the DG not to close the category of 'stakeholders' and with this the circle of potential participants. Using a too-definite definition might lead to leaving potentially important agents without consideration. On this note, 'stakeholders' also include those who have not yet realised their stake: 'I mean here they [the stakeholders] are not necessarily *active* within the social OMC, but they are concerned, they are aware of the – no, they should be aware, they should be active, and there is a legitimate role for them in the process' (Interview no. 8). The ideal governance process is thus one where all relevant groups have representatives who participate in policy making, and, what is more, where they have in fact a *right* to be represented on the basis of their affectedness (*see* Chapter Eleven).

Using the stretched and confused term 'stakeholder' makes it possible for DG Employment to be imprecise about the characteristics of the representatives they prefer to involve as well as about which concrete groups (constituencies) they would like to see represented in the social OMC. This particularly concerns the position of the civil society and that of the Member States. Concerning the latter, it is difficult to say on the surface level of the text whether they are part of the 'stakeholders' of the social OMC or whether their role is different. Although 'Member States' or 'governments' are often included as one among others in lists of 'stakeholders', they are also often mentioned separately as a special group of actors, such as 'Member States and other stakeholders'.[21]

---

20. E.g. European Commission Communication COM(2003)312 of 2 June 2003.

21. European Commission (2010) 'European Year for Active Ageing 2012: questions & answers'. Online. Available http://ec.europa.eu/social/BlobServlet?dicId=5702&langId=en, accessed 15 September 2010.

If the writers of different texts within the DG have no clear and common line about whether 'stakeholders' include the Member States or not, this is not necessarily because the DG does not have a clear or common idea of who their stakeholders are. On the contrary, it is because they share the conscious strategy of keeping the category open in order to have the opportunity for themselves to involve any actor that may turn out to be *important* for any (future) issue or situation they may deal with. As one interviewee put it, in response to the following question:

How would you define what makes one a stakeholder, or who your stakeholders are? How would you put the criteria?

I wouldn't, I would try to avoid that [...]. A vague, but common-sense understanding, rather than a kind of precise, legalistic [definition].

(Interview no. 4)

Similarly, the Commission's Civil Society website (for the Commission in its entirety) avoided fixing who exactly is meant, and stated the following under the heading 'Definition of civil society':

There is no commonly accepted or legal definition of the term 'civil society organisation'. [...] It should be noted that in its policy of consultation the Commission does not make a distinction between civil society organisations or other forms of interest groups. The Commission consults *'interested parties'*, which comprises all those who wish to participate in consultations run by the Commission.[22]

The Commission eludes strict categorisations of functional representatives that would openly or officially create different statuses for different actors and through this limit their freedom to manoeuvre. By consistently avoiding committing themselves to any formal obligations to consult specific agents (i.e. legal rights to be consulted or a formal accreditation system) (Geyer 2001: 488–90; Greenwood 2003: 272; Smismans 2007: 14), and by employing a governance buzzword to refer to those they involve, they make it difficult for others to tie them down to involving this organisation and not that. On this note, the decision of who to involve and in what way is not only a matter of reaching declared outcomes such as reducing poverty, but also has to be seen in the context of the Commission's institutional aims and its interaction with the Member States. I deal with this issue in the following chapters.

---

22. European Commission (no date) 'The European Commission and civil society: general over-view'. Online. Accessed 7 October 2010. No longer available.

Public administrations and social partners

Above, I have already briefly examined those 'stakeholders' named in the DG's text that do not, strictly speaking, have any special stakes in social policies, *viz.* experts, the media, and 'everybody'. In the second half of the present chapter I deal with the most prominent group of stakeholders – NGOs – in detail. Before that, I briefly take a look at two other groups of actors that stand out in DG Employment's lists: the first, public administrations, differ from all other participants in that they execute the policies in question rather than being affected by them; the second, social partners, are peculiar in the sense that their institutional position contrasts with the role they play in practice.

Public administrations – i.e. national, regional, and local authorities – are usually mentioned ahead of all other actors to be involved. A very frequent formulation is 'Member States and (other) stakeholders'. Apart from the confusion about whether or not Member States are stakeholders (*see* above), this also indicates their special role among all those involved in OMC governance: all others can influence policies, but Member States make policies. On this note, mentioning them first also has a diplomatic-hierarchical rationale. When the DG talks about involving functional representatives, it is often careful to state that this includes first of all the Member States, with the addition of others – thus indicating that the Commission, in its networking activities, respects the national competences and does not seek to go around them. At the same time, however, it uses a language of national *responsibilities* rather than 'competences'. This also points to the Member States' (normative) *obligation* to act in order to achieve particular political objectives. The DG uses this as an argument to promote putting certain issues on the agenda by drawing attention to particular problems and the Member States' 'responsibility' to tackle them. The involvement of non-governmental functional representatives, as well as the European dimension, is then presented as an added value to the governments' efforts:

> Much of the responsibility for addressing the challenge of Roma integration lies at the national, regional and local level. The actors of civil society, the Roma themselves, also have a capital role to play. But the EU has an important role to play in supporting and complementing these efforts.[23]

Member States are represented in the OMC by ministerial officers, and very rarely by government members (in high-profile events, and for decision making in the Council of Ministers or the European Council). Although the DG speaks of these national executives as 'stakeholders' of the OMC, they are not functional but territorial representatives, representing the residents of their territory. Seen from another angle, since the OMC is an intergovernmental process, it cannot be said

---

23. European Commission (2005) speech by Director (Horizontal and International Issues) Luisella Pavan-Woolfe, 23 November 2005. Online. Available http://ec.europa.eu/employment_social/speeches/2005/lp_231105_en.pdf, accessed 26 September 2008.

that the Member States are involved because of their special affectedness, but they are the very actors affecting others. The Commission for its part coordinates the Member States' cooperation, rather than involving them because they are affected by this coordination. By inserting Member States in the 'stakeholder' discourse, the DG obscures these hierarchical and power relations by subsuming national governments under the same category as NGOs and experts, albeit giving them a special position within this group. This talk diminishes the Member States' authority and increases that of other actors involved by the DG, and thus enhances the position of the DG itself. Although on the text surface it is often emphasised that social policy is a national competence, describing all involved parties as 'stakeholders' of these policies presents social issues as common issues that are tackled together. Member States are thus implicitly denied their door-guard position concerning who is an actor in their social policies.

The case is somewhat different with *subnational authorities*. These may or may not enact their own social policies, but they are in any case affected by the national policies, for example in the sense that these impact on their administrations' work and financial situation. Accordingly, representatives of subnational public authorities are depicted as representing their executive administrations rather than their residents. This is functional representation, based on their function of implementing social policies, and it is on these grounds that the DG advocates the involvement of regional and local authorities in European OMC processes. These administrations also have common organisations to represent them collectively at the EU level. For example, Eurocities, a network of big cities, actively lobbies in Brussels on many issues, and RETIS, a network of regional and local authorities, is focussed on social inclusion issues and operates specifically within the OMC. Both have received core funding from the Progress programme or its predecessor, the Social Exclusion Programme. Also, the Committee of the Regions has occasionally participated in OMC processes, but their ties to the OMC governance networks are rather loose, and they are not mentioned in the DG's text. The DG's direct networking with subnational units weakens the Member States' door-guard position (Palola 2007: 43, 60) and shows that the OMC governance networks are not necessarily nested territorially. However, the role of subnational administrations in the OMC remains in general rather weak, in spite of the DG's emphasis on them (Interview no. 8). This emphasis mainly indicates that DG Employment would like to see regions and municipalities play a bigger role in the social OMC. Yet, it is questionable how far these perceive the process as relevant for them, or are aware of it at all.

The *social partners* have long-established umbrella organisations at the EU level, the biggest ones being the European Trade Union Confederation (ETUC), Business Europe (formally UNICE, the Union of Industrial and Employers' Confederations of Europe) and the CEEP (European Centre of Enterprises with Public Participation and of Enterprises of General Economic Interest). Social dialogue at the EU is strongly institutionalised up to the point of rights to be consulted by the Commission and the possibility to negotiate binding agreements.[24] However, their involvement even in the employment OMC (EES) is 'patchy' (de la Porte and Pochet 2005: 365), and in the social OMC they are yet less present. Especially for ETUC, the liberalist orientation of the EU discourses has been unfavourable, and their member organisations have preferred to advance domestic interests seen from a national point of view. The European peak organisation therefore relies much more on the support of DG Employment (including funding) than on its constituents (Greenwood 2003: 266; de la Porte and Pochet 2005: 364–5). Curiously, when listing the organisations involved in the social OMC, the DG nearly always mentions the social partners, but they almost never expand on them by detailing the role they play or by giving concrete examples. Compared to the text about NGOs, the difference is striking; the latter are dealt with in detail, as a sector as well as individually, and are given extensive visibility in the DG's publications, notably on their Internet pages that frequently link to campaigns of NGOs in the OMC governance network, for example. The textual presence is here directly proportional to the role these organisations play in the social OMC. These discrepancies are astonishing considering that the involvement of the social partners in the social OMC is guaranteed by the Treaty, while that of NGOs is not. Article 160 (ex-144) of the Treaty on the Functioning of the European Union lays down that '[i]n fulfilling its mandate, the [Social Protection] Committee shall establish appropriate contacts with management and labour'.[25] The SPC does this by organising a formal annual joint meeting. By comparison, between civil society organisations and the SPC, contacts are less structured and work on a smaller scale, but it is difficult to say whether this in effect means less contacts. The DG also sees its role as 'liaising [...] between the [Social Protection] Committee and NGOs' (Interview no. 6).

Notwithstanding, seen from a policy content point of view, it is not surprising that the social partners are not prominent actors in the social OMC, since the latter mainly deals with issues that are not of central importance for them.[26] In fact, the only concrete topics mentioned in the DG's text in relation to the social partners are those of preventing unemployment in times of economic crisis[27] and of integrating poor people into the labour market.[28] The former is more related to

---

24. On the European social dialogue from the perspective of representation, *see* Smismans 2004: 315–403.

25. The social partners and the European Economic and Social Committee (EESC) are the only functional organisations mentioned in the Treaty's 'Title X' on social policy, which also includes employment and labour policies, such as occupational health and safety, vocational training, working conditions, the rights of the social partners, etc. The Common Objectives of the social OMCs mention both social partners and NGOs.

26. Cf. de la Porte and Pochet 2005: 375. Referring to the Lisbon Strategy as a whole (including the EES), Pfister (2009) points to the fact that trade unions are also likely to 'promote alternative visions of Europe' and are therefore not encouraged to participate actively.

27. European Commission staff working document SEC(2010)98 of 8 February 2010: 129.

28. European Commission (2004) speech by Director-General Odile Quintin, 18 October 2004. On-line. Available http://ec.europa.eu/employment_social/speeches/2004/oq181004_fr.pdf, accessed 16 October 2008.

employment policies, and the latter is dealt with as part of the 'active inclusion' strategy (comprising access to services, employment, and adequate income), which is not particularly prominent on the social partners' agendas either. From this perspective, what is peculiar is rather their being mentioned consistently when the 'stakeholders' to be involved are listed. Although the social partners do participate in consultations and interact with the DG also in OMC issues, they are not among the more important functional representatives, and yet are referred to much more often than other lower profile actors.

Although the concept of the 'stakeholder' is firmly tied to the relevance-for-policy-outputs perspective, which holds a dominant position in the DG's text, it is not the only one. Functional representation is also presented as a matter of input legitimacy and 'good governance', whereby affectedness or concern as such justifies a group's involvement in policy making. This is especially the case when it comes to the citizens in the street, i.e. 'civil society', or specifically people living in poverty. The representation of ordinary citizens is an important legitimatory argument for DG Employment, and this representation is primarily provided through NGOs. NGOs are by far the major 'stakeholder' that the DG refers to, quantitatively as well as qualitatively. The subsequent chapters analyse in depth in which senses their participation in OMC policy making is seen to generate legitimacy for these processes, and what the relation of the output legitimacy based on relevant contributions is with other forms of legitimacy. I begin here by examining the representative claims DG Employment makes about NGOs, i.e. whom they say NGOs represent, and how they perceive this representation to work.

NGOs: multi-representatives

NGOs play an exceptional role among the functional representatives involved in the OMC. It is special in two respects: Firstly, social NGOs are extremely present in the OMC governance processes at the EU level, and this is well reflected in the prominence they are given in the DG's text about these processes. Secondly, NGOs differ from the other 'stakeholders' in the ways they are seen to represent. Simplified, service providers represent themselves or their sector, and the social partners' organisations[29] and public administrations represent their members (citizens, in the latter case). NGOs, by contrast, are claimed to represent a variety of constituencies simultaneously, and therefore also to represent in several different ways.

To start with the former, NGOs are so ubiquitous in the DG's text about functional representatives in social inclusion that the term 'stakeholders' is in fact often used as a synonym for 'NGOs', and NGOs are usually the first kind of actors

---

29. It is possible to argue that in some instances social partners (claim to) represent their respective sectors beyond official members, i.e. unions sometimes speak for workers in general, and management organisations for employers in general. This happens in situations where they are not negotiating agreements binding only for their membership, but where they speak out about interests they argue are shared by all workers or all employees. Equally, Member States also represent non-national residents in some respects. Constituencies' limits are almost always fluid.

that DG officials mention when asked who the 'stakeholders' in the OMC are. What is more, they are not merely mentioned in the DG's texts, but extensively talked about, and their importance is continually stressed. Moreover, DG Employment's Internet pages frequently inform about the campaigns or conferences of central NGOs in their 'News' and 'Events' sections, and the *Social Agenda* magazine published quarterly by the DG contains a section called 'Other Voices', where a 'stakeholder' is given a page to present her views; in issues concerning the social OMC this is generally an NGO representative. The contacts between the DG and NGOs are correspondingly dense. In 2001, Commissioner Anna Diamantopoulou estimated that '[i]n an average year, my services are in close contact with around 700 NGOs' (European Commission 2001a). In 2011, there were more than 1,100 organisations in the Commission's 'register of interest representatives' who declared 'employment and social affairs' as one of their fields of interest.[30] Yet, especially in the case of social inclusion, relations with NGOs are remarkable not only for their quantity, but even more so for their quality. Policy officers in what used to be the Social Inclusion Unit have daily contact with at least one NGO representative; one of them referred to the DGs and national civil servants engaged with the OMC and the inner circle of involved NGOs collectively as 'the OMC community' (Interview no. 5). The individual people working for social NGOs in Brussels are often in this community for a long time and are networked accordingly; however, this is not necessarily the case for Commission officials. Notwithstanding, the former Social Inclusion Unit of DG Employment, which managed the social inclusion part of the OMC until the end of 2010, had a long tradition of working with NGOs that was distinctive of this particular unit, and they were widely known to be one of the organisations most open to NGOs within the DG, if not the entire Commission. The former Directorates, E (Social Protection and Integration) and G (Equality between Men and Women, Action against Discrimination, Civil Society) were the places within DG Employment where the involvement of NGOs was more 'in the culture' (Interview no. 1) than in other parts of the DG. Last but not least, the DG has a long history of funding NGOs that they work with on the European level; they themselves thus ensure to a decisive extent the presence of NGOs in the field (*see* Chapter Eight). As Justin Greenwood establishes, the widely held 'business rules OK' thesis does not apply to European social policy, but quite the contrary; public interest groups are the most influential kind of functional representatives in this area (Greenwood 2003: 275; cf. pp. 175–85, 209–29, 259–64).

In addition to their omnipresence, social NGOs in the OMC also stand out in terms of whom they are seen to represent. Contrastingly to other functional groups, NGOs are described by the DG as representing as many as three constituencies: specific groups of people affected by OMC policies; the NGO sector, including

---

30. European Commission (no date) 'Register of interest representatives'. Online. Accessed 11 January 2011. No longer available. Today, the Commission and the European Parliament maintain a joint register. *See* http://europa.eu/transparency-register/index_en.htm. Accessed 5 March 2013.

their member organisations; and 'civil society'.[31] This also means that their stakeholding is based on several rationales and that they represent in different ways simultaneously.

To start with the last of these constituencies, in academia *civil society* is generally understood as a sphere of collective action and public discourse between the private and the state, excluding organisations seeking political office and profit-seeking businesses, and preferably subscribing to a basic normative consensus including tolerance and non-violence (Thiery 2005: 1175). DG Employment takes a much wider perspective: 'The involvement of civil society is based on a broad definition and encompasses a broad range of actors, in particular NGOs, regional and local authorities [!], trade unions and employers organisations'.[32] Yet, although in the Commission's express definitions NGOs are only a part of civil society, in the DG's text 'civil society' is frequently used as a synonym of 'NGOs'.

So what exactly does 'civil society' mean in relation to NGOs? When the DG speaks about NGOs representing 'civil society', this refers to citizens as individuals, 'real people' like you and me, as it were, in contrast to politicians and bureaucrats. Involving NGOs thus 'ensure[s] that our policies meet the real needs of people' (European Commission 2003b). Accordingly, the picture of NGOs that the DG evokes is that of '[g]rassroots organisations, such as youth organisations, family associations and all organisations through which people participate in local and municipal life' and that 'bring people together in a common cause, such as environmental, human rights, and charitable organisations' (2003b). NGOs represent the man in the street on account of their 'closeness' to the everyday life of individual citizens. At the same time, however, the DG stresses that it is the task of the Member States and their subnational authorities to involve local, regional, and national NGOs. The Commission for its part engages mainly with European-level organisations. Yet, these are associations of national organisations, which again have (sub)national member organisations, which then, finally, have individual supporters. The idea is that the views of the individual citizens are transported from the bottom up to the European level through this chain to provide the DG with the grassroots perspective. The different aggregative levels of these organisations are thus seen as an organic whole. The DG often speaks of NGOs as 'an essential bridge between the European Union and its citizens'.[33] On a bridge,

---

31. For an analysis of DG Employment's discourse on 'civil society', *see* Smismans 2003.

32. European Commission Communication COM(2002)89 of 19 February 2002: 20. The Commission's White Paper on European governance gives the following definition: 'Civil society includes the following: trade unions and employers' organisations ('social partners'); nongovernmental organisations; professional associations; charities; grass-roots organisations; organisations that involve citizens in local and municipal life with a particular contribution from churches and religious communities. For a more precise definition of organised civil society, *see* the Opinion of the Economic and Social Committee on 'The role and contribution of civil society organisations in the building of Europe', OJ C329, 17.11.99 p. 30' (European Commission Communication COM(2001)428 of 25 July 2001: 14n9).

33. European Commission (no date) 'A quick guide to EU employment and social policies. 14. Dialogue with civil society'. Online. Available http://ec.europa.eu/employment_social/social_model/14_en.html, accessed 18 September 2008.

there are no obstacles to moving from one side to another; quite to the contrary, bridges are constructed to do exactly this – connect two sides. This connection works independently of how long the bridge is; in fact, the bridge becomes all the more necessary the greater the distance it crosses. The closeness of grassroots NGOs to the people thus directly moves the DG itself closer to the citizens, if this local NGO is part of a larger organisation with a representation in Brussels which cooperates with the DG.

What is more, the civil society that NGOs represent consists not only of the individual members in local associations, but it is also 'the society at large',[34] i.e. the citizenry in general. In other words, NGOs are presented as an additional pillar of popular representation, which is aggregated in parallel with the territorial pillar, so that the European-level organisations are 'relaying the views of stakeholders and society at large'.[35] They not only ensure that 'you can get involved and have your say',[36] but also function as a two-way information channel that 'make[s] sure that Europeans are well-informed regarding these policies'.[37] Consequently, the Commission supported the inclusion of functional representation as one of the elements of the 'Democratic Life of the Union' in the 2003 Draft Constitution[38] because

> [t]he draft Constitutional Treaty makes the participation of civil society one of the three pillars of European democracy, alongside representative democracy [!] and the social dialogue. This is an acknowledgement of the NGOs' role that the intergovernmental conference must preserve, and I hope that our common efforts will achieve this.[39]

34. E.g. European Commission (2008) 'What social Europe can do for you'. Online. Available http://ec.europa.eu/employment_social/publications/booklets/general/pdf/ke0008001_en.pdf, accessed 23 September 2008.

35. European Commission Decision C(2009)143 of 23 January 2009: 27.

36. European Commission (no date) 'Partners'. Online. Available http://ec.europa.eu/social/main.jsp?langId=en&catId=85, accessed 22 October 2010.

37. European Commission (no date) 'A quick guide to EU employment and social policies. 14. Dialogue with civil society'. Online. Available http://ec.europa.eu/employment_social/social_model/14_en.html, accessed 18 September 2008.

38. 'Article 46: The Principle of Participatory Democracy
    1. The Union Institutions shall, by appropriate means, give citizens and representative associations the opportunity to make known and publicly exchange their views on all areas of Union action.
    2. The Union Institutions shall maintain an open, transparent and regular dialogue with representative associations and civil society.
    3. The Commission shall carry out broad consultations with parties concerned in order to ensure that the Union's actions are coherent and transparent.'
    (European Communities 2003). The quoted provisions are now Article 11 of the Treaty on European Union.

39. European Commission (2003) speech by Director-General Odile Quintin, 21 October 2003. Online. Available http://ec.europa.eu/employment_social/speeches/2003/oq211003_fr.pdf, accessed 16 October 2008. Author translation.

If NGOs represent the citizenry in its entirety, the question arises of what the point is of representing this constituency twice, i.e. through territorial legislatures and through associations. One answer is the alleged 'closeness' to 'the ground',[40] which is depicted as an intrinsic characteristic of NGOs and often contrasted with the distance politicians and bureaucrats have from those who are affected by the policies they make (*see* Chapter Ten). NGOs are described as participative associations that are natural places for all citizens to engage themselves in, and in this they differ from electoral representation. This also explains why Odile Quintin, Director-General of DG Employment from 1999 to 2005, in the above citation contrasts 'the participation of civil society' with 'representative democracy': the former is conceptualised as *participative* – not representative – democracy. '[T]he European model of modern democracy is built on three pillars – representative democracy, participative democracy and social dialogue. Employment and social policy is where all these forms of democracy and governance meet' (European Commission 2003b). In the view of the DG, NGOs do not in fact *represent* civil society, but they *are* civil society. In other words, civil society is constituted through association; it is in fact *organised* civil society. The democratic ideal informing this interpretation is one where citizens actively participate in civil society organisations and through this take part in political processes in which NGOs 'play a full and active role' (2003b). Associational life is thus an essential element of full citizenship, and at the same time a natural way of taking part in social life.

Although this is described as 'participative democracy', what is taking place is certainly a form of representation, especially when it comes to the EU level of aggregation. The NGO officers working in Brussels are not grassroots activists engaging with 'the ground' in their everyday work, but part of the 'OMC community'. From this point of view, it sounds somewhat peculiar to 'represent civil society' – it seems questionable whether civil society can be represented as such, and unclear how this might work. It does not help to adopt the Commission's stance that NGOs are themselves (part of) civil society, because the NGOs (or their officers) interacting with the Commission will never be the entire civil society, and thus always represent those parts not physically present.

The claim to represent 'civil society' – in the meaning of 'the society at large' – has to be understood in the sense that NGOs represent *a different dimension* of the citizens than political parties, legislatures, and executives. In other words, they have the capacity to represent aspects that others cannot or do not represent. From the perspective of the citizen, this makes sense; it is plausible to assume that most people perceive that the families association or the environmental organisation they belong to, for example, represent different things about them than their district's MP or the national government. From the perspective of the Commission, this interpretation makes sense as well. First of all, the Commission's fundaments

---

40. E.g. European Commission (2005) speech by Commissioner Špidla, 7 November 2005. Online. Available http://ec.europa.eu/employment_social/speeches/2005/vs_051107_fr.pdf, accessed 22 July 2008.

of territorial representation are weak in general and for the OMC in particular. Secondly, their tight relationships with civil society organisations, which allegedly provide them with a direct connection to 'the Europeans', give them an alternative representative channel to the one the Member States' representatives are based on. In the OMC, Member States are represented by their executives, i.e. politicians with a certain distance from 'the ground' (although they are recommended by the Commission to engage with national functional representatives to overcome this distance). By contrast, the Commission claims to have a more or less direct channel to knowing what the citizens really feel. What is more, they have a vantage point on the views of the *European* citizens collectively, while each national representative only has information about their respective country. On the basis of their governance network, the Commission thus claims to represent Europeans as ordinary citizens with their needs and wishes.

Now, the social NGOs involved in the OMC do not have 'representing civil society' as their missions, but their *raison d'être* is the representation of specific functional groups, such as families, the homeless, or the mentally ill. It is only collectively, as a sector, that these associations add up to representing 'civil society' from the DG's point of view. In turn, this means that in order to be itself representative of 'civil society', the DG has to interact with an extensive range of NGOs speaking for many different groups. Representativity is here defined not in terms of how many individual members an organisation has, for example, but functionally, as covering a large number of diverse groups within society through their respective associations:

> The European Commission is in regular contact with the Platform of European Social NGOs (the Social Platform), as well as with a number of EU umbrella networks. The Social Platform was created in 1995 and has over 40 member organisations operating in the social sector. Through these members, it brings together over 1,700 organisations, associations and other voluntary bodies at local, regional, national and European level, representing a cross-section of civil society. These include organisations of women, older people, and people with disabilities, people who are unemployed, migrants, people affected by poverty, gays and lesbians, young people, children and families.[41]

Curiously, this list contains solely groups considered to be especially affected by social and anti-discrimination policies, while 'civil society' also includes healthy, rich, employed, single, heterosexual men, for example. Representativity as diversity is here bent towards privileging those groups that are normally at risk of being underrepresented, which at the same time could suggest that 'civil society' is mainly socially disadvantaged groups. It is improbable that this is the meaning intended by DG Employment; more likely the intention is to involve those parts of civil society that are particularly affected by their policies, and

---

41. European Commission (no date) 'Non-governmental organisations'. Online. Available http://ec.europa.eu/social/main.jsp?catId=330&langId=en, accessed 26 October 2010.

emphasise that this deliberately includes weaker groups, so that the DG's contacts with functional representatives do not replicate existing inequalities.[42] However, if this is the case, there is a contradiction between the claim to work together with organisations representing, collectively, 'society at large' and the declaration to involve associations speaking for the affected. The contrast between the DG's talk about 'involving civil society' and the inevitable practice of working with *particular* subgroups of civil society suggests that civil society is here above all seen as a pool of non-governmental actors, who are *potential* participants in OMC governance processes. In this view, the choice of actual participants in a given case indicates who the relevant groups are for the purpose. Through this, lists such as the one cited above also advance specific interpretations of what kinds of actors legitimately act in the name of 'civil society' in a given case.

In any case, NGOs are depicted by the DG to represent both 'civil society' in its entirety and their *specific functional constituencies*. Concerning the latter, this representative claim is based on three different, though related and overlapping relationships between the representing and the represented: NGOs can represent their constituencies on account of working for them (advocacy), providing services to them, and involving them in their own work.

The first, advocacy, is practiced by all the NGOs involved. Notwithstanding, there are NGOs for which this is their primary occupation and the key justification for their representative claim. Advocacy by definition implies a claim to represent the group whose views one advocates (cf. Urbinati 2000). It is on the basis of successfully making such a claim to DG Employment (and the public) that these NGOs participate in the OMC: if one wants to involve the affected, one needs someone to represent them, and advocacy NGOs offer themselves as the key actors doing exactly this; in fact existing for this purpose.

But how exactly does advocacy link to representation? Why is the Commission – and why are we – prepared to accept the claim of some association to speak for 'the poor'? The DG is here drawing on a very common logic based on the assumed 'motivational distinctiveness' (Goodin 2003b: 372) of NGOs. These organisations raise a lot of their resources through voluntary work and donations 'rooted in altruistic concern with "the cause"' (Goodin 2003b: 372), and their staff is committed to this cause – rather than to maximising efficiency or profits – out of inner conviction: 'Voluntary and non governmental organisations exhibit a shared *commitment* by individuals to address discrimination and inequality' (European Commission 2000a; emphasis added). We therefore tend to trust them to have internalised their professed goals, and to really strive to represent the best interests of, in this case, the poor. NGOs thus work essentially on reputational capital. This can clearly be seen in the DG's text, which often builds on the presumption that 'NGOs' and 'civil society' evoke the image of dedicated actors for a good cause:

---

42. Cf. also Rosanvallon's analysis of the 'legitimacy of proximity' (*légitimité de proximité*) (Rosanvallon 2010: Ch. IV).

From a historical point of view, civil society was always at the heart of the struggle against poverty and social exclusion. I am referring of course to the usually non-profit-making voluntary organisations which intervene where the state and the private sector either do not wish to or are unable to take effective action. (European Commission 2003c)

It is this assumption of sincere personal dedication to a cause which does not cater for any special advantages that makes it credible that '[n]on-governmental organisations [...] give a voice to the poor, the homeless, the unemployed',[43] because we trust their *intention* to speak with the voice of those they lobby for rather than their own.

Importantly, this motivation is more important than an organisation's formal authorisation by those they represent, or their representatives' belonging themselves to that group. When DG Employment presents certain NGOs as representing particular social groups, they never refer to the formal structures of authorisation and accountability inside these organisations, other than mentioning that their European level is constituted by national member organisations. The internal make-up of these national associations is not addressed. Although the dedicated, often voluntary, work of the grassroots level and its closeness to the represented is frequently evoked, the text does not deal with the question of how views are mediated from the local to the European level. Instead, the NGOs are taken as an organic whole, which is held together by the shared commitment to the joint cause of all staff members on all levels. It is this commitment that constitutes the 'bridge' that NGOs provide between policy makers and citizens: since the Brussels-based officers of European networks of NGOs are equally motivated by the idealistic cause their local staff works for (often voluntarily), they represent their constituencies in spite of their distance. In this perspective, the decisive thing for representation is not so much how views are mediated through different aggregative levels, but the basis of the representatives' motivation.

The topos of authentic intentions serves as the fundament of representative claims about NGOs; it has of course to be supplemented by evidence of how they pursue those intentions and how they in fact represent the groups they claim to speak for. This is generally built on assertions to the effect that the NGO possesses special knowledge about the real situation and needs of those it represents. Both together provide the basic legitimation of the representative claims about advocacy NGOs: empathy for and knowledge about their constituencies (cf. O'Neill 2001: 490). Out of these, the former is primary, since it motivates the acquisition of expertise and because of this also generates trust in the quality of this expertise. At the same time, the knowledge NGOs have about their constituencies is the main reason for involving them in the OMC. They provide necessary information 'from the ground' (European Commission 2008b). However, in order to be heard, this information has to be presented effectively. It has to come in such a form that

---

43. European Commission press release SPEECH/02/367 of 5 September 2009.

it can readily be used by policy makers. Additionally, for the DG, 'philanthropy alone is not enough', but in order to 'effective[ly] represent' their constituencies, NGOs have to engage in governance networks and cooperate with each other from the local through to the European level to 'make an effective and constructive contribution to shaping and implementing social policy' (European Commission 2003c). This is what makes an advocacy NGO a 'relevant' stakeholder in the OMC.

> You might argue that expertise involves elements of advocacy, and advocacy must, if it is to be credible, involve elements of expertise. *But*, let's put it that way, expertise is usually what is produced when the Commission asks for it, and advocacy is what the NGOs start [from], what is their starting position. (Interview no. 4)

Thus, for the DG, the *activity* of 'effective representation' is essentially information provision, while the *legitimacy* of this activity (the trust that the representatives' message really represents their constituencies) comes from the NGOs' motivational distinctiveness. But how can this authenticity be proven for an individual NGO? As stated above, the authenticity of an NGO is mainly a question of reputation, which is based on information collected about that organisation over time. This includes information about its financial sources,[44] its history and members, for example, but why not also observations about its representatives' comportment? DG officers also mention their respect for the visible dedication with which the NGO representatives work, referring, for example, to their long working hours (Interview no. 5) or their extensive and persistent efforts in pushing for certain political results. Many of the NGOs in the OMC governance network also have a long history of cooperation with the Commission, so that the authenticity of their missions can be assumed to be traditional knowledge, as it were, within the DG. Towards the outside, where the DG itself has to argue for the legitimacy of the NGOs they involve, they sometimes refer to the voluntary work at the organisations' grassroots level and to the cause they work for, but in most cases the text simply relies on the positive connotation of 'NGO'.

NGOs representing their constituencies on account of providing services to them, like for example FEANTSA (the European Federation of National Organisations Working with the Homeless), of course also practice advocacy for these constituencies in the OMC. Being not-for-profit organisations, the same assumption of motivational distinctiveness applies to them as to pure advocacy associations, i.e. their activities are motivated by their inner convictions and personal commitments to helping their beneficiaries. On this note, lobbying for the interests of these groups is part of their work. The difference from pure advocacy NGOs is that here representative claims are above all based on the fact that through

---

44. These have to be provided when registering in the EU's (formerly the Commission's) register of interest representatives, and they must also be opened and approved to obtain financing from the Commission.

'working with people in poverty',[45] these associations are especially close to the groups they speak for, and thus know their situations and needs through direct contacts 'on the front line'.[46] This knowledge distinguishes them from other actors who lack direct contact with the poor. The fact that NGOs do not make a profit with the services they provide adds to their legitimacy as representatives, making it credible that their true intention really is nothing other than to represent the best interests of their beneficiaries. After all, when FEANTSA launches a campaign called 'Ending Homelessness'[47], this ultimately calls for abolishing the need for their own existence. Hence, the logic of representation is here the converse of the pure advocacy NGOs' case: while for the latter, representation is legitimated by empathy, backed up with knowledge about their constituencies, service-providing NGOs' legitimacy as representatives is based on knowledge, backed up with empathy. Both speak for people they feel concerned for, and who themselves 'find it hard to express their experiences and opinions' (European Commission 2007a) or even 'cannot speak for themselves'.[48]

The third rationale for NGOs representing their constituencies is that of involving people from these groups in their own organisation. The association emphasising this most is EAPN (*see* EAPN 2009). However, this representational logic is not referred to in the DG's text addressed to the public, and since 2008 has no longer been a condition to receive core funding.[49]

In addition to 'civil society' and the affected, there is a third constituency that NGOs are said to represent in the DG's text about them, namely NGOs themselves as a *sector*, or collectively as actors in the field of social policies. NGOs are themselves affected by the OMC policies, because they work within areas influenced by these. This is especially true for those NGOs that also provide social services, but pure advocacy NGOs are political actors in the field as well,

---

45. E.g. European Commission (no date) 'A quick guide to EU employment and social policies. 6. Eradicating poverty and tackling social exclusion'. Online. Available http://ec.europa.eu/employ-ment_social/social_model/6_en.html, accessed 18 September 2008.

46. European Commission staff working document SEC(2010)98 of 8 February 2010: 129.

47. European Commission (2010) 'Homelessness – a major challenge for Europe'. Online. Available http://ec.europa.eu/social/main.jsp?langId=en&catId=89&newsId=869&furtherNews=yes, accessed 14 September 2010.

48. European Commission (2010) 'Commissioner vows to speak for the "forgotten people" in Europe'. Online. Available http://ec.europa.eu/commission_2010-2014/andor/headlines/articles/2010/02/20100121_en.htm, accessed 14 March 2011. Originally published by *Touteleurope.eu* (21 February 2010). Online. Available http://www.touteleurope.eu/fr/en/news/actualite-vue-detaillee/afficher/fiche/4181/t/85293/from/4487/breve/commissioner-vows-to-speak-for-the-forgotten-people-in-europe.html?cHash=f0c2d36f05, accessed 14 March 2011.

49. The call for proposals to receive core funding from 1 January 2007 to 31 December 2007 still contained the award criterion 'the degree of participation of key institutions or actors, including people exposed to social exclusion and poverty, in the work of the network and in the design and implementation of each of the foreseen activities' (European Commission 2006a: 12; similarly, in European Commission 2005a and 2002a). For the periods of 1 January 2008 to 31 December 2010 and 1 January 2011 to 31 December 2013 this was no longer required (European Commis-sion 2007b; 2010b).

because they lobby for particular types of policies. According to the DG's text, social NGOs are represented as a sector because they work for the same goals as the OMC (or the Commission within the OMC), namely 'combating poverty and social exclusion'.[50] In the same vein, one of the priorities of the Progress programme is 'strengthening networks: especially those that support and promote policies and actions which are covered by the programme's remit'.[51] This connects back to what was defined above as the central criterion of what makes an actor a stakeholder for DG Employment, i.e. *relevance* with respect to reaching defined policy goals. NGOs are here represented because they have important competencies in social policies,[52] such as providing social services, which not only makes them *affected* when political conditions change,[53] but also gives them the capacity and the *'responsibility* for fighting exclusion'.[54] In other words, their participation is not only 'a matter of administrative efficiency' or due to 'the multidimensional nature of social exclusion',[55] but the idea is also to commit them to contribute to the common effort and engage themselves. This logic is based directly on the 'working together, working better' topos underlying the greatest part of the DG's discourse about functional representation in the OMC, and which ultimately makes 'everybody' a stakeholder, at least potentially. On this note, the central role given to NGOs is understandable, because they represent a whole range of actors that can possibly contribute to the joint endeavour of 'fighting exclusion': citizens in general, the especially affected, and NGOs as social policy actors. They are thus especially relevant with respect to reaching the policy goals striven for.

The representation of all these three constituencies is in the DG's text based on epistemological assumptions. NGOs are claimed to represent 'civil society' or citizens in general on account of their intrinsic closeness to them, thus knowing their real needs and thoughts. They represent the affected by virtue of knowing them because they care for them and feel concerned by their cause, or because they also encounter them in their work. Finally, they represent their own non-governmental sector on the basis of being themselves part of this, thus knowing the NGOs' perspectives. On the contrary, the DG does not much address the institutional structures linking NGOs with their constituencies. The role of individual supporters and the formal and informal relations of authorisation, accountability, and deliberation within NGOs are not dealt with. However, relationships between the grassroots and the EU level are necessary in practice to make the epistemological

---

50. European Commission Communication COM(2001)565 of 9 October 2001: 60.

51. European Commission (2008) 'Programme offers real PROGRESS for EU citizens'. Online. Available http://ec.europa.eu/social/main.jsp?catId=370&langId=en&featuresId=11&furtherFeatures=yes, accessed 18 September 2008.

52. European Commission Communication COM(2001)565 of 9 October 2001: 60.

53. European Commission staff working document SEC(2010)98 of 8 February 2010: 129.

54. European Commission Communication COM(2001)565 of 9 October 2001: 60. Emphasis added.

55. *ibid.*

representative claims plausible, because the Commission mainly interacts with EU-level representatives. Notwithstanding, the level of aggregation is only very rarely specified when the involvement of NGOs is brought up.

There is a gap between the representative claims made about NGOs and the reality of NGO officers firmly based in the OMC governance networks in Brussels, which is not filled by the DG's text. In other words, there is no indication how the 'closeness' of the grassroots level to the everyday issues in social policy is mediated to the EU level, suggesting that either the functioning of this link is taken for granted or it is unimportant for the purpose of involving NGOs. One reason for not addressing the issue of representational structures within NGOs more can indeed be seen in the roles these NGOs are assigned in the OMG governance. This role is analysed in the following chapter.

Chapter Seven

The Role of NGOs in the Social OMC

As shown in the previous chapter, the main reason DG Employment gives for involving functional representatives in the social OMC is the idea that '[w]e *all* must pull together'.[1] This 'working together' topos informs the lion's share of the DG's text about their work with 'stakeholders'.[2] On the one hand, it serves to assure that the Commission does not act alone or seek to impose measures on others, but cooperates: 'The EU does not only respect subsidiarity towards the Member States. EU social policy is also always carried out with as much involvement of the social partners and civil society as possible'.[3] This implies that the Commission's own legitimacy is not deemed sufficient to act on its own, even where EU competences are concerned, but needs to be complemented with the legitimacy functional representation can provide. This twofold legitimation of Commission activities – acting within the limits set by the treaties and involving functional representatives when acting on the European level – is also called 'double subsidiarity'.[4] On the other hand, working together is also seen as *necessary* to achieve the objectives of European social policies – '[s]uccess rests on participation'[5] – and therefore everybody with the possibility to make a contribution (i.e. all relevant actors) *should* do so. In other words, attaining these political goals is also a *responsibility* of all those involved, '[b]ecause fighting poverty is not only an issue for Governments [*sic*]. It is for civil society too'.[6] On this note, 'the involvement of all relevant actors' more generally, i.e. a society where all stakeholders do in fact participate in policy making, is also promoted as an ideal mode of governance.

1. European Commission press release SPEECH/06/19 of 20 January 2006.
2. Cf. the title of Commission Communication COM(2005)706 of 22 December 2005: 'Working together, working better [...]'. The same phrase has also been used as a programmatic heading in a leaflet presenting the social OMC to the public at large (European Communities 2007a).
3. European Commission (2005) 'Was heißt "soziales Europa"?' ('What does "social Europe" mean?'). Speech by Commissioner Špidla, 7 November 2005. Online. Available http://ec.europa.eu/employment_social/speeches/2005/vs_051107_de.pdf, accessed 26 August 2008. Author translation.
4. European Commission (2008) 'Welcome word'. Online. Available http://ec.europa.eu/employment_social/spsi/welcome_word_en.htm, accessed 18 September 2008.
5. European Commission (2006) speech by Commissioner Špidla, 16 March 2006. Online. Available http://ec.europa.eu/employment_social/speeches/2006/vs_060316_fr.pdf, accessed 22 July 2008. Author translation.
6. European Commission press release SPEECH/2010/30 of 18 February 2010.

In this chapter, I enquire more deeply into what is meant by this 'working together'. I first explore how it is to come about, before looking at the role NGOs are given in this context. When they are involved in OMC policy making, what are they supposed to do? And, complementarily, what role does the DG assign itself?

Mobilising partners

The governance philosophy advanced by the DG for the OMC rests on the recognition of 'the necessity to mobilise and involve *all* concerned actors'.[7] It is continually stressed that this should involve the widest possible range of organisations: 'By partners I mean everybody'.[8] This requires activating those not yet represented in the process. Accordingly, great emphasis is placed on awareness raising, i.e. potential functional constituencies and their representatives are to be made aware of the OMC, the social problems meant to be tackled, their own stakes in the matter, and their opportunities to contribute to the process. In short, awareness is to lead to engaging oneself in the undertaking:

> The main objective of this Year [the 2010 European Year for Combating Poverty and Social Exclusion] is to *raise awareness*. Citizens awareness, stakeholders awareness, decision makers [*sic*] awareness. Only with the combined *commitment* of all can we bring people *together* to fight poverty and social exclusion.[9]

The need to first of all inform potential stakeholders about the existence and functioning of the OMC is well recognised in the DG. Knowledge of European social policy is confined to a comparatively small insider circle:

> [I]t still remains a well-kept secret, as we say. It's not like the anti-discrimination issue that is much more well known than what social inclusion is about. (Interview no. 7)

> To me, it's very clear that the strategic goal should be to involve much better local authorities, and also to some extent national administrations; I mean, of course national administrations are represented at the Social Protection Committee, but the reality is that in many of the countries[...] I mean, most of the national administrations work on policies which are at the core of the social OMC without even, I would say, an awareness of the existence of the social OMC – let's be clear on this. (Interview no. 8)

---

7. EAPN (2001) speech by Director (Directorate E, DG Employment) Gabrielle Clotuche at an EAPN conference, 22 November 2001. Online. Available http://www.eapn.org, accessed 28 July 2008. Emphasis added.

8. European Commission press release SPEECH/02/367 of 5 September 2002.

9. European Commission press release SPEECH/2010/30 of 18 February 2010. Emphases added.

Thus, although according to Eurobarometers, 'almost three out of four Europeans would like the European Union to play a more active role in the fight against poverty',[10] even those who are in a position to engage themselves in this process do not necessarily know about this possibility. Therefore, awareness raising is necessary in order to 'make more visible the positive role played by good social protection and inclusion policies and to support the modernisation of policies'.[11]

Raising awareness of the OMC's existence goes hand in hand with promoting the 'recognition' of its key objectives and of one's opportunities, indeed one's 'responsibility', to get engaged in the process. Recognising the problem and knowing that one can and should take part in existing processes aimed at tackling it then ideally leads to taking 'ownership' of and 'commitment' to the attainment of the OMC's goals:

The 2010 European Year aims to reach EU citizens and all public, social and economic stakeholders. Its four specific objectives are:

- *Recognition* of the right of people in poverty and social exclusion to live in dignity and to play a full part in society;
- An increase in the public *ownership* of social inclusion policies, emphasising *everyone's responsibility* in tackling poverty and marginalisation;
- A more cohesive society, where *no one doubts* that society as a whole benefits from the eradication of poverty;
- *Commitment* of all actors, because real progress requires a long-term effort that involves all levels of governance.[12]

Mobilisation thus means activating all possible actors specifically to *support* the ongoing process and its goals: 'Another feature of the [open] method [of coordination] is the emphasis on mobilising all actors [...] in support of the process'.[13] The ideal evoked here is a society where the awareness of problems leads first to a principled support of the good cause, and then to activities in the service of that cause. Each actor has the possibility to contribute according to their own functional role or position, so that in the end everybody is working together by bringing in their own particular resources (cf. the previous chapter). A curious characteristic of this line of reasoning is the automaticity with which awareness is linked to support. The DG's text assumes that someone informed about the OMC will approve of it. This automaticity is made plausible by keeping the text

10. European Commission press release SPEECH/10/12 of 21 January 2010.
11. European Commission (2008) 'Awareness-raising projects'. Online. Available http://ec.europa.eu/employment_social/spsi/awareness_raising_projects_en.htm, accessed 18 September 2008.
12. European Commission press release IP/07/1905 of 12 December 2007. Emphases added.
13. Eurofound (2002) draft speech by Director (Directorate E, DG Employment) Gabrielle Clotuche for a conference of the European Foundation for the Improvement of Living and Working Conditions (Eurofound), 16 May 2002. Online. Available http://www.eurofound.europa.eu/ewco/employment/documents/clotuche.pdf, accessed 25 September 2008.

concerning political goals in the OMC on a very general level and excluding any allusion to different actors' interests or preferences. Thus, what remains is the goal to 'tackle poverty and social exclusion' (European Commission 2007c), which appeals to the support of every rational being, or at least cannot be publicly contested. In this way, everything undertaken within the OMC framework is identified as 'fighting poverty',[14] i.e. by definition leading to a widely accepted goal. Framing things in these very broad terms not only serves to support the argument that everybody should take part in the process – because such vague formulations make the objectives seem universal values (cf. Perelman and Olbrechts-Tyteca 1969: 76) – but it can also be utilised to pressure actors who oppose the OMC, or specific approaches, as the *instrument* to deal with social issues, because they can be made to seem like they are disagreeing with the value of promoting wellbeing (*see* Bauer 2002: 390). But what does functional representatives' 'support of the process' mean here, more concretely? Since the functional representatives who are given by far the most prominent position in the DG's text are NGOs, I will next take a look at the roles these are assigned in the OMC.

NGOs: invited lobbyists

The NGOs' first task, from the perspective of DG Employment, is to provide the latter with *information* 'from the ground' which is necessary for policy making,

> [b]ecause one of the objectives, and one of the implementations, of the social OMC is to help identify key issues that can and should be addressed in order to achieve the common social objectives. And this can only be done if governments and those who are responsible for policy making are really in continuous contact and have a clear picture of the social situation. And [...] the contacts with the NGOs should of course be seen in that respect. (Interview no. 6)

> Let's have a few examples. What's the impact of the [financial] crisis on microfinance institutions? They [the NGOs] would have a view on this before anything is published. So it's interesting for me to know. (Interview no. 8)

Through Brussels-based European networks of national NGOs, the DG has access to extensive expertise independently of the information the Member States transfer to the EU level. This is based on national member organisations' close relations to 'the ground', i.e. those ultimately affected, and their resulting knowledge about the lives of the poor and the concrete work done to help them: '[O]ur policy development needs the expertise of NGOs that tackle social issues, locally and nationally' (European Commission 2000a). This means that the information available from these sources is more of a qualitative nature; its value

---

14. E.g. European Commission Communication COM(2002)89 of 19 February 2002.

lies in leading to a deeper *understanding* of social phenomena, including wider contexts, causal relations, emerging or overlooked problems, experience of means to tackle them, and the real lives of those living in poverty.

> We're talking about social objectives, social cohesion issues, which means how a society should develop in a cohesive and sustainable [...] manner. [...] So, in order to understand how this can be done, you can only do this in close contact with all those concerned, to understand *why* there's still a problem of exclusion; issues like new elements coming up the horizon, for example the questions of migrants, ethnic minorities – these are also linked, all [...] new developments that can only be monitored and closely studied, analysed, if you have close contact with the ground. (Interview no. 6)

> Such [European] networks [of social NGOs] have an important contribution to make [...] towards a better understanding of the most concrete forms of social exclusion [...].[15]

This qualitative nature of the information provided by NGOs is what distinguishes them from academic or think-tank experts. Their knowledge is not presented as based on research but on representation and experience. In this sense, it can be compared to the knowledge a Member of Parliament has about her district, for example. The role assigned to NGOs in terms of information provision thus takes into account the fact that NGOs are not expert as such, but mostly advocacy organisations, i.e. providing expertise is part of and instrumental to their advocacy work. The information they feed into OMC processes is not described as the professional knowledge of Brussels-based officers, but as citizens' or social workers' views that are mediated from the grassroots level through the NGO structures. NGOs are thus 'vehicles through which to communicate', 'promoting and representing the views of specific groups of citizens to European institutions' (European Commission 2000a). On the one hand, this representation of qualitative information about citizens' lives is maintained to make the DG closer to the people; on the other hand, the DG also needs this sort of expertise for particular cases or about particular issues, which is why expertise from NGOs is also produced upon the DG's request (Interview no. 4).

Providing knowledge, based on their activities 'on the ground', is the most salient feature of the NGOs' role in the DG's text, especially on its surface level. It is also the standard explanation scientific literature gives for the Commission's openness towards organised interests, considering its notorious shortage of staff (and, consequently, in-house expertise), the functional need to propose acceptable legislation or initiatives, as well as its lack of democratic legitimacy through territorial structures of representation (e.g. Tanasescu 2009: 56–7; Hix 2005: 227–

---

15. European Commission (2008) 'Key European Networks'. Online. Available http://ec.europa.eu/ employment_social/spsi/european_networks_en.htm, accessed 21 November 2008.

8; Laffan 2002: 129–30; Mazey and Richardson 1994: 170–4, 177–8; cf. Sbragia 2000: 228–31). Without wanting to contest this causal explanation, I would like to show that the role which DG Employment depicts for NGOs in the social OMC is more faceted.

First of all, the mediation of information is meant to take place in two directions: from 'the ground', i.e. the grassroots, through the national level to the Union; and from the EU down to the individual members. The rationale is closely related to that of mobilising stakeholders outlined above: NGOs are seen as channels to *inform citizens* about OMC policies and through this ensure their support. This again is premised on the image of NGOs as having particular close and direct ties with the citizens. They can thus convey information to them about the processes they are involved in at the European level, whereby their participation gains a double value for the DG:

> It is vital that stakeholders are actively involved in order to ensure that our policies meet the real needs of people. NGOs can be the bridge between citizens and authorities. Civil society representatives can also help make EU policy better known or understood by the citizens of Europe. (European Commission 2003b)

Thus, as representatives of the citizens, NGOs are to function as a link between the DG and the people, representing the people to the DG and the DG's policies to the people. On its Internet page about 'non-governmental organisations', the DG even calls them 'an *essential* bridge between the European Union (EU) institutions and citizens',[16] i.e. a necessary representational structure.

What is more, the intention is not merely to inform, but also to educate citizens:

> [W]e will further step up our efforts to raise public awareness and *convince* citizens of the relevance of our policies and instruments in their daily lives.[17]

The DG perceives a need to explain to the citizens what they are doing and how these policies benefit people in their everyday life. Their concern is that many popular policies are not recognised by citizens as originating in the EU, and that conversely, most citizens do not know that there are European policies dealing with issues they perceive as pressing problems, such as social exclusion. The reasoning is that if people's knowledge about these things improved, they would support the Commission much more. This involves informing them not only about the existence of the social OMC, but also convincing them of the DG's problem definitions and promoting European policies as a solution. However, the DG recognises the difficulty of getting their messages across to the individual citizens:

---

16. European Commission (no date) 'Non-governmental organisations'. Online. Available http://ec.europa.eu/social/main.jsp?catId=330&langId=en, accessed 12 November 2010. Emphasis added. Cf. European Commission Communication COM(2008)412 of 2 July 2008: 18.

17. DG Employment (2009) *2009 Annual Management Plan*: 4. Emphasis added.

The new focus on better communicating policies and their benefits to citizens, as well as key stakeholders, means that people must be able to identify easily with EU employment and social policies. They need to see the real human, economic, social or political consequences of the EU actions and understand how these actions relate to daily life in the EU. They also need to see that their public concerns and aspirations have been acknowledged, reflected upon and acted on by the Community and Member States. This implies that there is a need to highlight the concrete benefits of policies related to PROGRESS in its communication activities. It also implies using a different language, less EU jargon-oriented and to focus upon what interests European citizens.[18]

Lacking the publicity infrastructure available to national administrations, one means of overcoming this communication difficulty is to communicate via NGOs:

Whenever possible, Progress-funded information-sharing activities are geared to utilize the 'multiplier effect', where, once generated, relevant information is further disseminated and exchanged within target groups using a variety of networks and partnerships. In this respect, the capacity of pan-European networks and NGOs to act as effective channels of information and active utilisation of that capacity are the key issues. [...]

To achieve the 'multiplier effect' [...], particular attention has been given to using the networking of stakeholders for communication purposes. Networking has provided opportunities for discussing social and employment policies, disseminating communication tools as well as exchanging innovative good communication practices. This, in turn, has helped the Commission to reach out to national stakeholders and also reconnect Europe with its citizens. (European Commission 2009a: 24, 28; emphasis omitted)

On the one hand, citizens are to be informed about the challenges to which the OMC provides solutions, and on the other hand, these policies conducted at EU level are to be made more concrete and understandable, so that people see how they relate to their own lives. The latter in particular is a difficult endeavour. NGOs are deemed to have a better connection to citizens, so involving them is also seen as one way of making citizens aware of European policies. Again, the presumption is that gaining support is a matter of spreading knowledge about the policies in question and explaining them properly. The aims of this communication strategy also go beyond the immediate context of social policies and include promoting a more positive image of the EU more generally. However, the functioning of such a strategy hinges on the capacity and willingness of the

---

18. European Commission (2007) call for tender VT/2007/013 of 13 March 2007 (specification to tender No VT/2007/013: 'Framework contract for services in support of communication activity concerning the PROGRESS programme and related policies'). Online. Available http://ec.europa.eu/social/main.jsp?catId=626&langId=en&callId=60&furtherCalls=yes, accessed 19 March 2013.

NGOs to communicate the processes they are involved in at EU level to the citizens. If this is a difficult task for the Commission with its public relations resources, it is no easier for welfare NGOs depending on public funding. What is more, it is highly questionable whether NGOs see the education of their supporters as their task. Generally, the internal flows of information about EU issues are weak. Already, the national member organisations of EU-level networks are often not very knowledgeable about European processes (Interview no. 2). Most NGOs see the EU first and foremost as a source of funding (Interview no. 8), or as an opportunity structure to advance their own objectives (Warleigh 2001: 622), and in view of their limited resources they tend to prioritise lobbying over educating their supporters, without the latter being unsatisfied with that state of affairs (Warleigh 2001; Sudbery 2003: 89–90; Maloney 2008: 75–7; concerning local organisations, see also van Deth and Maloney 2008; van Deth 2008: 335–7). In this regard, the continuing esotericism of the social OMC among the general public seems to call the functioning of the DG's strategy into question.[19] While the DG depicts NGOs as highly participative organisations of citizen activists, in fact they often function, and are seen by their supporters, as gyroscopic representatives. Moreover, while DG Employment counts on (sub)national NGOs' dense connections to public deliberations to Europeanise social policy discourses, these may themselves be unaware of or uninterested in the European dimension.

Having said this, the main task assigned to NGOs in the social OMC remains communication in the opposite direction, towards policy makers. Notwithstanding, this communication goes well beyond simple information and mediating constituencies' views. The NGOs involved in the OMC are 'social NGOs', i.e. their raison d'être is to lobby for public policies that pursue certain welfare objectives. Some of them are so-called 'thematic NGOs', concerned with specific social policy areas, such as supporting people with mental health problems, reducing child poverty, or helping microenterprises; others work more globally on poverty in general. Yet, all of them have as their functional logic the campaigning for specific policy orientations to all those actors who participate in defining relevant policies. For the social OMC, this includes, besides the Commission, mainly the national governments and, since the ratification of the Lisbon Treaty, also increasingly the European Parliament. Within and between these institutions there are subgroups whose views diverge, so that those concurring with the aims of particular NGOs have an incentive to cooperate with them or support their having an influence on the policies in question. In other words, when DG Employment promotes the involvement of social NGOs, they also open the process for organisations who advocate the boosting of social policies in general, and for whom the OMC is one opportunity structure to advance their views. A social NGO operating in Brussels can almost invariably be expected to call for EU action against poverty. The DG in turn promotes the stepping up of social policies in the EU. It thus not only receives information, but also assistance in the advancement of broad political goals. These

---

19. See also the study by Alex Warleigh (Warleigh 2001) and the criticism in Smismans 2003: 493.

alliances can work and be used in many different configurations, reflecting the variety of actors involved in the OMC and the methods of policy making.

Since the OMC's logic is to impact on national social policies, the Member States are obvious objects of the DG's attempts at persuasion. In addition to influencing them directly, the DG also works with NGOs that pursue similar policies. A policy officer in the DG explained this strategy in the following way while drawing the sketch reproduced in Figure 7.1:

> With the social OMC, we do not build an autonomous process, but we [seek] to influence the policies in the Member States. This can be done only on the condition that we get influence on the different actors. […] I'm here [the Commission] and I want this actor [a Member State] to have a certain view here. I can try to influence him directly, but I can also try to get an influence on *this* actor, on a side actor [a stakeholder], so that they [the Commission and the stakeholder] become partners in the influence of *this* [the Member State]. And that's the reality of potential partnerships in the countries. (Interview no. 8)

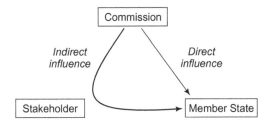

Figure 7.1: Indirect influence via functional representatives (from Interview no. 8)

This strategy is most effective if the DG supports the NGOs in their activities in the Member States, for example by insisting on their involvement in national OMC-related policy making. The rationale is as follows. In the framework of the OMC, the Member States have agreed to common objectives such as making 'a decisive impact on the eradication of poverty and social exclusion', and the Commission acts as 'the guardian of the objectives' (Interview no. 8), as it were. Many social NGOs work towards the same aim (though not necessarily with a similar philosophy and approach to the policies carried out under the OMC), and thus lobby governments to take action in order to decrease poverty. References to commitments signed on the European level can be used as an instrument in this advocacy work, and vice versa the DG benefits from the NGOs making use of that instrument, because this strengthens the OMC role in social policies. They thus have a strong incentive not only to promote the role of social NGOs in general, but to engage them specifically in the *European* framework of social policies. Accordingly, the DG actively offers the OMC as a tool for NGOs: 'And you will find my door wide open in terms of support to you in translating the new EU competencies in [...] combating social exclusion into action on the ground' (European Commission 2000a). What is more, DG Employment works towards both sides – the Member States and the NGOs – to increase the impact of this strategy:

> It seems to me extremely important when preparing these action plans, and *we will tell the Member States* this very clearly, that all relevant players should be involved. This includes the social partners and non-governmental organisations. Since the Member States are going to be implementing these national plans *I can only encourage you as the NGO sector to lobby your governments* and to make them aware of your concerns and the way in which you would like to see disabled people included, and social exclusion avoided. I think this is an extremely important *tool for developing community action* that makes it possible to include disabled people in social and economic life.[20]

Alliances with functional representatives also work between different parts of the Commission itself, vertically as well as horizontally. Vertically, the two units managing the social OMC (until the end of 2010: E/2 and E/4) may avail themselves of the NGOs' influence in order to advance their initiatives *vis-à-vis* the DG's or the Commission's internal hierarchy. Since the advancement of projects also depends on other policies and other units' or DGs' priorities, the individual units are, as it were, lobbying for their initiatives within their own organisation, and find themselves on the same side as NGOs sharing similar policy priorities:

> [Involving functional associations] helps a lot because, truly speaking, sometimes we contact them in order to lobby for issues that, when we requested them from the hierarchy, they did not receive a favourable follow-up, [...] while, you know, when there is NGO pressure, it seems that the hierarchy responds more favourably. You know, it's [...] a fact. (Interview no. 7)

Horizontally, NGOs help feeding the policies of one unit, directorate, or DG into policies defined elsewhere in the Commission. In its strongest version, this is called 'mainstreaming', meaning the systematic consideration of certain issues, such as poverty or non-discrimination, in all Commission policies. Mainstreaming is essentially based on the logic that reducing poverty also requires the use of policy tools that are held by DGs other than DG Employment. However, this horizontal spreading of ideas presupposes that different units know what others are doing, and to achieve this, policy officers and functional representatives work together:

---

20. Director-General Quintin, quoted in European Commission (2000) *Combating Discrimination Against Disabled People in the Labour Market*, conference report. Online. Available http:// ec.europa.eu/employment_social/disability/combat_en.pdf, accessed 17 October 2008. Emphases added.

[T]hey use me, and I use them, most of the time explicitly, I would say. It's a kind of alliance, so that when DG Markt [Internal Market and Services] or DG Sanco [Health and Consumers] works on a topic which is very much of importance for social inclusion, they take into consideration these [social OMC] objectives or the needs of […] those consumers who are not average consumers but the third or the fifth of the European population which is more fragile. (Interview no. 8)

All these three strategies mean that certain DG services and certain NGOs form networks of people concerned with the same matters and having common or similar understandings of them. From this perspective, it becomes impossible to distinguish between 'good' democratic input and 'bad' lobbying. Also, the argument that functional representation improves output legitimacy appears in a new light. It can well be asked from whose point of view political output improves, or what kinds of outputs are advanced, when NGOs are involved in policy making. What is more, the borderline between public administrations and non-governmental actors is relativised, in the sense that 'there are inside the Commission some actors who try to develop things, and outside some actors who try to develop things' (Interview no. 8). In other words, if actors developing similar 'things' on either side of the institutional walls work together, the result is a win-win situation. Consequently, both parties also support each other's political leverage. The DG promotes the involvement of stakeholders in all social policies and gives a place to major NGO campaigns in its publications, and European NGOs, for their part, lobby for a higher priority of social policies in general and a strengthening of EU competences in them. The DG even occasionally quotes NGO representatives to underpin the argument for involving them:

For PROGRESS to be [a] success, partnership must extend to social partners and non-governmental organisations (NGOs). Their input is essential, according to Roshan di Puppo, Director of the Social Platform, who said: 'If you don't have mobilised actors, you can't fulfil goals. We need to figure out if we have identified the right actors to move forward. This is where we need to reach out and look at the composition. Are there NGOs? Are there trade unions?'.[21]

Utilising lobbying capacities of NGOs in these ways implies that the organisations participating in such strategies are politically in line with the respective units' views and have compatible interests. Indeed, many of the principal NGOs active in the social OMC also see themselves as DG Employment's partners in spirit:

---

21. European Commission (2008) 'Strategic framework working group: third meeting'. Online. Available http://ec.europa.eu/employment_social/progress/framework3_en.htm, accessed 28 November 2008.

> [W]ithin every system, every government, within the Commission, there are people who are struggling to achieve the things we want to achieve. And so we try to be allies to them, to make their jobs easier and more effective. And overall, then, DG Employment fits that description. And the Inclusion Unit even more so. (Interview no. 2)

This view is a perfect match for the DG officer's statement quoted above, that

> there is no on one side the European institutions and on the other side the European NGOs [...]. The sociological aspect is that there are inside the Commission some actors who try to develop things, and outside some actors who try to develop things. (Interview no. 8)

Engaging successfully in these activities requires a number of *competences* on the part of the NGOs, in particular the capacity to utilise the OMC 'infrastructure' efficiently to influence policies. This implies two skills: being acquainted with the OMC procedures and being able to lobby professionally.

Knowing the procedures of the OMC is essential to address one's views to the right person at the right time in the right way. This starts with being acquainted with the roles and competences of the different political institutions involved and timing one's interventions according to their schedules:

> To interact in the appropriate way, this means not only to present the issue, which is the legitimate task or work of the network, but also to do it in the appropriate timing with the appropriate language [...] because the social OMC [...] is a process with [...] defined steps during the year or during a cycle, [...] which is three years. And so [...] if there is a way to really prioritise [...] a specific issue [...] then if there is a clear message that the NGOs can provide in the right moment when the Member States start discussing on it, then it can be much more fruitful – effective – as an input, rather than presenting these issues [...] in other moments. (Interview no. 6)

Thus, practical conditions mean that input from functional representatives has different chances to influence outcomes at different policy-making stages. Choosing the best moment requires following OMC politics closely and having insider information about current affairs. The second key capacity demanded from NGOs seeking a central role in the OMC is experienced lobbying. This includes the ability to present their messages in an effective manner, for example by using the language of the OMC governance network. In this way, the message is smoothly inserted into the ongoing discourse and recognised as a part of it.

It is these competences that distinguish more substantial influence from mere information giving. Although the DG does need both, there is a clear qualitative difference between their relations with NGOs that have these capacities and with those that do not:

[T]he main difference is really that people from the Social Platform and these organisations which are within the Social Platform are really Brussels insiders – seasoned Brussels insiders of the European institutions – while people from organisations which don't have this affiliation – […] the really big ones, big international ones – have some understanding of what is Commission, what is Council, what is Parliament, but they are making an effort – tendential, I mean […]. And you could say grassroots – small grassroots, local or national ones – may not be very knowledgeable about these systems here at all, so they may be more idealistic, but also more naïve about […] what they propose. (Interview no. 4)

All European networks are not necessarily advocacy groups to the European institutions, and why not? But of course if they are not aware of the European agenda, if they do not [seek] to have an influence on it, they can nevertheless be interesting for us; they can give us information about their members, about the situation in the different countries and so on, but it will not be the same type of interaction. (Interview no. 8)

Thus, the capacity to push for policies effectively in the OMC environment is key to building closer relations with the DG. Although the DG also has contacts with NGOs that do not have these competences and seeks to build their governance networks as broadly as possible, they clearly express the need for an inner circle of associations that play a stronger role and are capable of 'making a difference' and 'influenc[ing] policy in the European Union and in the Member states [*sic*] through their national members' (European Commission 2010b). This influence includes both raising awareness of European social policies on the ground and promoting certain policies to other policy makers.

All this means that the ideal role that the DG outlines for NGOs in the OMC goes well beyond being able to provide relevant input in the form of information or advocacy, important as that is. The closest insiders are to form a qualitatively different 'partnership' with the Commission and are not seen as external influence groups but as an integral part of the OMC governance community. In the DG's vision, they work hand in hand with it to achieve the OMC's political aims. In other words, these NGOs are not described as using their lobbying power *towards* the DG but in a common effort *with* them. This is the core of the 'partnership approach'[22] that the DG is promoting for the OMC. This partnership approach is based on the already familiar idea that

[g]overnments *cannot* deliver sustainable development and ambitious strategies alone. Business, workers and civil society *must* be involved at *every* stage – from formulation to implementation and delivery. And at *every* level: European, national, regional and local.[23]

22. European Commission press release SPEECH/02/122 of 21 March 2002.
23. European Commission press release SPEECH/01/173 of 22 March 2001.

In other words, in order to arrive at the outcomes desired by public administrations, 'all relevant actors' have to 'work together'. At the European level, this means in the first place DG Employment and NGOs. Their ideal relationship is described as follows:

> At European level, the growth of NGOs has led to *constructive*, organised partnerships with institutions rather than confrontation. The [Social] Platform's meeting here represents a further step in developing *synergies* and partnerships with political decision-makers and I am happy to be part of it. (EC SPEECH/01/173; emphases added)[24]

The Social Platform is an umbrella organisation of a good forty European networks of social NGOs, including all those in close cooperation with the Commission. The DG's aim in this relationship is here depicted as 'developing synergies', i.e. through joining forces, both parties together can achieve results that could not have been arrived at by each working separately. The tacit presumption that gives sense to this expression is that both parties are *already* working in parallel for similar goals, otherwise their combined action would not lead to increased achievements. The way that this synergy is meant to be generated is through 'constructive, organised partnerships' as contrasted with 'confrontation'. Hence, the DG does not wish to see NGOs oppose their policies, but to 'contribute helpfully'.[25] NGOs are expected not only to advance their own objectives, but to build up (construct) something together with the other involved actors. The OMC is not (only) a forum where everyone interested in social policies is invited to give their views, but a joint undertaking meant to arrive at results: '[T]he social policy agenda is based on building partnerships, which boils down to involvement of all actors and a *focus on delivery*' (European Commission 2003b; emphasis added). This logic works only if the partners agree on the aims to be pursued as well as on the broad approaches to go about realising them through.

In the DG's text, that agreement is implied to exist, but never addressed explicitly. The political objectives themselves are formulated in ways general enough for a universal audience of 'every rational being' to agree, such as 'a modern social policy which accompanies social and economic changes'[26] or 'tackle child-poverty'.[27] Having said that, the DG is of course referring to the Common Objectives as adopted by the Member States, which form the fundaments of the OMC, and which are rather general. The specific ways of realising these shared objectives are up to the Member States, and the OMC is depicted as a process to find the best political techniques for doing this. This involves setting priorities concerning areas of political action and promoting particular policies that are perceived to be especially successful ('good practice'). However, there is no

---

24. The meeting referred to here is one of the regular bi-annual meetings of the Social Platform with DG Employment.

25. *Oxford English Dictionary Online*, 'constructive, adj.', accessed 30 November 2010, http://www.oed.com/view/Entry/39904?redirectedFrom=constructive#eid.

26. European Commission press release SPEECH/05/749 of 1 December 2005.

27. European Commission press release IP/09/360 of 5 March 2009.

allusion to the possibility that different actors might have different understandings of the aims themselves or of the global approach that should be taken towards them. In the DG's text, finding successful problem solutions is a matter of information, knowledge, and political will, not of interests or ideological orientations. Thus, NGOs are involved in 'arena[s] for exchanging knowledge, experience and good practice, making commitments for initiatives and [...] monitoring progress achieved'.[28] Specific alternative measures or approaches to realise the OMC's objectives are not discussed in the same context as the involvement of functional representatives; rather, this involvement itself is presented as a means to achieve the desired outputs. So how does the DG characterise the NGOs' role in these partnerships?

When the DG speaks about 'partnerships' between those involved in OMC policies, the central objective of these is building *consensus*: 'Strengthening partnerships with key EU and national policy-/decision-makers and stakeholders will contribute to building consensus and creating momentum for change in support of EU objectives and priorities' (European Commission 2010a: 28).[29] However, the consensus referred to here is not one that is expected to be built between the partners themselves, but more broadly in society: 'Stronger partnerships are expected to exert influence and motivate change in support of EU law and policy objectives by increasing their visibility and prominence on the political agenda' (2010a: 28). In other words, it is assumed that the partners themselves already endorse the European policy objectives, and that by working together they can also convince other actors of these objectives. It is remarkable that the DG speaks of a 'consensus *in support of* EU objectives', i.e. the text does not refer to EU objectives as the *outcome* of a process of consensus finding, but seeks to build consensus for the objectives that are already there. This consensus is meant to 'create momentum for change' or 'motivate change', i.e. the underlying idea is that consensus is a necessary condition for desired changes to happen. In short, only if everybody in society works together, in consensus, can the social situation be changed. Arriving at this consensus is also a responsibility of the participating NGOs:

> But partnership is not an innocuous or theoretic term. It requires everybody to contribute. In a good partnership, the individual has responsibilities as well as rights. It is here that you must also make a contribution today. Building bridges requires work from both sides. The civil society has to participate actively. Not only to advance this or that idea, but also to act on the ground. Without the capacity to build shared consensuses about the necessary reforms, it is difficult to have durable success.[30]

---

28. European Commission (2009) '2nd meeting of the integrated platform on Roma inclusion'. Online. Available http://ec.europa.eu/social/main.jsp?catId_88&langId=en&eventsId=206&furt herEvents=yes, accessed 7 September 2009.

29. The cited phrase features in most strategic documents of the Progress programme and also of the DG in general.

30. European Commission (2005) speech by Commissioner Špidla, 7 November 2005. Online. Available http://ec.europa.eu/employment_social/speeches/2005/vs_051107_fr.pdf, accessed 22 July 2008. Author translation.

This specific passage, or parts of it, was used in at least five speeches by Commissioner Špidla and Director-General Quintin in October/November 2005, speaking to very diverse audiences. In addition, the argument presented here is put forward in a great number of other texts. It is worth looking at this excerpt in some detail, because it summarises one of the key ideas of functional representation in the social OMC. The central proposition here is that (organised) 'civil society has to participate actively', also by 'acting on the ground'. This is based on two premises. The first defines 'partnership' as a *symmetric* relationship. There is symmetry between the partners in the sense that all have to contribute, and also between the different characteristics of each individual party: each has responsibilities as well as rights, i.e. each is characterised by complementary attributes, one of which cannot be held without the other. The familiarity of the responsibilities-cum-rights topos supports this condition. As well as that, the bridge metaphor makes it seem obvious that 'work from both sides' is needed, leading directly to the proposition that the audience – civil society organisations – have to do something too. The symmetry between the parties in the partnership also appeals to notions of fairness: it feels just that both cannot only demand things but also have to contribute something. Briefly, the argument is constructed in such a way to make the proposition appear self-evident. The underlying implication here is that NGOs would otherwise prefer to have only rights ('to advance this or that idea'), instead of also doing their share of work. Next, this share of work, assigned to the NGOs, is described as 'acting on the ground'. What this means in practice becomes accessible only through what follows: 'Without the capacity to build shared consensuses about the necessary reforms, it is difficult to have durable success'.

This assertion is the second premise supporting the proposition that NGOs should 'participate actively': their contribution is prerequisite in order to have 'durable success' concerning 'necessary reforms'. In other words, the required NGO activities are means to achieve a goal. 'Reforms' refers to different areas of social policy in different speeches, but they are not singled out in detail. Yet, they are defined as 'necessary'. The civil society organisations are asked to 'act on the ground' in order to build a consensus about these reforms. Their own support is already implied, so that the necessity of the reforms itself does not need to be justified. This technique not only excludes those from the envisaged partnership who disagree with or wish to discuss that necessity, but also avoids drawing attention to the substance of the reforms (cf. Perelman and Olbrechts-Tyteca 1969: 144). In brief, the political objectives themselves are not opened to discussion but presented as self-evident, and what is at stake is their realisation, which is constructed as a shared goal by the DG and the addressed NGOs. It is on this basis that the audience is to be convinced to enter into a division of labour with the DG and employ their own capacities in the service of a joint purpose. 'Acting on the ground' is something that is difficult or impossible for the DG to do themselves, but nonetheless essential to achieve the goal that is implicitly taken as agreed by all partners. In accordance with the logic set by the definition of a partnership as requiring everybody's contribution, this responsibility is therefore assigned to the NGOs.

But what does 'acting on the ground' and 'building a consensus' mean in practice? The immediate context of the passage does not dwell on this, but on the basis of other texts it becomes clear that NGOs are meant to use their specific capacities to win support for the social OMC's objectives. This includes mainly three things.

Firstly, as already noted above, they are expected to relay the European reform process via their member organisations to other societal actors, including organisations as well as individuals, making them active participants in the process and through this, winning their support: 'Creating the political space and legitimacy necessary for building inclusive policies requires building awareness and consensus among a broad range of actors. This is greatly facilitated by involving them in the policy process'.[31] The argument is based on the aforementioned notion of functional representatives as two-way channels of communication: they can inform others of the processes going on at the EU level, and through their own participative structures offer opportunities to get involved and thus be represented in these processes. Interestingly, the cited argument is presented as a 'legitimacy argument' for the involvement of stakeholders. Thus, the 'legitimacy' of a political goal is here not understood in the sense of something the presence of which impacts on whether or not the policy in question should be realised. Rather, legitimacy is here something malleable that needs to be *created* in order to realise intended policies. Building on the notion of NGOs as participative organisations close to the citizens, the idea is that they can engage their suborganisations and individual people in the common cause, and that this engagement generates ownership and therefore support, because 'participation breeds commitment' (European Commission 2008c), both on the level of individuals and organisations. 'Participation', however, is here understood as getting involved in an existing project, becoming part of something that is already ongoing, rather than participating in the design of the project itself. The mechanism by which participation is supposed to lead to support is nowhere explained. Instead, NGOs are perceived as a pool of potential supporters that need to be 'empowered' and 'activated' in order to be able to play their role as allies, and that offering them partnerships, i.e. access, will in response generate support from their side:

> PROGRESS aims to empower partners to have effective impact. Technical adviser Mark Schacter said [in the third meeting of the Strategic Framework group]: 'Partnerships gain support and activate groups of stakeholders who can in turn support objectives of PROGRESS'.[32]

---

31. Background paper for workshop 2a in the European Commission conference 'Learning Together' – Lessons Drawn from the Community Action Programme to Combat Social Exclusion, 29–30 March 2006. Online. Available http://ec.europa.eu/social/BlobServlet?docId=358&langId=en, accessed 19 December 2008.

32. European Commission (2008) 'Strategic framework working group: third meeting'. Online. Available http://ec.europa.eu/employment_social/progress/framework3_en.htm, accessed 28 November 2008. The quoted technical adviser is an external consultant.

NGOs are thus assumed to support political processes they are involved in, but they may not be aware enough to get involved by themselves. On this note, support can be seen as a return for giving access.

Secondly, the NGOs' 'advocacy role is at the centre of changing public attitudes and in combating prejudice' (European Commission 2000a). They should thus 'contribut[e] [...] to promoting a fairer and more inclusive society' (European Commission 2003b) in the frame of their role as public deliberators, i.e. communicate not only with their own particular constituencies but also with society at large. This corresponds to a deliberative understanding of representative democracy, where the people's views can change in interaction, and representatives and the represented communicate with and try to convince each other. Notwithstanding, the emphasis in the envisaged communication with the citizens is clearly on the top-down path. Its aim is to convince citizens of the DG's points of view – which are seen as identical to those of the addressed NGOs – rather than to mediate the citizens' views to the DG. This influence on public opinion also works indirectly towards the Member States' governments, since the NGOs' participation is expected to 'enhance [the] visibility' of the process, 'encourage ambition in objective setting and increase the focus on policy implementation',[33] in other words pressure the Member States to deliver on social policies.

Finally, NGOs should adopt the Commission's network-governance approach and cooperate with other involved organisations horizontally as well as vertically:

> Across the EU there are thousands of different organisations doing excellent work. But, to be successful partners, civil society must [...] develop lasting partnerships and networks with all actors. It must coordinate efforts at local, regional, national and European level. (European Commission 2003c)

This includes, for example, 'extend[ing] their networks and contacts with each other' and also 'co-operat[ing] with the social partners and develop[ing] together initiatives on issues of common concern' (European Commission 2003b). This presupposes that the addressed NGOs in the social sector (as well as the social partners, in the latter case) have common views and objectives, and are similarly interested in working within the frame of the social OMC. At the same time, the appeal to network with others in the field encourages those NGOs already participating (and therefore receiving the message) to involve others too.

To sum up so far, the role assigned to NGOs in the social OMC is based on the 'working together' topos, i.e. the idea that objectives can only be or can be better achieved if everybody pulls together and contributes their particular resources to the common purpose: '[W]e all have a part to play in tackling social exclusion and poverty, and [...] real progress requires a long-term commitment from all actors and levels of policy-making'.[34] This in turn means that NGOs

---

33. European Commission Communication COM(2005)706 of 22 December 2005.

34. European Commission (2008) 'What social Europe can do for you'. Online. Available http://ec.europa.eu/employment_social/publications/booklets/general/pdf/ke0008001_en.pdf, accessed 23 September 2008.

carry a part of the responsibility for the achievement of those objectives; working together is not an end in itself but a means to arrive at an outcome. The envisaged partnership is a partnership *for* something, namely a 'partnership for change and modernisation'.[35] It thus requires that the NGOs 'commit themselves to delivering concrete results – for example in the framework of the European strategy against exclusion' (European Commission 2003b). Committing oneself means pledging oneself to a course of action,[36] for example by making a promise in such a way that it is very difficult to change one's plans, or by binding oneself in practice, so that alternative actions become impossible. The very frequent use of the term 'commitment' illustrates the extent to which NGOs are seen to become *part* of the OMC policies – integrated actors rather than external influences. This logic is premised on the implication that the involved NGOs share the objectives of the OMC, i.e. that those objectives are also their own. On a very general level, this is indeed the case: reducing poverty and social exclusion is the proclaimed *raison d'être* of the social OMC as well as the NGOs invited to enter into a partnership with the DG. In the DG's text, this serves as such as the basis for working together. Concretely, the collaboration refers particularly to activities seeking to convince third actors of the envisaged policies. 'Working together' is thus presented as a technique to solve given problems or achieve given aims. It refers both to the cooperation between DG Employment and social NGOs and to a broader societal consensus that involves as broad a range of organisations and individual citizens as possible. The former cooperation is to an important extent meant to bring about the latter. 'Working together' is instrumental to and necessary for political output.

The ideal presented here is one of a society where everybody participates in a joint effort to realise a shared vision. This includes not only providing input into policy-making processes, but also a positive view of non-state actors and individuals providing or contributing to welfare services. Based on the concept of symmetry, the functional difference between public officers and NGO representatives is here reduced to a mere labour division where each actor does what she is best at and provides her specific resources. *Politically*, the two no longer belong to clearly different societal sectors in the sense that one represents the political system and the other the civil society interacting with the former but remaining a separate sphere with a certain distance. When comparing the Commission's network-governance model to Easton's classical simplified model of a political system (Easton 1965: 32; *see* p.12 of this work), the question of whether to locate a functional organisation more on the inside or on the outside of the box called 'the political system' is here not only a question of societal function, but also one of political orientations. In other words, how far an NGO is seen as an integrated part of the political system depends not in the least on how much they agree politically or ideologically with the public administration. Those NGOs with

---

35. European Commission press release SPEECH/05/58 of 31 January 2005. Emphasis omitted; author translation.

36. *Oxford English Dictionary Online*, 'commit, v.' (draft additions January 2002), accessed 30 November 2010, http://www.oed.com/view/Entry/37160?redirectedFrom=commit#eid.

which DG Employment seeks to work in partnership are not seen as an external influence, a counter-democratic force, or a critical corrective, but as functional parts of an integrated societal project. I will come back to the NGOs' tasks in the social OMC in the next chapter about the financing of NGOs through the OMC's financial programmes, SEP and Progress. Before that, the present chapter is concluded with a brief look at the role the DG gives itself in its partnerships.

DG Employment: catalyst or partner?

If the role of functional representatives is seen as carrying the OMC process to the citizens and raising support for its objectives, the DG's role is described as being the 'guardian of the objectives' (Interview no. 8), who on the basis of the Common Objectives as approved by the European Council points the Member States in the right direction. For one thing, this means reminding the latter of the goals they have subscribed to and pushing them to achieve progress. Thus, the DG 'encourages EU countries to examine their policies critically, and highlights how some perform well in certain areas, spurring others to perform better'.[37] For another thing, the Commission also interprets these objectives by framing the main goals, prioritising issues, and raising new ones to the agenda. Overall, the DG sees itself as 'a *catalyst* for reform, a *facilitator* and *broker* between the main governmental and non-governmental bodies and between public and private actors'.[38] All these three terms refer to a more or less impartial actor, who advances the interaction between other agents in order to bring about a certain shared result, without herself being a party to that result. The DG's role is thus described as one of bringing those parties together that need to cooperate if political goals are to be attained; it seeks 'to *help* guide EU countries in their strategies to tackle poverty'.[39] It leads the Member States and other involved actors on the right track by pointing to political goals and problems, by commissioning and issuing information about these and possible solutions, and by prompting the countries to cooperate and coordinating this cooperation. At the same time, it stresses that it is the national governments that have to do the actual work. They remain sovereign in their decisions concerning the implementation of reforms, yet the necessity and general direction of those reforms themselves are stated as a fact that serves as the starting point – not the object – of argumentation:

---

37. European Commission (no date) 'Poverty and social exclusion'. Online. Available http://ec.europa.eu/social/main.jsp?langId=en&catId=751, accessed 9 September 2010.

38. European Commission (2008) discussion paper for working group 3 at the Commission conference Responding to New Social Realities: Towards a European Agenda for Opportunities, Access and Solidarity, 5–6 May 2008. Online. Available http://ec.europa.eu/employment_social/empl-web/social_agenda/documents/library/wg_3_en.pdf, accessed 30 September 2008. Emphases added.

39. European Commission (2008) 'EU boosts national efforts to fight poverty and social exclusion'. Online. Available http://ec.europa.eu/social/main.jsp?catId=437&langId=en&newsId=401&furtherNews=yes, accessed 14 September 2010. Emphasis added.

EU countries have to adapt and modernise their socio-economic model. Each will have to choose how they do it based on their level of prosperity, their traditions, and policy choices. The EU has an important role in helping governments, who are the main actors of change, by supporting, accompanying and coordinating their efforts to reshape their employment and social policies. [...] Member States have the main responsibility for employment and social policy. The EU's role is to be a catalyst for change and modernisation. (European Communities 2007b; emphasis added)

The DG thus presents itself as an actor, who knows what has to be done, and animates those who possess the means to do what is right. Its role is presented in as neutral terms as possible. In the same vein, the DG (or the Commission, in whose name the DG acts) often refers to itself and the OMC with terms such as 'the EU' and 'the process'. In identifying itself with 'the EU', the Commission reduces complexity for the reader, but simultaneously obscures responsibilities and invokes an opposition between 'the EU' and 'the Member States'. Overall, when the DG speaks about its own role, the stress is less on the substantial goals than on fostering coordination, on 'rally[ing] the Member States and all the other stakeholders in Social Europe, and get[ting] them involved in a common project'.[40]

Functional representation is an integral part of this coordinative role. The DG not only promotes cooperation between national administrations, but – equally importantly – 'the EU can help by fostering partnership between trade unions, the business community, research institutes, health organisations and local and regional authorities. And, above all, between representatives of civil society' (European Commission 2003c). Crucially, involving NGOs, supporting cooperation among them, and promoting their role in policy making plays a double role: for one thing, functional representation serves to legitimate the DG's guiding role in the OMC; for another thing, it also functions as an important instrument of these steering activities.

Regarding the former, the DG builds its *legitimacy* as a facilitator who can guide others on the claim to represent the common interest of the Union (the role given to it in the treaties), thus standing outside the particular national interests; from this relatively neutral position, it finds out what is best for all by listening to all those affected. Through the involvement of NGOs, the DG has a connection to 'the ground', and its policies become not only representative of the affected, but also efficient problem solving. Accordingly, upon the publication of each major initiative, DG Employment emphasises the broad consultations among 'a wide range of stakeholders'[41] upon which the proposal is based.

---

40. European Commission press release SPEECH/08/223 of 5 May 2008.

41. E.g. European Commission (2000) speech by Director-General Quintin, 14 March 2000. Online. Available http://ec.europa.eu/employment_social/speeches/2000/000314oq_en.pdf, accessed 20 October 2008.

In cooperating with NGOs, the DG lays great emphasis on its openness towards these organisations. The involvement of NGOs in the social OMC is visibly present on the OMC-related websites, and the officials working in this area consistently stress their willingness to talk to potential actors in the field. Together with the former Directorate G (Equality between Men and Women, Action against Discrimination, Civil Society), the former Directorate E (Social Protection and Integration) is one of the places within the entire Commission that is most open to NGO representatives and considers the cooperation with them as part of their everyday work.

This openness is frequently expressed as the willingness to *listen* – indeed, the recognition of a normative necessity to listen – to what the representatives of affected groups have to say:

> I am delighted to be here. For the European Commission, taking part in a regular exchange of views with an organisation like EURAG [European Federation of Older People] is essential. Over the last few decades, older citizens have come to represent an important sector of the non-governmental scene, as well as a real political constituency in their own right. I look forward to listening to your views and experiences.[42]

> We need, all of us, to listen, to understand and to respond. We need to diversify the political dialogue. That means we need to find new vehicles through which to communicate. A significant part of this must be to help to develop the capacity and the voice of the constituencies that gather around the voluntary ethos, on the basis of specific issues, political principles or basic solidarity. That, of course, means you. Your role in promoting and representing the views of specific groups of citizens to European institutions means that you bring a particular credibility to the table. (European Commission 2000a)

What is more, when addressing NGOs, as in the above two quotations, the DG also expresses its intention not only to listen, but also to 'understand' and to 'exchange [...] views' and 'respond', i.e. to have a dialogue with NGOs rather than simply receiving input. It is this willingness to listen in order to take all views into account that legitimises the DG's position as facilitator, because it enables it to propose solutions that are in the common European interest.

Regarding the second purpose of involving NGOs – their use as *instruments* in the steering of policies – I have shown above how strategic partnerships are meant to work in order to pursue shared goals. Importantly, the legitimising function of functional representation is also used to support this strategic dimension, namely when DG Employment actively promotes the involvement of NGOs more broadly,

---

42. European Commission press release SPEECH/05/565 of 30 September 2005.

also *vis-à-vis* other actors. Such promotion is justified with the same normative values that are used to argue that involving NGOs makes the DG's policies more legitimate:

> The European institutions need to be clearer about the immense value of the voluntary and NGO sector in the process of social and economic integration, within and across the Member States. I can assure you that I understand and acknowledge that value. [...] We need to create the conditions, the structures, the climate and the opportunity for *citizens to have a greater say* in their governance, in the management of change, at all levels. (EC 2000a; emphasis added)

Furthering the leverage of functional organisations in general can well be seen as part of a symmetric partnership, in reciprocity to the DG's expectation that these organisations for their part further the popularity of the OMC among their constituencies. Advancing the NGOs' role includes taking a certain responsibility for their financial resources, since many of them depend on grants or other payments from the Commission:

> But you must be equipped to play your full part. That means responsibilities for the European institutions. It also means your obligations, your own capacity and willingness to participate, as representatives of a coherent civil dialogue and as high quality service providers. Some of the task of building your capacity to play a stronger part in the European policy process is about the institutions supporting you more effectively. That means more efficient payments for social and employment policy action. I can assure you that I am addressing this with the urgency it demands. It means ensuring that your contribution is encouraged and welcomed in new programmes. (EC 2000a)

As well as that, promoting the influence of NGOs also includes pressing the Member States to involve them more and better, and adopt a network culture of governance themselves. This is done regularly, for example in the DG's evaluations of the OMC and the National Action Plans. In 2008, this evaluation states under the heading 'Weaknesses in the Open Method of Coordination':

– Participation of stakeholders leaves a lot to be desired

> The involvement of stakeholders in the policy process is both a question of democracy and a pre-condition for the efficiency and effectiveness of policies. However, this [is] only rarely internalised in national decision making processes, and a culture of partnership and cooperation is often at an embryonic stage. Although progress has been made in recent years, there is still a lack of transparency and openness of the Social OMC process, also linked to its limited visibility. Much more attention needs to be given to the quality of stakeholder participation, which needs to be both supported

(capacity building) and sustained. Today, it is often limited to the first stages of the policy process (information, consultation). Stakeholders are less involved in policy implementation, monitoring and evaluation, and often receive no feedback on the impact of their input.[43]

Contrarily to many other texts justifying the promotion of functional representation in the social OMC, appeals to the Member States to involve NGOs more do not contain references to their role in 'supporting the process' or 'building consensus', but put the focus on gathering input in an open and democratic way and designing responsive policies. The DG seems to expect that functional representation as such is beneficial to bringing the OMC forward nationally, which raises some questions when considered in the context of the DG's own ways of selecting partners who bring together national NGOs. More to the point, notwithstanding the fact that DG Employment demands ambitious standards concerning functional representation in the Member States, when it comes to the 'quality of participation' at the DG itself, it is difficult to find any concrete commitments from their side.

---

43. European Commission staff working document SEC(2008)2169 of 2 July 2008.

Chapter Eight

The Key European Networks

In this chapter and the following one, I look at two instances of functional representation in the social OMC that are exceptional for different reasons. The first case is the so-called 'Key European Networks', i.e. EU-level networks of social NGOs that receive core funding for their running costs from DG Employment through Progress, the OMC's financial programme (p.97). In the subsequent chapter, I examine how DG Employment justifies the funding of these organisations, how they see their role between financial dependency and influencing policies, and how the role of these organisations differs from others that do not receive this form of funding.

The second special case is the descriptive representation of the poor, i.e. the representation of poor people by poor representatives on the European level, which the DG has been actively promoting. In Chapter Nine, I analyse how this form of representation is related to other ways of representing 'people experiencing poverty', i.e. what its specific function is, and how representation is seen to work here.

DG Employment has a long history of financially supporting social NGOs, i.e. NGOs representing those especially affected by social problems and policies (*see* pages 96–99). The social OMC has set this funding on a sound legal basis through the Social Exclusion Programme (SEP) (2002–6) and Progress (2007–13), the latter of which gathered existing funding in the areas of social exclusion, social protection, employment, working conditions, non-discrimination, and gender equality into strands of one programme. There are two clearly distinct forms of financial support for functional representatives in the social sector, namely project funding and core funding. The former is meant to finance specified and limited activities and can be accorded to European, national, or subnational organisations, not necessarily non-governmental ones or representatives. Core funding, by contrast, is restricted to European networks of functional representatives – so-called *Key European Networks* – and finances a share of these associations' running costs, i.e. contributes to the basic budget for their day-to-day activities and expenses.[1] Funded networks have to be made up of national member organisations covering at least fifteen EU Member States (before 2008: at least twelve Member States). They must be non-governmental, not-for-profit, and independent of commercial interests, and their main purpose has to be in line with the goals of the social OMC. Concerning their internal structure, the European-level network must be authorised by and accountable to

---

1.   *See* Table 5.1 p.97 for a list of the organisations funded during 2002–2013.

a board or a similar body representing the national member organisations, and it needs to have a sound administration, also in terms of its staff's professionalism (European Commission 2010b; cf. 2007b; 2006a; 2005a; 2002a). Under the SEP, up to 90 per cent of eligible expenditures were covered by these funds; for Progress, the limit was lowered to 80 per cent 'as a general rule'.[2] However, taking account of the previous level of financing and the 'pivotal position and expected contribution in support of EU objectives and priorities',[3] the Commission has implemented higher funding levels and applied a 'degressivity rule', i.e. support started at up to 86 per cent of expenditure in 2008 and has since been at one percentage point less each year, so that in 2011 it was up to 83 per cent (European Commission 2007b; 2010b).[4] In any event, DG Employment financially ensures the functioning – and thus in many cases the existence – of the very networks whose *raison d'être* it is to influence the policy made by this DG. Their *justifications* for this practice tell a lot about how they conceptualise the role of functional representation in policy making. I first analyse this argumentation in detail, and after that look at how the relationship between the DG and the funded associations works in practice.

A strategic partnership

The Strategic Framework of the Progress programme is structured strictly along a particular type of enthymeme known as practical inference. The basic pattern of this logic is the following: 'One wants to attain x. Unless y is done, x will not be attained. Therefore, y must be done' (von Wright 1963: 161). In Progress's strategy, this pattern is applied through five levels, namely ultimate outcome, intermediate outcomes, immediate outcomes, strategies corresponding to each immediate outcome, and activities to implement these strategies. There is one ultimate outcome, three intermediate outcomes, and five immediate outcomes with one to four strategies and activities each. Concerning the core funding of the Key European Networks, the main paths are as follows:

---

2. Decision No 1672/2006/EC of the European Parliament and of the Council of 24 October 2006. For the SEP, *see* European Commission 2002a; 2005a; 2006a.

3. European Commission Decision C(2009)143 of 23 January 2009.

4. According to the 'degressivity' rule, '[u]nless otherwise specified [...], when operating grants are renewed, they shall be gradually decreased' (Council regulation (EC, Euratom) No 1605/2002 of 25 June 2002, as amended by Council regulation (EC, Euratom) No 1995/2006 of 13 December 2006). In the Progress programme, the Commission and the funded NGOs sign Framework Partnership Agreements covering up to three years, but grants are fixed on an annual basis in separate agreements, i.e. renewed annually. In 2011, €10.3 million was budgeted for these funds, which amounts to 36.24 per cent of the expenses in the social protection and social inclusion section of Progress ('Progress Programme – annual financial envelope 2011 – operational expenditure', Annex to European Commission document PROGRESS/008/2010 of 24 November 2010).

Ultimate outcome:	To ensure that Member States implement laws, policies and practices in a manner that contributes to the desired outcomes of the Social Agenda.[5]

Intermediate outcomes:	Help positively change understanding and promote ownership of EU objectives and priorities among key EU and national policy/decision-makers and other stakeholders.	Help strengthen partnerships with key EU and national policy/decision-makers and stakeholders.

Immediate outcome:	Build greater capacity for national and pan-European networks to support, promote and further develop policies and objectives relating to PROGRESS policy areas.
Corresponding strategy:	Investing strategically in the capacity of key EU networks to participate and influence policy-making and policy implementation at EU and national level in support of EU objectives and priorities.
To that end, PROGRESS will support:	NGOs and networks active in PROGRESS policy areas.

(European Commission 2008a; layout adapted)

According to this strategy, the involvement of functional representatives is thus *necessary* in order to achieve desired *outcomes*. It is seen as such an important prerequisite for political output that it is justified to financially support organisations to fulfil this function. In the texts relating to this funding, the DG explicates in more detail how output legitimacy is supposed to result from functional representation. Their line of reasoning starts with arguments for the necessity of functional representation for social policy making *in general*, upon which the justifications for the need to *finance* such associations are built.

Some of these broader arguments substantiating the involvement of functional representatives in policy making have already been analysed in the previous chapters. However, in the present context of funding such organisations, they are presented from a slightly different perspective: the texts analysed before deal with the involvement of NGOs from the point of view of the *DG's* policies' legitimacy – here, it is proposed to spend common money on NGOs, so that one may expect argumentation on a more general level as to why it is *overall good* or *right* to involve them. Therefore, I first take a look at how this is substantiated in the specific logic of the SEP and Progress strategies, and then see how the bridge is built from there to funding functional associations' running costs.

---

5.   The desired outcome of the Social Agenda is '[m]ore & better jobs, & more cohesive societies that offer equal opportunities for all, in Member States' (European Commission 2008a: 8).

   The Social Agenda is DG Employment's political reference framework for the modernisation of social and employment policies in response to the challenges of economic and technological changes, globalisation and demographic ageing. *See* European Commission Communication COM(2008)412 of 2 July 2008.

One of the arguments that has already appeared in different contexts is that functional representation in policy making is necessary because NGOs, too, are *responsible* for the attainment of political goals: 'Delivering on the objectives agreed at European level is a joint responsibility between the Commission, the Member States and other relevant stakeholders, including social partners and civil society' (EC 20008a: 4). This reasoning is presented to underpin the intermediate outcome, 'help strengthen partnerships with key EU and national policy/decision makers and stakeholders'. It is thus another instance of the 'together' topos: if we are all responsible for achieving some joint objective, it is a matter of common sense to work together. In principle, this can be based either on concepts of fairness (everybody has to do their share) or on the expectation of a resulting win-win situation (synergies). As in previous contexts, both logics are evoked; yet, the Strategic Framework does not explicate the responsibility argument any further.

A line of reasoning specific to the justification of financing Key Networks draws on the *complexity* of the issues to be dealt with. This complexity is used to justify functional representation in two ways. The first connects to the previous argument: social policy issues are complex in the sense that they cover 'a wide range of policy areas such as employment, social protection, education and training, health and housing'.[6] Therefore, they require an 'integrated approach' that links these policies together, and 'experiences of Member States as well as of the Community [...] have [...] shown the importance of partnerships bringing together all those involved in these policies to ensure this integrated approach'.[7] Again, this is a pragmatic, common-sensical argument appealing also to the audience's own experiences with managing issues that involve many different parties. As well as that, the experiences of the Member States and the Commission are referred to as a supporting fact: involving stakeholders not only improves policy making in theory, but there is evidence of this effect.[8]

Secondly, complexity is also understood on a more abstract level, directly connecting to governance and participation literature: '[T]he growing complexity of governance and the expectations of stakeholders require a new approach based on public engagement principles' (European Commission 2008a). This 'requirement' is explained with several arguments:

> Public engagement can help policy and decision-makers and other stakeholders, and ultimately European citizens, understand the complex problems facing Europe and their implications, involve those who are normally excluded from policy debates, promote public dialogue and create momentum for change by building common ground, managing differences and creating new partnerships. (EC 2008a)

---

6. European Commission proposal COM(2000)368 of 16 June 2000.

7. *ibid.*

8. At the same time, it is worth noting that speaking of the 'multidimensional nature' of 'social exclusion' (instead of poverty, for example) also constructs the subject matter as a complex one and serves to integrate new policy areas into the process or 'mainstream' social exclusion policies in more and more sectors.

In other words, where issues are complicated and the affected demand to be heard, involving them is necessary in order to improve the flows of information between policy makers, the affected, and the public at large, including weaker groups, in order to achieve common understandings of political objectives, so that, ultimately, reforms can be carried through efficiently.

As already noted, functional representatives are meant to 'relay the views of stakeholders and society at large'.[9] Within the Progress strategy, these 'views' are essential inputs for policy making, which is justified with one of the programme's key principles, namely 'evidence-based' policy making. Progress is meant 'to ensure that EU policies and legislation are based on evidence and are relevant to the needs of, and challenges faced by, Member States'.[10] To achieve this, 'the Commission will collect information that is relevant, credible and accurate on what stakeholders need, expect and are concerned about and it will use statistical tools, methods and common indicators that can stand EU-wide support'.[11] Importantly, 'the evidence base for EU policies and legislation consists not only of hard facts and their analytical interpretation, but also comprises the opinion of the stakeholders, their needs and expectations' (European Commission 2010a: 53). Representation is thus here conceptualised as mediating *information* that is necessary for decision-making, in the same way as statistical indicators. It is therefore important that this information be collected at one point to be made useful for everybody, and that it be ensured to be 'relevant, credible and accurate' to fulfil its function as evidence. As the coordinator of the OMC, the Commission offers itself to take on this task, which thus includes managing relationships with functional representatives. From the strategic point of view, information about opinions and needs (together with other data) allows policy makers not only to learn and to 'understand the complex problems facing Europe and their implications' (European Commission 2008a), but also to 'take ownership of EU objectives and priorities', because

> positively changing the understanding of these parties [key EU and national policy- and decision-makers and stakeholders] will enable national policies to converge further towards those of the EU. [...] PROGRESS will seek to motivate these actions by collecting and analysing relevant and accurate evidence.[12]

In short, the information available through functional representation can serve as knowledge about how to reach political goals agreed at the EU level, such as 'more cohesive societies', and by involving functional associations, DG Employment makes this knowledge available to other actors, notably national

---

9. European Commission Decision C(2009)143 of 23 January 2009.

10. European Commission (no date) 'Immediate outcomes'. Online. Available http://ec.europa.eu/social/main.jsp?catId=663&langId=en, accessed 25 January 2011.

11. *ibid.*

12. European Commission (no date) 'Intermediate outcomes'. Online. Available http://ec.europa.eu/social/main.jsp?catId=664&langId=en, accessed 25 January 2011.

policy makers. This is expected to induce learning, not only about the utility of specific policies for specific problems, but also in the sense of internalising political goals. Thus, the 'evidence' to be presented is not neutral data, but provided for a purpose.

In the context of involving 'all stakeholders', it is often emphasised that one of these groups is especially important to involve, namely the poor.[13] This refers both to descriptive representation through participation of poor people in policy debates (European Commission 2010a: 53) or governance processes, and to the non-descriptive representation of people living in poverty through NGOs.[14] Conversely, because the latter is more feasible, 'European networks have a key role to play in representing, promoting and defending the rights and interests of their constituencies at EU level'.[15] The importance of representing this particular group is not explicitly substantiated, but the value of taking 'into account the experience of people exposed to social exclusion'[16] is often taken as self-evident. Sometimes, it appears in a strong connection to a general 'closeness' of social policies to those most directly affected by them. Social NGOs not only feed the views of poor people into policy making, they also, through their representation, 'foster a better understanding of the most concrete forms of social exclusion' and 'ensure a regular monitoring of the implementation of the national action plans at a level closer to their main beneficiaries' (European Commission 2005a). They can thus provide information that otherwise would be inaccessible to policy makers, because it is poorly or not at all mediated through executive bureaucracies and territorial representation.

However, closeness is not only about information. It is noteworthy that the DG speaks about '*involv*[*ing*] those who are normally *excluded* from policy debates' (European Commission 2008a: 4; emphases added) and 'ensuring that this [European] strategy *takes into account* the *experience* of people exposed to social exclusion'.[17] '[I]nvolving those normally excluded' is based on the opposition between inclusion and exclusion. The latter is presented as the normal situation and the starting point for any activity. The passively excluded are then included by some agent (here through 'public engagement' introduced by policy makers), i.e. they are brought from the outside to the inside of the process and given an agency of their own. This inclusion takes place through representation, i.e. those not normally represented are now given presence through having their representatives involved in policy making. The purpose of this is to 'take the experience of the

13. European Commission proposal COM(2000)368 of 16 June 2000.

14. European Commission proposal COM(2000)368 of 16 June 2000.

15. European Commission Decision C(2009)143 of 23 January 2009.

16. European Commission (2008) 'Key European Networks'. Online. Available http://ec.europa.eu/ employment_social/spsi/european_networks_en.htm, accessed 21 November 2008. Cf. European Commission 2005a.

17. European Commission (2008) 'Key European Networks'. Online. Available http://ec.europa.eu/ employment_social/spsi/european_networks_en.htm, accessed 21 November 2008. Emphases added.

poor into account' politically. 'Experience' contrasts with 'opinions', 'interests', and 'needs', mentioned elsewhere as the substance of functional representation. At the same time as having a value as information, an experience is also something inherently subjective that is difficult to aggregate and mediate. Taking this mental perception 'into account', i.e. considering it in policy making, indicates an attitude of attention to what is particular and singular (cf. Rosanvallon 2010: 17–18 and Ch. IV), and does not have a direct instrumental value for the efficiency of policy making. The kinds of experiences to be represented here are experiences of immediate affectedness of poverty, and it is this type of affectedness that justifies special attention to those exposed to it. Affectedness is thus not only a position that endows a person with special information that is useful for policy making, but also a condition that as such legitimises a demand to be represented – so that this representation in turn legitimises policy making, because exclusion would conflict with this norm. This again makes it important to involve social NGOs in OMC governance, because they are the main representatives of socially excluded citizens. Hence, the task of 'voicing the concerns of [...] people exposed to social exclusion [...] and formulating them to influence policy making' (European Commission 2010b) also goes beyond providing evidence needed by policy makers to produce the desired outcomes; it is also based on a notion of input legitimacy that is not only instrumental to output.

As was shown in the previous chapters, NGOs are seen to represent not only especially affected groups, but also citizens in general. In the case of both constituencies, they are seen to function as two-way avenues of communication, i.e. another reason for their importance is that they are meant to 'serve as a channel for the dissemination of information' (European Commission 2009a: 20). This is necessary because '[t]here is a clear need to increase the awareness of the stakeholders and the general public about the EU policies pursued'[18] and European networks of NGOs can 'help reach a greater awareness for the social inclusion process' (European Commission 2005a). They are thus not only providing important input but also mediating a 'dialogue' (European Commission 2002a).

While all these aspects are substantiated in the texts relating to the financial programmes funding European networks of NGOs, the most explicit reference to democratic norms is found in one sentence, which is repeated in several documents, but never elaborated: 'Furthermore, such involvement fosters accountability and transparency, and increases the relevance of policy measures'.[19] 'Relevance' can be understood as 'effectiveness and efficiency' of policies,[20] but it is nowhere explicated whose accountability functional representation is meant to improve in which ways, and in what ways transparency should increase. This suggests the interpretation that accountability and transparency are no *major* considerations

---

18. European Commission proposal COM(2004)488 of 14 July 2004.
19. European Commission document PROGRESS/008/2009 of 10 December 2009. Cf. European Commission 2009a: 51.
20. European Commission proposal COM(2000)368 of 16 June 2000.

for the importance of involving social NGOs in the OMC, but nevertheless seen as suitable arguments supporting the case. As well as that, elaborating on the relationship between functional representation and accountability in greater length could also easily lead the argumentation into difficulties. Hence, it is easiest to refer to the very common association of 'involvement' and 'accountability and transparency' only in passing.

In brief, in the context of funding NGOs at EU level, their *involvement in general* is justified with the democratic norm to represent the most affected and above all with the need to include their resources (particularly information) in a common effort. Now, when turning to the *specific* arguments for *funding* such organisations, these resources are to be directed to a particular aim. The line of reasoning mainly concentrates on the need to 'strengthen partnerships' with European networks of NGOs and make these partnerships 'effective' (European Commission 2008a: 4) for the purpose of supporting the social OMC.[21] As could be seen in the previous chapter, 'partnership' between the DG and NGOs refers to a relationship where both sides work for similar goals and support each other. In their argumentation to support the Key European Networks' funding, the DG concentrates on the NGOs' contributions in this partnership, i.e. they argue that because the latter can support the OMC, partnering with them (i.e. financing them) will advance the achievement of the OMC's political goals. The expected contributions of the funded networks are depicted as follows.

The main task of Key European Networks is 'to participate in and *influence* policy-making and policy implementation at EU and national level'.[22] They do this in several ways: '1. provision of evidence base for policy (and legislation); 2. participation in policy debate; 3. information sharing and learning' (European Commission 2010a: 52–3), both within the network itself and between the network and policy makers. Moreover, influence 'is also gained through the setting-up of coalitions capable of affecting change' (European Commission 2005a), i.e. networking in the OMC community. In other words, the Key Networks are expected to engage in typical advocacy or lobbying activities. The internal network structure of the funded organisations – i.e. their constitution of national member organisations that often for their part consist of single NGOs – is seen as instrumental to reaching also the national level by partnering with the European level (European Commission 2007b; 2010b). However, it is only the European-level organisation that is funded, and these funds must not be given to national members. That is, the network in its entirety is seen as one organic whole

---

21. On a broader level, the referred to partnerships as such are not restricted to relations between the DG and NGOs, but include 'key EU and national policy/decision-makers' and are meant to work across all territorial levels and phases of policy making. This stands in the known logic of the together-topos (achieving political objectives works better when all affected work together). However, out of this network of partnerships, the core funding of EU-level networks fosters specifically the cooperation between the latter and DG Employment, so that it is this relationship that is in the focus of the argumentation supporting these financial programmes.

22. European Commission document PROGRESS/008/2010 of 24 November 2010. Emphasis added.

(cf. Chapter Six), so that supporting them at the EU level impacts also on the knowledge and influence of the national level.

The influence Key Networks exert is meant to 'affect [...] and/or accompany [...] *change* in employment and social policies and legislation'.[23] The direction of this change does make a difference: Key Networks are thought 'to participate in and influence policy-making [...] *in support of* EU objectives and priorities'.[24]

It is a general feature of the DG's text to talk about *involving* functional representatives and *raising support* for OMC policy goals in the same breath:

> [T]he Employment, Social Affairs and Equal Opportunities DG will support the Member States in delivering on the EU 2020 Strategy and Social Agenda goals by: [...]
>
> – Rallying support and promoting the involvement of key EU and national stakeholders, by actively encouraging a culture of social dialogue and partnership.[25]

'Support in delivering goals by rallying support' suggests actively lobbying for the political goals in question so that it becomes easier for national governments to implement them. The partnership with Key Networks is an important part of this strategy. Since the 'mission of Progress is to strengthen the back-up provided for EU objectives',[26] the programme's evaluation procedures include paying attention to the Key Networks' contribution to 'shaping and achieving EU policy goals' by monitoring that their 'advocacy goals and social agenda goals [are] closely linked, so that it is clear how and where advocacy is intended to contribute to the achievement of desired outcomes' (European Commission 2009a: 51). The funded organisations should 'promote, support and further develop EU policies and objectives'[27] by 'increas[ing] visibility about particular policy issues, which helps to ensure that positive publicity is achieved on these issues' (European Commission 2010a: 53). This then 'helps to develop and strengthen *consensus* and *support* from the grassroots level upwards for *action* to be taken in particular areas of social and employment policy' (EC 2010a: 53; emphases added).

As I have already shown in the previous chapter, a supportive consensus among the population at large is seen as the legitimatory basis that makes change in the desired direction possible. This consensus is meant to be 'built', and 'impulse for change in support of EU objectives and priorities' is to be 'created' by partnering with Key Networks (European Commission 2008a: 4). In other words, the legitimacy aimed at through involving them is not only based on their

---

23. European Commission Decision C(2009)143 of 23 January 2009. Emphasis added.

24. European Commission document PROGRESS/008/2010 of 24 November 2010. Emphasis added.

25. European Commission document PROGRESS/008/2009 of 10 December 2009.

26. European Commission Decision C(2009)143 of 23 January 2009.

27. European Commission document PROGRESS/003-annex 3. Untitled working document from the inaugural meeting of the Progress Committee, 12 December 2006.

representing their constituencies' views or experiences in the policy-making process (i.e. bottom-up mediation), but also on using them to consciously change their constituents' views in favour of the DG's objectives (top-down mediation). This includes all three constituencies assigned to them, i.e. especially affected groups, citizens at large, and the NGO sector. In brief, legitimacy is sought through adapting policies to citizens' preferences, *and* conversely, through trying to adapt citizens' preferences to policy agendas. As for the latter, those whose views are to be influenced also include national and subnational policy makers.

Remarkably, in the DG's vision, these two legitimatory mechanisms, as well as the different activities assigned to the Key Networks, do not conflict which each other but form different aspects of their role. Raising awareness of the social OMC among the public, advocacy work in favour of EU political goals, providing information, and representing their constituencies are depicted as mutually complementary activities that all add up to advance the implementation of OMC objectives.

Therefore, since all of these contributions can raise the legitimacy of the social OMC and through this promote the achievement of its objectives, it is justified to *ensure* these contributions by establishing *strong, stable* and *lasting* partnerships with some NGOs,[28] and by enhancing the 'quality'[29] of functional representation through improving their *capacity* to be effective partners in the sense described above. This is done through funding them.

The funding provided to the Key Networks is meant as a support to improve their professionalism, including organisational management, 'which will in turn increase their legitimacy, [...] transparency and public accountability' (European Commission 2007b; 2010b). Above all, however, professionalism is needed 'to secure quality and a maximisation of results' (EC 2007b; 2010b). This is why the main purpose of core funding is to increase their capacity 'to meaningfully and fairly partner with the Community to achieve shared EU objectives and policies'[30] and 'to participate in and influence policy-making and policy implementation at EU and national level in support of EU objectives and priorities'.[31] Hence, it is clear that 'funding is not used to build capacity simply for capacity's sake, but rather to help key EU networks to better contribute to shaping and achieving EU policy goals' (European Commission 2010a: 52). It is mainly three overlapping types of capacity that the DG seeks to improve on the side of the Key European Networks: the capacity to provide information, the capacity to influence policies, and the capacity to represent their constituencies. As shown above, all three are

---

28. Blank model for the Commission's Framework Partnership Agreements with the Key European Networks, version of 18 June 2004, updated April 2009, Preamble and Article I.1.1. Unpublished document. Cf. European Commission 2007b; 2010b.

29. DG Employment (2009) *2008 Annual Activity Report*.

30. European Commission document PROGRESS/003-annex 3. Untitled working document from the inaugural meeting of the Progress Committee, 12 December 2006.

31. European Commission document PROGRESS/008/2009 of 10 December 2009.

seen as activities in support of the social OMC and the political objectives agreed in its framework.

The first, providing information, or the 'consulting capacity' (EC 2010a: 54) of the Key Networks, involves analysis and knowledge based on the work of their members at local level, monitoring and evaluation of national social policies (European Commission 2005a), making proposals for 'innovative approaches' (European Commission 2006a), and thus contributing to a better understanding (EC 2006a) of social issues and better ways of tackling them. This type of input is thus seen as expertise that mainly furthers efficient problem-solving by decision makers.

The 'capacity to influence policy-making and policy implementation' for its part has a very clear purpose: it is 'a precondition for the achievement of the Social Agenda goals' (European Commission 2009a: 51). Hence, the expected influence is of a specific type. It is meant to 'produce effective policy proposals requiring action by others' (European Commission 2002a) and 'exert [...] pressure on policymakers in the relevant policy area' (European Commission 2010a: 11); in other words, engaging in advocacy towards European as well as (sub)national actors to support the achievement of the OMC objectives (European Commission 2009a: 51). Financial support increases the networks' capacity 'to address social exclusion and poverty effectively' (European Commission 2006 a), i.e. augments the impact their lobbying work has. The immediate purpose of this can be to advance particular policies as well as to 'put pressure on the system so that the fight against poverty and social exclusion is not forgotten' (Commission official, quoted by Bauer 2002: 389), i.e. 'raising awareness' (European Commission 2010a: 53) and also specifically promoting the social side of political issues (to counterbalance the dominating economic perspective, for example).

The capacity to represent refers in this argumentation mainly to the representation of especially affected groups and the networks' national member organisations (which can also be service providers), and to a minor extent to the representation of citizens in general. Primarily, representation is here understood as mediating information about disadvantaged groups, including information of a qualitative kind that allows policy makers to better understand social phenomena, and that is otherwise difficult to access (European Commission 2005a). However, representation also includes mediating the poor's opinion (in singular form), needs, expectations (European Commission 2010a: 53), views,[32] rights, interests (European Commission 2007b; 2010b), and experiences,[33] so that they become participants in the process.[34] Moreover, representing includes communication in

---

32. European Commission Decision C(2009)143 of 23 May 2009.

33. European Commission (2008) 'Key European Networks'. Online. Available http://ec.europa.eu/employment_social/spsi/european_networks_en.htm, accessed 21 November 2008; European Commission 2005a.

34. European Commission document PROGRESS/008/2010 of 24 November 2010.

both senses, i.e. the establishment of a dialogue.[35] The capacity to do this hinges most of all on the internal structure of the Key Networks. Therefore, the funding they receive is also meant to improve the internal links between the different levels of the network, so that the (sub)national associations and their constituencies are represented at the EU level (towards European policy makers), and vice versa are informed about the processes there (European Commission 2010b; 2007b; 2005a). Additionally, member organisations are not only important as representatives of their constituencies, but also as sources of expertise and experience regarding social policies and as advocacy actors. The representative capacity of the Key Networks is therefore the essential factor of their *legitimacy* as functional representatives in the social OMC: 'The legitimacy of European networks is also dependent on the representativeness and official recognition of their members in their own countries, as well as on their professionalism' (European Commission 2006a: 8). This 'will in turn increase the probability of meeting their [the Key Networks'] objectives' (European Commission 2002a: 6), i.e. serves mainly output legitimacy in terms of the outputs expected by the DG. Representativity is based on a 'solid membership' including a 'geographical diversity' of 'relevant members' with effective advocacy capacities that follows the enlargement of the EU itself, i.e. expands into new Candidate and Member States (European Commission 2006a). Part of the Key Networks' tasks is hence mobilising and training new members (2006a: 8). Under the SEP, networks in the process of establishing themselves were also accepted, while under Progress, candidates for Key Networks have been required to be already properly constituted and registered at the time of application (since 2010: for at least three years prior to the application). Thus, the focus has been shifted from creating networks to supporting organisations with an existing track record and the according capacities. In brief, 'representativeness' is here understood both in terms of territorial extension (coverage of (future) Member States) and relevance, i.e. the member organisations' size, resources, and status as national governance actors. Finally, the network's decision-making processes should also be open and transparent, which refers mainly to the European networks' accountability to its members.

The Key European Networks are thus to be funded *in order to* strengthen their capacities in these areas *in order to* make them stronger partners of DG Employment *in order to* impact together on the political outputs of the social OMC more efficiently. The following section deals with how this partnership functions in practice.

---

35. European Commission proposal COM(2000)368 of 16 June 2000.

Partners by design

The fundamental principles of the partnership between DG Employment[36] and the Key European Networks are the same as those described in the previous chapter for social NGOs in the OMC in general. The relationship is built on the notion of a joint responsibility for achieving political outcomes and, following from this, a spirit of 'doing it together' where both parties contribute and support each other. In the case of the Key Networks, core funding is one major part of the DG's support to strengthen their position:

> But you must be equipped to play your full part. That means responsibilities for the European institutions. It also means your obligations, your own capacity and willingness to participate, as representatives of a coherent civil dialogue and as high quality service providers. Some of the task of building your capacity to play a stronger part in the European policy process is about the institutions supporting you more effectively. That means more efficient payments for social and employment policy action. I can assure you that I am addressing this with the urgency it demands. It means ensuring that your contribution is encouraged and welcomed in new programmes. [...] And some of it is the nature of your 'place at the table' of European dialogue and policy co-operation. (European Commission 2000a)[37]

Consequently, these partnerships imply responsibilities and obligations also on the side of the NGOs: '[T]here are two sides to any bargain' (2000a). Since the Key Networks receive special support, they are also expected to make special contributions going beyond those of other functional associations. Being funded by the DG means entering a formal contractual relationship that includes, firstly, a framework partnership agreement for the entire period covered by the call for proposals (usually three years), which specifies the general conditions and both parties' responsibilities; and secondly, specific yearly agreements for annual operating grants, which are signed after the DG's approval of the organisation's annual working plan and budget (European Commission 2007b; 2010b). As a representative of EAPN – one of the closest and most longstanding funded partners of the DG – put it: 'They don't fund EAPN to be EAPN. That has to be very clear, and this is not a civil society funding; they fund networks to contribute to the European programme' (Interview no. 2). As noted above, this view is the same from the other side. In particular, Key Networks are expected to evaluate the National Action Plans for inclusion policies, take part in the DG's consultations

---

36. My focus is here on the Key Networks funded under the social inclusion and protection strand of Progress, whose principal point of contact in the DG is the (now former) Inclusion Unit, that manages the OMC's general coordination and its social inclusion strand. The following therefore pertains only to the relationships of this unit with 'their' Key Networks.

37. It should be noted that at the time of this speech, the funding of social NGOs from the EU budget was less secure than it then became with the SEP and Progress programmes, so that the 'urgency' Commissioner Diamantopoulou mentions was indeed a critical concern of many NGOs.

and conferences, raise awareness of the social OMC, push its issues on the political agenda of other European institutions and in connection with related policy areas ('mainstreaming'), network with other functional associations to build 'coalitions capable of affecting change' (European Commission 2005a), support the capacity of their member organisations to influence national social politics and support the European process, as well as extend their membership into new Member States and Candidate countries. The abilities of the different Key Networks to meet all these expectations vary. In particular, enhancing the capacities of the national networks is often difficult because of the very limited resources these have. Different Key Networks also perceive their tasks differently. An NGO such as Caritas, with a history before 'social Europe', strong national organisations, and strong relations beyond Europe, can see their OMC-related activities as obligations that also prevent them from doing other things they used to do more, before becoming one of the Key Networks in 2005. This shows how the core funding provided to social NGOs also redirects their activities to make them a part of the OMC 'universe'. EAPN, by contrast, was decisively involved in the lobbying for the setting up of the OMC and actively worked for it to be what it then became, such that they perceive it more as a framework of their own in which they do what they aimed for in the first place (Interview no. 2).

The example of EAPN also shows how closely interlinked some of the Key Networks are with the Europeanisation of social policies as such. Organising at the European level goes hand in hand with doing advocacy work addressed to EU institutions, i.e. urging them to tackle poverty or specific aspects of it; in other words, European associations have as their *raison d'être* the lobbying for doing social policy in the EU as well. Funding such associations is thus one means of ensuring a strong civil-society voice advocating European solutions to social problems, in addition to national ones. Doubtlessly, this is one of the Key Networks' main tasks; but as the case of EAPN shows, this mechanism is older than the OMC, which is in fact an example of its success. In the words of the EAPN Europe Director: 'EAPN aims to put the fight against poverty within the EU, [*sic*] high on the EU political agenda' (Farrell 2008: 128). In institutionalising the EU poverty policies, EAPN's strategy went hand in hand with that of the DG:

> We first did the lobbying to get the Articles 136 and 137 in the Amsterdam Treaty. And that's the basis for the social OMC. And then between the Amsterdam Treaty and 2000, we developed and said okay, now we have a treaty base, now we need a strategy based on that treaty, and on that treaty base. And then we talked about how it should look like, what it should do. Of course, then you had the model of the Employment strategy, you had the Employment OMC, and so we said okay, well that's a model we could follow, and then we talked about how the model should look like, and then we produced this document which

was called 'A Europe for Everybody' [*sic*],[38] and we outlined what should be the pillars of the social OMC. [...] [A]nd this was produced then in 1999, with assistance from the Finnish Presidency, and then you will see a very strong correlation between this proposal and what became the social OMC when they developed the Objectives in Nice in 2000. [...]

Though when the social OMC came into place, the Commission at that moment said we shouldn't push so hard to have that, that it was going too far, not because they didn't believe in it, but because they thought it was impossible. And [...] we said no, well we want it, and it's necessary to make this step. And we pushed through the governments for it. (Interview no. 2)[39]

The publication mentioned by the interviewee and other EAPN documents of the epoch support this version of the course of events. More recently, DG Employment describes EAPN's role in the following way:

EAPN is one of the main partners of the European institutions on the European strategy to combat social exclusion. It lobbies for the integration of the fight against poverty and social exclusion into all Community policies, ranging from Structural Funds and employment policies to economic and monetary policies and builds alliances with relevant actors to create a stronger voice in favour of social inclusion. (European Commission 2009a: 60)

Thus, its main tasks are seen to be mainstreaming and building advocacy coalitions with other actors to create a strong supportive lobby for European social inclusion policies.

The advocacy activities of the Key Networks not only 'contribute to the objectives of the Community policy'[40] as such, but are in addition used by the DG as references legitimising their own efforts in the same direction. In particular, DG Employment quotes NGOs' calls for more action at the EU level to achieve the general goals of the OMC. Almost invariably it is appeals by the Key Networks that are cited:

[S]takeholders and policy makers met at the Seventh Eurochild annual conference in Örebro, Sweden to discuss *how to work together* to end child poverty. [...] These [the final conclusions of the conference] included recommendations to the European Union. One of these *asks the EU to adopt a comprehensive and ambitious EU strategy* on the rights of the child, and a Recommendation on child poverty and well-being. The Eurochild conference

---

38. EAPN (1999) *A Europe for All: For a European strategy to combat social exclusion. EAPN contribution to the European Commission Conference of May 6–7 1999.* Online. Available http://www.eapn.eu/images/stories/docs/EAPN-position-papers-and-reports/europeforall1999-en.doc, accessed 7 February 2011.

39. Cf. Farrell 2008: 128.

40. Blank model for the Commission's Framework Partnership Agreements with the Key European Networks, version of 18 June 2004, updated April 2009, Preamble. Unpublished document.

also asked Member States to *strengthen cooperation and exchange at an EU level* on child poverty and well-being, while maintaining budgets for children and families.[41]

FEANTSA, the European Federation of National Organisations working with the Homeless[,] held a European seminar last June [...]. Ending homelessness requires much investment (time, expertise, research) but the crucial element is cooperation. [...] For this reason, it is very important to encourage local authorities *to develop a European forum* where they can *regularly exchange good practices and ideas* on effective ways to reduce homelessness. http://www.feantsa.org/code/en/pg.asp?Page=981. (European Commission 2008d: 3; emphases added)

This fits well with what was said in the previous chapter about the cooperation between DG Employment and NGOs in the social OMC as 'working together on the same side'. However, this partnership appears in a slightly different light when taking into account that the closest partners are financed by the Commission to organise events that are then quoted by the DG in support of their own position.

The DG's relations with the Key Networks are clearly much closer than with other NGOs. Most DG officers first think of them when asked about NGOs: 'When referring to NGOs, I refer mostly to European Networks, of course, and mostly to those who are currently supported by Progress' (Interview no. 8). This results from involving the Key Networks in almost everything the former Inclusion Unit does, which is not the case for other NGOs. As shown in the previous chapter, being involved in these processes requires quite substantial capacities on the side of the NGOs, so that being less involved is not necessarily due to being expressly shut out, but can also be a result of not having the means to contribute to the highly specialised processes. On the other hand, it is not least the core funding provided to some NGOs that gives them these means. At the same time, the status of a Key Network entails by definition a *privileged access* to the DG. This privileged access means first of all a continual, regular contact with the DG as well as the Cabinet of the Commissioner (Interview no. 4). Therefore, when 'NGOs' are to be involved or consulted in some specific context, the Key Networks are readily there and prepared to contribute, for example to the Social Protection Committee representing the Member States and the Commission (Interview no. 6). Privileged access also means the possibility to meet high-ranking officials and the Commissioner, and have them participate in events of the network (Interview no. 4). Sometimes it is astonishing where Key Networks can be involved. For example, at least three representatives of the Social Platform[42] (including two Key Network

---

41. European Commission (2010) 'Eurochild annual conference looks at ways to end child poverty'. Online. Available http://ec.europa.eu/social/main.jsp?langId=en&catId=89&newsId=945&furth erNews=yes, accessed 8 February 2011. Emphases added.

42. The Social Platform (Platform of European Social NGOs) is not funded by DG Employment but through the Europe for Citizens programme (2007–2013), managed by DG Communication (2004–2006, the Community Action Programme to promote active European citizenship at DG

officers) participated in the Strategic Framework working group of the Progress Committee, which drafted the strategy (outlined above) of the programme that finances many of the Platform's members' running costs.[43] However, the members of the Progress Committee itself do not include functional representatives.

Having special relations with the funded networks does not mean, however, that the Inclusion Unit has neglected the other social NGOs active in the sector. In fact, they are aware of them, and some associations without core funding in the OMC framework do have close relations with them. Yet, these are mostly associations funded by other strands of the Progress programme (for example, anti-discrimination, which until the end of 2010 was located in DG Employment) and the Social Platform (*see* above). The general tendency, then, is that the Key Networks and other NGOs form three layers around the unit managing the OMC:

- A close inner circle of the Inclusion Unit's 'own' Key Networks.
- A middle layer of networks funded by other units within DG Employment, or other DGs with close relations to DG Employment. These networks have a privileged access to 'their' units, and easy access to Inclusion.
- An outer layer of NGOs without substantive EU funding, but having some interest and capacity to engage in OMC processes. Obviously, there is a lot of variation in this group.

Strikingly, when DG officers are asked about the differences in their contacts with Key Networks and 'other NGOs', they speak mostly about the first two layers:

[T]hese [Key] Networks are really our main partners. But then, we're well aware that there are other networks, and there's a second layer. If you look at DG Employment, [...] [there] are similar networks that are funded not by us, on Social Inclusion, but by, for instance, the Anti-discrimination Unit, the Gender Equality Unit, the Disability Unit, and so these are in a kind of second layer, and we do take care that if we organise things, there will be specific meetings only with our inner, the twelve Key Networks we finance, but when

---

Education and Culture). Notwithstanding, the Platform is a privileged partner of DG Employment, its member organisations being European networks of NGOs active in the social sector, including the Key Networks. The location of its funds is a consequence of the social NGOs' funding crisis in the nineties, when the ECJ ruled that their funding through the Commission had been without legal basis (cf. Chapter Five), and the subsequent attempts of the Commission to find or create robust funding bases to ensure the existence of these organisations and stabilise their budgets.

43. European Commission (no date) 'Strategic framework working group: first meeting'. Online. Available http://ec.europa.eu/employment_social/progress/framework1_en.htm; 'Strategic framework working group: second meeting'. Online. Available http://ec.europa.eu/employment_social/progress/framework2_en.htm; 'Strategic framework working group: third meeting'. Online. Available http://ec.europa.eu/employment_social/progress/framework3_en.htm. All accessed 27 November 2008. Cf. European Commission (no date) 'About the Strategic Framework working group'. Online. Available http://ec.europa.eu/employment_social/progress/framework_en.htm, accessed 28 November 2008.

we recognise that there's a broader issue, we will involve the others also. And this is for instance the European Year on Poverty and Social Exclusion, which will be next year [2010]; it's clear that we want to involve as many networks as possible, supporting this, and you really need to reach out, [...] so we'll try to broaden the circle when there's a broader issue. (Interview no. 5)

Necessarily, we have more contacts; [...] they differ in the sense that they have to [...] produce a certain input into the social OMC; for example, ENAR [European Network Against Racism] [...], they're also very active, AGE as well, but they're not funded by our strand, they're funded by the Anti-Discrimination Unit, and [...] they don't have this obligation of [...] reporting on the social OMC, and when it comes to [...] meeting with them, we have two types of meetings: one where we discuss work, let's say the work programme, and this takes place only with twelve networks that we fund, and then more broad ones, for example for the preparation of the Round Table, where, you know, in cases we need to discuss policy, where we involve all the others. [...] [A]nd we also address an invitation to the Social Platform, [...] for other organisations who would eventually [...] like to participate and with whom we do not have direct contacts. (Interview no. 7)

Table 8.1: Key elements of pluralist and corporatist functional representation

	Pluralism	Corporatism
Number of functional organisations	Unspecified	Limited
Functional categories	Self-determined	Differentiated
Organisations in one functional sector	Multiple	Singular
Membership	Voluntary	Compulsory
Relations between organisations	Competitive Non-hierarchical	Non-competitive Hierarchical
Representative monopoly	No	State-granted
Relation to the state	No special statuses or recognition as representatives Independent creation Financial independency Independent leadership selection and interest articulation	Special licenses or recognition as representatives May be state-founded Public funding Some state control on leadership selection and interest articulation

Source: Schmitter 1979: 13, 15.

This shows how inseparably Commission financing and privileged access to the Commission belong together. Importantly, however, Key Networks are not privileged *because* they are funded, but both funding and privileged access are intrinsic elements of the partnership they have entered into.

The privileged access for the Key Networks to DG Employment raises the question of whether functional representation in the social OMC can be understood as a kind of corporatist arrangement. Certainly, the OMC is neither 'pure' corporatism nor 'pure' pluralism, but analysing it through the elements of each ideal type offers interesting insights. Pursuant to Philippe C. Schmitter's classic definitions, pluralist and corporatist functional representation are characterised, respectively, by the elements listed in Table 8.1.

As the juxtaposition shows, the functional representation scene in European social policy is of course formally organised according to pluralist principles. However, as the characteristics of the associations' relations to the state (here, the Commission) in particular indicate, the DG's funding practices introduce distinctly corporatist elements. Paying the running costs of and granting special access to a limited number of networks creates a special status for some in relation to others. Furthermore, the DG has purposefully assisted the creation of several of these networks (*see* Chapter Five and below). I come back to the question of how much control the DG exerts over the Key Networks at the end of this chapter; for the moment, I would like to draw attention to another pivotal difference between pluralist and corporatist systems, namely that of *competition* between functional associations. As shown above, funding the Key Networks is essentially meant to create a stable, 'ongoing, formalised relationship of co-operation',[44] which is also necessary regarding the task assigned to the funded organisations (support the OMC), that requires work over a longer period of time. However, calls for proposals are issued at least every three years, so that there is a formal competition for these funds at relatively short intervals. This provokes the question of how much competition there is de facto; is there a theoretical possibility, for example, that EAPN, which has always been funded since its setting up, will not be among the chosen organisations one day?

> Yes, it's more than theoretical, it's very real. [...] [I]t's an open competition, every year, [...] depending on the criteria they apply, because if the criteria isn't strong of having a track record in this role, if they put more emphasis on innovation, then groups who don't have the constraints of developing all this through all their members [are] likely to be more innovative. So, yes, it's a real possibility. [...]

---

44. Blank model for the Commission's Framework Partnership Agreements with the Key European Networks, version of 18 June 2004, updated April 2009, Article I.1.1. Unpublished document. Cf. European Commission 2007b; 2010b.

So, there's different possibilities – they develop a programme that we don't like, and that we don't want to put our energies into contributing. So that would be one sort of possibility. I don't think it will happen; this period, now that we have the poverty target, whatever way it's designed, it will be something that EAPN members will want to work on. The other possibility is that they think: now you have a lot of talk about social innovation, and if they were to reflect that back in the criteria then, as I say, our job has been more about: we build it on our members, we build our work programme with our members, […] and we build it on a belief that by and large the public authorities have the responsibility to arrange the systems that distribute the wealth, and if you start going into more innovative approaches, with NGOs or the private sector or others delivering the services as the key, then we could be in a very different position. (Interview no. 2)

The DG carefully avoids committing themselves to safeguarding certain organisations' financing or existence – even those whose godparent they are – but follows a pragmatic approach by funding such associations that pursue the kinds of activities that match their political strategy. The competition for funding is one way to ensure this; it is thus mainly an instrument of control. At the same time, however, the bureaucratic complexity of the selection process also allows for a certain amount of discretion in the choice of their partners.

As well as that, it is worth considering that having been a Key Network for several years provides an association with better resources for its next application than most other associations can possibly have. That said, looking at the list of funded organisations since 2002 (*see* Chapter Five), how lasting are the relationships with the Key Networks in practice?

As Figure 8.1 shows, there is considerable variation in the length of funding, i.e. quite some turnover of Key Networks. The mean duration of financial support is six years, i.e. about two consecutive programme cycles (under Progress, one cycle is three years; under SEP, cycles were one, two, or three years long). Out of nineteen organisations, only three (EAPN, FEANTSA, and Eurochild) have

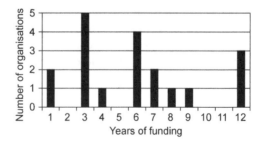

Figure 8.1: Duration of core funding per NGO in the social OMC, 2002–13 (own compilation)

been funded over the maximum period of time (twelve years); two of these have been godfathered by DG Employment. Discounting these three networks in the calculation results in a mean of 4.75 years, which also amounts to two cycles. There is no instance of an association that stopped being funded at some point in time and was financed again later. Hence, there is real competition for funding and partners are changed according to the DG's needs. At the same time, the DG also has a need for stable partnerships. For the most longstanding Key Networks, an end to this relationship is rather improbable because of their tight community with the Inclusion Unit and their concordant agendas. An end of their funding would thus be a sign of major changes in the DG's overall OMC policies and strategies.

Another aspect of the Key Networks that is reminiscent of corporatist structures is the specific support for the *aggregation* of social NGOs at the European level, i.e. their representation through umbrella organisations in Brussels. The DG does provide project funding to national, regional, and local NGOs, but operating grants for running costs are reserved for EU-level networks. For one thing, aggregating the vast field of social NGOs across Member, Candidate, and Associated States in Brussels is simply practical: '[W]orking with European NGOs is the most easy indeed for the Commission. I mean, they are here in Brussels, they speak the same language as we do [...]' (Interview no. 8), and they are also much more knowledgeable of EU processes and procedures (Interview no. 4). Over and above this, however, aggregation is also necessary. As Director-General Odile Quintin explains:

> The social security institutions will have an important role to play in this new form of cooperation [the OMC]. The German association of pension funds is particularly active in this respect and has already organised several seminars about the Open Method of Coordination, jointly with the Federal Ministry of Labour and Social Affairs. But I confess that it would be difficult for the Commission to participate in such deliberations – very useful otherwise – if they had to take place in each of our 15 Member States separately![45]

Yet, the problem is not only the number of Member States, but also the number of Commission officers. Just before the reorganisation of DG Employment at the end of 2010, the then dissolved Inclusion Unit (E/2), which managed the OMC's social inclusion strand, had thirteen staff members responsible for policy development, in addition to eight employees in charge of administrational and technical issues (finances, contracts, statistics). Out of these thirteen officers, at least two were seconded experts, i.e. employees of national ministries who remain on their ministry's payroll while working for the Commission for a period of six months to four years. Therefore, the DG's relationships with NGOs not only

---

45. European Commission (2001), Director-General Quintin's speech at the 5th anniversary of the European Social Insurance Partners. Online. Available http://ec.europa.eu/employment_social/speeches/2001/010920oq_fr.pdf, accessed 17 October 2008. Author translation.

depend on what they would like to do, but also on what they are able to do with the resources they have:

> I think, certainly, here, we are aware of the existence of all the other NGOs, of course, in view of… if you look at the human resources we have for supporting the social OMC, it's ridiculous sometimes. If you look at the ambitions and you look at the number of people here, that need to do everything; the analysis, I mean, supporting the Commissioner in writing briefings and so on, doing projects, doing studies, doing all kinds of supporting work. I mean, there's a limit of what you can do […].

> So you don't have the opportunity, […] we don't also have the budget to go and the time to travel through the European Union to visit all kinds of […] which you should do in fact… […].

> But it's true that […] we talk to them [the Key Networks] a lot – we go to their offices a lot, we participate in their events a lot, and so it's also up to us to make sure that this is not a closed circle, because this is the danger, of course – that you create this secretariat of people who are very aware of the jargon and you see everywhere with them. There would be a danger of really being too focussed on these people and not seeing any more the broader circle. There is a danger there, and so it doesn't help if you really […] there's time pressure and the workload is […] that's true, that there is a problem there. (Interview no. 5)

The Key European Networks institution is thus also a strategy to deal with these practical restraints. DG officers can neither meet functional representatives from or in all Member States, nor deal with large amounts of lowly aggregated information. However, they do need information and contact with functional representatives. In the interviews, they all emphasise that for policy making 'you need partners' and 'someone to talk to'. Importantly, they do not primarily put the 'need for partners' in the context of the strategic partnership dealt with in the previous chapter (i.e. lobbying together for certain political goals *vis-à-vis* other actors), but, rather, stress that *practically*, policy making is impossible in isolation: '[T]he policy creates the partnership, but the partnerships also create the policy. If you don't have partnerships, […] or at least potential partnerships, you can't create a policy; if you have nobody to talk with, you can't develop a policy' (Interview no. 8). Consistently, partners are here referred to as someone 'to speak with at the EU level' (Interview no. 5), as 'interlocutors' (Interviews no. 2 and 7), who provide 'another view' (Interview no. 7), ideally that of the directly affected or the public more generally, and who 'stimulate' (Interview no. 8) the DG through their participation. Thus, NGOs are here not only sources of information and advocacy agents towards third parties, but also a professional network, in which ideas are created and shaped. However, such partners have to be organised in particular ways for this communication to work:

If the national NGOs are not connected between themselves, being able to represent a viewpoint at the Commission, with the Commission the interconnection is very difficult. It was already the case in the 90s; it has become, of course, even more needed in the EU-27 Union. (Interview no.8)

The DG has therefore purposefully and in a long-term strategy created the partners it needs. EAPN is a textbook example of this strategy.

EAPN itself describes the history of its foundation as follows:

The European Anti-Poverty Network (EAPN) was established in 1990 and emerged, with support from the European Commission, from the contacts NGO representatives built up through their involvement in the EU Poverty Programmes which ran from the late 1970's to the early 1990's [sic]. (Farrell 2008: 128)

[A]nd then the people who had got to be in contact with each other through these Poverty Programmes [...] wanted to have a more permanent network to share and to continue to look at the question of poverty and try to push for the question of poverty [to] be higher in the EU agenda. So that was the bottom-up [...] development of the network; and then top-down, the Commission was interested, because within the complex European Union mechanisms, you need a civil society engagement to try – and even with that it's very hard still – but to try and engage the different levels in the European policy making. So the Commission was interested to have an interlocutor on the question of poverty and social exclusion, and so they were very supportive from the beginning of setting up EAPN, and have been funding the network ever since [...]. So that was kind of the top-down interest in having the network, and the two coincided and kept together. (Interview no. 2)

The decisive point in this story, however, is that it was not just a coincidence that social NGOs from different parts of the EU met in the context of the Poverty Programmes. Rather, one of the main purposes of these programmes was to generate such contacts:

[I]t's not by chance that the Poverty Programmes were launched in the 70s and [...] that during the 90s the Commission started developing and pushing [...] for some of these networks – they were not being there; but really the Commission was very much involved in this, because the Commission wanted them very much, that they were funded – founded first and funded second, structured and so on and so on, [...] so, this is not by chance. We needed to build partners. (Interview no. 8)

Moreover, setting up EAPN was not an easy thing to do. Especially in the southern Member States, there was not much tradition of national social NGOs, and in Germany, Commission funding was seen as incompatible with the network's independence (Cram 1997: 127, 131). Therefore, 'far from displaying the automatic coming together of interested parties, the establishment of such (national member) networks has required sustained effort on the part of some dedicated individuals' (Cram 1997: 127). In her analysis of organised interests in European social policy, with EAPN as one example, Laura Cram therefore comes to the conclusion that the standard explanation of 'a collaboration of interested parties from different Member States in response to changing [i.e. growing] EU powers' (p. 128) in order to influence European policies cannot alone account for the formation of European networks of social NGOs. Not only did the setting up of EAPN require support and funding from the Commission as well as strong efforts from above (the network's European level), many national NGOs do also (still) not perceive the EU as an important actor in social policies (apart from being a source of funding), and the possibility to receive funding can indeed be a more important motivation to join a network than the desire to influence European policies (pp. 123–8). Hence, DG Employment was a decisive catalyst in the setting up of EAPN, as well as of FEANTSA.[46]

Furthermore, also beyond these midwife activities, through the conditions it sets for receiving core funding, the DG critically influences how the main functional representatives in European social policy are structured internally, namely in the form of a network of national organisations. Both under Progress and the SEP, funded organisations are required to be European-level networks of national members in a given minimum number of Member States. For DG Employment, the national NGOs participating in European networks are primarily *resources*, which are pooled at EU level and therefore accessible to them. As pointed out above, these resources are mainly information 'from the ground' and advocacy impact. Therefore, the DG sets value on the 'quality of the membership':

> Yes, if we ask it, yes, we can have an access to this [input from the grassroots level]. We can know, for example, what's happening in this or that country. But again, a lot depends on the quality of the membership. For me, it's not important to have only many organisations; it's, let's say, the quality of the organisations – when I say 'quality', one of the issues is the scope, let's say, what population, how strong they are at national level. Again, to give you an example, […] Eurochild has many organisations as members, but in Belgium they have very small organisations with no significance, like Dyslexia International, and one of the things I have been pushing them for is to get as members the two big children organisations, Kind en Gezin from the Flemish and O.N.E. from the Walloon side, which is the case for Coface, for example: they've got this membership, it's a strong membership, and then you can have some influence when it comes to European issues. But when you have small-scale organisations: [scoffs] – even if they're many in number, they don't have the necessary impact. (Interview no. 7)

---

46. For FEANTSA, *see* Cram 1997: 129; Greenwood 2003: 216, 260.

As noted above, the legitimacy of European networks to act as functional representatives in the social OMC, i.e. the weight their messages can have, also depends decisively on the quality of their membership in these terms; that is, the number of people the member NGOs can claim to represent and the status they have in national governance processes. These assets translate into valuable information input to the Commission and into influence on all OMC actors; in other words, it makes the network a strong and desired partner of the DG. This is why a social NGO without national foundations, organised exclusively at EU level, would neither meet the DG's need for partners, nor be able to make a credible claim to represent those especially affected by social policies.

However, effectively maintaining such networks is difficult, because the national NGOs often have scarce resources and do not necessarily see EU processes as especially relevant for their work. European networks often face the dilemma that, on the one hand, their members are the basis for their influence in the EU, but on the other hand, having an impact on policy making in Brussels and communicating the European work to the membership require different approaches:

> That's a great weakness of our network: that often, even where we have strong networks, it's really in the hands of a few people who really can follow. Partly, that's to do with the way we work [...]. Our power is to contribute quite detailed into key moments; we're not able to mobilise thousands of people, and even when you see the trade unions mobilising thousands of people, you're not sure what impact it has. So that's our power: to be able to make timely contributions into very detailed processes, and so that's very often why they're not able to communicate beyond a narrow few. (Interview no. 2)

Hence, DG funds for the European level are not sufficient to decisively increase the capacity of a network to represent the members and the grassroots level, but these lower levels also have to be resourced accordingly. Ultimately, then, the Commission's abilities to create an efficient system of functional representation are very limited. The DG itself notes that 'key EU networks are significantly more successful at the EU than at national level'.[47]

Similar considerations are all the more true concerning the Key Networks' communication with the public at large. It seems that raising broad awareness of the topics the social OMC deals with is not decisively easier for civil society organisations than for the DG: 'And I mean we'd love to think it's for the general public, but the reality of trying to reach the general public is quite difficult' (Interview no. 2).

---

47. DG Employment (2009): *2008 Annual Activity Report*, p. 20.

Representation: supporting the representation of the poor or creating a lobby of one's own?

DG Employment's practice of funding their main non-governmental partners raises the question of how far the financial dependence of the latter entails their being controlled by the DG; and, given the obviousness of this issue, what are the DG's concepts of representation and democracy relating to this particular practice?

The question of *dependency and control* gains significance from the fact that many of the funded organisations could not exist without the DG support, which became clear in the funding crisis of 1998 (*see* pages 96–97). Thus, although the DG justifies the so-called degressivity rule of its grants with the intention to

> ensure that the renewal of such grants does not increase the beneficiary's financial dependency on the Commission and thus to sustain artificially the existence of bodies which would reduce their activities or disappear entirely without substantial and repeated Community intervention.[48]

This reasoning is obviously counterfactual. Even though not all Key Networks would cease to exist, all of them would have to 'reduce their activities' substantially without this core funding from the EU budget. For example, European networks that existed prior to the OMC have been able to employ additional staff and strengthen their vertical relationships with the national level through the Commission funds. Hence, without being funded, European social NGOs could not play the role they now have: 'We are also conscious of the necessity for the Commission to support civil dialogue financially, otherwise it would not be happening at European level' (European Commission 2003b). The Key Networks are thus critically dependent on the DG.

On the other hand, the issue of dependency and control is only relevant from a political point of view if the Key Networks do indeed have substantial influence in or on the social OMC. As is often the case with advocacy, this is difficult to assess on a more general level than mere anecdotal evidence, and would also require a more detailed discussion of what exactly is meant by 'influence'. Globally, the social OMC's principal objective – reducing poverty – has not come much closer, so that in terms of ultimate outcomes the achievements of the Key Networks are also modest. Moreover, today, the Key Networks and much of the DG's Inclusion Unit find themselves on the weaker side of a divide between an economic perspective oriented towards market competitiveness and a social perspective oriented towards a more even distribution of wealth. In other words, the Key Networks are not determining the general direction of European social policies. However, from the perspective of social policies' incremental development and Europeanisation, Key Networks can have a decisive influence on single decisions,

---

48. European Commission (2010) 'Frequently asked questions'. Online. Available http://ec.europa. eu/social/BlobServlet?docId=4878&langId=en, accessed 17 February 2011.

which often may not have great importance in themselves, but can turn out to be significant through their (unintended) consequences. A case in point is EAPN's lobbying for the establishment of the OMC (*see* above). The organisation's strategy is to concentrate on single political steps and invest their resources in pushing these in their preferred direction. Success in one step may provide the basis for further action, but the overall impact is visible only in the longer term.

> [I]f you take the active inclusion approach, with its three pillars of access to services, access to employment – decent employment we would always say, or quality employment – and access to adequate income, in a way it has developed as a theme under the OMC, but it's more than a theme, it's a kind of a philosophy and a way of thinking, and a very global [one], and so, even with the worst case scenario, this thematic approach will continue. And that has been a big push from EAPN to get the Recommendation in this area. That wasn't easy, and I think it was a lot of the influence of EAPN that that Recommendation came true. So, I think there's no getting back from that now they've only written it two years ago. So, that will be a space, a thematic space for us to advance on the agenda. (Interview no. 2)

Hence, without going too deep into the possible influence of the Key Networks, one can work on the assumption that they do have some impact on OMC policies.

Obviously, a similar assessment is also the reason for DG Employment to finance their running costs. Heeding that this expense item is a relatively large one for the DG, how much control do they exercise over the use of this money? The DG's main instruments and moments of control are the funding decision itself and the signing-off of the Key Networks' annual work plans, the acceptance of which is the prerequisite for the next annual grant payment. Here, it is ensured that the activities of a network are in line with the DG's interests and expectations. While the choice of the Key Networks is made by the Unit, the work plans are approved by the DG officer who is responsible for the respective network. Each Key Network is assigned an officer who works as their main contact person within the DG and is in charge of the relationship. Concerning the details of the Key Networks' day-to-day activities, these officers have a lot of discretion about how to arrange the relations with 'their' network, which results in different ways of doing things. The tendency in the Inclusion Unit is towards overseeing the general orientations of the NGOs' activities rather than controlling single activities, but not fully as a matter of course:

> [T]here was a debate, in fact, of this, because some colleagues who were responsible for a number of networks – who were for example contacting directly the members of the Social Protection Committee, or they were issuing reports without us being aware of them beforehand – were upset; but we said, you know, the fact that we provide them part of their funding [...] does not mean that we control them. (Interview no. 7)

Despite this formulation – it 'does not mean that we control them' – the question that poses itself within the DG is evidently not whether to control the Key Networks, but how far to do so; how much autonomy should these partners be given? The Key Networks themselves attach importance to also having initiatives that are not directly funded by the DG, and to designing their strategies autonomously. However, 'autonomy' is a very relative term in this context: '[M]y idea certainly is to leave them [i.e. EAPN] a lot of autonomy, so it's just checking whether what they're proposing [in their annual work programmes] is really in line with what we normally expect the networks to do, the role we expect them to play' (Interview no. 5). Ultimately, then, the real degree of control is elusive. As one officer put it: '[T]o some extent they are under our control, because we pay them quite heavily. Even if we respect their independence, nevertheless there is this aspect' (Interview no. 8).[49] Already through the tasks entailed in being one of the Key Networks and through their often rather dense contacts with the DG, these organisations become in a sense a part of the system and are no longer external influences on the OMC. Most networks do not have as long a background of working in the EU as EAPN, and also not the power that EAPN may have had in influencing the design of the tasks assigned to them, so that becoming a Key Network changes the way they work. Yet, this type of control is a rather subtle and indirect one and therefore difficult to demonstrate. What is more, the Key Networks can also be expected to anticipate Commission control and to some extent adapt their activities to the DG's presumed expectations. For example, it is common for them to copy 'their' DG officer into important communications with third actors (Interview no. 5) to keep the DG informed of their activities. Pursuing activities that are not coordinated with the DG beforehand does thus not mean activities the DG does not know about. Finally, the conditions set in the calls for proposals require the funded organisations' 'mission' and 'main purpose' to be in line with the OMC and the tasks given to the Key Networks (European Commission 2010b) – this clearly includes activities not pursued in direct cooperation with the DG. A cautious estimation is thus that the control over the Key Networks is considerable.

This is of course not surprising, considering the resources invested in them. More surprising is the fact that the DG officers do not perceive these mechanisms as controls proper, but describe the position of the Key Networks as independent within the framework given by the Commission. When they stress that the funded associations 'remain free' (Interview no. 7), this is thus a *contained freedom*, the boundaries of which are taken for granted. From within this perspective, all interviewed officers emphasise that completely remote-controlled Key Networks are not what the DG needs:

[T]here is also this tension – which I think is visible for some of the networks or the platforms – that being so used to talk[ing] with the Commission, some

---

49. The interviewee mentions the DG's control here without me having brought up the issue.

of them are including the censorship or including the vocabulary they are expected to bring. So you like some freshness, and sometimes you like free activity and innovative ideas, because they are already incorporating what *they* think *you* expect them to say. (Interview no. 1)

As noted above, the DG needs the Key Networks, among others, as interlocutors with whom to develop policies with, and therefore 'they need to keep their independence, because for us, it's an added value to have as interlocutors stakeholders who are independent' (Interview no. 7). Many officers cite the 'frank criticism' that many Key Networks frequently aim at the Commission as evidence of their autonomy, and in particular as evidence that neither does the DG seek to make these organisations their agents, nor would these organisations indeed accept such attempts. These public criticisms from the side of Key Networks do in fact take place and can be rather outspoken. Notwithstanding, when this criticism concerns the social inclusion strand of the OMC, it usually does not animadvert on policy goals but on the means to achieve them. Criticism of the general orientation of EU social policies in turn is usually primarily addressed at those actors or parts of the Commission whose views differ from those dominating in the Inclusion Unit. In both cases, statements generally call for greater ambition and action on the EU level. Hence, the main control over the activities of the Key Networks is exercised through funding such organisations that are *already* largely in line with the Inclusion Unit. The strength of this instrument makes it possible to leave the Networks some freedom within defined borders. Control is thus more structural than coercive.

This means that there is a tension between the Key Networks' function as *partners* of the DG, striving for similar goals together, and the Key Networks as *representatives* of functional constituencies, such as the poor, children, or the mentally ill. Those NGOs that are granted core funding do have a contained autonomy to represent their constituents' views within the borders of the OMC. Yet, constituencies with views that are incompatible with those held by DG Employment are not likely to receive funding for representation. In consequence, dissident NGOs – demanding, for example, that social policies should be dealt with exclusively nationally – have entirely different possibilities to be heard in OMC matters.

How, then, does DG Employment see the role of the Key Networks as *representatives*? Representing especially affected groups is one task assigned to the funded organisations and one justification for financing them. They are a vital representative structure for the DG, because 'how do you get out and [...] find who lives in precarity and what the concerns are?' (Interview no. 7). Talking to DG officers reveals that in addition to the practical necessity of political partners, values of equal representation also play a role in their funding: 'I think [...] it's fair to give back money from the taxes to the people who are representing civil society, otherwise those people have no voice, and they are never represented' (Interview no. 1). Sometimes documents also present the representation of the poor as a value as such:

> For the social protection/social inclusion section [of Progress], this [Key Network core funding] is the largest spending item (around 36%) and reflects the importance of the stakeholders' participation, including people experiencing poverty and social exclusion, in the relevant policy areas.[50]

Here, the 'importance' of functional representation serves without further substantiation as the justification for financing representatives. The emphasis DG officers lay on this value varies; some have obviously thought more than others about the relationships between individual people threatened by poverty and the Commission. Nevertheless, for all of them, the primary rationale of creating and maintaining the Key Networks is: 'We need them' (Interview no. 7). It should also be noted that, in this specific case, balancing existing inequalities in functional representation sits well with DG Employment's agenda in the social OMC, so that it is easy for them to uphold normative convictions supporting this practice.

The representative claims that the DG makes about the Key Networks build on their member organisations, i.e. on the formal relations between the European network and its immediate constituents (national NGOs), and implicitly beyond this on the 'closeness' of the member organisations to those ultimately affected. Accordingly, representativity is defined through the territorial coverage of the membership and the recognition of the member organisations as legitimate functional representatives of the grassroots.

Representing disadvantaged groups through functional associations also requires a certain *internal democracy* of these organisations. As mentioned before, one of the conditions of being accepted as a Key Network is being 'mandated by its members, through a Management Board or other administrative forum, to represent these members at the EU level and to be responsible for the activities of the network' (European Commission 2010b). In other words, DG Employment requires formal relations of authorisation and accountability between the EU-level network and the immediate member organisations. Furthermore, they also pay attention to the less formal communication between these levels:

> The effective and efficient organisation of work will be judged against the extent to which the applicant [...] presents its relations with its national members, including arrangements to ensure involvement of membership organisations in policy development and policy statements, goal-orientation and planning practices, [and] reporting methods [...]. (European Commission 2007b: 16)[51]

However, the DG does not refer to procedures further down in the chain of delegation – i.e. below the top level of the national NGOs, which is in most cases still a considerable distance from the grassroots and those ultimately represented. This has to do with resources as well as priorities – the DG does not have the

---

50. European Commission document PROGRESS/008/2010 of 24 November 2010.

51. The quoted passage is part of the award criteria against which applications of NGOs to become one of the Key Networks are assessed.

resources to scrutinise with much detail what goes on within the Key Networks (or other NGOs) beyond the EU level. Notably, the lack of resources is also a key reason for possible shortcomings in the NGOs' internal democracy:

> [M]ore directly, we're accountable to our members, which are our national networks, and our European organisations. And hopefully those national networks are accountable to grassroots organisations fighting against poverty and social exclusion. But the level of accountability has to be somehow proportional to the level of resources. So if a network is trying to build a network with absolute volunteering on top of heavy daily commitments, okay. Their ability to be accountable [...] they can have a clear structure, but it's not so easy, so I think the proportionality between accountability and resources – there's a relationship between these two things. (Interview no. 2)

The funding provided by the DG is restricted to the EU level and does not impact on the financial situation of the lower levels, for which the DG can take no responsibility. As already noted, the 'capacity-building' that the DG seeks to generate with its funds means primarily '[i]mproving the organisational capacity and management of the European networks' and '[r]einforcing the advocacy and campaigning skills of the European partner organisation and those of its national members to advance, support and further develop EU objectives and priorities at EU and national level' (European Commission 2010b). Put differently, the DG's purpose is to increase the Key Networks' influence on policy making, which stands in a certain tension with ensuring democratic structures of representation through the levels of the associations up to the ultimate individual constituents. Thus, DG Employment gives priority to the former. Notwithstanding, the internal flows of information between the grassroots level and the European networks are a key resource for the DG, so that they do have an interest in functioning representation. These considerations raise two important questions: Firstly, is representation here prioritised over democracy, and what kind of representation would that mean, from the point of view of DG Employment? Secondly, given the constraints of scarce resources (both at the Commission and the NGOs), financial dependency, and high aggregation from the local to the European level, can the functional representation of socially disadvantaged groups at the EU be realised in a democratic way at all? Given that functional representation often works differently than territorial representation, what could democracy look like in these conditions? These are questions I return to in the last chapters.

Chapter Nine

The Descriptive Representation of the Poor

So far, I have mostly been dealing with social NGOs, which are the major functional representatives of those especially affected in the OMC. Nevertheless, there is another form of functional representation in the sector, which, albeit of much smaller weight, is particularly interesting: the EU-level descriptive representation of people living in poverty. Analysing this mode of representation broadens the picture of functional representation in the social OMC, because poor citizens cannot be treated by the DG as collaborators in a similar way to Brussels-based NGOs. Their descriptive representation thus has to follow a different logic. I first briefly present the ways in which poor people are represented descriptively in the social OMC, before taking a detailed look at DG Employment's argumentation for this special mode of representation. Finally, I enquire into how representation itself is thought to function here.

The descriptive representation of the poor – i.e. their representation by representatives being poor themselves – can take place within NGOs involved in the OMC and outside of them as an additional mode of representing this constituency. Many social NGOs involve descriptive representatives in their work in various ways. Under the SEP, this was one of the conditions to receive core funding from the DG (European Commission 2006a: 11–12; cf. 2005a; 2002a); since 2007, under the Progress programme, this is no longer explicitly required, although the participation of 'relevant constituents' still appears among the award criteria (European Commission 2007b; 2010b). Involving people living in poverty in NGO work means representing the poor *to* the NGO, which can then build *their* claim to represent this constituency on this involvement – yet, in any case, it remains the NGO that does the representing towards third parties. By contrast, in the present chapter, I look at instances where this NGO mediation is absent and poor citizens represent their peers to EU-level policy makers directly.

The single main forum for this is the annual European Meeting of People Experiencing Poverty, which has been taking place since 2001. These meetings are held under the political responsibility of the EU Presidency of the first semester, in cooperation with DG Employment, which also provides part of the funding, and with EAPN, which deals with the practical organisation, and recruits as well as prepares the participants through their national member organisations. The first Meeting was organised by the 2001 Belgian EU Presidency, which built its initiative on national experience with this type of event. Since 2003, the Meetings have been annual events and are today an established part of the yearly EU agenda (Dierckx and Van Herck 2010: 10–11; Interview no. 2).[1]

---

1.   The annual meetings are still supported by the Belgian government.

It is important to note that the European Meetings of People Experiencing Poverty differ a lot from usual EU conferences. Well over half of the participants are descriptive representatives (about 130 in the EU-27), who are termed 'delegates', while policy makers are called 'guests' to emphasise that they are invited by those living in poverty. Delegates are prepared for the Meeting in their home countries in long processes (around four months) that can also include citizens who are not part of the delegation but have in this way the opportunity to provide input for the European Meeting. As well as that, there are national follow-up processes. During the two-day meetings in Brussels, facilitated workshops take the central role, and the main emphasis is placed on the delegates getting the chance to express themselves. Policy makers are expected to listen and respond to the delegates, and to use common language (Interview no. 3; EAPN 2009: 71–3). The guests include mainly Social Protection Committee (SPC) members, MEPs, representatives from national ministries (especially from the presiding Member State and the country to organise the next Meeting), officers of the Key Networks and other Brussels-based social NGOs, and DG Employment officers. Among the plenary speakers is usually a Presidency Minister and the Employment Commissioner or other senior Commission officials. Some delegates from the Meetings also participate as invited speakers at the annual Round Table on Poverty and Social Exclusion, which is the main yearly conference for politicians, officers, and functional representatives dealing with European social policy.

The cooperation of the spring Presidency, DG Employment, and EAPN means that the European Meeting is not fully 'owned' by any of these three parties. However, all three seek to make sure that the Meeting corresponds to their expectations, because all three invest considerable resources in it and therefore aim to capitalise on the political significance that the Meeting has gained over time. For the Presidency and the DG, this means above all influencing the topics of the Meeting. Since the delegates' messages are used to legitimate political initiatives, policy makers have an interest in focussing these messages on topics that suit their agenda (Interview no. 2). DG Employment, the spring Presidency, and EAPN each refer to the European Meeting to legitimise their own position and activities. Especially for DG Employment, the Meetings of People Experiencing Poverty are an argument for the legitimacy of their policies, claiming direct input from the affected, better outputs as a result, and not least an attitude of attention and respect towards the concerned citizens: '[The] EU listens to people experiencing poverty to help improve their lives'.[2] The DG develops two main lines of reasoning to underpin the need for the descriptive representation of the affected (in addition to their representation through other structures): giving voice and receiving unique input. I look at each of these in turn before I analyse how DG Employment presents these Meetings in terms of political representation.

---

2. European Commission press release IP/08/753 of 16 May 2008.

The right to speak and be listened to

Existing social inequalities are replicated, if not amplified, in functional representation due to the structurally different capacities of functional groups to organise and lobby for their preferences (cf. Chapter Four). This is especially true for those most directly affected by social policies, i.e. people living in poverty. DG Employment ties these circumstances in with the European Meetings of People Experiencing Poverty to argue that the deliberate descriptive representation of disadvantaged groups can counteract this structural inequality. The central premise here is that all those affected by a policy have a *right* to 'have their say'[3] in 'decisions that affect their lives'.[4] This refers to a basic democratic principle, which therefore should be equally valid for all citizens. The formulation 'their say', instead of the similarly possible 'a say', suggests that this 'say' intrinsically belongs to the affected – the issue is thus not whether they should have an influence, but whether this influence is realised. Hence, the DG goes beyond the right to speak and to get involved in policy making, which is also guaranteed by formal constitutional citizenship rights, such as the freedom of expression and of association. In order to make these formal rights effective, DG Employment calls for more equality on the receiving side: the affected not only have a right to speak, but also a complementary – informal – right to be *listened to*. In other words, for the implementation of fundamental democratic standards, formal rights to have an influence are not sufficient, but need to be supplemented with mechanisms that ensure the ability of everyone to exercise these rights effectively. Just as the right to vote is not worth much if one's vote counts less than others' or has no impact, the right to express oneself does not allow one to influence policies if one does not have the social capital needed to mobilise, or if no one takes account of what one says. The DG condenses this idea with the help of the concept of *voice*: 'People experiencing poverty have the right to a voice, and that voice must be heard'.[5] Having and using one's voice means here speaking for oneself, instead of being spoken for by others who do not share one's situation. The concept of voice in connection with descriptive representation also suggests something unmediated, i.e. the direct self-expression of people living in poverty through the mouth of a sample of them.

3. European Commission (2007) 'Tackling social exclusion: people experiencing poverty have their say'. Online. Available http://ec.europa.eu/employment_social/emplweb/news/news_en.cfm?id=233, accessed 23 October 2008.

4. European Commission (2010) 'New strategy will help poor sections of society'. Online. Available http://2010againstpoverty.eu/export/sites/default/downloads/newsletter/Newsletter_3_EN_EY_2010_100909.pdf, accessed 18 March 2011.

5. Commissioner Špidla's closing speech at the 8th European Meeting of People Experiencing Poverty, 16 May 2008. Czech Presidency of the European Union (2009) *Where We Live, What We Need*. Conference report. Available online at http://eapn.eu/images/stories/docs/eapn-report-2009-en-web2-light-version.pdf, accessed 14 March 2011.

The key problem concerning the poor is that they 'are generally unable to have their say'.[6] This inability results partly from their structural lack of capacities, which is a consequence of their situation: 'People living in poverty face many barriers when it comes to taking part in decision-making. Not enough money. Not enough information. Not enough confidence. The list goes on'.[7] Therefore, disadvantaged people 'find it hard to express their experiences and opinions' (European Commission 2007d), to the extent of becoming 'forgotten people in Europe, who cannot speak for themselves'.[8] However, the latter expression is singular in the DG's text. The general message, by contrast, is 'that people experiencing poverty ha[ve] the knowledge and expertise to analyse exclusion, and aim [...] to take part in society and the decisions that affect their lives'.[9] Thus, since both the right and the motivation to do so exist, it is the task of those with more powerful positions in society to create the circumstances for the socially disadvantaged to act as equal citizens. Put differently, all those with the right to have a say have to be *given* a voice in case they are not in a position to *take* that voice themselves. Voice is hence something the possession of which is contingent on one's social status, and persons of low status, who do not have voice by themselves, depend on elites to be provided with it:

> The purpose of the meeting is to *give* a voice to those who are living in poverty and/or experiencing social exclusion and *offer* them the chance to directly voice their concerns and aspirations at a forum of decision-makers and anti-poverty support organisations.[10]

From the perspective of the policy makers, giving a voice to marginalised people and listening to them requires the creation of special conditions adapted to their specific needs. In this sense, the European Meetings of People Experiencing Poverty are a process, where the structure and methodologies of the conferences have been continuously developed in order to improve the communication between delegates and guests (cf. EAPN 2009: 71–3; Dierckx and Van Herck

---

6. European Commission press release SPEECH/08/244 of 17 May 2008.

7. European Commission (2007) 'Active participation of the poor vital to fighting social exclusion'. Online. Available http://ec.europa.eu/employment_social/spsi/network_of_media_en.htm, accessed 24 September 2008.

8. European Commission (2010) 'Commissioner vows to speak for the "forgotten people" in Europe'. Online. Available http://ec.europa.eu/commission_2010-2014/andor/headlines/articles/2010/02/20100121_en.htm, accessed 14 March 2011. Originally published by *Touteleurope. eu* (21 February 2010). Online. Available http://www.touteleurope.eu/fr/en/news/actualite-vue-detaillee/afficher/fiche/4181/t/85293/from/4487/breve/commissioner-vows-to-speak-for-the-forgotten-people-in-europe.html?cHash=f0c2d36f05, accessed 14 March 2011.

9. European Commission (2008) 'The first Meeting of People Experiencing Poverty – 1 to 2 December 2001 – Brussels'. Online. Available http://ec.europa.eu/employment_social/spsi/events_en.htm, accessed 16 October 2008.

10. European Commission (2010) 'Media Alert. EU anti-poverty meeting: "Starting point for a new deal"'. Online. Available http://2010againstpoverty.eu/export/sites/default/downloads/Events/20100624_Media_Alert_PEP.pdf, accessed 13 December 2010. Emphases added.

2010). To give poor citizens the chance to speak and be listened to, attention has to be given to the preparation of and follow-up for the delegates (the latter including feedback), the organisation of the workshops (number of participants, length of presentations, length of the workshop slots in the programme, working modes, facilitation, etc.), the time for informal contacts, the ratio between delegates and guests, the attitude of the participating politicians (including particularly their comportment in personal interaction, but also the length, language, and content of their speeches), the topics discussed, the language(s) used, and lots of small organisational details that go unnoticed in conventional events (such as dealing with the fact that most delegates are unaccustomed to travelling and moving in unfamiliar places and complicated buildings, do not speak foreign languages, and have great difficulties paying their travel costs in advance) (Dierckx and Van Herck 2010: 53–64). In short, providing the necessary conditions involves both resources and, above all, a respectful attitude:

> The previous three meetings made clear the importance of having sufficient financial and human resources to enable effective participation by people experiencing poverty. But allowing the time needed for that participation, and an attitude of confidence and respect, are just as necessary.[11]

Most of the DG officials I interviewed spoke about the challenges of engaging in genuine communication with people living in poverty and understanding each other:

> I remember one of the first [Meetings I took part in], where I was asked, in the Round Table I was sitting in, to provide my own experience of social exclusion, and it was, you know, it was very hard. (Interview no. 7)

> I remember when I was coordinating a working group on National Action Plan indicators; we tried to ensure that people living in poverty would [...] participate in the process of defining indicators [of social exclusion]. Of course, if you want to have something which is really difficult, it's indicators, because you need to know what statistics are, margins of confidence and this kind of things, reliability, and so on. [...] There was a project launched whereby there was a group of people living in poverty, and there was a group of people in government and academics, and they tried to discuss together what are priorities when measuring poverty, and how to measure it. It was a long process – took, I think, more than two years – it was a difficult process. [...] It was a project about indicators, but the first six months they never mentioned the word 'indicator'. So they really started with the personal experience of people, what is social exclusion [...]. (Interview no. 5)

---

11. Director-General Quintin, speech at the 4th European Meeting of People Experiencing Poverty, 10 June 2005. Luxembourg Presidency of the European Union (2005) *Images and Perceptions of Poverty*: 20. Conference report. Online. Available http://www.eapn.eu/images/stories/docs/EAPN-position-papers-and-reports/4EUmeetingPEP/4thpep_en.pdf, accessed 15 March 2011.

Overcoming these difficulties is the task of the policy makers. This means that the constellation of these Meetings is necessarily top-down, i.e. based on the willingness of the privileged to challenge their own habits and ways of thinking, to encourage people to speak to whom they would not normally have contact with, and to listen. Listening cannot be commanded by the person who takes the floor, but whether those present really listen remains their own decision.

Notwithstanding, the fact that some decision makers do listen is also seen to change the *agency* of people living in poverty from objects into subjects. By taking part in the European Meetings, they become people who are listened to and who have something important to say:

> Representatives of the estimated 72 million Europeans living in poverty will today *have their say* in Brussels *on how to tackle social exclusion* in the EU at a major event organised by the German Presidency and the European Commission. The sixth annual 'European meeting of people experiencing poverty' will assess results achieved so far and help develop strategies for the future.[12]

In other words, those affected by poverty are recognised as political actors among others:

> The European Commission has always supported these initiatives, which show the vital need to involve people experiencing poverty in policies to tackle exclusion. European coordination of national policies on exclusion is based on involving and mobilising *all the actors* in those policies.[13]

This recognition gives the participants the dignity of self-dependent citizens who take part in collective decision-making. This is not only 'because it shows that everyone, with or without a job, can be and can feel useful to society',[14] but this dignity is also part of democratic citizenship.

Dignity also comes through the European Meeting in a second way, namely by representing an anonymous mass of people through concrete individuals: 'The annual meetings [...] have given a voice *and a face* to "the poor"' (European Commission 2007a; emphasis added). Seeing these descriptive representatives

---

12. European Commission (2007) 'Tackling social exclusion: people experiencing poverty have their say'. Online. Available http://ec.europa.eu/employment_social/emplweb/news/news_en.cfm?id=233, accessed 23 October 2008. Emphases added.

13. Director-General Quintin, speech at the 4th European Meeting of People Experiencing Poverty, 10 June 2005. Luxembourg Presidency of the European Union (2005) *Images and Perceptions of Poverty*: 19. Conference report. Online. Available http://www.eapn.eu/images/stories/docs/EAPN-position-papers-and-reports/4EUmeetingPEP/4thpep_en.pdf, accessed 15 March 2011. Emphasis added.

14. Director Jérôme Vignon, quoted in EAPN Europe (2009) 'EAPN releases a new publication on participation'. Online. Available http://www.eapn.eu/index.php?option=com_content&view=article&id=855%3Apress-release-eapn-releases-a-new-publication-on-participation&catid=7%3Apress-releases&Itemid=100002&lang=en, accessed 22 March 2011.

reminds others 'that whenever we talk about targets and percentages we are in fact not talking about figures, we are talking about people and their potential and talents'.[15] Individualising people counteracts widespread stereotypes and thus gives them dignity in the perception of *others*:

> These people experiencing poverty and social exclusion also wanted to break the negative image of 'layabouts who don't want to work' which tends to surround them. They felt that it was vital to include them in this type of meeting in order to recognise their intelligence, the benefit of their experience and their ability to make constructive suggestions. (European Commission 2008e)

The main impact on the agency of the poor aimed at through the European Meetings consists of representing them – or giving them the chance to present themselves – as competent experts on social policies (on the basis of their direct affectedness), and on the consequent change of attitudes among the more privileged. Both of these ideas are central for the DG's second line of reasoning justifying the descriptive representation of people affected by poverty.

Unique expert input

The argument of descriptive representatives as valuable experts is about as equally strong in DG Employment's text as that of a right to a voice. The gist of this reasoning is that people affected by poverty are *experts by experience*, i.e. their experience gives them knowledge of the matter that is valuable for decision-making. This input differs from that of all other involved experts or functional representatives, in that this expertise stems directly from 'the situation [...] on the ground' (Interview no. 6). It is unique because of its *authenticity*, i.e. its 'first hand'[16] quality, which no other representative could pass on without losing something essential: '[I]t's more genuine' (Interview no. 7).

DG Employment illustrates the special character of this input by continually contrasting 'policy makers and people who experience poverty in their every day life [*sic*]'.[17] This rhetoric creates a clear difference in positions between the descriptive representatives and the other governance actors involved: there is a division between those who 'make' and those who 'experience'. In other words, there is a passive role for those 'most *affected* by social exclusion' and an active

---

15. European Commission (2007) 'Tackling social inclusion: people experiencing poverty have their say'. Online. Available http://ec.europa.eu/social/main.jsp?catId=89&langId=en&newsId=27&furtherNews=yes, accessed 22 October 2008.

16. European Commission (2009) 'European media seminar: "poverty and media"'. Online. Available http://2010againstpoverty.eu/export/sites/default/extranet/Newsletter_EN_EY_2010_091208.pdf, accessed 16 March 2011.

17. European Commission (2010) '2010 Starting point for a new deal. 9th EU Meeting of People Experiencing Poverty'. Online. Available http://2010againstpoverty.eu/news/news/news101.html?langid=en, accessed 13 December 2010.

role for those 'who can *help* improve their lives',[18] implying the need to be helped on the part of the former. At the same time, there is also explicit reference to the differences in power between these two groups: 'This is why we are gathered here today: so that decision-makers, those in a position to swing the balance and reduce poverty, can hear what the people affected have to say'.[19] Finally, the distance is also manifested spatially and cognitively: 'Around 200 Europeans on the *front line* of the battle against social exclusion met EU and national policy makers in *Brussels* for a direct dialogue' (European Commission 2008f; emphases added); '[The participants] also emphasised that their *experience* of social exclusion was quite distant from the *perception* of decision makers' (European Commission 2007e; emphases added). The emphasis on this distance firstly serves to point out the special value of the input that descriptive representatives can provide: it is something that professional policy makers (including NGO officers) almost by definition have no access to themselves, because in general they have no personal experience of poverty. This is why this specific kind of experiential knowledge can only be related by those who have had that experience themselves, and it is in this sense that the poor 'understand their own problems the best' (European Commission 2008e). Secondly, accenting this gap is used to establish the argument that sound policy making cannot be based on involving only one of the two groups (the elites), because the authentic input of the other group (the poor) is essential information about practical matters. This links directly to the basic governance philosophy whereby all those connected to an issue should be involved in the political process. The implicit point here is that the different perspectives and resources of the poor and the officers complement each other, and in this way lead to outcomes that would otherwise not be possible. However, this mutual complementing is not meant as joint policy making, but in a one-directional way, i.e. policy makers receive the input provided by people living in poverty and progress it further in designing their policies.

Yet, what they receive here is a unique resource that is different from other input not only because of its authenticity and the insider information it contains, but also because of the effect it can have on the policy makers: through listening to those with an immediate experience of poverty, they can *understand* them. The aim of descriptive representation is thus not only to *know* something *about* poverty but also a deeper level of comprehension, which is just as necessary and only possible through 'talking face to face' (European Commission 2007e):

> Even the best intentioned and best informed policy makers cannot claim to be able to develop policies, programmes and practices to combat poverty and

---

18. European Commission (2009) 'Statement by Commissioner Vladimír Špidla on the 8th European Meeting of People Experiencing Poverty'. Online. Available http://ec.europa.eu/social/main.jsp?langId=en&catId=89&newsId=513&furtherNews=yes, accessed 2 June 2009. Emphases added.

19. European Commission press release SPEECH/08/244 of 16 May 2008.

social exclusion if they do not understand *what [it] is like* to be poor. And the only people who can tell them are those who live in such situations.[20]

Understanding 'what it is like to be poor' is intended to change the perspective of decision makers more deeply and broadly, which is ultimately expected to have an impact on the implemented policies.

Both in the general discourse of 'involving all relevant actors' and 'working together, working better', and in the argument that descriptive representation can lead to a more profound understanding, the main value given to the descriptive representatives' inputs is that they are meant to lead to political *outputs*.

Generally speaking, descriptive functional representation is smoothly inserted in the broader discourse of taking 'all relevant actors' on board in order to achieve something together. That is, to begin with, people living in poverty are a group of stakeholders among others. Consequently, their input stands on the same level as that of other functional groups, and by being involved they play the normal role that citizens are expected to play. If they are mentioned with special emphasis among other functional representatives, this is also to argue that descriptive representation should be seen as normal by all parts of the audience, contrarily to what is assumed to be the case. Conversely, the DG takes credit for involving *all* affected. In this line of reasoning, the reason for seeking the input of the affected is that '[t]he times when these policies were developed by some officials, who "knew" what was good, are over';[21] 'To successfully tackle poverty in Europe, we need to involve everyone, and particularly the people most affected'.[22] In other words, functional input is needed to produce better output (i.e. 'successfully tackle poverty'). Among this, the input of the poor fulfils a particular function: 'The direct involvement of people experiencing poverty and social exclusion in the development, delivery and monitoring of policies and programmes is crucial to ensure the design of more *focussed* and *relevant* action' (European Communities 2007a; emphases added) because 'their direct experience and knowledge contributes important insights to what does and what doesn't work'.[23] This suggests that the basic political orientations are not discussed in this context, but it is more a question of choosing particular issues to focus on and of adjusting measures. The expertise of those directly affected allows policies to

20. Deputy Director-General Lenia Samuel, speech at the 5th European Meeting of People Experiencing Poverty, 12 May 2006. Austrian Presidency of the European Union (2006) *5th European Meeting of People Experiencing Poverty – How do we cope with every day* [sic] *life?*: 13. Online. Available http://www.eapn.eu/images/stories/docs/EAPN-position-papers-and-reports/5EUmeeti ngPEP/5thpepreport_en.pdf, accessed 16 March 2011. Emphasis added.

21. European Commission (2004) Director-General Quintin's speech at the 3rd European Meeting of People Experiencing Poverty, 28 May 2004. Online. Available http://ec.europa.eu/employ ment_social/speeches/2004/oq280504_fr.pdf, accessed 16 October 2008. Author translation.

22. European Commission (2009) 'Statement by Commissioner Vladimír Špidla on the 8th European Meeting of People Experiencing Poverty'. Online. Available http://ec.europa.eu/social/main.jsp? langId=en&catId=89&newsId=513&furtherNews=yes, accessed 2 June 2009.

23. European Commission Communication COM(2003)773 of 12 December 2003.

be 'adapted to the situation really on the ground' (Interview no. 6) and therefore to be 'more effective and efficient' (Interview no. 5). Yet, this may also involve taking account of the poor's own problem perceptions: 'You need to consult the beneficiaries of your policies in order to know what the *needs* – the specific needs – are, and be able to better respond to these needs' (Interview no. 7; emphasis by the interviewee). Inputs are thus both meant to adapt existing strategies and to participate in shaping the definition of the goals to be aimed at. Yet, the stress is clearly on the former of the two.

If the expertise of those affected by poverty is meant to improve policies, what evidence is there of any substantial impact of these descriptive representatives' input on DG Employment's political output? It is worth mentioning that receiving feedback on their messages' concrete impact has been one of the central demands of the delegates to the European Meetings of People Experiencing Poverty. In 2009/2010, when I interviewed the officers in charge of the Meetings, all of them spontaneously mentioned that this was a key task and something that needed to be improved. At the 2010 Meeting, the DG provided for the first time an overview of demands presented at past Meetings and corresponding Commission responses.[24] Notwithstanding, the political influence of these Meetings is difficult to assess, because causalities are hard to establish and the ultimate outcomes are the results of a great many influences. The DG itself makes assertions of substantial, concrete impact only in connection with the 'active inclusion of people excluded from the labour market', a basic approach developed within the OMC that includes the three strands of adequate income support, inclusive labour markets, and access to quality services.[25] The formulation of the strategy formally started in February 2006 with a Commission Communication[26] and a general consultation. In October 2007, the Commission published a second Communication[27] on the matter, followed by another consultation, and finally a third Communication[28] and a Recommendation[29] to the Member States in October 2008. This last Communication was accompanied by a Commission Staff Working Document laying out the various inputs that had influenced the process at its different stages. Among these, the 2007 European Meeting of People Experiencing Poverty is mentioned as a 'useful contribution', and, what is more, the central messages of this Meeting are listed.[30] Although this does not prove how much substantial influence the Meeting had on the policy, it is the only instance where such influence is officially claimed. Apart from this, evidence of political influence is scarce, anecdotal, and scattered.

---

24. Spanish Presidency of the European Union (2010) *2010 Starting Point for a New Deal*: 8. Online. Available http://www.dejavu.pl/eapn/Report_2010/Report2010EN_web.pdf, accessed 17 March 2011.

25. European Commission Recommendation C(2008)5737 of 9 October 2008.

26. European Commission Communication COM(2006)44 of 8 February 2006.

27. European Commission Communication COM(2007)620 of 17 October 2007.

28. European Commission Communication COM(2008)639 of 9 October 2008.

29. European Commission Recommendation C(2008)5737 of 9 October 2008.

30. Commission Staff Working Document SEC(2008)2590 of 3 October 2008: 12.

A realistic assessment of the effect of the descriptive representatives' input on the DG's outputs is seeing them as part of the bigger governance picture, where policy initiatives are developed through discussing topics in many different forums, of which the European Meetings of People Experiencing Poverty are one among others. Conversely, the fact that action on a particular issue has been demanded by those most directly affected is then used *vis-à-vis* other actors in the subsequent debate in order to legitimate efforts to bring about European initiatives. It also has to be taken into account that the agenda of the Meetings is decided upon in advance by the joint organisers, so that the topics of the conference are coordinated with ongoing political processes. However, the discussions there can direct the DG's attention to specific aspects of the issue, which may well influence further action taken:

> [I]t will happen only very rarely that something completely new comes up, but you will get an idea of how does the problem present itself, [...] in how many of the Member States is this an issue. And so, I really have the impression that our previous Director really took this into account, [...] for instance, now on [...] housing exclusion and homelessness, we really have a thematic focus this year,[31] and so we really took this up. As I said, it's a major issue. (Interview no. 5)

It is instructive that in Progress' Strategic Framework, the organisation of the European Meetings of People Experiencing Poverty figures as a means to 'support [...] policy debate' (European Commission 2010a: 25), i.e. it is part of the 'information and communications activities, networking between and with stakeholders and events on issues relating to Progress policy areas' that are meant to bring about Immediate Outcome no. 3.5, *viz.*: 'Promote high-quality, participatory policy debate at EU and national levels on law, policies and objectives in areas relating to Progress'.[32] This again should '[h]elp positively change understanding and promote ownership of EU objectives and priorities among key EU and national policy/decision-makers and other stakeholders' (Intermediate Outcome 2.2).[33] Accordingly, descriptive representation is not only an input channel, but also an instrument for the organisers to advance their goals in a setting where discursive influence is virtually the only influence they have on other involved actors:

> What is also clear [...] is that the Commission is trying to help Member States cushion the social impact of the economic and financial crisis. This is wholly true to the EU's approach, but our hands are relatively tied in what we can do

---

31. In the social OMC, the years during which the Member States do not submit National Strategic Reports (the so-called thematic light years) are assigned a specific theme on which to work in particular. In 2009 this was homelessness and housing exclusion.

32. Progress document PROGRESS/009/2007- revised of 24 October 2007. Online. Available http:// ec.europa.eu/employment_social/progress/docs/progress_009_07_en.pdf, accessed 27 November 2008.

33. *ibid.*

in Europe. We need very strong political support. I hope that the outcomes and conclusions of this 8th Meeting will help strengthen our efforts.[34]

This is why, as mentioned at the beginning of the chapter, all three organising organisations (the spring Presidency of the EU, DG Employment, and EAPN) seek to give the Meeting a topic that suits their respective agendas. This again means that the central topic is not least determined by the political responsibilities of the national Ministry in charge and of DG Employment, who will 'of course [...] want the Meeting to pick up themes which are very current or are very much the responsibility of that particular Ministry' (Interview no. 2) or the DG. Conversely, if the issues raised by the delegates concern other executive departments, they are less likely to have an impact.

> The limit of this is that there are too many situations in which this participation is not effective. [...] [F]or instance, what is the European Commission's or what is DG Employment's capacity to use what we can learn with these people [...]? Have we been in the capacity to influence DG Comp[etition] or DG Trade? The answer is no. (Interview no. 8)

Among the issues that DG Employment has been advancing through the European Meetings of People Experiencing Poverty is the above-mentioned housing, which was on the agenda of the 2008 and 2009 Meetings and was a thematic focus in 2009, so that it was also discussed in many other forums. Yet, it is difficult to pinpoint the exact influence the input of the poor has had:

> I mean, [...] this is a process that is not one-to-one in the sense that if something is said by some of the participants at the conference, we take it up, we modify, we amend a document, and then it's... It doesn't work like this, but it does have an impact. I remember the thing on housing, for instance – it came up so clearly – that this is something that was really taken up by our Director in different meetings, and he really pointed to it [...] and he also translated it to the members of the SPC [...] But there is not like... one person says something – it's like the general messages are a support of some of the things we're doing. (Interview no. 5)

Another example is financial inclusion (the right of each person to basic banking services, such as a bank account), which 'through these Meetings we managed to have [...] on the top of the agenda' (Interview no. 7), but which was also discussed, among other things, in the 2007 Single Market Review,[35] in a study commissioned by the Commission and a subsequent conference about that

---

34. Commissioner Špidla, closing speech at the 8th European Meeting of People Experiencing Poverty, 16 May 2009. Czech Presidency of the European Union (2009) *Where We Live, What We Need*: 38. Online. Available http://www.eapn.eu/images/docs/8thpepreport_en.pdf, accessed 5 March 2010.

35. European Commission Communication COM(2007)724 of 20 November 2007.

study in 2008,[36] before it was talked about in the 2009 European Meeting. This illustrates well the DG's way of working, of which the Meetings are a part: '[Y]ou launch an idea, and then the next thing is to get the facts, get the evidence. Then you try to see whether there is political support to develop some kind of initiative, and then you go a step further' (Interview no. 5). In fact, financial inclusion is also an example of where DG borders were crossed, as DG Employment and DG Internal Market and Services were both involved. Minimum income, in turn, is an example of where this strategy has so far not led to many results, although the DG and EAPN have been working on the issue for years, and it has also been discussed in the European Meeting (in 2008).

By way of conclusion, it is difficult to evaluate the concrete influence that the descriptive representation of people living in poverty has had on the DG's political output. While the evidence is scarce, it is nevertheless worth noting that many of the officers involved in the organisation of the European Meetings are sincerely committed to the idea that what the immediately affected say should have a concrete influence on policies:

> But still I think that there's an issue – it's not only about being able to express yourself once and then that's it; I mean, you're relieved because you've been able to say it and there was some press. It's not only about this, I think, because it's also a kind of a clear message to people that are there, […] like if you think that there's an important problem with housing – and this was something that came up very strongly over two consecutive Meetings – it's a valid question. If Europe is organising and paying for this conference, this is wanting you to participate in this – it's a valid question to ask them, you know, when we... Last time we were here, we pointed to some problems – has anything happened that year, then? Have you done something? (Interview no. 5)

In the setting of the OMC, it is a general structural characteristic that political outputs are the result of complex and lengthy processes with a great number of inputs, so that it would require in-depth case studies to assess the influence of any of these inputs. Notwithstanding, the DG itself has continually demanded the Member States to document the impact that the descriptive representation of the poor (as well as other functional representation) has had on the national social policies, and repeatedly criticised the fact that the relationship between this input and political output is not clearly established in the national reports:

> But it also has to be underlined that in most cases [of the 2003 National Action Plans] one does not find a single element demonstrating that the increase of this participation [of people experiencing poverty] has had a direct impact on the design and implementation of policies. This impact is very difficult to measure, but one can assume that it is in general very weak.[37]

---

36. *See* European Commission press release IP/08/805 of 28 May 2008.
37. European Commission (2004) Director-General Quintin's speech at the open plenary of the

Ultimately, then, DG Employment acknowledges the need to demonstrate the impact that some particular functional input has had, and it has also started making efforts in this direction.

Gaining access to expertise that serves to better design policies is the DG's main argument relating to the special input that people living in poverty can provide. Yet, they also expect another effect on political outputs, which is more indirect. Meeting poor people face to face and talking to them can change the general *perspective* of the guests of the European Meetings of People Experiencing Poverty – i.e. politicians and executive officers – and through this can impact on the ways they deal with social problems. This effect connects back to what was said at the end of the previous section about increasing the poor's dignity from the point of view of the more privileged. However, while the DG's public text mainly refers to this as a goal in itself that has to do with basic democratic norms of equality, interviews with DG officers suggest that, in addition to this, changing the attitude of the Meetings' guests is also meant to subtly influence the policies that these people participate in developing.

Participating in a European Meeting of People Experiencing Poverty can be an eye-opening moment for policy makers:

[T]he Meetings themselves – those that I did participate in – actually left a more – much more – profound impression on me than I thought they would, because these were real people and you did get the real-life stories, usually in informal chats afterwards, and so, and of course, ultimately it does impress.

[…] [W]hen I say it worked, I mean it did generate the impact – or it seemed to me – that it was intended to. But what is the impact, I mean, that's intended is of course, apart from giving a few people, poor people, the chance to experience something else than poverty for a moment, and to speak to some officials or whatever, but the other intended impact is of course that the officials actually meet real-life poor people, and that they come home with an imprinting of a concrete person rather than just an archetype or a statistical number. So in the end, I guess it works at least to some extent. (Interview no. 4)

3rd European Meeting of People Experiencing Poverty, 28 May 2004. Online. Available http://ec.europa.eu/employment_social/speeches/2004/oq280504_fr.pdf, accessed 16 October 2008. Author translation.

The quoted passage is an almost verbatim excerpt from European Commission Communication COM(2003)773 of 12 December 2003. For this criticism, *see also*: European Commission Communication COM(2001)565 of 9 October 2001; European Commission Staff Working Paper SEC(2005)256 of 14 February 2005; European Commission Staff Working Paper SEC(2006)410 of 23 March; tender specifications for call for tender VT/2008/059 of 3 May 2008. Online. Available http://ec.europa.eu/social/BlobServlet?docId=1179&langId=en, accessed 4 March 2013.

Indeed, a change in attitude is meant to be achieved through breaking stereotypes and making the guests realise that, 'What would these people say? It's: "We're not different from you. We have exactly the same expectations from life as you do. But what we need is to have some support in order to be able to realise these expectations"' (Interview no. 7). In other words, the intention is to reduce the tendency of the privileged to view marginalised groups with less empathy than groups who are socially more similar to themselves: '[T]here is a tendency to look at people in precarious situations as if they are animals in a zoo' (Interview no. 7). Personal contact should help overcoming this distance and fostering an attitude of respect for people living in poverty on the part of the policy makers, and, following from this, a stronger personal *commitment* to improving their condition (Interview no. 5). Those officers more closely involved with the organisation of the European Meetings and related processes see a real issue in the relationship between the attitudes of the responsible policy makers and the approaches taken towards social problems:

> Let's be honest: not everybody dealing with these issues has the same feeling about them. Some colleagues, they see their position in this Unit, despite the commitment, as a means to go forward. For them, it's a file. Some others, […] and I include myself there, we're more committed than the others. And we don't see this as a means only for career progression; we're really involved in this […]. But you see, we're different people in this Unit, and each one sees this place differently; but again, I do consider that when you deal with these issues, you have to have some specific feeling. (Interview no. 7)

Direct contact not only breaks stereotypes, it also makes political issues concrete, which it is hoped will change the approaches taken towards them:

> [M]any of the people in the Commission are economists, even when we're working on social policies. Economy is not the only rationale of our lives. I mean, there are political aspects, there are other aspects of importance […] [S]tatistics is not the only source of knowledge in our society. I rely very much on figures, but there are things about […] how people live, what they expect, or what we should do, or how we could find the way to improve things, which will not be given only by economists. (Interview no. 8)

This is why the 'idea of a *dialogue* lies at the heart of the meetings of people experiencing poverty' (European Commission 2007e).

> Decision makers and politicians are asked to exchange information with people experiencing poverty, to answer their questions and to take their recommendations. In 'classical' events it's the opposite: some people experiencing poverty are invited by decisions makers to give their testimonies. (Interview no. 3)

A genuine dialogue requires an open mind of the interlocutors, which raises the question of whether this strategy of changing attitudes through direct contact with descriptive representatives also works for those whose perspective is furthest from the attitude aimed at. Put differently, are the guests of the Meetings predominantly people who do not need to be convinced of its goals? Concerning these people, it is more realistic to assume that the Meetings primarily 'give [...] them new energy for their commitment' (Interview no. 2). In this respect it is also worth recalling what was said at the beginning of this chapter about the Meetings being tied to the issues within the DG's and the responsible Ministry's responsibilities. In line with this, the participating politicians and officers are almost exclusively working in the area of social policies, while people from other departments, such as economy, employment, education, or urban planning, for instance, are missing. In any case, out of those policy makers who did participate and who took part in the EAPN-commissioned impact study about the Meetings, 93 per cent declared that the Meetings helped them 'to understand the situation of people experiencing poverty', 80 per cent said they were acting 'differently in the fight against poverty after these meetings', 43 per cent judged that 'the meetings stimulate policy makers to fight poverty', and 50 per cent found that 'the discussions and recommendations of the meetings [are] translated into policies' (Dierckx and Van Herck 2010: 15–16, 34–5). This suggests the interpretation that the Meetings do have some impact on the way of thinking of the involved policy makers (whether or not this is eased by a previous inclination of those who take part), but their influence on political outputs remains a question that is difficult to answer.

Representation: experience or expertise?

DG Employment conceptualises the descriptive representation of people living in poverty as 'involvement' or 'participation' rather than representation. Apart from the fact that this phraseology is common well beyond the Commission, in policy texts as well as governance literature, it is also directly in line with the DG's arguments of giving voice and providing expert input. Both voice and expertise are presented as something unmediated, coming directly from 'the ground', which is also reinforced by the emphasis on the 'direct dialogue'[38] between poor people and decision makers. However, in practice, the delegates at the European Meetings of People Experiencing Poverty are clearly meant to speak also for those who live in poverty as well but are not present at the event. For one thing, this is a logical consideration: what would be the sense of listening to any limited group of citizens, if what they say has no bearing on other citizens?[39] After all, one of the reasons given for these events is the aim to better understand 'poverty', i.e. a social condition concerning millions. Put differently, if the Meetings are to provide input into policy making, what would be the democratic value of input formulated

---

38. European Commission (2010) 'The fight against poverty in the EU takes centre stage at the 9th Meeting of People Experiencing Poverty'. Online. Available http://www.2010againstpoverty.eu/export/sites/default/downloads/Press/EN_Diary_Note__9th_PEP.pdf, accessed 23 March 2011.

39. Alcoff (1991) demonstrates that it is indeed impossible to speak exclusively for or about oneself without what one says having some relevance for others.

by 120–30 citizens, if these were not speaking for a larger group? For another thing, the representative character of the European Meetings does come through when one looks closely at the news that the DG publishes about them: accounts of the participants include '*delegations* of people experiencing poverty from 27 countries',[40] delegates are called 'first hand witnesses of *poverty*',[41] i.e. people talking about a larger phenomenon beyond their own lives, and often the size of the affected group – the functional constituency – is given in this context: 'There are still 79 million Europeans at risk of poverty across the EU'.[42] It is thus not merely an imposed interpretation to analyse these practices as descriptive representation. Apart from the question of whether we are de facto dealing with a situation of representation, it is also worth noting that the terminology of 'participation' makes it possible to avoid difficult questions about the choice of participants and their relationship with those they speak for. These issues are not addressed in the DG's text. Yet, what can be concluded from this text about how the European Meetings are meant to work in terms of representation?

The descriptive representation of poor citizens practised by the Commission is widely recognised to be legitimate, despite the circumstance that it is organised very differently from conventional forms of democratic representation and that its impact is unclear. In fact, its ramifications for political outputs have long been only of minor importance for its perceived legitimacy:

I think that it is very important that it [the European Meeting of People Experiencing Poverty] *exists*, but I think that it's not so effective. The Commission has managed to develop views that participation of people is legitimate […]. There is no reference actor in the European Union […] who could develop the view that it's not important. So this is an important vector, an important *aquis* from the last decade. […] So, it's important that it exists, […] for a democratic and very political factor, for the fact that nobody can *contest* that it's legitimate; you see? (Interview no. 8; emphases by the interviewee)

Besides the fact that this status of legitimacy makes it possible for DG Employment to legitimise their own position by drawing on the European Meetings (whose delegates will inevitably call for EU action to reduce poverty), the circumstance that this status has been achieved without much emphasis on (or impact from) concrete, substantial contents indicates that representation has here an important *symbolic* dimension. Symbolic representation means that the

---

40. European Commission press release IP/08/753 of 16 May 2008. Emphasis added.

41. European Commission (2010) 'The fight against poverty in the EU takes centre stage at the 9th Meeting of People Experiencing Poverty'. Online. Available http://www.2010againstpoverty.eu/export/sites/default/downloads/Press/EN_Diary_Note__9th_PEP.pdf, accessed 23 March 2011. Emphasis added.

42. European Commission (2009) 'Statement by Commissioner Vladimír Špidla on the 8th European Meeting of People Experiencing Poverty'. Online. Available http://ec.europa.eu/social/main.jsp?langId=en&catId=89&newsId=513&furtherNews=yes, accessed 2 June 2009.

delegates to the Meetings are representative mainly by virtue of symbolising their constituencies, rather than, for instance, by mediating the aggregated views of the represented or by being formally authorised. Symbolism is at work in at least two aspects of the Meetings: the delegates represent symbolically by sharing the condition of, and also visibly resembling, their constituency, and the EU symbolically demonstrates that they are listening to the poor and respect them as full citizens by inviting them to venues reserved for high-profile conferences, such as the EP and Charlemagne buildings in Brussels. These two aspects together make up much of the legitimacy of the event and create an influence beyond 'mere symbolism':

> I was responsible, for instance, last October for a conference about media and poverty, which was a conference organised in the main conference hall of the Commission for 130 people. They were among the public NGOs, but also journalists, […] and at the end of the conference, thanks to the partnership with the NGO, ATD Fourth World, we gave the floor to two people – two persons experiencing poverty. These two persons, […] for half an hour they explained how they live, what it is to be poor […] and what they expect from the different actors. […] [E]ven in terms of visibility, I mean, everybody could notice that these people were not officials or they were different. They were different. But when they took the floor to tell people that their expectations, for instance, are not necessarily different from ours, so they are not a separate category – I mean, indeed I never heard such a quality of silence in a European conference, and it was the end of the day, and some of the people had started at four o'clock in their country before arriving in Brussels […] and I struggled inside, for instance, to get them, and to get them in the main conference room – in the main building of the European Commission – with the same standard of service, including web-streaming and so on and so on, because I wanted people experiencing poverty to be speakers in this conference on the same seat as the one as Mr. Barroso has sat one day before and maybe the foreign minister of one of our countries the day after. This matters also. (Interview no. 8)

Hence, these symbolic aspects are important for attaining the intended influence on the attitudes of the listeners and on the ways in which the agency of the poor is seen. However, achieving such substantial consequences with symbolic means is only possible if the latter are complemented with appropriate contents. The impression that instances of descriptive representation make on the more privileged is a result of the specific combination of visibly poor people appearing in a context of political power and the experience that these representatives have constructive and relevant things to say. This is why, to ultimately have an impact on policies, descriptive representation has to be organised as a structured, long-term process that is not only geared to symbolic effects, but also makes sure that concrete contents are fed into the policy-making process. This involves not only a receptive attitude on the part of the policy makers and clear messages from the representatives, but also structures that make communication between the two possible.

[T]o give you an idea, when our Head of Unit came, she told us: why don't we do a wide consultation like [Commissioner for Institutional Relations and Communication, Margot] Wallström has done. And the citizens, […] there were 20,000 people, I don't know how many thousand, who came here in Hazel, and there was a public consultation, because this was a media show! It was not a real consultation. We want to have consultations which will allow us to go ahead, if you like; not just to make a 'mediatic' show.

[…] [S]ince 2006, we have this strategy on the Rights of the Child […] and one of the issues they want to do is this EU Forum with participation of children and lots of blah blah. The NGOs were very keen on it. I kept telling them: be realistic – this cannot be done at European level. If you need to consult children, first of all you have to identify the structures in which you do it, and then you start from the local and national level. You don't bring children here to Brussels, you know; the same way we do not bring people [living in poverty] here without any preparation. Preparation is a *year*-long process that takes place at the national level, even at regional, local level. (Interview no. 7; emphasis by the interviewee)

The European Meetings of People Experiencing Poverty build their legitimacy on both symbolism and substantial input, which is what makes them vulnerable to recent demands for political outputs responding to the representatives' messages over the years.

What distinguishes the Meetings from conventional conceptions of representation is the *relationship* between representatives and represented. The selection of the representatives is organised by the national EAPN networks and is done differently from one country to the next. Some networks have a series of big conferences with elections of the delegates; others recruit the representatives among people they know through their work (Interview no. 3). In any event, it is never the whole intended constituency (the poor) that authorises their representatives, which would obviously be impracticable. Concerning the deliberative relationships between representing and represented, little is known and variation can be assumed to be significant. Presumably, people with contacts to a social NGO also know a range of others in similar situations through this NGO. One can also expect EAPN's member organisations to choose delegates on the basis of such considerations, among other criteria. Moreover, it is conceivable that being part of a wider community of peers can mobilise people to volunteer as a representative, and conversely, having been a delegate to the European Meeting can motivate people to create more contacts with others. The impact study on the Meetings indicates that many participants have been empowered, have learned new skills, have networked among each other, and have engaged more in civil society and other political arenas after the Meeting (Dierckx and Van Herck 2010: 17–24). Hence, in all likelihood there is considerable communication between representatives and represented. Nonetheless, the fact remains that the national EAPN networks (or, sometimes, their member NGOs) have a great say in the choice of participants in the Meetings. Moreover, they apply their own criteria, too, which can also be inspired by the logics of scarce resources and practicability. For example, it is easier for the national networks to have the same people participate several times, because in this way they do not need to start their preparation from the beginning (Dierckx and Van Herck 2010: 62). At the same time, many new participants are so overwhelmed by the new situation (the Meeting itself, but also travelling to an unknown place, etc.) that they only manage to fully contribute at their second attending (p. 59). Yet, a number of representatives had been there so many times that the DG asked EAPN to bring new faces to the 2009 Meeting (Interview no. 7).[43] Another issue in the choice of representatives is the fact that some of them are people who have actually overcome poverty and are now in a less precarious situation. With them, it is easier for the more privileged to engage in a dialogue, so that they become translators between the remotest parties, and 'act as advocates for vulnerable groups' (European Commission 2010c).

> I wonder whether you could organise it if there was not this layer between people who have been in poverty but have then managed to get into social service providing, and so on, who know – can be a bit the link. [...] I mean, if people are really living in poverty, are really excluded, this means a kind of a barrier, and so a kind of not wanting to participate in things where these difficult words are used, and so on. So it is something you need to really work on. (Interview no. 5)

This shows the importance of the Meetings' content dimension in addition to the symbolic aspect, i.e. besides having poor citizens representing poor citizens in Brussels, the aim is also to generate genuine communication and make the messages of the affected understood. Besides, the presence of these translators gives an additional twist to the question of what exactly the representative claim the DG makes about the European Meetings is, and what it is based on, if not all of the representatives are in fact poor.

Representation is based on an agreement between the representatives and their audience, i.e. the conference guests and, in a second layer, those reading the DG's text about the Meetings. By contrast, most of those claimed to be represented have in all probability never heard of the events; their approval is thus not critical to bring representation about. Consequently, also the choice of the representing and their concrete relationships with their constituencies is not seen as relevant to the case. Instead, representation comes about through two mechanisms, *viz.* firstly, symbolising the represented by (visibly) resembling them, and secondly, having empathy for and deep experiential knowledge about their situation (cf. O'Neill 2001: 490). This latter condition is still valid for those representatives who have

---

43. It is perhaps also worth considering the fact that if the delegates are different individuals every year, their demands for concrete consequences following their inputs may be less insistent, since they have not been witnessing a series of Meetings while their life situation has remained unchanged. Cf. Dierckx and Van Herck 2010: 24.

overcome poverty; yet, the DG's text about the Meetings never mentions these translators. On the whole, the logic of the European Meetings is strongly based on the combination of both representative mechanisms, i.e. representation here has an aesthetic as well as an epistemic dimension, which are mutually dependent. The legitimacy of this form of representation rests on the credibility, in the eyes of the audience, of the representatives as 'being poor' and of what they say as authentically based on this poverty. For this kind of authenticity, it is largely irrelevant which individuals, out of millions of poor people, do the representing. Moreover, the fact that the representatives share the condition of the represented and speak out of their personal experience suggests that representation is here something unmediated, thus providing a direct view on the represented. That said, who precisely, or what aspect of the constituents, is claimed to be represented here?

The functional constituency represented in the European Meetings are 'people experiencing poverty', i.e. the poor. Notwithstanding the intuitive simplicity of this concept, it is worth noting that it is impossible to delimit this group clearly. Due to the diversity within the EU, a relative definition of poverty is applied in the OMC, going back to a Council Decision of 1975, whereby 'persons beset by poverty [are] individuals or families whose resources are so small as to exclude them from the minimum acceptable way of life of the Member State in which they live'.[44] Statistically, this is defined as people living in households whose total equivalised income (in purchasing power standards) after social transfers is below 60 per cent of the national median. In 2008, this was 17 per cent of the population (85 million people) (European Commission 2010d: 1). Yet, 'given the conventional nature of the retained threshold, and the fact that having an income below this threshold is neither a necessary nor a sufficient condition of being in a state of poverty' (European Commission 2005b: 1), precisely speaking, only poverty *risk* can be measured in this way. In 2010, this indicator was complemented by two additional ones.[45] The first, material deprivation, refers to the inability to afford goods, services, or activities 'that are ordinary in the society or that are socially perceived as "necessities"' (European Commission 2010e: 134). The second new indicator is the number of people living in households where none of the adult household members is working (p. 126). In 2008, 120.3 million Europeans (23.6 per cent[46]) fell under at least one of these three definitions, and 6.9 million belonged to all three categories (pp. 126–9). This demonstrates how difficult it is to determine what poverty actually is and who is affected by it. The situation is further obscured by the equally used term 'social exclusion', which takes a more multi-dimensional perspective and is defined as

---

44. Council Decision 75/458/EEC of 22 July 1975.

45. European Council (2010) *European Council 17 June 2010: Conclusions.*

46. Eurostat (2013) Table t2020_50. Online. Available http://epp.eurostat.ec.europa.eu/tgm/refreshTableAction.do;jsessionid=9ea7d07e30ea4d64a5498634427181a2dfc03c61186f.e34OaN8Pc3mMc40Lc3aMaNyTaNiPe0?tab=table&plugin=1&pcode=t2020_50&language=en, accessed 17 November 2011.

a process whereby certain individuals are pushed to the edge of society and prevented from participating fully by virtue of their poverty, or lack of basic competencies and lifelong learning opportunities, or as a result of discrimination. This distances them from job, income and education opportunities as well as social and community networks and activities. They have little access to power and decision-making bodies and thus often feeling [*sic*] powerless and unable to take control over the decisions that affect their day to day lives.[47]

Ultimately, poverty and social exclusion remain intuitive concepts; although it is not difficult to understand who is referred to, it turns out to be impossible to specify the group unambiguously. Nonetheless, the same is true for most representative claims.

In light of this, it is conclusive to note that the standard expression used by DG Employment is 'people experiencing poverty', i.e. the defining characteristic in the claim they make is personal *experience*. This circumvents the problems of statistical measurement and refers back to the audience's intuition and the self-definition of those who perceive themselves to be poor, on whatever grounds.

Experience is also the foremost *aspect* of the represented that the delegates to the European Meetings are said to represent. The experience of poverty and the practical knowledge resulting from this are the main inputs intended to be gained through descriptive representation. This comes close to what Iris Marion Young has called 'perspective', i.e. the specific point of view people have, on the basis of their social location (Young 2000: 136–41). For DG Employment, this experience of poverty has a special value as expertise, which is relevant for policy making. However, it is something that is not only generally unknown to the more privileged, but also very difficult to represent for people who do not share this condition themselves, and therefore has to be mediated through descriptive representation in order to become accessible for executive officers and politicians. Descriptive representation provides 'first-hand information from the front line of poverty and suffering in our society',[48] and 'is an essential reminder of what the reality is'.[49] Representing this experience thus opens a source of *information* and has an important instrumental value, allowing the DG 'to successfully tackle poverty in Europe' because it 'help[s] develop solutions, strategies and policies to improve the lives of those most affected by poverty and social exclusion'.[50] By presenting the descriptive representatives' input as valuable knowledge, the DG also makes a claim that the poor are here represented *as* responsible, politically mature *citizens*.

---

47. European Commission Communication COM(2003)773 of 12 December 2003: 9.

48. Commissioner Andor, quoted in European Commission (2010) 'Media Alert. EU anti-poverty meeting: "starting point for a new deal"'. Online. Available http://2010againstpoverty.eu/export/sites/default/downloads/Events/20100624_Media_Alert_PEP.pdf, accessed 13 December 2010.

49. European Commission press release SPEECH/08/244 of 16 May 2008.

50. European Commission (2009) 'Statement by Commissioner Vladimír Špidla on the 8th European Meeting of People Experiencing Poverty'. Online. Available http://ec.europa.eu/social/main.jsp?langId=en&catId=89&newsId=513&furtherNews=yes, accessed 2 June 2009.

Contrarily to widespread attitudes, people living in poverty are here described as those 'who understand their problems best' (European Commission 2008e) and therefore have something relevant to say. Relating their experience thus has little to do with a value in itself given to self-expression, or with recognition of the cultures of the poor, but it is depicted as representation with the specific purpose of influencing political outputs and eventually changing these very experiences into something better.

When looking for exact characterisations of the delegates' speech acts in the Meetings – such as expressing interests, giving opinions, relating their life experience, giving advice, demanding action, etc. – most texts, by far, remain on a rather indeterminate level by referring to 'dialogue' and 'discussions' along the following lines:

> Around 200 Europeans on the front line of the battle against social exclusion met EU and national policy makers in Brussels for a direct dialogue. They discussed issues ranging from minimum income to housing, social services and services of general interest. The aim of this annual event is to include marginal groups in the process of seeking solutions and building policies to improve their lives. (European Commission 2008f)

> This meeting is essential in giving a voice to those who we usually hear all too little: those experiencing poverty. It is also part of an ongoing dialogue between people most affected by social exclusion and the policy makers at European and national levels who can help improve their lives. [...] To successfully tackle poverty in Europe, we need to involve everyone, and particularly the people most affected. This meeting will help develop solutions, strategies and policies to improve the lives of those most affected by poverty and social exclusion, focusing in particular on housing, financial inclusion and access to services.[51]

Giving a 'voice' or a 'say' to the affected and 'involving' them in a 'dialogue' in order to find 'solutions' is the dominant meaning given to the descriptive representation of people living in poverty – a language inserting itself smoothly in the Commission's general governance discourse of 'working together, working better'. In this perspective, giving a voice to the marginalised is the prerequisite to including their 'contribution'[52] in the common effort, which again is a precondition for success.

---

51. European Commission (2009) 'Statement by Commissioner Vladimír Špidla on the 8th European Meeting of People Experiencing Poverty'. Online. Available http://ec.europa.eu/social/main.jsp?langId=en&catId=89&newsId=513&furtherNews=yes, accessed 2 June 2009.

52. European Commission (2008) 'The second Meeting of People experiencing poverty – 10 to 11 May 2003 – Brussels'. Online. Available http://ec.europa.eu/employment_social/spsi/events_en.htm, accessed 16 October 2008.

However, it is seldom that the text refers more concretely to what those involved actually say. The delegates' messages are very rarely cited,[53] but usually dealt with on the aggregate level. In most cases, their input is classified as relating 'experience', which makes a 'better understanding of poverty' possible (European Commission 2007e). By contrast, *interests* are never mentioned explicitly,[54] and implicitly only once:

> But this reform can only succeed if the people living in poverty actively participate in the policies to fight exclusion. Because Social Europe has to benefit everybody, by creating employment and by fighting against exclusion. It would make no sense if it existed only for business and politicians.[55]

This implies the argument that if one is not represented by people sharing one's life situation, one's interests will not be considered (possibly irrespective of good intentions), and one will thus benefit less from the decisions made.[56] The argument resurfaces nowhere else in the text about the European Meetings. Otherwise, 'opinions'[57] and 'expectations' (European Commission 2009b) are mentioned once, and 'concerns',[58] 'needs', and 'aspirations'[59] repeatedly, but not dominantly.

By designating the content of what the descriptive representatives say as 'experience' – always in singular – the text suggests that what people living in poverty have to say is a rather uniform message. Even where plural 'concerns' or 'opinions' are mentioned, there is no allusion to the possibility that the poor might have a plurality of different views or disagree among themselves. This has to do with the presentation of the descriptive representatives as *experts* who provide a 'reality-check'[60] for policy makers, tell them about 'current conditions and

---

53. One of the few isolated cases is European Commission 2008e.

54. The interests of people living in poverty are, however, mentioned a couple of times in connection to NGOs said to represent these interests. E.g. European Commission 2010a: 50.

55. European Commission (2004) Director-General Quintin's speech at the 3rd European Meeting of People Experiencing Poverty, 28 May 2004. Online. Available http://ec.europa.eu/employment_social/speeches/2004/oq280504_fr.pdf, accessed 16 October 2008. Author translation.

56. Cf. Mill [1861] 1991: 245–7. John Stuart Mill makes this case in his *Considerations on Representative Government* to argue for the extension of suffrage to the working class. It was commonly assumed among supporters of universal suffrage that if workers had the right to vote, they would elect their peers to parliament, which would then mean that their class perspective would be considered more strongly in decision-making. This presumption has since turned out to be partly wrong (*see* Manin 1997: Ch. 4).

57. European Commission press release SPEECH/08/244 of 16 May 2008.

58. E.g. European Commission press release SPEECH/10/30 of 18 February 2010.

59. E.g. European Commission (2010) 'European Year for Combating Poverty and Social Exclusion'. Online. Available http://ec.europa.eu/social/home.jsp?langId=en&catId=637, accessed 5 March 2010.

60. Commissioner Špidla, quoted in Czech Presidency of the European Union (2009) *Where We Live, What We Need.* Conference report. Online. Available http://eapn.eu/images/stories/docs/eapn-report-2009-en-web2-light-version.pdf, accessed 14 March 2011.

national differences',[61] and help them understand 'what [it] is like to be poor'.[62] If experience is treated as expertise, it becomes a piece of information about facts and is thus largely unambiguous. At the same time, questions about recruitment, representativity, and accountability can be neglected, because in this perspective it is not of major importance who relates the expertise. As well as that, since the representatives are defined by their experience of poverty, it would be rhetorically problematic to dwell on differences between their experiences while still treating them as one functional group. What is more, however, this way of presenting things renders the descriptive representation of the poor much less political than it could be. Ultimately, the *political* messages that remain from the DG's accounts of the Meetings are, firstly, that descriptive representatives of people living in poverty should be involved in policy making, and secondly, that an effort should be made to reduce poverty. This can well be seen as a message directed particularly towards political actors preferring a more narrowly economic perspective on social policies, while at the same time giving new impetus to those already agreeing. Yet, undoubtedly, listening to people from marginalised social groups contains much more political potential than this. Notwithstanding the facts that the contents of the representatives' inputs are important to the involved officers at DG Employment's former Inclusion Unit, and that the delegates have brought the DG to provide them with feedback about what has resulted from their demands, in the DG's text directed at the public the substantial dimension is still very weak. In most cases, the reader is not told what the representatives said. Ultimately, then, the political potential inherent in descriptively representing those who are normally marginalised and spoken for by more privileged people is not realised. If instead of 'giving *a* voice' to people living in poverty one would listen to their 'voices', one could possibly hear something radically new. However, these messages would also be very likely to conflict with established points of view and collide with the formal limits of competencies between DGs, ministries, and territorial layers of government. Instead, the European Meetings are integrated into the DG's general governance discourse of involving the resources of every possible party in order to achieve a common goal, which is not itself discussed. Descriptive representation differs from other functional representation in its authenticity and in that it is also about the agency of the represented, but in the end it is mostly about a specific kind of expertise that harmoniously complements the expertise provided by others. Yet, it is dubious whether everything poor people would like to tell decision makers can easily be subsumed under 'expertise by experience', and above all, whether

61. European Commission (2010) 'Media Alert. EU anti-poverty meeting: "starting point for a new deal"'. Online. Available http://2010againstpoverty.eu/export/sites/default/downloads/Events/20100624_Media_Alert_PEP.pdf, accessed 13 December 2010.

62. Deputy Director-General Lenia Samuel, quoted in Austrian Presidency of the European Union (2006) 5th *European Meeting of People Experiencing Poverty – How do we cope with every day* [sic] *life?* (conference report): 13. Online. Available http://www.eapn.eu/images/stories/docs/EAPN-position-papers-and-reports/5EUmeetingPEP/5thpepreport_en.pdf, accessed 16 March 2011.

putting together the parts contributed by different functional parties does by implication result in a synergetic whole. The question, therefore, is what happens to those messages that do not fit the given frame.

In conclusion, DG Employment's reasoning contains many arguments for descriptive representation that are also developed in the relevant literature, with the exception of any treatment of questions concerning the representatives' authorisation and accountability, as well as the relationships between representing and represented more generally, which is hardly surprising. The principle advanced in their argumentation whereby the affected have a right not only to speak but also to be listened to promotes a strong conception of democracy; this principle is enhanced by the European Meetings' strong symbolic dimension. However, this democratic potential is countered by treating the experience of poverty as largely uncontroversial information and as contributions to a joint governance project. This observation leads us back to Anne Phillips's (1995: 171–8) considerations about why it is so difficult to apply theories of descriptive representation to social class (cf. Chapter Three). By dealing with women and ethnic minorities, these theories conceptualise descriptive representation also as a means to strengthen the position of these groups *against* the dominant majority *without* overthrowing the existing social order in which particular elites govern the political system. In the case of people living in poverty, the latter condition seems less secure. In addition, descriptive representation in the social OMC is part of a larger governance context, and therefore mostly follows the general logic of functional representation in this setting. The remaining chapters bring out this general logic.

Chapter Ten

The Commission's Concept of Representation: 'Closeness' on All Levels

The analysis of DG Employment's argumentation about functional representation in the social OMC has raised a number of issues that deserve further consideration. In Chapter Six, it was found that the functional groups to be represented are identified on the basis of their relevance to the policy in question – 'relevance' meaning their representatives' capacity to contribute to the attainment of envisaged political goals. The most prominent actors – social NGOs – are claimed to represent three different constituencies simultaneously, *viz.* civil society, especially affected groups, and the NGO sector. Out of these, the representation of the first two is based on epistemic claims about the NGOs' inherent closeness to, empathy for, and knowledge about these constituencies. However, the centrality of 'closeness' to the man in the street for this claim stands in tension with the fact that the internal relationships of Brussels-based umbrella organisations to the grassroots-level associations are not dealt with. In other words, these mediating structures are considered irrelevant to the claim made about the NGOs. How, then, does DG Employment consider this representation to work, more precisely? In Chapter Seven, another tension was revealed between the role of NGOs as representatives and their role as partners of the DG, working together with the latter to achieve common goals. How are these two brought together? This issue is further aggravated in the case of those NGOs funded by DG Employment (Chapter Eight). According to the funding strategy, the main aim of this financing is to increase these associations' capacity to influence policy making, which is not necessarily the same as representing constituencies, and can indeed be incompatible with functioning internal structures of communication (Halpin 2001). How are representation and influence related to each other? The case of descriptive representation (Chapter Nine) has different starting points, but leads in part to similar questions. Representative claims are here based on both symbolic and epistemic mechanisms, which make this form of representation especially authentic. This authenticity is independent of how the representatives are recruited, so that the arrangements for choosing them become irrelevant. At the same time, representation is here depicted as something direct, unmediated. The descriptive representation of the poor distinguishes itself also by the emphasis given to its impact on the constituents' agency. People living in poverty are represented as responsible, politically mature citizens, whose dignity should be acknowledged. The unique input they provide is presented as expertise based on experience, which is free of conflicts within the constituency or between the poor and other policy makers, but is one – special – contribution to a joint project. This raises the question of how the inclusion of this form of representation in the frame of 'working together' in order to achieve common goals is made compatible with the mediation of the constituents' views. Hence, the essential issue with all these practices is how representing a functional group and collaborating with an executive relate to each other, or, put differently, how representation itself is supposed to function in the DG's model. In order to work this out, in the following I look into the DG's model through the lenses of the three theories of representation outlined in Chapter Two – i.e. simple principal–agent models, deliberative representation, and the representative claim.

Two levels of representation

DG Employment's discourse about functional representation through social NGOs contains two representative claims, one based on what these NGOs do on the EU level, and one based on what they do on the local or regional level. It is worth stressing here that this refers to the *DG's portrayal* of NGOs' roles and characteristics rather than empirical data about the latter. The two claims are related to each other, but they emphasise different things.

The claim based on what NGOs do *on the EU level* defines representativity as the aggregation of information or views from the national to the European level. According to this claim, a European NGO represents especially affected functional groups on the basis of four criteria:

– Geographical coverage of member organisations (number of Member States)
– Recognised status of the member organisations in the Member States
– Significance to the policy issue (i.e. both the member organisations and the European secretariat are specialists on the group(s) to be represented, such as families, for example.)
– Effective mediation of information and views from the national to the European level, to the DG and into the EU policy discourse.

The first of these, extensive geographical coverage, is a quantitative criterion which does not relate to the number of natural persons involved on the lowest organisational level (such as members, donors, voluntary workers, participants, beneficiaries, etc.), but to the amount of Member States in which the EU-level network has member organisations. The representativity of these member organisations is evaluated based on their recognition in their respective countries. Thus, the member organisations' legitimacy to speak for their claimed national constituencies is to an important extent established elsewhere. The DG does not spell out how they assess the legitimacy an NGO has in a given country, or what kinds of criteria it would like to see being used for the recognition of national NGOs, but it concentrates on the European secretariat's relationship with the national members' highest organisational level. The NGO's and its members' specialisation on the political issues dealt with is a criterion aiming at the quality of the input to be expected. Legitimacy is here based on knowledge.

All these three criteria are geared towards giving European NGOs quantitatively and qualitatively representative foundations on the basis of which they can legitimately speak for functional groups across the EU. Nevertheless, they only become truly representative if they do in fact use this potential and indeed efficiently and effectively mediate information and views from the national to the European level, making these available to EU policy makers. What may seem to be a circular argument (European social NGOs are important because they are important for the DG) is in fact a representative claim based on what these NGOs are doing:

> European networks have a key role to play in representing, promoting and defending the rights and interests of their constituencies at Community level, *by virtue of their position* as the European Community's main contacts in the implementation of policies. (European Commission 2007b; emphasis added)

Put differently, representation is more than structures, status, and knowledge; these are necessary but not sufficient. In addition, a legitimate representative is a political player taking part in the relevant policy discourses and interacting with the other involved actors.

> [The European Association of Service Providers for Persons with Disabilities is a stakeholder] [b]ecause they do represent a huge potential in terms of employment; a huge intellectual potential as well, in terms of their expertise, whom they're able to bring to the table, to take part in deliberations […]. (Interview no. 4)

It is striking that the criteria of representativity in this claim are the same as the criteria the DG uses to define the relevance of stakeholders (cf. Chapter Six) and for selecting NGOs to fund (cf. Chapter Eight). In other words, the DG chooses as its partners such NGOs whose *EU level* is representative, in the way conceptualised by the DG.

While the claim about the representativity of NGOs' EU secretariats strongly emphasises representing *to* the DG or the wider OMC network, the claim based on NGOs' *local or regional activities* puts the focus on the representation *of* constituents. Here, representativity is defined as 'closeness' to those 'on the ground', which is achieved through activities that equally take place 'on the ground' and thus bring the NGOs into direct contact with the represented individuals. When making this claim, the text does not specify NGOs' local activities, but largely works on the image of 'good' social NGOs that help people in need out of moral motivation. The closeness of this practical work to the affected individuals creates an unmediated relationship between the latter and the (often voluntary) NGO workers, who therefore have unique insights into the lives and views of the represented. This makes a special quality of empathy and knowledge possible, on the basis of which NGOs are claimed to be a form of 'direct [!] representation' of their constituents: they know 'the real needs of men and women on the ground' (European Commission 2001a). The location of this relationship 'on the ground' creates an opposition to those political actors who are by nature located further up, which is especially true for the DG itself, but also for the national executives, for example. The metaphor of 'up' and 'down' is a familiar one for the extent of aggregation and for the abstractness of information (single individuals' lives vs. statistics). At the same time, however, it points to the distance between the two positions. When the DG claims that social NGOs represent 'men and women on the ground' on the basis of their contact with them, this also implies that DG Employment itself does not have this direct relationship; they thus depend on functional representatives to represent a specific dimension of the affected, *viz.* the practical knowledge of their needs based on a deeper understanding of their situation than is possible when looking at things from Rue Joseph II in Brussels. The representative claim made about descriptive representatives is similar to this in the sense that it is also based on a special quality of knowledge resulting from direct contact. Closeness is here brought to its maximum level, i.e. personal experience. In brief, functional representation is meant to make up for the DG's institutional distance from the people, and through this, also to overcome a key difference from national governments, *viz.* the latter's closer relationships to 'men and women on the ground'.

Locally helping people in need is the main basis of representing those especially affected by social policies. Another way in which the local activities of NGOs are used to justify representative claims made about them is their function as arenas of participation, both of those to be assisted and of those engaging in voluntary work to help others. It is through this that NGOs are claimed to represent not only the especially affected, but also civil society more widely. They

> bring people together in a common cause, such as environmental, human rights, and charitable organisations. [...] [They are] [g]rassroots organisations, such as youth organisations, family associations and all organisations through which people participate in local and municipal life. (European Commission 2003b)

> It is certainly the case that they generate and focus active citizenship along with solidarity. (European Commission 2000a)

Closeness is therefore not only direct contact with those represented, but also a structure where the represented actively engage with the organisation. Put differently, being represented not only means being spoken for in the relevant policy arenas by someone who knows one's situation, but also practically engaging in communal activities and thus actively forming a functional constituency of people concerned by a particular issue. From the perspective of this claim, NGOs are thus essentially grassroots associations where people come together, help each other, and work for aims that are valuable to them.

The differences and points of contact of these two claims become clear when analysing them in terms of the modes of representation they imply. The claim about NGOs' representation at *EU level* is essentially based on a principal–agent logic: the European umbrella organisation is made up of national members, and the EU secretariat is formally authorised by and accountable to representatives of these national associations. Their representation is thus founded on formal institutions, and they are usually presented as constituted by their members: 'Eurochild *is a European network of organisations* promoting the rights and welfare of children in Europe'.[1] Logically, this implies a pyramid structure, but the DG does not address the NGOs' institutional setup in detail. Only the funded organisations are formally required to be 'mandated by their members, through a Management Board or other administrative forum, to represent them at the EU level, and to be responsible for the activities of the network' (European Commission 2007b: 14).

The condition that the national member organisations be recognised themselves as legitimate representatives in their respective countries adds deliberative elements. Representativity in this sense can often not be verified with formal criteria, but depends on the societal status of an actor, which can be assessed, for example, through discourses in policy networks. At the same time, major parts of the evaluation of representativity are delegated to others. Different criteria of recognition can be applied in different Member States, and the Commission has very limited possibilities to influence this. On the other hand, this reliance on national processes can also itself justify the representative claim as an argument from authority. National discourses are here presented as a suitable instance to ascertain the legitimacy of functional representatives, which works on the assumption that they are seen as such by the audience as well. By using this criterion, the DG also indicates their remaining within the boundaries of EU competences and responsibilities, i.e. their own area of legitimate action.

On top of this, the criterion that the EU-level umbrella organisations participate actively in policy discourses also means that representation here has strong deliberative elements. It is understood as the activity of speaking for a functional group in joint policy-making forums with other representatives in order to find solutions together:

> The Round Table will establish a fruitful dialogue between representatives from national governments, EU institutions, NGOs, trade unions, academics as well as citizens who live in poverty and experience social exclusion. The two-day event will also be a key opportunity to exchange best practices among the 27 EU Member States. Above all, it will aim at seeking solutions for those living in poverty and suffering from social inclusion [*sic*].[2]

---

1. European Commission (2010) 'Eurochild annual conference looks at ways to end child poverty'. Online. Available http://ec.europa.eu/social/main.jsp?langId=en&catId=89&newsId=945&furth erNews=yes, accessed 14 December 2010. Emphasis added.

2. European Commission (2009) 'Social inclusion in times of recession'. Online. Available http://ec.europa.eu/social/main.jsp?catId=88&langId=en&eventsId=210&furtherEvents=yes, accessed 9 October 2009. The news refers to the 8th annual European Round Table on Poverty and Social Exclusion.

Consequently, representativity is also to some degree the contribution to a governance process with its own political agendas and internal ways of working. Together, these three criteria define representing at EU level as having a formal institutional setup and being acknowledged as legitimate political actors in national governance spheres (as concerns the member organisations) and in the European OMC arena, on the basis of their activities in the relevant governance processes.

Two characteristics of the NGOs' style of representing are attributed to both the European and the local level and thus connect them to each other. These are: the quantitative dimension of geographical coverage, and the question of what aspect of the constituencies is represented.

Geographical coverage means, at the EU level, to aggregate national organisations from as many Member States as possible. It is on this basis that umbrella organisations are claimed to represent a *European* constituency. The best example of this is the Social Platform, which has extensive membership not only geographically but also in terms of different functional groups, so that it can represent European civil society:

What is the EU support to promoting dialogue with civil society?

Since 1995, consultation with civil society organisations in the employment and social field has included a 'structured dialogue'. The main partner in this context is the Platform of European Social NGOs, which brings together 40 European level organisations representing a wide range of civil society [...].[3]

This 'structured dialogue' is elsewhere known as the 'European civil dialogue',[4] i.e. the dialogue with *European* civil society. Concerning the local level, geographical coverage refers to NGO activities in many places across the EU. However, rather than having direct contact itself with many local associations, the DG, as it were, outsources the aggregation of all these voices to European NGOs. For one thing, this makes functional representation more efficient for them and thus creates an important resource of political input without causing too much work for the DG officers. For another thing, this strategy creates structures that specifically represent *European* functional constituencies. Since the OMC is concerned with finding European ways of developing social policies, it makes a difference whether the DG can refer to functional representatives speaking for affected citizens throughout the EU (thus claimed to voice what citizens in the EU need), or whether they refer to a great number of associations speaking for the affected in Brittany, Lapland, Gdansk, Sicily, etc. The latter would imply that

3.   European Commission (no date) 'A quick guide to EU employment and social policies. 14. Dialogue with civil society'. Online. Available http://ec.europa.eu/employment_social/social_model/14_en.html, accessed 18 September 2008.

4.   European Commission (no date) 'Partners'. Online. Available http://ec.europa.eu/social/main. jsp?catId=85&langId=en, accessed 18 September 2008.

poor people in Brittany and in Lapland, for example, could have different views, or even that being poor in Gdansk could be a different situation from being poor in Sicily (thus directing attention to a need for different political approaches rather than European ones). For the Commission, which speaks for European interests, such a representation would have much less potential to create legitimacy for their policies, because they would need to demonstrate how they derive a common European good from all these different views, a claim that would be relatively easy to contradict. Now, by contrast, they can draw on organisations which themselves claim to speak for poor people in Europe, and through that representation the view of the affected Europeans is already there as such, ready to be taken into account. I will come back to this issue later. For the moment, it is to be noted that the geographical extension of the lower levels of representation is important for both representative claims, at EU and at local level. Concerning the former, it is based on formal membership of the national level and serves to justify the claim to speak for a European constituency. Concerning the latter, it is based on a presentation of local associations as being active everywhere, thus being close to their constituents wherever these may be and knowing their specific situation from direct contact. By implication, all these pieces of knowledge are transferred from the grassroots level through national organisations to the EU-level secretariat. Therefore, the claim of closeness made regarding the local associations is important for the umbrella organisations; it is the basis of the pyramid on which the top rests, and from which it draws its legitimacy as representative. In other words, formal membership and recognised political activities alone are not sufficient to represent European constituencies, but broad, concrete contacts with these constituencies are also necessary. 'Closeness' is thus essential for the way NGOs represent, at all levels. The case of descriptive representation is structurally similar. Here, the local and the EU level coincide in the same representatives, because the participants physically travel from 'the ground' to the EU. In other words, the geographical diversity of the European level is assured through formal structures involving representatives from all Member States (correspondingly to the national membership of European NGOs), while local closeness is achieved through having several representatives from each country and especially through their personal experience of what they represent.

In the same manner as geographical coverage, the aspect that NGOs are claimed to represent about their constituents functions as a staple between their modes of representation at the local and at the European level. Both the local staff and the European secretariat, based on the latter's knowledge, mainly represent the 'needs' of those 'on the ground':

> It is vital that stakeholders are actively involved in order to ensure that our policies meet the real needs of people. NGOs can be the bridge between citizens and institutions. (European Commission 2003b)

I would like also to extend a special welcome to all those representatives and volunteers of charities and NGOs who are here today. I very much look forward to hearing your views on how you feel the [National Action] Plans are operating on the ground.[5]

Again, descriptive representation has similarities: 'If we politicians wish to take the measure of your needs and assess what impact the measures to tackle poverty and social exclusion are having, we must heed what you have to tell us'.[6] Concerning the EU level, the needs of the represented are the substance of the content that the representatives pass on, and to which European NGOs have access through their lower levels of organisation. Regarding the local associations, knowledge of people's needs comes through their experiences in their activities, as can be seen in the above quotation where the knowledge mediated by NGOs is based on 'how [they] *feel* the Plans are operating on the ground' (emphasis added). In other words, the ability to represent something substantial is based on experiential closeness to the represented individuals at the lowest level of organisation, so that the substance of representation connects to geographical coverage. In addition to this, the two are also related in that the 'needs on the ground' are here constructed as needs on a *European* ground. The central opposition constructed in the text is that between European policy makers (or policies) and 'the real needs of people', which is bridged by NGOs. The key role given to this juxtaposition serves to justify the importance of NGOs as representatives of the affected citizens: '[V]oluntary and non-governmental organisations serve to bring the needs of the people closer to the decision-makers' (European Commission 2000a). Because of the significance of this argumentational structure, there is no room to dwell on differences within each of the groups, i.e. either politicians or those on the ground. Any indication that different people on the ground might have different needs (or that the ground itself could be internally heterogeneous, i.e. consist of several grounds) would weaken the argument that NGOs are needed to represent those on the ground, and undermine the legitimacy of European umbrella organisations as representatives of affected people across the EU. Consequently, the needs on the ground appear as unproblematic.[7]

---

5. European Commission (2002) speech by Director-General Quintin, 3 October 2002. Online. Available http://ec.europa.eu/employment_social/speeches/2002/031002oq_en.pdf, accessed 17 October 2008.

6. Commissioner Špidla, welcome speech at the 6th European Meeting of People Experiencing Poverty, Brussels, 4 May 2007. Quoted in: German Presidency of the European Union (2007) 6th *European Meeting of People Experiencing Poverty – Progress made, future steps* (conference report): 15. Online. Available http://www.eapn.eu/images/docs/6theuropeanmeetingofpep_en.pdf, accessed 20 March 2013.

7. An occasional exception are the Roma, whose internal differences of opinion and needs are sometimes addressed. Cf. European Commission press release SPEECH/06/415 of 26 June 2006; European Commission (2005) speech by Commissioner Špidla, 9 December 2005. Online. Available http://ec.europa.eu/employment_social/speeches/2005/vs_051209b_en.pdf, accessed 26 August 2008.

As all this shows, the representative claim made about the NGOs' *local level* is essentially based on their closeness to the represented, which comes about through their activities that bring their staff into direct contact with those they speak for. In light of the evoked distance between 'people' and 'decision-makers' (EC 2000a), this closeness also means that NGOs represent people in the sense of common people with everyday concerns related to practical life situations. This aspect applies to their representation of both especially affected groups and citizens in general. The mode of representation this implies is mainly gyroscopic. The claim is above all based on assumptions about the motivation of the people working for NGOs, i.e. the attitude out of which they act. Helping and speaking for the weak out of moral conviction and for small or no remuneration creates a quality of trust that is difficult to achieve for executive officers and elected politicians: 'Your [social welfare organisations] role in promoting and representing the views of specific groups of citizens to European institutions means that you bring a particular credibility to the table' (EC 2000a). Importantly, although this claim of a specific ethical motivation is established on the basis of local activities, it is applied to all levels of organisation:

> Voluntary and non-governmental organisations exhibit a shared commitment by individuals to address discrimination and inequality. They tackle these on the level of helping the individual; but they have also increasingly called on the political level to make the necessary adjustments and policies to combat exclusion and discrimination. (EC 2000a)

This general trust of social NGOs that renders a continual scrutiny of their activities unnecessary is in part based on people's knowledge of NGOs in their own environment, but also largely relies on the positive image of social NGOs in general. In this respect, it has an important symbolic dimension, i.e. already the term 'NGO' symbolises something irrespective of its exact content. 'NGO' often stands for 'the good' – who help the weak and small out of moral conviction – against the 'big and evil', who for their part act for money and power. Social NGOs are typical examples of this widespread image, but environmental NGOs or humanitarian and development aid NGOs, for example, are also identified with this idea. In addition to their motivation, NGO officers are also more generally seen as a category of policy makers on their own. They are neither politicians nor bureaucrats or lobbyists but fairly close to common people themselves in a way that might be called 'social closeness'. On this note, the label 'NGO' functions as such as a statement regarding an association's representativity of marginalised constituencies. It is essentially based on their local activities in direct contact with the man in the street.

This gyroscopic representation based on symbolism as well as the assumptions of motivational distinctiveness and social closeness mediates the needs of the constituencies 'upwards' into political processes; it thus makes policies representative of the constituents' views by transporting the latter into decision-making arenas. However, the local level of NGOs is also expected to represent anticipatorily, i.e. in addition to the mediation of information about needs, representation is an ongoing communication between representatives and represented, in which they mutually adapt to the changing views of each other (Mansbridge 2003: 516–20). In other words, policies become representative of people's views not only by taking these views into account, but also by educating people about the way things are seen by policy makers ('building awareness') and by achieving a common understanding about issues among the affected ('building consensus'):

> [C]reating the political space and legitimacy necessary for building inclusive policies requires building awareness and consensus among a broad range of actors. This is greatly facilitated by involving them in the policy process.[8]

Awareness and consensus are closely linked in the DG's perspective, the tacit assumption being that awareness of European policies leads to support (cf. Chapter Seven). In this vein, awareness raising is defined as 'mak[ing] more visible the positive role played by good social protection and inclusion policies and support[ing] the modernisation of policies'.[9] By virtue of their direct contact with people 'on the ground', NGOs have a key role in making them aware of European political processes; they are thus supposed to function as intermediates between citizens and the DG in both directions, which 'is vital in order to ensure that EU policies meet the actual needs of EU citizens, and that citizens are informed about them'.[10] In a way, one might say that policies become more representative when people *realise* that their concerns are in fact being taken into account in policies they did not know of before. NGOs are thus a kind of hybrid structure, representing functional groups and the people more broadly to the DG, as well as the DG to the citizens. The underlying assumption is that they are basically in line with DG policies, and their representative function is thus seen as part of their role as partners of the DG. They are not entirely external influences to the political institutions, but an essential party in a common effort, where one of their tasks is getting others on board. Related to this, learning about policies is also the prerequisite for becoming active oneself. The 'active engagement of all citizens',[11] which is among the aims of the social OMC, primarily refers to their participation in functional associations. The latter are thus also a vehicle to make social policies more participative, based on their closeness to the citizens.

---

8. Background paper for workshop 2a, European Commission conference 29–30 March 2006. Online. Available http://ec.europa.eu/social/BlobServlet?docId=358&langId=en, accessed 19 December 2008.

9. European Commission (2008) 'Awareness-raising projects'. Online. Available http://ec.europa. eu/employment_social/spsi/awareness_raising_projects_en.htm, accessed 18 September 2008.

10. European Commission (no date) 'Relations with civil society'. Online. Available http://ec.europa. eu/employment_social/fundamental_rights/civil/civ_en.htm, accessed 18 September 2008.

11. Background paper for workshop 2a, European Commission conference 29–30 March 2006. Online. Available http://ec.europa.eu/social/BlobServlet?docId=358&langId=en, accessed 19 December 2008.

All these modes of representation are deliberative, i.e. they work through communication between representatives and represented, either directly or through the public sphere. The DG focuses on the role of direct contact between NGO workers and their constituents. In their account, deliberative representation is mainly based on practical knowledge through doing and on direct contact with common people in their everyday lives. Both are forms of closeness that allow NGOs to represent their constituents as people like you and me, or, put differently, to represent the voice of common sense as opposed to complex bureaucratic processes dominated by political interests. This opposition is constructed through emphasising the distance between 'politicians' and 'the ground', or 'policies' and 'the real needs of people' (European Commission 2003b), i.e. the abstract and the concrete, or the system and the individual. A tacit subtext of this argumentation is the identification of complex political processes with formal procedures, i.e. in the case of the OMC the representation through Member States and intergovernmental decision-making. Through stressing, on the one hand, the closeness of NGOs to the man in the street, and on the other hand, the DG's close cooperation with these NGOs, the DG implicitly claims to have a more direct channel to 'the ground'. NGOs thus provide a less mediated access to 'the *real* needs of *people*' (as opposed to views of detached administrations), and in this way bridge the distance between the DG and the citizens.[12] This is why they are sometimes termed 'direct representation':

> Greater direct representation is, therefore, crucial. First to ensure that policies are technically viable, practically workable and acceptable to all stakeholders. Meeting the real needs of men and women on the ground. And secondly to help the Union to reconnect with its citizens. Closing the gap between rhetoric and reality. (European Commission 2001a)

As this quotation shows, the DG recognises a need for such a bridge and a more direct connection to the citizens. Social NGOs are suitable for this task. Firstly, they are perceived as authentic representatives of the weak and of common people. Importantly, the opposition between policy makers and 'the ground' is used by many NGOs, too, to claim their position as representatives of the latter. Involving them in policy making is thus also a strategy to deal with a growing gap between 'the politicians' and 'the people':

---

12. It is striking that this argumentation has structural similarities with a typical characteristic of populist political movements, *viz.* the claim to represent the voice of the people *immediately*, together with the claim that the people did indeed speak with one voice which could be accessed or 'read off' (Saward 2006: 310, 312) by the movement. The DG does certainly not claim (as populists do) that they could directly convert the wishes of the people into concrete policies; however, they do suggest that European civil society could be represented in a very direct way through European umbrella organisations, without alluding to the possibility of internal conflicts and differences within that civil society.

Let us not forget that we would not speak that much about 'civil society', if the governments and the institutions were not confronted with new forms of political radicalism. Sometimes, this radicalism expresses itself violently in the contestation of 'globalisation'. But for some time, it has been contributing to making 'institutions' and policies appear cut off from the societies and their people. (European Commission 2001b; author translation)

Secondly, NGOs bypass the national executives as representatives of national peoples and thus establish the DG's 'own' structures of representation with their own alternative form of legitimacy:

[The involvement of stakeholders is a means to increase the democratic legitimacy of the social OMC] [i]n the way, in the extent that... I mean, the knowledge is gathered, the interests are not the same, it's – well, it's not something we refer [to] explicitly, but the fact is there are conflicts. There are conflicts of legitimacies, or... and if we do not address the different – one of the most important conflicts is that there is quite a, well, quite a very frequent conflict between the national government, of the local authorities and the organised civil society. If the Commission has a dialogue only with the governments – governments are supposed to represent Member States, and Member States are not only the national administrations and the ministers, but the fact is that the viewpoints are more those of national administrations than those of local authorities or [...] So, there is a permanent challenge here. (Interview no. 8)

Thirdly, based on their aggregation to the European level, NGOs can also be claimed to represent European civil society, whereas all territorial representatives (except for the EU institutions) represent by definition only a national, regional, or local constitution. Altogether, they thus provide a possible source of representative legitimacy for the Commission that corresponds to the latter's role as representative of the European interests. The same considerations are true for the descriptive representation of the poor in their European Meetings.

The representative claims made about the NGOs' European level (representing national member organisations) are firmly based on those about the local level (closeness), and are only possible on these fundaments. The modes of representation working at the grassroots level are claimed to constitute the *essence* of what NGOs are, and accordingly, that essence is inherently present also at the highest level. In other words, the intrinsic 'closeness' of NGOs holds also for their Brussels secretariats, irrespective of whether the employees there have direct contact with their constituents. On the rhetorical level, 'closeness' is associated with 'NGOs', so that a generalised connection is created between the two. In short, closeness is made an intrinsic characteristic of NGOs as such.

A gap bridged by personal commitment

Seen from the institutional point of view, these representative claims do not dissolve the contradictions specified at the beginning of this chapter. On the contrary, it becomes clear that these contradictions are inbuilt in the way representation is conceptualised here. Firstly, if representativity is defined as broad coverage aggregated to the EU level, this is in tension with sensitivity to the diversity of local conditions, i.e. closeness to the individual representees. Secondly, if representativity is defined as mediating the needs on the ground, this is not necessarily compatible with the capacity to take part efficiently in EU governance processes.

Evidence suggests that the DG is aware of these contradictions, although they are not addressed in public. Concerning the conflict between broad coverage and the representation of all the views thus covered, an interviewee spontaneously brought up existing differences when reflecting on my question of how 'the involvement of NGOs […] can add to the democratic legitimacy of a policy':

> One more example, ILGA [the International Lesbian and Gay Association] is the organisation of gay and lesbian, bisexual and transgender people; obviously, these are people of quite varied political preferences, who vote for various, very different political parties, and while ILGA has been pushing very, very hard for non-discrimination law, I'm sure there're many homosexuals who are in politics and who are against non-discrimination law. I know a few. (Interview no. 4)[13]

The DG is thus not unaware of diverse views within functional constituencies, but prioritises high aggregation of a broad coverage over the mediation of diversity. In this way, they construct one European voice for a defined functional group: '[Y]ou know, we consult "youth" through the Youth Forum' (Interview no. 7).

The tension between mediating needs on the ground and the capacity to influence EU-level governance processes is brought up in relation to representational elitism and, above all, the role of the Key Networks. The elitism inherent in representation is raised as a justification for involving as many actors as possible, as well as to justify the Commission's taking discretionary decisions:

> There're difficulties that sometimes NGOs try to say 'we are'; a disability NGO would say 'we are the disabled, we alone should be heard', and that is not the case, actually. Because obviously, I mean, a classical case is: in many Member States you have the issue of individual accounts for services, from which disabled people could be able to pay for services. Which is a great idea that gives them much more independence, […] but there now the experience from several Member States has shown that there need to be quite strict rules for that, that you actually are only able to buy services for it and not something

---

13. Non-discrimination policies were at the time handled by DG Employment, and belonged to the portfolio of the interviewee, in addition to social inclusion.

else, because otherwise the families of the more severely disabled people may abuse those resources in different ways. Of course, this is an argument you won't hear from most of the NGO activists, because the classical NGO activist for disability has two university degrees, and of course doesn't necessarily perceive the problem in this context. So, the more severely disabled people who are from poor families are not necessarily – I mean, when you speak about this, it's good to take this into account; at the same time, one does have to see from contacts with NGOs that the activist's viewpoint is – while being in favour of a vulnerable group – isn't entirely the same as necessarily the interest of every single individual from that group. And so, ultimately we have to take our own responsibilities – we're a public authority, [...] and sometimes we do make our NGO partners happy, and sometimes less so. (Interview no. 4)

Hence, knowing the conditions on the ground can sometimes require social positions (contact with the most disadvantaged within the constitution) that rarely go together with the requirements for working in the OMC sphere in Brussels (two university degrees). Therefore, the DG cannot ensure full information about the 'needs on the ground' through European NGOs, but needs to involve other actors as well, such as local authorities, for example. Obviously, this issue is related to the previous one about the internal diversity of functional constituencies.

The DG also perceives a problem concerning the combination of mediating views from the grassroots and acting on the EU level in the case of the funded organisations. From their perspective, the dilemma presents itself as one between receiving useful input and creating dependencies:

And also the fact – there is also this tension, which I think is visible for some of the networks or the platforms – is that being so used to talk with the Commission, some of them are including the censorship or including the vocabulary they are expected to bring. So you like some freshness and sometimes you like free activity and innovative ideas, because they are already incorporating what *they* think *you* expect them to say. This is very visible with the European Youth Forum, which... I used to work for youth policy, and at some point they were less young than I – in terms of really, you know, contradicting and challenging our ideas – and they were already integrating the things they thought we wanted them to say. And I don't think they are paid to tell us what we want them to tell. [...]

There is there an issue, whether at a certain point, after a certain period of time, are they really representing the basis, the membership at grassroots level? Or are they disconnected from their membership? So I think here there is an issue, of course [...]. (Interview no. 1)

[T]his is a difficult thing; it's this tension between... an autonomous voice you want to talk to, and you want to have represented at the EU – you know if you don't finance it you would probably not have this partner to talk to – and it's difficult to have a real dialogue if you only have partners in the Member States, [...] and you maybe don't have any voice in certain of the Member States, so it's a bit artificial. We create it – we have created partners to speak to at the EU level, to organise towards autonomy, and still trying to make sure that it's in the spirit of the social OMC and they are really representing the people they say they represent [...]. (Interview no. 5)

However, the DG is also aware that the issue is not only one of financial dependency, but also one of the role as partners that the funded organisations are given:

Therefore, in the area of social policy, the NGOs have become indispensable and often powerful partners. I am thinking of women's rights, disabilities and the fight against poverty. For this reason, NGOs become policy-makers and beneficiaries of considerable public subsidies. They thus have to conciliate their mission as 'advocates' and this reality of policy-making. Consequently, they oscillate between autonomy, contesting the institutions, and partnerships with them. (European Commission 2001b; author translation)

The DG is thus conscious of the contradictions observed in their public argumentation. Their public argumentation does not address these issues, but cannot be said to virtually conceal them either. Rather, it leaves a *gap* between what is said about the NGOs' grassroots level and about their European activities, which is not filled. As shown above, the representative claims made about social NGOs are based on their local and European activities; however, nothing is said about what happens in between these levels, i.e. how the vertical mediation inside the NGOs works or should work. This is how the contradictions arise between, on the one hand, local and social closeness to the represented and knowledge about their needs, and, on the other hand, the aggregation of these needs at the European level and the participation in governance processes as partners of the DG.[14] At the same time, it would indeed be difficult to eliminate these contradictions by dwelling on NGOs' internal representative processes, which in part explains why these are not referred to at all. Instead, the DG's text spans this gap by presenting NGOs as *bridges* between the individual citizens and the EU (cf. Chapter Six), which are constituted by a shared *commitment*:

Voluntary and non-governmental organisations exhibit a shared *commitment* by individuals to address discrimination and inequality. They tackle these on the level of helping the *individual*; but they have also increasingly called on the *political* level to make the necessary adjustments and policies to combat exclusion and discrimination. (European Commission 2000a; emphases added)

Hence, in terms of what connects the NGOs' local and European levels, the DG does not speak about the organisations' formal or institutional structures,

---

14. A similar gap appears in the text about descriptive representation at European level, which speaks about the representatives' individual experience of poverty and their role as active participants at the EU level, but leaves out how they are chosen, whether they disagree about some issues, etc.

but stresses their staff's dedication to a cause. Put differently, NGO officers are claimed to be representative on the basis of their attitude rather than on the basis of institutionalised communication between the different aggregative layers of the organisation. In a way, then, as one moves up from the local to the European level, physical closeness turns into a sort of psychological closeness, since NGO representatives at all organisational levels share empathy for the represented. Because their work is generally perceived to be motivated by such empathy and personal commitment, and because they are known to work on small budgets and with little possibilities for personal gain or power, they receive special trust as representatives of the weak. In short, representative claims about NGOs rest strongly on gyroscopic and symbolic elements, which work on widespread epistemic assumptions rather than on formal authorisation and accountability. Presenting NGOs as steadily turning gyroscopes oriented towards generally valued goals makes it possible to depict them at the same time as mediating needs on the ground and as acting as partners of the DG. This allows the DG to 'listen […] to those on the ground' (European Commission 2008g) through European NGOs without having to dwell on the exact ways in which the views of those 'on the ground' are channelled to the EU level. This argumentational construction does not resolve the contradictions between partnerships or efficient policy making at EU level and the mediation of views, and between a broad coverage and taking account of intra-constituency diversity, but it makes them seem irrelevant within this particular notion of representation. In other words, the NGOs' internal structures and procedures between their European and local level are insignificant to the DG's representative claim. Their formal institutional make-up is only of importance concerning the link between the national and the European level, but for the general picture it is not a major issue. Rather than organisational structures, NGOs are presented as organic entities, held together by a commitment and a moral attitude that are manifest in their 'closeness' to those 'on the ground'. Making such a claim is only possible if the audience in fact perceives NGOs as moral agents. Indeed, this image is strong enough for the DG to rely on it without detailed proof. Thus, the argument that NGOs are representative because of their attitudes and the trust placed in them is not invented by DG Employment; rather, they reinforce this view by referring to it.

Evidence that the DG is concerned about the NGOs' institutional structures is scarce but indicates that they seek to know for whom exactly an association is speaking, and to ensure that the views advocated by an NGO do in fact originate in the people they claim to represent.

[T]he social partners have over the years built up platforms of dialogue and procedures ensuring their representativity. The movements making up civil society are just starting to sketch this out. [...] I do not resist posing a provocative question: Can one really aim to organise a 'civil society' with NGOs about whose functioning and representativity one does not know much, but who sometimes have more political and media handling means than a multinational or a state? [...] All this raises two questions. That of the

NGOs' representativity, and, following from this, that of their responsibility. NGOs are often born out of individual initiatives: Whom do they thus really represent? And this question is all the more important at the Union level, where our interlocutors are not the NGOs themselves but federations or networks of national NGOs. Are these European NGOs representatives of civil society? Or are they principally oriented towards financial support, permitting them to maintain structures without any democratic responsibility really taking place? The question poses itself all the more since one often has the feeling that NGOs talk to us to gain credit, and not really to design policies [...]. (European Commission 2001b; author translation)

These critical questions were posed by Director-General Quintin at an internal forum. At single instances, similar issues have also been raised in conferences with NGOs, but never in great detail:

A second [important question the NGOs need to address] is the matter of accountability. It is not only who NGOs represent, but how they conduct their business that is important. How do NGOs consult with their members? Are they democratically organised? Do they practise equal opportunities policies? It is not only in the interest of the broader EU interest that NGOs that participate in the consultation processes with the institutions are accountable. It [is] also in the interest of the NGOs themselves. I know that the NGO community is well aware of these issues and questions. I know that NGOs are well aware that they need to be resolved if we are to be able to help you to make the civil dialogue as effective as the EU needs it to become. (European Commission 2000a)[15]

Hence, the DG is aware that the internal structures of representation between the NGOs' local and European level matter, and they also seem to be conscious of the fact that how these structures work is not only an issue for the NGOs, but also for themselves as the NGOs' high-profile partners. However, dwelling on NGOs' subnational structures would make it more difficult to construct a neat representative claim and would risk having to address challenging questions – such as the ones quoted above – in public.

The role of the constituencies

The issue of the NGOs' internal structures of mediation can also be regarded in light of the question of what role the *represented* are given in evaluating an NGO's representativity. The DG judges NGOs to be representative on the basis of information about their work, not on the basis of expressions of the affected themselves. In other words, the decisive approval is that of the institution towards which an association represents – the DG – and not of the constituency that is claimed to be represented. Certainly, the latter approach would also be difficult to

---

15. Note that addressing the aforementioned issues is presented as necessary in order to make the civil dialogue more 'effective' rather than to make it more democratic, for example.

realise, because those especially affected by social policies are mostly uninformed, unorganised, and politically passive precisely due to their social situation:

> [O]f course, the NGOs, the people who work in those NGOs, and who are from the group in question – obviously, they're not entirely representative, in the sense that you might have, you know, given Roma in general, and they're Roma intellectuals, these people, and of course the Roma for whom we are trying to, well, create – Member States should try to create policies – are people who live in slums. So – and it's very good, of course, to have advice from people who, being Roma themselves, have the empathy, feel very strongly about anti-gypsyism, racism, who have collected lots of evidence from the ground about which policies work and not – I mean in this sense they are; they both in terms of their understanding, in terms of their knowledge can be very valuable, but at the end of the day, they're not – let's say – the full-blown representatives of the people who are in that poverty ghetto, because those people in that poverty ghetto very likely have not heard about them, or do not necessarily identify with them. (Interview no. 4)

This quotation shows two important characteristics of how representation is conceptualised by the DG. Firstly, as already noted, representation is mainly perceived in a deliberative way. To be a 'full-blown representative' one does not need to be formally elected, but the main criterion is whether the represented 'identify with', or 'feel represented' (Interview no. 1) by a representative on the basis of the views she advocates. This implies a central role for the public sphere as a medium of communication, and connects to the notion of gyroscopic and symbolic modes of representation resting on the notion of NGOs as being characterised by a distinctive moral commitment. Secondly, however, the DG also realises that this communication between European NGOs and their constituencies often does not take place, and, what is more, faces severe structural obstacles. In view of this situation,

> their [the NGOs] role is a bit different: they're an interlocutor, rather than a political representative of all these groups whose interests they represent; they lobby on their behalf, but you couldn't say that they represent them in the sense how we understand – I mean a narrower sense of how we understand political democracy. (Interview no. 4)

This means that representation is to an important extent advocacy *for* a group rather than a mediation *of* expressed preferences, which fits together with the emphasis placed on the representatives' knowledge about and empathy for the represented (closeness). From the fact that it is difficult or even impossible for the DG to communicate with marginalised groups it also follows that the interested public is at least as important an audience for the DG's representative claims as those claimed to be represented. In order to build their own legitimacy on the involvement of NGOs, they first of all need to convince the public at large of the representativity of those organisations.

This brings us to a last consideration concerning the ways in which representation by NGOs is conceptualised by the DG, *viz.* the relation, via NGOs, to the *European public.* As was shown in Chapter Six, NGOs are claimed to represent not only those especially affected, but also 'the society at large',[16] mainly in the sense of common people with their everyday concerns. In NGOs' mediating role between the people and the DG, one of their tasks is the top-down communication, with the aim of raising awareness of the goals of the social OMC and building support for them (cf. Chapter Eight). Based on their 'closeness' to the citizens, they are seen to be in an advantageous position for this anticipatory form of representation, although their European secretariats still need to '[r]einforce the advocacy and campaigning skills [...] of [their] national members to advance, support and further develop EU objectives and priorities at [...] national level' (European Commission 2010b). This educational activity is not so much meant to boost support for specific policies by convincing citizens of their advantages, but the intention is above all to create diffuse support for the DG (and the EU more generally) as an actor in social policies. Therefore, NGOs are expected to create links between the citizens and the EU by inducing people to see themselves as represented (also) by the Commission, i.e. to identify with the EU.[17] The DG thus seeks to utilise NGOs to constitute a constituency for themselves, namely a European civil society:

> You also contribute to European integration as a whole. By encouraging national NGOs to work together to achieve common goals, the European NGO networks are making an important contribution to shaping what President Prodi has called a European public opinion. (European Commission 2000a)[18]

This is an additional way in which NGOs are supposed to function as bridges between the DG and the citizens, namely as advocates of European integration. Encouraging their aggregation at EU level also serves this intention. As already noted, European umbrella organisations formally create a representation of *European* constituencies simply through their institutional setup.

Following the theory of the representative claim, all constituencies are first constructed rhetorically. Whether or not the claim to represent such-and-such a constituency is legitimate depends on whether the audience acknowledges it as referring to something they perceive as real. In other words, they recognise themselves, or a third group referred to, in the portrayal presented by the claim-

---

16. European Commission (2009) Commission Decision C(2009)143 ('Annual work programme of grants and procurement contracts for 2009 (update) – Programme PROGRESS').

17. Also, *see* the objectives of the 'Europe for Citizens' programme, which to an important extent relies on supporting civil society organisations. European Commission (updated 13 February 2012) 'Action 2: active civil society'. Online. Available http://ec.europa.eu/citizenship/about-the-europe-for-citizens-programme/overview/action-2-active-civil-society/index_en.htm, accessed 13 February 2013.

18. For the speech by Commission President Romano Proda that Commissioner Diamantopoulou refers to, *see* European Commission press release SPEECH/00/157 of 28 April 2000.

maker (Saward 2006; esp. 301–3). One could thus ask whether Europeans see themselves as part of a European civil society as represented by the DG, and whether the DG's plan to constitute such a constituency with the help of European NGOs is plausible. The latter can be seriously doubted (e.g. Warleigh 2001; cf. Smismans 2003); at the very least, it is based on dubious presuppositions, such as strong communicative relations between the European associations and the citizens, or the commitment of their national and local levels to advance the European integration of social policies. However, to stay on the level of the DG's text, their argumentation rests on an invitation to the people to *feel* represented on the basis of the involvement of NGOs, which are portrayed in a particular way, namely as close to the ground, as knowing and caring for the concerns of the man in the street and the socially marginalised, and as therefore representing them. Although this claim evokes direct contact between NGOs and the citizens, accepting it would merely require acknowledging the picture drawn of NGOs as close to the people. If I as a European inhabitant perceive European social NGOs as close to me (or to socially marginalised people) and therefore qualified to represent my (or their) concerns on the EU level, the DG's claim is successful in my case. Yet, 'European civil society' can only be constituted as a constituency if the same agreement is made by a considerable share of the people. This presupposes that the DG's discourse is received by a sizeable public. For this, one can reasonably assume that direct channels remain of minor significance with regard to communicating with the general public, and that different media continue to function as the main link between public administrations and citizens. Based on everyday experience of following a range of leading European newspapers, it can safely be said that European social policy is almost absent in these forums. DG Employment's goal to build a European constituency by presenting themselves as close collaborators with social NGOs thus faces strong structural challenges, on the part of the NGOs as well as concerning their possibilities of reaching their intended audience.

To conclude, the concept of representation put forward by DG Employment for social NGOs reconciles authentic knowledge of constituents' concrete needs, the mediation of these needs to the EU level, the capacity to efficiently feed this information into OMC governance processes, and partnership with the DG, by presenting these organisations as intrinsically motivated by a sincere commitment to a good cause. In this view, the representatives' attitude is more significant than the associations' institutional structure and formal processes. Representation is primarily a deliberative process building on, and renewing, the reputation of 'NGOs' as representatives of the man in the street – it is trust rather than control. In addition, it is also meant as a means to build a European functional constituency out of those affected by social policies, as well as a European civil society. In this sense, it can be seen as an attempt to construct a particular structure of representation between citizens and the Commission, generating its own form of legitimacy. In the following chapter I look at these issues from the perspective of democracy.

Chapter Eleven

The Commission's Concept of Democracy: 'Working Together'

When I spoke to Commission officers about the role of functional representation in the social OMC, I waited during most of the interview to see whether they would themselves mention democratic legitimacy as one aspect of the issue. Only when the concept was not brought up by the interviewee did I ask towards the end whether 'one could say that the involvement of NGOs as such can add, or could add, to the democratic legitimacy of a policy'. One person's answer began in the following way: 'It's a complicated question, because we could start discussing what is democratic legitimacy, and that would be a long discussion' (Interview no. 4). In this chapter, I look at the DG's contribution to this discussion, i.e. at how democratic legitimacy is conceptualised in their text about functional representation in the social OMC. In principle, democratic legitimacy on the basis of functional representation has two levels: the legitimacy of political actors and the political process is affected, firstly, by how functional representatives are involved, and secondly, by the internal legitimacy of the functional associations. Concerning the latter, I have already shown how the DG presents the ways they represent their constituencies. In the following, I concentrate on how this is related to the wider picture of democratic legitimacy for the DG and its policies. I first analyse their argumentation through the elements of the working model of democracy laid out in the Introduction (Chapter One), *viz.* output legitimacy, input legitimacy, and political accountability. After that, I look at the overall concept of democratic legitimacy that is formed through the specific interpretations of each of these elements and the relationships between them.

Output legitimacy

In the DG's text, the output legitimacy of the political process is conceptualised as policies that efficiently and effectively lead to the desired results, as envisaged by the OMC's common objectives, e.g. ensuring 'access for all to the resources, rights and services needed for participation in society'.[1] Functional representation can help to achieve this efficiency in two related ways: first, the nature of the matter necessitates an approach that involves all affected, and second, functional organisations know the needs of the especially affected. To start with the latter, in order to be able to solve social problems, policy makers need to know what the

---

1.   European Commission Communication COM(2005)706 of 22 December 2005: 6.

'*real needs*' (e.g. European Commission 2008h) of the people are, and 'needs on the ground' are what NGOs are primarily seen to represent. They can thus provide the information necessary to adapt policies to these needs on the ground, and through this increase output legitimacy, i.e. 'ensure [...] the design of more focussed and relevant actions' (European Communities 2007a). Although the distinction between needs on the one hand, and opinions, interests, or preferences on the other hand is not unambiguous, it becomes clear that in the DG's argumentation, the needs of the most affected are above all a piece of information. Rather than a kind of input that influences the course of politics more substantially, they are thus a resource for policy makers that is conceptualised as expertise:

> [I]f you want to develop policies that address problems people are confronted with, you should – well, the *experts* are also the people who are really living in this kind of situation. So we should listen to them, because it is on the basis of what they are telling us that it would be possible for us to make our policies more effective and efficient. (Interview no. 5; emphasis added)

'Needs' are here something unpolitical; they are facts about the conditions 'on the ground', knowledge based on personal experience or direct contact. They do not conflict with each other or with the needs of other actors, and the decisive imperative is to *know* what they are, so that policies can respond to them.

The other output-based argument in favour of functional representation states that since the matters dealt with are multidimensional, the political process needs to involve all those affected in different sectors of society in an 'integrated approach':

> Social exclusion is multidimensional in nature. As a result, measures to combat social exclusion have to be developed in a wide range of policy areas such as employment, social protection, education and training, health and housing. The experiences of Member States as well as of the Community have demonstrated the importance of an integrated approach which succeeds in linking and 'proofing' different policies to combat social exclusion. They have also shown the importance of partnerships bringing together all those involved in these policies to ensure this integrated approach. Experience has demonstrated the need for ensuring an active participation of all stakeholders, especially those excluded or exposed to social exclusion as well as the organisations working for their interests including social partners and other civil society actors such as non governmental and voluntary organisations.[2]

Output is thus seen as depending on the efforts and cooperation of different actors, among which NGOs play an important role. Functional representatives not only bring information about the needs of the affected to the table, but also contribute by working towards the same goals as the OMC. Therefore, integrating their work into the common framework and supporting them financially promotes the achievement of political objectives:

---

2. European Commission proposal COM(2000)368 of 16 June 2000: 4.

The EU's *contribution* to breaking the hereditary chain of poverty

[...] The European Union also provides support for the operating costs of European networks, such as Eurochild, which are devoted to the fight against child poverty.[3]

The political goals that are to be pursued in this way are not themselves dwelt on in this context. Output legitimacy is not presented as concerning the achievement of such results as the people or the represented wish, or that emerge from public debates, but as achieving goals that have already been defined. In the social OMC, these goals are adopted by the Member States as the common objectives, to which the DG frequently refers. The common objectives are the formal, authoritative framework within which the Commission operates. However, these objectives remain on a very general level and deliberately leave a lot of room for different ways of pursuing them, and as the coordinator of the process, the DG can advance particular policies, approaches, and emphases. For example, if the common objective is to have 'a decisive impact on the eradication of poverty and social exclusion by ensuring [...] the active inclusion of all, both by promoting participation in the labour market and by fighting poverty and social exclusion',[4] this does not specify the balance between employment and other means of reducing poverty, which are themselves referred to by the very general expression 'fighting poverty and social exclusion'. The objective as such thus does not prescribe much. Notwithstanding, the DG does not present itself as bringing in the voice of the people or of the affected concerning *how* these objectives should be implemented, but depicts itself as a mediator ensuring *that* they are achieved. The goals themselves are not opened to interpretation in this context, but achieving them is presented as concerning technical questions, necessary information, and cooperation.

This shows that output legitimacy is here given priority over input legitimacy in the sense that inputs are mainly instrumental to outputs rather than determining what outputs are aimed for. In this frame, political inputs in the sense of preferences and interests are more likely to impact on details than on general orientations. However, the meaning given to input legitimacy does go beyond this.

Input legitimacy

The most obvious ways in which functional representation can increase input legitimacy are that through involving representatives of affected groups, the policy-making process can receive quantitatively more input as well as qualitatively more diverse inputs from more sources. DG Employment uses both arguments

---

3. European Commission (2008) 'Fact sheets'. Online. Available http://ec.europa.eu/employ-ment_social/spsi/network_of_media_en.htm, accessed 24 September 2008. Emphasis added.
4. European Commission Communication COM(2005)706 of 22 December 2005: 5.

and continually stresses the wide range of 'stakeholders' they consult with.[5] Also more generally, the Commission has consistently established and promoted the view that extensive consultations ('governance') self-evidently increase their democratic legitimacy:

> *Would you say that the involvement of these organisations could also be seen as a way to improve democratic legitimacy?*
>
> Yes. Governance. Yes, of course.
>
> *In what way would you say it...*
>
> First of all, you know, that they give another view; second, because through them there is a broader range of stakeholders which is consulted – we include the wider public, and for me this is added value, because through them you can have access to, let's say, to the beneficiaries, if you want. (Interview no. 7)

As was shown in the previous chapter, this increased input is also meant to function as an alternative channel to the input from or through national executives. Notwithstanding, the claim that more input leads to more legitimacy presupposes some argumentative underpinning.

The key argument presented by the DG in this regard is that functional representation is a *right* of the affected citizens:

> [A]part from this [efficiency and effectiveness], I think one major other reason [for involving functional representatives] is that it's simply a kind of right thing. It's also a rights-based thing. So, if you're developing policies that adjust the problems that certain people are faced with, people should have a right to have a say in this, and to give you their opinion on what's happening. So it's not only the efficiency and effectiveness, it's also kind of a basic right. [...] If there's a policy about you, you should be able to give input into this policy. (Interview no. 5)

The fact of being affected by some policy thus gives citizens the right to express themselves on that policy and, what is more, to be listened to by the policy makers (cf. Chapter Nine). In practice, this means a right to be represented in their capacity as affected. Although the DG conceptualises this chiefly as 'participation' and confines the term 'citizenship' to refer to formal rights (Smismans 2007: 2–9), they do advance a strong argument that affectedness entitles one to being represented in policy making, which in effect comes down to a sort of informal 'governance citizenship' (p. 13). On the local level, this citizenship is built on issue-specific engagement and support, i.e. participating in a common cause (such as reducing poverty). At the European level, this representation is mostly based

---

5. E.g. European Commission (no date) 'Partners'. Online. Available http://ec.europa.eu/social/main.jsp?langId=en&catId=85, accessed 13 February 2013.

on the role of NGOs as speakers for the common people (as opposed to political elites) and as being rooted in the grassroots of civil society, which qualifies them to provide the relevant input concerning their functional constituency. The focus is not so much on the contents that are represented, nor on the exact ways in which these are mediated to the Brussels secretariat, but on the fact that *all* relevant functional groups are represented in the first place.

Regarding social policies, this fact itself is not trivial. In pluralist systems of free and voluntary association, functional representation favours groups with specific interests, superior financial means, and superior social capital (Olson 1965), all of which is usually not the case for those most affected by social policies, who tend to be marginalised groups. By deliberately giving access to organisations representing the weakest in society and going as far as to financially ensure their existence and capacity to act, the DG creates an *equality of representation* that otherwise would not be possible: 'The EU also seeks to increase public engagement in governance by involving those who are usually excluded from policy debate, for example ethnic minority groups or people experiencing poverty' (European Commission 2010a: 28). In this sense, inputs are not exclusively treated as instrumental to effectively achieving defined outputs, but there is also a link to the idea that an equality of outputs (i.e. producing outputs that benefit all parts of the population) hinges on equal input. This could imply that the input provided by functional representatives goes beyond facts about needs and also consists of preferences and interests. However, instead of this, the provision of input is framed as participation and contributing to a joint effort.

A strong role for the equality of representation is also played by the descriptive representation of poor people, which not only increases the representation of the most affected as such, but also creates more equality in terms of political agency. People living in poverty become more equal by being given the opportunity to 'speak for themselves' instead of being spoken for by the better-off. This also affects the contents of representation, because descriptive representation is presented as relating views that other forms of representation cannot. Equality of input thus goes beyond quantitative equality.

Having said that, by far the main way of representing weak social groups remains functional associations with non-descriptive representatives. Concerning their prominent role, the deliberate creation of more equal input inevitably also means that the DG creates and controls a privileged access for some functional associations to the policy-making process by choosing organisations to fund and setting the criteria for their cooperation. The decisive question, then, is how it is determined what groups are represented by whom.

In this context, one first notes that the DG's text never defines or delineates very precisely the functional constituencies to be represented. This fits the fluid nature of the constituencies themselves, to which the styles of representation that the DG depicts are also adapted. The fact that there is no clear-cut outline of the social OMC's functional constituencies also means that any functional association wishing to enter the process needs to argue for their affectedness, while the DG retains considerable flexibility as to possible invitations. This flexibility paired with discretion puts the criteria applied by the DG for giving access to functional representatives at the centre of attention. These criteria are all the more important as the large and heterogeneous constituencies concerned (such as the poor or families) rarely have one obvious association to represent them, but there are several possible organisations. Which of them will be funded or invited to the table?

First of all, participation in the governance processes of the social OMC is of course non-actionable. Thus, the 'right' to be represented in the making of policies one is affected by is a moral one, a normative principle proclaimed by the DG that cannot be enforced if some organisation perceives itself unjustifiably excluded. Also more generally, the DG presents itself as open to any interested actor, but avoids specifying their own responsibilities towards the latter in great detail. The calls for proposals to become one of the funded Key Networks are the only documents listing clear criteria of access for functional organisations, i.e. these concern only the access to the innermost circle. The numerous criteria mainly refer to five areas:[6]

- The formal set-up of the organisation, including geographical coverage, not-for-profit character, and independence of commercial interests
- Administrational capacities and sound organisation
- The compatibility of the organisation's purposes with the objectives and priorities of the social OMC
- The capacity to contribute efficiently to the OMC and to promote EU objectives
- The capacity to represent their constituencies' views efficiently in the policy-making process

Concerning the OMC's governance processes more generally, involvement presupposes above all networking with other actors on the European level and the capacity to provide inputs efficiently in a form that is useful for policy makers. Remarkably, the DG never mentions the numerical or otherwise-observable basis of support of an association among the represented or the public as a criterion of access. Instead, the focus is clearly on the *capacities* to efficiently *support* the political process.

The tension between representatives' capacities and constituencies' support is a structural problem of democratic functional representation on the EU level in general, due to the high professionalisation necessary to influence policies in Brussels.[7] Certainly, involving associations that are unfamiliar with the relevant procedures or do not have the resources to act within them would not necessarily amount to more input, while demanding much more resources on the part of the DG. However, the requirement of strong capacities furthers the development of well-established and tightly networked Brussels insiders who

---

6. European Commission 2007b; 2010b.

7. On the professionalisation of functional representation in the EU, *see* Saurugger 2006.

risk becoming increasingly detached from their constituencies, and it structurally disadvantages the greatest part of the existing associations representing the socially marginalised. The DG does not try to counter these tendencies, but underpins them by advancing the conception that the main thing with regard to democratic input is to be professionally represented by actors who are able to impact policies in one's favour, rather than to be represented by a specific actor of one's choice. By implication, the definition of what is good for a particular group is not established by that group itself, at least not primarily. What is more, the need for capacities also favours the DG itself. This is problematic since, in the OMC, the DG is not a neutral administration but has vested interests, in particular concerning the further Europeanisation of social policies. In particular, the amalgamation of representation and 'advancing EU objectives and priorities' (European Commission 2007b: 16), together with the process's informality and the inevitable elusiveness of the functional groups to be represented, makes the DG's discretionary role problematic.

Seen from another angle, the criteria applied by the DG emphasise more the provision of input for the *benefit* of the represented than input *originating* from them; they thus envisage governance for rather than by the people. Considering the situation of those to be represented, this can also be seen as a practical necessity, particularly since the DG makes an effort to include input from those directly affected as well, in the form of descriptive representation. However, in view of the professionalisation of representation in Brussels and thus the growing distance between represented and representing, the *communication* between them becomes especially important.

All this means that the DG's political *accountability* for how and to whom it gives access is decisive. In particular, the criteria of involvement need to be discussed publicly, both concerning the choice of individual associations and the representational landscape on the whole. While Olson's thesis holds true in general, the social inclusion strand of the OMC evidently does not attract many functional representatives of elite interests.[8] Rather, the *equality* established here is one between the representation of national executives on the one hand (who represent the entire people of their states), and of the affected people and the civil society sector on the other hand (as well as subnational administrations, to some extent). In combination with the alliance between the involved NGOs and the DG, this boils down to bending representational equality towards supporting the DG *vis-à-vis* the Member States. Hence, it would be indicated to publicly debate the question of whose input should be sought and which functional groups should be supported in which ways in providing input, and thus to make these choices accountable. In addition, accountability of the DG as well as the involved organisations can function to test the proclaimed intrinsic closeness of social NGOs to their constituencies, i.e. verify whether inputs are in fact grounded in the 'real needs' of the affected.

---

8.   Greenwood (2003: 275) denies that the 'business rules OK' thesis was valid even for the EU as a whole.

Political accountability

Accountability is the crux of democratic legitimacy in functional representation. It has three main dimensions, *viz.* the functional organisations holding public institutions to account, the accountability of public institutions for their practices of involving functional representatives, and the accountability of these representatives themselves for their activities in the political process (*see* Chapter Four).

In the first case, *functional associations act as part of the public sphere*, towards which political actors are held accountable. In their capacity as advocacy organisations, they regularly scrutinise public policies and publish information as well as their possible concerns about them, which can then be taken up by the public. In case of widespread disagreement, the resulting pressure can lead to policy changes, to changes of politicians or civil servants, or can translate into electoral decisions, if applicable. Also, DG Employment sees this mechanism as one reason to involve functional organisations:

> The development of the European social model is increasingly conditioned by the active participation of citizens in public affairs, which of course does not replace the state or the market but contributes to monitoring all the authorities, and therefore to participatory democracy. (European Commission 2003c)

> By concluding alliances with relevant institutions or actors, European networks can contribute to make other actors, also involved in employment and social issues, acknowledge problems and be accountable to commitments they have made. (European Commission 2010b)

Yet, in both of these statements as well as in the DG's text in general, NGOs are primarily meant to monitor the Member States. The former quotation refers to national settings; the latter, by speaking of 'commitments', inserts itself into the DG's framework discourse drawing on the goals the Member States have set for themselves in the common objectives. The DG has no comparable commitments, but depicts its role as assisting the Member States to achieve theirs. There is no allusion to the idea that NGOs might hold the DG publicly accountable in any strong sense. Rather, the fact that they are involved is as such meant to demonstrate that the process and the DG's role conform to principles of good governance.

The DG is very conscious of their culture of open doors towards all kinds of actors, and sees this as part of their accountability in the sense that they work in an open and transparent way:

> [W]hatever the newspapers are writing about us, [...] it's very easy to meet with functionaries; I mean, in France [...] you would not be invited like this, and you would not have a 'yes' if you ask to meet any civil servant from the French administration. So here, it's a different culture, and I think to some extent a very open one. (Interview no. 1)

However, the discourse about this openness, framed as 'working together' and listening to the affected, does not refer to the possibility that those involved may have fundamentally different views. Although accountability through functional representatives does not necessarily mean criticism by these actors, it does mean that the public evaluation of DG policies by NGOs can in principle be positive as well as negative. Certainly, one cannot expect the DG to actively promote the notion that their openness could also facilitate the challenging of their policies in public. Yet, evidence of such occasions suggests that when those NGOs who are closely affiliated with the social OMC criticise European social policy, this criticism is rarely addressed at the Social Inclusion Unit. Nevertheless, these instances are cited in order to demonstrate the political independence of the funded NGOs:

> [I]n particular, in the beginning of the mandate of this Commission [2004–9] you saw a lot of verbal radicalism on part of the Social Platform, which [...] [was] not that much even on specific issues, but on the whole kind of orientation of the first Barroso Commission, on the Lisbon Agenda and how they felt that the new Commission was too pro-business and not social enough. So this is kind of very general, and [...] that is a case which I referred to when I said [...] [some NGOs are] overcompensating for the, let's say, *potential* criticism that they are the Commission's paid NGOs, by making very broad, I'd say political, statements that the Commission is going too far to being pro-business. I'm not evaluating whether they had a point or not, but [...] it was in a way moving out of the specific NGO focus into, let's say, a world-view criticism. (Interview no. 4)

> I would say that [...] if you would screen EAPN communication for the last two or three years, I mean they've been very critical of Commission initiatives. [...] And there's this tension also within the Commission, of course, because you have the Social Inclusion Unit, which would often be on their track, but then [...] many of the decisions of the Commission are collective decisions, so it means then you have a complicated process going on of trying to convince people in other DGs [...]. (Interview no. 5)

Unsurprisingly, forming mutually supportive partnerships with functional associations is difficult to combine with making oneself publicly accountable through these same associations. Rather, what can be expected are forms of network or peer accountability among the DG or the Social Inclusion Unit and its partner NGOs. It is evident that basic values and convictions about social policies are internalised and shared among this community, and being part of such a network can generate mutual commitments, 'monitoring and reputational sanctioning' (Goodin 2003b: 376). However, this kind of accountability is primarily accountability of the DG *to* functional representatives (and vice versa) instead of *through* them to the people.[9] It can only contribute to democratic accountability if the public has possibilities to oversee and sanction public institutions' activities within such networks; in other words, it has to be looked at in the context of the DG's accountability *for* their governance practices (*see* below).

---

9. *See* Papadopoulos (2007), who denies that network or peer accountability were democratic accountability.

Given the partnership setting, public accountability *through* functional representation is allowed for, mostly in the sense that different services within the Commission, or different political institutions within the EU, are associated with different groups of functional actors, who monitor actors other than their respective 'hosts'. In other words, the Social Inclusion Unit's 'own' functional partners would publicly criticise Council decisions or policies by other parts of the Commission, while functional groups connected to economic politics, for instance, would possibly publicly hold DG Employment to account for their social policies. This is the arrangement evoked by the DG in the statement quoted above, maintaining that '[b]y concluding alliances with relevant institutions or actors, European networks can contribute to make other actors [...] acknowledge problems and be accountable to commitments they have made'. This arrangement, however, replicates existing inequalities in functional representation. Hence, two levels of argument need to be distinguished. First, on the systemic level of the political system on the whole, public institutions form alliances with functional actors, who contribute to holding other actors to account through the public sphere. The functioning of this arrangement is based on different organisations having different interests or missions and therefore incentives to control each other. In this view, the DG's involvement of NGOs first of all advances the public accountability of political actors other than the DG itself. The idea that functional representatives cooperating with other political actors could for their part hold the DG to account for their policies within the OMC does not figure in the text. Second, on the level of the individual actor (here the DG or its Inclusion Unit), functional representation is described as part of that actor's 'good governance', *viz.* openness and transparency. It is depicted as partnerships to achieve common goals rather than as a relation of accountability in a strong sense, i.e. one that could lead to consequences for the accountee. The problem here is not so much the fact that the DG of course avoids inviting opposition, but more the synonymous use of NGOs or other functional representatives and 'partners' with whom the DG 'cooperates'.[10] This language leaves potential critical voices altogether without attention by positioning them outside the framework of functional representation in the social OMC. It thus constructs possible criticism as an exception.

Ultimately, then, the strongest sense of accountability *through* functional organisations evoked by the DG is their use of NGOs as information resources about the conditions 'on the ground'. Yet, it is questionable whether this is political accountability proper. The DG itself conceptualises the process as the receiving of information about facts – which allows them to make better policy recommendations – rather than as a forum to which they would explain and justify their policies. Their notion is reminiscent of Easton's classical simplified model of the political system (*see* p.12), where the policy-making process is situated in a feedback loop between inputs from the environment and outputs impacting on

10. European Commission (no date) 'Partners'. Online. Available http://ec.europa.eu/social/main. jsp?langId=en&catId=85, accessed 13 February 2013.

that environment. However, this feedback loop as such does not ensure that policy makers explain their choices and that the citizens can impose consequences on them, but it remains subject to the DG's discretion how to proceed with the inputs received. Moreover, the information given by NGOs about social conditions is not mediated through the public sphere but mostly given to the DG directly.

The second dimension of political accountability is the *accountability of the DG for their practices of functional representation*. In this regard, they refer above all to their responsibilities concerning how to deal with the input they receive and to principles of good governance. The DG is very conscious of the fact that notwithstanding extensive input from functional representatives, it is them who take the final decisions about their policies, also taking into account considerations other than the NGOs' inputs. In the same vein, they do not see themselves as responsible to the NGOs for their policies in the first place.

> They [NGOs] are an important vehicle of views and issues that are in our societies on certain aspects, et cetera, but [...] it is also the responsibility of those who deal with them to understand the kind of stakes and positions that they bring, and how to use them, etc. (Interview no. 6)

> And of course [...] we have to take it [the NGOs' messages] with a pinch of salt. One shouldn't, as public officials... we should not fall into the opposite extreme and assume that when you have an organisation for and of people with a particular disability or with disabilities in general, or of Roma, that their perspective necessarily is shared by that whole group. I mean, [...] yes, it's very nice to hear the slogan 'nothing about us without us', and we fully support that these organisations should be there; we shouldn't, however, fall into the opposite mode of thinking – to have all Roma impersonated by Roma NGOs, let alone one Roma NGO, or all disabled people by, let's say, a disability advocacy NGO, because of course, the NGOs, the people who work in those NGOs for and who are from the group in question – obviously they're not entirely representative [...] you know, given Roma in general, and they're Roma intellectuals, these people [...] I mean [...] they are, both in terms of their understanding, in terms of their knowledge, [they] can be very valuable, but at the end of the day, they're not, let's say, the full-blown representatives of the people who are in that poverty ghetto, because those people in that poverty ghetto very likely have not heard about them, or do not necessarily identify with them. So [...] there're difficulties that sometimes NGOs try to say 'we are' – a disability NGO would say 'we are the disabled, we alone [...] should be heard', and that is not the case, actually. [...] I mean, [...] it's good to take this into account; at the same time, one does have to see from contacts with NGOs that the activist's viewpoint [...], while being in favour of a vulnerable group, isn't entirely the same as necessarily the interest of every single individual from that group. And so, ultimately we have to take our own responsibilities; we're a public authority, [...] and sometimes we do make our NGO partners happy, and sometimes less so.

[…] [S]ometimes you could fall into the track of trying to do things in order to be applauded by NGOs. […] [W]e value a lot the input of NGOs, but one shouldn't be too afraid to also […] defend the position of the public authorities when we believe that a particular NGO or several have a one-sided view, which can happen. (Interview no. 4; cf. Chapter Ten)

The forum that the DG sees itself as accountable towards is not so much the Member States, but rather directly 'the citizens to whom we have a duty to make enlightened and just choices'.[11] This may in part be due to the fact that the corpus of the present study consists of public texts, much of which are not primarily addressed at national executives, but above all at the OMC's governance networks and the interested public. At the same time, however, the minor role assigned to the Member States as a forum of accountability – in spite of the OMC's formal setup and the key role played by the intergovernmental Social Protection Committee – is also a sign of the DG's endeavour to build an additional source of direct legitimacy based on the citizenry in its entirety, bypassing the national administrations. This cannot only be seen in their justifications for individual choices, but also in those for being active in social policies at all:

We need to ask ourselves whether European taxpayers know and understand where their money is going? Can they see and understand what we are doing? And we need to ask ourselves whether we are doing things as simply and efficiently as possible? And whether action at European-level [*sic*] brings real added value? [*sic*] (European Commission 2001a)

Their arguments build partly on outputs (first part of following quote), and partly on procedural legitimacy through functional representation (second part):

Citizens will ultimately benefit from PROGRESS as Member States will promote laws, policies and practices in line with Social Agenda goals – more and better jobs and a more cohesive society. And EU and national policy/decision-makers and other stakeholders will be in a better position to meet the challenges of a social Europe in a globalised world.

How do citizens benefit?

[…] The EU has also created a sound basis for policymaking by involving a range of actors such as non-governmental organisations, social partners and local and regional authorities, as well as those affected by poverty and those working with people in poverty.[12]

---

11. European Commission press release SPEECH/08/223 of 5 May 2008.

12. European Commission (2008) 'What social Europe can do for you'. Online. Available http://ec.europa.eu/employment_social/publications/booklets/general/pdf/ke0008001_en.pdf, accessed 23 September 2008.

The DG speaks about their *responsibilities* concerning their practices of involving functional representatives, rather than about accountability. Principally, they refer to their adherence to principles of 'good governance', i.e. 'participation, openness, accountability, effectiveness and coherence' (European Commission 2003b). The most significant of these is 'participation', referring to the 'involvement of all actors' (2003b), thus 'ensur[ing] full participation' (European Commission 2000a). The DG asserts that it attaches great importance to the fact that all potential functional groups are represented in the process. This requires financial support in order to ensure an equality of political inputs:

> High-quality and participatory policy debate […] can be achieved only […] when all relevant target groups, including weaker, non-governmental and subnational actors, are involved. The active participation of non-governmental actors in the policy debate is the result of capacity building of organisations. (European Commission 2010a: 53)

Accordingly, the stabilisation of NGO funding, created with the OMC's funding programmes, is part of good governance. The DG sees 'improv[ing] the management grants awarded to NGOs' and thus 'building [their] capacity to play a stronger part in the European policy process' as belonging to the 'responsibilities [of] the European institutions' (European Commission 2000a), since 'otherwise [the civil dialogue] would not be happening at European level' (European Commission 2003b). Additionally, regularisation is sought through structuring the DG's relationships with functional representatives, in particular through the biannual meetings with the Social Platform, the umbrella organisation involving all social NGOs active in the OMC. In the same vein, the DG's support *vis-à-vis* other institutions for the NGOs' 'place at the table' (European Commission 2000a) more generally is mentioned in the context of the negotiations of the Draft Constitution and the Lisbon Treaty. After the Treaty's entry into force and the introduction of the grant programmes underpinning the OMC, these issues have been much less emphasised; also, the 'civil dialogue' and further measures to institutionalise functional representation have not been among the central topics in recent years.[13]

Stronger measures of accountability proper – be it under this designation or others – are difficult to find in the DG's text. They usually deal with it in terms of *transparency* and 'openness', but it is nowhere specified what exactly is meant with these expressions. In the 'General principles and minimum standards for consultation of interested parties by the Commission', the principles of 'openness and accountability' mean the visibility of consultation processes as well as the Commission's duty to explain their actions and take responsibility for them.[14] This again is intended to make policy making understandable and credible (i.e.

---

13. Cf. Greenwood (2003: 218–20, 272–3) on the civil dialogue.
14. European Commission Communication COM(2002)704 of 11 December 2002: 17.

legitimate).[15] Elsewhere in the Communication, it is stated that 'more involvement of interested parties through a more transparent consultation process [...] will enhance the Commission's accountability', because publishing documents about the consultation process 'give[s] the legislature [i.e. the EP] greater scope for scrutinising the Commission's activities'.[16] It is also interesting to note that in this connection, 'awareness-raising publicity' is mentioned as a measure to ensure that every potential functional representative receives the information about open consultations (COM(2002)704: 20). Although this document does not concern the social OMC, where the largest part of functional representation processes does not take place in the form of formal consultations leading to official Commission documents, let alone legislative proposals, it does give an idea of how the Commission approaches the issue of accountability in general, namely in terms of openness to every possible functional input, as well as transparency and clarity of the process (European Commission 2010a: 49). The assertions about this procedural legitimacy are meant to generate trust in the Commission as an agent who acts publicly and in communication with society. Transparency of procedures implies justifying them, and together with opening the process for all interested parties, this entails that the Commission's practices of involving functional representatives are subject to challenge and debate.

Yet, the proof of the pudding is in the eating. Contrary to public consultations, in the OMC a great part of the contact between the DG and functional representatives is informal and non-public. Processes of functional representation in the OMC cannot be learned about through a one-stop Internet portal (such as for consultations), but finding the existing dispersed information requires substantial knowledge about the policy area's structures and processes as well as the ability to read policy documents in English, French, or German. For the general public it is thus extremely difficult to verify the DG's assertions about their responsible conduct, and even more difficult to enforce changes on them. The DG itself states that a substantial amount of its contact with the organisations it finances is unofficial, which is why the 'outputs' delivered by these organisations cannot be measured for evaluation purposes:

> In 2009, PROGRESS-supported key EU networks and NGOs produced 263 reports aimed at providing policy advice, research and analysis and 161 reports aimed at identifying good practices in the policy areas of anti-discrimination, social protection and social inclusion, and gender equality. The networks/NGOs also convey their views on possible legislation or events happening in these areas to policymakers through meetings, official questions and more informal discussions at conferences. [...] PROGRESS-supported key EU networks and NGOs respond to the [Commission's] consultations by submitting official written opinions, but they also provide numerous informal consultations, written and oral, at both EU and national levels, which are impossible to quantify. (European Commission 2010a: 53)

---

15. Cf. also European Commission Communication COM(2001)428 of 25 July 2001.

16. European Commission Communication COM(2002)704 of 11 December 2002: 3, 5.

On top of this informality, the shadow of publicity for OMC policies, i.e. the potential for their politicisation in public, can be considered fairly weak. Consequently, the forum which *can* hold the DG to account consists mainly of functional organisations with access to EU processes and of Member States administrations. However, especially for the former, access and transparency is limited as well. Ultimately, then, this leads us back to the network accountability to the inner circle of social NGOs, dealt with above, as well as to the national executives (mainly via the Social Protection Committee), who may in some cases be in the position to enforce consequences on the DG for their practices. Yet, access to this inner circle of NGOs, as well as these organisations' core funding, is controlled by the DG itself, which refers to them as partners rather than as a forum of control. The national executives in turn are not depicted as an accountability forum in the DG's text, but mainly as those who profit from the DG's involving functional representatives through the comparative knowledge this creates. In short, the DG's 'good governance' concept builds on elements of deliberative accountability, but does not live up to the demands of transparency and visibility that could make such accountability democratic.

Approaching accountability as 'good governance' shows that the DG's concept of their accountability mainly boils down to ensuring the possibility of all interested to provide input into the process, i.e. making themselves accountable means here demonstrating the willingness to hear all views. The political process itself is described as a combined effort among those expressing their views; in other words, the views heeded are framed as contributions to the achievement of a common goal rather than as part of a dialogue about those goals themselves or about evaluating the DG's performance. This becomes clear, too, when looking at the role given to political debate, the major locus of deliberative accountability. One of the tasks of the Progress programme is to support 'high-quality and participatory policy debate'.

> If partnerships are to be successful, all partners need to be able to have their say and feed into public policy debate in an effective way. The Commission therefore will ensure that there is productive debate at EU and national levels on law, policies and objectives relating to PROGRESS, with the participation of all stakeholders. For this, the Commission will increase public engagement in line with EU rigorous governance principles.[17]

'Public policy debate' evokes associations of deliberative accountability for the DG's policies through the public sphere. Indeed,

> [t]hrough PROGRESS, the European Commission creates an enabling environment in which the voices of different stakeholder groups can be heard and *arguments for and against specific policy changes* can be advocated. To

---

17. European Commission (no date) 'Immediate outcomes'. Online. Available http://ec.europa.eu/social/main.jsp?catId=663&langId=en, accessed 31 May 2011.

achieve this, PROGRESS supports activities that generate evidence for policy debate to underpin the arguments [i.e. policy studies] and activities that enable different stakeholder groups to express their *position* with regard to EU policies and legislation. (European Commission 2010a: 49; emphases added)

This paragraph is one of the very rare occasions where the DG's text refers to the possibility that arguments and positions concerning specific policies might oppose each other. In general, however, debate is associated with building consensus and support for 'EU objectives', as the same document states further down:

The greater involvement of stakeholders [in policy debates] helps foster a sense of shared ownership and joint responsibility for the implementation of legislation and policies developed in common. Among the major achievements of high-quality and participatory policy debates are the strengthened political commitment of Member States in PROGRESS policy areas, the establishment of common ground/consensus between and among policy- and decision-makers and stakeholders on EU objectives, and the identification of more effective policy measures. (European Commission 2010a: 50)

Participation in these debates is part of the tasks of the Key Networks (pp. 52–3), which thereby

increas[e] visibility about particular policy issues, which helps to ensure that positive publicity is achieved on these issues. This promotes increased knowledge and awareness about particular issues which in turn helps to develop and strengthen consensus and support from the grass-roots level upwards for action to be taken in particular areas of social and employment policy. (p. 53)

Throughout this argumentation, it is suggested that participating in the debate leads to supporting the eventual policies. Furthermore, the text remains ambiguous as to whether policies are supposed to be defined in the debate, or whether consensus is sought regarding policies that are already formulated. Yet, even assuming the first case, it is expected that all involved will take ownership of the decisions arrived at. As well as that, it is clear that support is to be generated for dealing with social policy issues at the EU level in the first place. The policy debate envisaged by the DG is not intended to entail consequences for them other than support, and the participation of functional representatives in public debates is not conceptualised as making the DG accountable through them (in the sense that functional organisations could use the debate to publicly evaluate Commission policies, and this could lead to public support or pressure), but it is seen as a way to generate awareness and commitment among their respective constituencies. Again, accountability is presented as a matter of ensuring the representation of all possible views in an open process, which ultimately leads to consensus. This conception raises the question of what it would mean to be accountable to groups who disagree.

Finally, it remains the *accountability of the functional organisations* themselves for their political activities within the OMC. It is part of the general accountability of functional representation in the OMC and concerns the DG in the sense that the democratic credentials of the associations they involve impact on the legitimacy of the process as a whole. As pointed out in Chapter Four, one can distinguish a continuum of three accountability forums for functional representatives, *viz.* their core network of active members or supporters, the wider functional constituency they speak for, and the general public. Out of these, it is the first that the DG's civil servants think of when asked about whom European NGOs are responsible to:

> Well, they're responsible to their members. [...] I think what we worry about is the normal procedures in which they work, so this we screen as contact persons from the Commission, and when we screen their new work programme for the next year, this is something we will always look into. So there needs to be a General Assembly, there needs to be regular moments throughout the year when new initiatives are checked with the members, and this we will look into, we'll make sure that this is happening. But the reality, of course, [...] in all organisations, there will be tendencies to decide on viewpoints and so on with a limited number of people present, and we understand it's here oligarchies of very few people are in the end... But [...] we try to ensure this thing that the members need to be involved, there need to be really be procedures and elections, and this kind of thing. Voting on issues [...]. Otherwise, of course it's not like that they're elected. It's a difficult question. (Interview no. 5)

As noted in Chapter Eight, the DG requires the networks it funds to have formal and regular relations of accountability with their national members:

Exclusion and eligibility criteria

Regarding the applicant organisation

Partnership agreements may be signed with European-level organisations [...] which are mandated by their members through a Management Board or other administrative forum, to represent them at the EU level and to be responsible for the activities of the network [...].

Award criteria

[...]

Effective and efficient organisation of work

The effective and efficient organisation of work will be judged against the extent to which the applicant [...] presents its relations with its national members, including arrangements to ensure involvement of membership organisations in policy development and policy statements, goal orientation and planning practices, [and] reporting methods [...]. (European Commission 2007b: 14, 16; cf. 2010b: 13, 15)

Also in a more general context, Commissioner Diamantopoulou defines the accountability of NGOs as concerning 'not only who NGOs represent, but how they conduct their business [...]. How do NGOs consult with their members? Are they democratically organised?' (European Commission 2000a). The DG thus sees the accountability of European NGOs to their core networks mainly in terms of formal principal–agent as well as deliberative relationships between the EU secretariat and the member organisations. Official measures of authorisation and accountability and continuous communication are both seen as important. In other words, the EU-level organisations are not seen as institutions standing on their own, but as firmly rooted in their national constituents. However, the DG is mainly concerned with the relationships between the European and the national level and much less with those between the national and subnational levels.

Extended deliberative accountability is required towards peer organisations in the NGOs' functional sectors. Among the criteria for Key Networks quoted above, there is the condition that a funded organisation '[d]emonstrates its ability to interact with external actors, including key institutions, other NGO networks and relevant constituents when designing and implementing each activity envisaged' (European Commission 2010b: 15).[18] Put differently, NGOs are demanded to be networked in their sector, which entails a certain degree of informal network accountability towards other actors in their fields. This requirement goes beyond funded organisations and is indeed something the DG would like to see as the hallmark of functional representation:

> But what is the recipe for a successful civil society? Philanthropy alone is not enough to make an effective and constructive contribution to shaping and implementing social policy. If civil society is to make a real difference, it must be structured and democratic. It must mobilise and exploit the full potential of all available resources. Across the EU there are thousands of different organisations doing excellent work. But, to be successful partners, civil society must ensure openness, accountability and effective representation. It must develop lasting partnerships and networks with all actors. It must coordinate efforts at local, regional, national and European level. (European Commission 2003c)

> [T]he role of civil society organisations goes beyond advocacy or influence; they should also build partnerships with other NGOs involved in different areas and commit themselves to delivering concrete results – for instance in the framework of the European strategy against exclusion. (European Commission 2003b)

As these quotations show, the DG perceives the sectoral networking among NGOs primarily as a condition of 'success', defined as making 'an effective and

---

18. Cf. European Commission 2007b: 16, where the formulation is less clear.

constructive contribution to shaping and implementing social policy'. As well as that, it is instrumental to including more associations in the OMC orbit than the necessarily limited number of those who are directly involved in Brussels, and to reaching out to national and subnational organisations. However, the demand for coalitions and coordinated action among social NGOs also implies peer accountability between them. The DG clearly would like functional representatives to form a more coherent movement that works together for shared goals, instead of each association pursuing its own agenda alone. Although it is clear that this de facto implication of network accountability is not the DG's primary intention in this context, it is not irrelevant either, since one major purpose here is that associations with direct contact to the OMC governance processes also bring in inputs from other organisations. This entails some relationship of accountability between them.

Now, turning to the accountability of functional associations to their wider functional constituencies (such as the poor, for example) – this is not very present in the text. There is no reference to direct relationships between the European NGOs and the represented 'on the ground'. Rather, relations between represented and representatives are implied to be taking place on the local level where the grassroots associations are concretely '*working with* the [h]omeless' (European Commission 2007f; emphasis added), for instance. However, it is not evident how possible relationships of accountability concerning local activities extend to accountability for political activities at the European level. This brings us back to the gap observed earlier between the representative claims the DG makes about NGOs at the local level and at the European level. The representativity of the EU-level networks builds on direct contact on 'the ground', which generates knowledge among the local staff, and on the mediation of this knowledge within their organisation through the different levels of aggregation. The link between the concrete and local on the one hand, and the abstract and European on the other hand is provided by the organisation's channels of information mediation and by the common ethical commitment that is shared by the representatives on all levels.

Similar considerations apply to the accountability of European networks of NGOs to the general public. When alluding to relationships between the functional representatives and the citizens at large, the DG often identifies the former with 'civil society' and evokes an image of NGOs firmly rooted in common people's everyday lives. The main way of extending this 'closeness' through to Brussels is the identification of civil society organisations as representatives of the public good and the man in the street.

To sum up, the accountability of functional organisations is described as based on principal–agent structures and deliberation between the European and national level, and on direct contact on the local level. The two are implicitly connected by the NGOs' internal channels of information and their staff's commitment to their shared cause at all levels. The latter points to a strong role given to functional representatives' internal accountability to their own consciousness (cf. March and Olsen 1995: 167; Mansbridge 2003: 522). By contrast, the functional constituencies are not given a major position as political actors in the DG's text. This conception of the NGOs' accountability is consistent with the gyroscopic and symbolic representation styles ascribed to them. If NGOs are representative on the basis of their reputation (i.e. generalised knowledge about NGOs) as reliably committed to their professed cause and as 'close' to the represented, the density of communication between the European associations and their ultimate constituencies becomes a secondary question. It is only with regard to the aggregation of national organisations to the European level that representation is seen to work along principal–agent structures, which ensure the representation of all national constituencies. One difficulty with this is the lack of visibility in and of the social OMC; i.e. the intrinsic closeness of NGOs to their representees is asserted or taken for granted rather than open for verification. Gyroscopic and symbolic representation, if it is to be democratic, does not mean the detachment of representatives and represented, but entails the continual *possibility* to scrutinise representatives, challenge their claims, give or withdraw support, and thereby influence the choice of representatives as well as the positions advanced by them. Democratic accountability is a means to *ensure* that the views of the represented are taken into account. In addition, a severe problem is the amalgamation of gyroscopic representation based on the reputation as speaking for the common people on the one hand, and the partnership with a political institution on the other. I discuss this issue in the Conclusions (Chapter Twelve).

Concerning themselves, the DG presents their involvement of functional representatives *as such* as an evidence of their accountability. The openness to NGOs' participation and the emphasis on principles of 'good governance' are intended to generate trust and legitimacy for this involvement. In other words, the DG underlines cooperation and 'working together' instead of debate and challenging as a means to make themselves accountable. The alleged possibility for everyone to engage and participate and the transparency of the process provide for a kind of cooperative accountability on the inside in the sense that policies are discussed *inside* the governance processes rather than in the space surrounding them. Although the DG justifies their policies to the general public outside, the forum that can ask questions, receive answers, pass judgements, and possibly impose consequences is the OMC community on the inside rather than the citizens at large. In the following section, I look at the overall concept of democratic legitimacy underlying this account of governance in the OMC.

Democracy as the participation in a joint project

All these elements amount to a concept of democratic legitimacy as *cooperation*. In the view of DG Employment, democracy means the participation and contribution of everybody in a common project. 'Working together' leads to legitimacy by strengthening the DG's position as the guardian of the European general interest, by bringing it closer to the citizens, by generating trust, and by being built on a 'participative' democracy that involves the individual citizen in the European process.

The DG presents itself as representing the European citizenry in its entirety and as working to ensure their welfare. This claim is based on the treaties[19] and is a form of what Pierre Rosanvallon (2010: Ch. II) has called the 'legitimacy of impartiality' (*légitimité d'impartialité*).[20] It is based on 'organic representation' (*représentation-organe*), a characteristic of independent authorities,[21] who claim to precisely not represent a subgroup of the governed, but to *embody* all of them as an indivisible whole (Rosanvallon 2010: 142–7). In this respect, the Commission's legitimacy is directly derived from not being elected. Instead, concerning the social OMC, the DG is mandated by the joint objectives adopted by the European Council, i.e. its task is to advance certain *goals*. In line with this reasoning, 'working together' with functional representatives improves the output legitimacy of the process, because issues are complex and achieving set targets requires involving the resources of all concerned actors. As well as that, a cooperative style of policy making underpins the claim to represent the public good and wellbeing of *all* Europeans.

However, the legitimacy of the Commission as the guardian of the European general interest remains relatively weak on its own. Moreover, it suggests a certain distance between the Commission and individual citizens. Hence, the DG's cooperative concept of democracy is mainly based on the representative legitimacy of functional associations, which represent a multiplicity of specific groups *to* the Commission and thereby create *specific* legitimacy for the issue at hand. Democracy is thus strongly founded on communicative ties with the represented. These functional representative structures are conceptualised as 'working together' with functional representatives, which brings the DG closer to the people because through these representatives they involve the wider citizenry in the process and gain 'legitimacy of proximity' (*légitimité de proximité*), to use Rosanvallon's felicitous terminology once more (2010: Ch. IV). '*Closeness*' to 'the ground' is maybe the single most important attribute that the DG attaches to social NGOs; and by involving them in policy making they claim to become closer themselves. The NGOs' closeness is understood physically (direct contact on the local level) as well as psychologically (empathy and commitment), and the latter dimension transmits the closeness of an NGO's local workers through to the European level. Hence, 'closeness' is primarily a matter of *attitude* on the part of the representative – of sincere attention, concern, and compassion. As a political institution, the DG cannot claim quite the same for themselves; rather, by cooperating with these organisations they demonstrate an attitude of sincere empathy by *listening* to representatives of the poor and by taking their views into *account* and giving them presence in policy making. They thus become close in their own way.

---

19. *Treaty on European Union*, Article 17(1): 'The Commission shall promote the general interest of the Union and take appropriate initiatives to that end'.

20. Cf. Saward's criteria of 'untaintedness' (Saward 2009: 19–20).

21. Cf. *Treaty on European Union*, Article 17(3): 'In carrying out its responsibilities, the Commission shall be completely independent'.

To claim such legitimacy of closeness, it is important to listen to *all* those affected. Hence, the concept of democracy as cooperation strongly depends on the legitimacy based on *equality*. This equality between functional groups has to be deliberately created and cannot be assumed to exist automatically. Equality is one of the greatest promises of democracy, and certainly a powerful argument of legitimacy in relation to social policies. The fact that it is here artificially created means that it is decisive to combine the equality argument with that of the NGOs' closeness – only if it can be claimed that the included NGOs are legitimate representatives of their constituencies can their deliberate involvement be said to increase legitimacy. In this way, the process does not present itself as giving access to some chosen actors (and not to others), who are maybe not mandated by their proclaimed constituencies, but rather in terms of opening the doors to a *type* of organisation that is known to give voice to the most affected and can be counted on to mean well (namely NGOs). It is also often emphasised that the DG listens to many different groups. At the same time, however, the continuous emphasis on the deliberate rebalancing of representation also reinforces the notion that the especially represented groups could not seize political space themselves and needed someone to speak for them.

This tendency is countered with the descriptive – albeit equally deliberately organised – representation of the poor. With descriptive representation, another dimension is added to equality by emphasising the political agency of the excluded, i.e. not only their capability to formulate reasonable input, but also the significance of this input for policy making. Importantly, however, the DG does not construct any opposition between the representation through NGOs and descriptive representation. Rather, the two are presented as complementary and equally necessary ways of involving the socially weak in policy-making processes that affect them. Based on the direct contact between NGOs and their constituents at the local level, both are seen as channels of 'participation'. As well as that, both are supported and advocated by the DG, although non-descriptive representation is by far the main mode of functional representation in use.

The notion that democracy essentially means 'working together' is crystallised in the concept of '*good governance*', which mainly refers to responsible conduct of the DG and its openness to all those who wish to get involved. Hence, good governance also refers to supporting the functional representatives of weak groups financially as well as structurally. This 'good governance' legitimacy takes the place of political accountability in the sense that it functions to emphasise that the DG does not act alone, arbitrarily, or behind closed doors, but is open to discussing policies with all affected. It is thus meant to create *trust*, contrarily to accountability proper, which compensates imperfect trust with means for control. The centrality of this argument also shows the DG's need for legitimacy stemming from representative structures that connect it to the governed more directly than its formal mandate through the Council and the EP.

What, then, is the role of the represented in this model? For them, the DG's cooperation with functional representatives means that they can themselves become part of the European process by engaging in NGOs on the grassroots level. The citizens' role is thus conceptualised in a framework of '*participatory democracy*' (European Commission 2003b; emphasis added) based on '*active citizenship*', which is

a means to ensure vibrant debates on issues that matter for its citizens. In democracies active citizenship involves voluntary work in organisations and networks, organising activities for the community, participation in interest groups and political parties, participation in forms of peaceful protest and in public debate on issues such as social inclusion, gender equality, human rights, employment, social services, environment [...]. (European Commission 2008i; emphasis added)

Hence, a primary role of civil society organisations is to 'generate and focus active citizenship along with solidarity' (European Commission 2000a), i.e. to channel and organise people's political and charitable activities. They are capable of doing this because they are firmly rooted in the local level, i.e. they are intrinsically 'grassroots organisations [...] through which people participate in local and municipal life', and 'which bring people together in a common cause' (European Commission 2003b). In this way,

Civil Society Organisations are the best placed organisations to work on some crucial issues because of their key role in engaging with communities at local, regional, national and international level. Engagement in voluntary and community activities is a way for people to contribute to public life. They can give their time or their money to support issues of concern to them. Civil Society Organisations have increasingly become places where people can debate and affect issues that matter to them, and where they feel they can be advocates for change. (European Commission 2008i)

NGOs are close to the people and deal with 'issues that are at the forefront of citizens' concerns' (European Commission 2000a). Crucially, these issues are primarily social ones, particularly involving the engagement for the benefit of weaker social groups. 'Active citizenship' thus does not refer to any collective action whatsoever, but is strongly orientated towards charity and the public good and essentially means 'the potential *contribution* of civil society to promoting a fairer and more inclusive society' (European Commission 2003b; emphasis added). In other words, functional associations are the channels through which citizens participate in the joint project coordinated by the DG.

Civil society thus understood is the core of the DG's model of democracy: 'A dynamic voluntary sector is an expression of a dynamic society. Through that expression, it generates a more participative democracy' (European Commission 2000a). As mentioned earlier (*see* Chapter Six), during the negotiations for the Constitutional Treaty (which then became the Lisbon Treaty), the DG advocated the view that the European model of modern democracy is built on three pillars – representative democracy, participatory democracy and social dialogue. [...] This is the 'triangle' of democracy in the Union, with different actors being given specific and complementary roles. (European Commission 2003b)

The *clou* of this is the rhetorical amalgamation of (a specific kind of) local engagement with EU-level functional representation into one organic whole, *viz.* 'participation', and on this basis the presentation of the DG as the bastion of a form of democracy that is particularly close to the people. Not only is it '[e]mployment and social policy [...] where all these forms of democracy and governance meet' (EC 2003b), but participative democracy is also 'something that Europe, as a whole, needs a great deal more of' (European Commission 2000a). DG Employment thus becomes the advocate of a modern, multifarious form of democracy that connects Europe to the people by reaching out to them and meeting them where they are in order to involve them as actively engaged citizens.

In this way, 'working together' includes all levels of functional organisation, down to the individual people. Concrete, often voluntary local work and advocacy in all political arenas are natural parts of one continuum of 'participation', through which all those who participate in one way or another become part of a common process.

At the EU, in the social OMC, this mainly means that the supporters at the local level, as well as the especially affected whom the associations speak for, become part of the process through being represented. European social NGOs are claimed to represent the wider public and the functionally affected in two main ways. Firstly, they represent Europeans *as* concerned by social issues and therefore 'giv[ing] their time or their money to support' (European Commission 2008i) social NGOs, or more passively accepting their representative claims. The social issues in question are broken down into more limited problems, such as child poverty or homelessness, which the DG works to solve and urges Member States to tackle. Secondly, social NGOs represent the especially affected *as* people with specific needs. The knowledge of these needs is the NGOs' main input, on the basis of which the DG designs their policies. They thus become themselves representative of those most affected by social policies as well as of 'the Europeans', who are concerned by social problems. This provides them with a distinct democratic legitimacy for initiatives in social policies. In particular, the existence of more direct channels of representation – bypassing the indirect representation through the Member States – creates the basis to claim a mandate by the people, in addition to that given by the national governments. This argument gives the DG the room for manoeuvre to promote specific policy orientations, rather than being restricted to acting as the Member States' agent.

What is more, local participation also makes people part of the common effort on their own grassroots level:

First, to overcome the extent to which poverty and social exclusion can undermine people's skills and self-confidence you need to develop policies and programmes which empower people and not make them dependent. This can best be achieved by involving them in the design and implementation of policies and programmes. Secondly, creating the political space and legitimacy necessary for building inclusive policies requires building awareness and consensus among a broad range of actors. This is greatly facilitated by involving them in the policy process.[22]

Interestingly, the quoted passage from a conference workshop background paper is said to present the 'arguments about legitimacy' (as additional to 'arguments about efficiency') 'for stressing mobilisation and participation as being essential elements in the struggle to prevent and eradicate poverty and social exclusion'.[23] The two 'efficiency arguments' essentially claim that including inputs (knowledge and resources) from all relevant actors improves policy outputs. By contrast, the two 'legitimacy arguments' quoted above put forward two slightly different perspectives. The first is a small sideline argument that is used only rarely. It is based on the idea that on the individual level, social exclusion also manifests itself in passivity with respect to civil society engagement. Conversely, therefore, activating the most affected to engage themselves in processes that concern them can in itself be part of the solution to their problems by *empowering* them to tackle their situation:

> [T]rying to have participation also means that indirectly perhaps you're also doing something about the situation people are in. It's… maybe an argument that's a bit more difficult to make, but by empowering people to enter into a dialogue, and facilitating this through all kinds of work, like pointing to good practice and so on […] and by inviting people to participate in policy preparation and so on, and the policy process, you kind of assist this process of empowerment. And I think this is also important. (Interview no. 5)

Evidently, this argument pertains mainly to very local 'outputs'; to apply it to the EU level, one would need to emphasise and use descriptive representation much more. Consequently, empowerment through participation is mostly evoked when the DG talks about increasing functional representation on the (sub)national level.

The second way in which 'participative democracy' with an 'active citizenship' through functional associations lets people become part of a joint endeavour is based on the assumption that grassroots-level participation makes citizens aware of social issues, helps to build a consensus supporting policies to tackle these issues, and through this creates citizens' *ownership* of the political process. In short, through becoming part of the process, people perceive the latter to be their own rather than something emanating from 'Brussels'. They thus become part of the cooperative framework of 'working together' for shared goals, which according to the DG's argumentation improves outputs.

---

22. Background paper for workshop 2a, European Commission conference 29–30 March 2006. Online. Available http://ec.europa.eu/social/BlobServlet?docId=358&langId=en, accessed 19 December 2008.

23. *ibid*

[T]here is a word which is particularly important in the implementation of the social OMC, [which] is the *ownership* of the process. This is a process that [...] should be seen as – perceived as a commitment from all the levels who are involved. The governments, here in Brussels, in the national Member States, at the local level in the Member States, as well as from those who are covered, who are involved by these policies, [...] the actors, those who have the stakes in these issues, etc. So, the most they feel that they are participating to the process, the best will be the effective use of the process, I would say, and the achievement of the results. So in this way the role of the NGOs should be seen – it's really to improve implementation, improve ownership of this process at all relevant levels, and to make it a success, an effective use. So, democratic in this way. (Interview no. 6)

Hence, 'active citizenship' and 'participative democracy' is not only a particular way of mediating citizens' concerns into the policy-making process, but also a way of reaching them in order to convince them of a political agenda. In terms of representation, this is a form of anticipatory representation where the DG, via NGOs, seeks to educate citizens about the values of European social policies (*see* Chapter Ten). In terms of legitimacy, it means that the legitimacy of specific policies is here not so much something that exists (or not) among the people to a given extent, but something that essentially has to be *created*. As shown earlier (*see* Chapters Eight and Ten), the idea is that political support can be generated through 'raising awareness' and 'building consensus', for which functional representatives are necessary because of their 'closeness' to 'the ground', i.e. their good connections to the people.

With regard to democratic legitimacy, the output orientation of this argument is striking. The inputs possibly generated through active participation at the local level are here conceptualised as contributions (i.e. resources) to a joint project, and the results of the latter hinge on the cooperation and synergies of as many contributions as possible. 'Support' and 'consensus' are much more present than other inputs. The legitimacy envisaged here is thus that of a broad *acceptance* of the DG's social policies among the public, which in turn is instrumental to political outputs. The DG presents itself as representing Europeans in their entirety and seeing to it that social policies in the EU further their wellbeing. This role is greatly eased if it is acknowledged by the people. Again, the supportive consensus sought is one that directly relates the citizens to the DG, bypassing the Member States. It is essentially meant to legitimate social policy making at the EU level in the first place.

Together, all these notions form a distinctly *cooperative* concept of democratic policy making, which is advanced consistently throughout the DG's text about functional representation in the social OMC. Politics is described as 'working together', and participating means contributing to a joint project. In this model, democratic legitimacy is essentially based on involving all affected or otherwise concerned. In other words, the opportunity of all affected to influence the outcomes is conceptualised as the opportunity to join a political project and contribute to the achievement of its goals.

The main justification for this view is the argument that through taking everybody on board, better results will be achieved, i.e. politics will be successful. 'Success' is defined on the basis of the OMC's common objectives, which lay out ambitious goals, such as having a

> decisive impact on the eradication of poverty and social exclusion by ensuring access for all to the resources, rights and services needed for participation in society, preventing and addressing exclusion, and fighting all forms of discrimination leading to exclusion.[24]

In other words, the common objectives (i.e. intended outputs) are used to define the rationality of policy making (cf. Buchstein and Jörke 2007: 186–7; Scharpf 1975: 22–4) in the OMC with respect to what should be aimed for. However, the text nowhere alludes to the possibility that there might be fundamental disagreements concerning the more detailed interpretation of these objectives and how to achieve them. Instead, their achievement is presented as a matter of commitment and of finding the most efficient instruments by involving all actors with relevant resources. This means that the DG's concept of democracy strongly *depoliticises* European social policy. Politics is here not a competition of different views or a search for compromises, but cooperation for joint goals. This becomes especially clear in the notions relating to political accountability. Accountability is not conceptualised in terms of answering a forum's questions and possibly facing consequences, but in terms of a cooperative, open attitude, and responsible conduct. Functional representatives are framed as 'partners' – i.e. by definition working *with* the DG for shared objectives – and citizens appear as supporting the OMC objectives in principle, as well as in practice by engaging in charitable or advocacy work, but often not being aware of the fact that 'the EU' works to advance aims that are important to them. Democracy thus appears as a rather harmonious pulling together. 'Working together', orchestrated by the Commission, is presented as the only rational option and as automatically resulting in 'working better'. Such automaticity is only plausible if the participants agree not only on the goals but also on the ways to achieve them. Hence, actors who potentially disagree with DG Employment's policies do not appear at all and are thus not part of this account of democracy.

Finally, is 'democracy' a category the DG thinks in terms of in the first place? The term 'democracy' itself figures very rarely; only twenty-three out of 544 documents mention 'democracy' and/or 'democratic', and none of my interviewees used the word spontaneously. When I asked them about it, all of them said (while emphasising different aspects of this) that the involvement of functional representatives increased the democratic legitimacy of the social OMC because through them the affected were represented in the process so that the DG could take their views into account – an argument consistently present throughout the DG's text. Looking at the results of the analysis, one can certainly say that the text does

---

24. European Commission Communication COM(2005)706 of 22 December 2005.

contain a particular concept of democracy, although it is mostly presented in terms of 'working together', 'listening' to the affected, or openness, rather than explicitly referring to 'democracy'. Although the interviewed civil servants did not describe their practices in terms of 'democracy', most showed a rather strong conviction that doing their work in the right way means to an important extent involving representatives of the affected and taking their messages into account. They also felt that the Social Inclusion Unit's culture of close cooperation with social NGOs distinguishes them in a positive way from other parts of the Commission. In this sense, legitimacy through functional representation is an internalised value. The fact that this is not referred to as 'democratic' may partly be due to the fact that democratic legitimacy is not pursued for its own sake but is one element of a political setting, which is maybe more generally perceived as 'doing things in the right way'. Beyond this, the choice of terms in the DG's publications may also be a strategy to avoid explicit discussions about 'democracy'. Since the Commission is rather vulnerable to common accusations of being 'undemocratic', it may not be an advantageous rhetoric strategy to expressly promote one's practices as 'democratic' and thereby provoke a debate about the meaning of this term and whether it is appropriately attached to them. Thus, to understand their concept of democracy, more important than the word itself are the more abstract notions I started from. If 'democracy' is thought of as a normative concept defined as comprising input legitimacy, output legitimacy, and accountability, only the first two of these are present in the text. According to DG Employment, it is important to listen to all affected and to produce policies that increase their wellbeing, but the idea that the people could potentially oppose or impose changes on the DG's policies does not appear. On the contrary, consent is presented as a function of awareness and rationality. Also, the involved NGOs are almost exclusively seen as partners who 'help' the DG promote their political goals, and together with what used to be the Inclusion Unit form the 'OMC community', even if they do not agree on everything. Altogether, then, although the DG consistently claims to act according to the will of the people, there is no dynamic notion of this will and its relationship with implemented policies, in the sense that the people's will could be contested, or change, or that policy orientations could change as a reaction to differences with the people's will appearing. Instead, the Commission's mandate and the involvement of all relevant actors are meant to make sure that the DG represents the European *volonté générale*, the existence of which is taken as an unproblematic fact.

Lastly, can one expect the DG to dwell on potential opposition to its policies? Clearly, their communication is strategic political text and not a study in democratic theory. Accordingly, I have analysed it as argumentation meant to legitimate their political activities. It is a common technique of such argumentation to present choices as having no alternative; nonetheless, the absence of any allusion to contestation remains striking and cannot fully be boiled down to the text's strategic purpose. However, what one may *expect* the Commission to do on the basis of their particular interests is something different from what one should *demand* them to do on the basis of normative standards for democratic governance. Irrespective of a text's immediate or conscious objective, all statements also present 'a way of being in the world' and offer this to others, whether intended or not, 'as one possible way to be' (Alcoff 1991: 21). In other words, the DG's text also promotes a particular vision of legitimate policy making, by presenting the virtues of their own model of governance and arguing that their policies are legitimate on the basis of this way of doing things. This argumentation is built on a model of democracy guided by strategic goals (cf. Smismans 2003). That is to say, DG Employment suggests that we conceptualise democratic governance according to notions that neatly fit their interests as an actor in the social OMC as well as their activities pursued in this interest. Hence, we maybe cannot realistically expect the DG to reflect democratic legitimacy more critically, but we should all the more expect other actors to challenge the concepts advanced by them, so that the public discourse about what democracy should look like in the social OMC is not dominated by one of the process's main actors.

Chapter Twelve

Conclusions

Democratic representation vs. partnership

In a nutshell, DG Employment advances the following concept of democratic legitimacy through functional representation. Social NGOs represent people living in poverty, as well as the European citizens at large *as* being concerned by social exclusion and possibly engaged in or supporting social NGOs themselves. They are ideally placed as functional representatives of these groups, because they work with and for the poor and therefore know their needs, they are motivated by personal concern, and they are rooted in society through the broad support of charitably engaged citizens ('closeness' to the common people). These NGOs are extensively and intensively involved in policy making by the DG, whose policies thereby gain legitimacy in several ways. Input legitimacy is increased, firstly because the NGOs provide information about the needs of the affected, and secondly because through them the process becomes more participative, thereby enhancing not only the involvement of the affected (the right to be listened to concerning issues one is affected by, increased political equality and legitimacy based on an attentive attitude towards the weak), but also active citizenship in general ('participative democracy'). Through the NGOs' inherent 'closeness', functional representation thus makes the DG itself 'closer' to (i.e. representative of) the people. This input legitimacy mainly leads to an increased output legitimacy, i.e. more efficient and effective policies to reduce poverty, which is the main element of the legitimacy claimed. These policies have to be implemented by the Member States, but they become possible through the DG's catalyst role; the latter thus acts as the representative of the European general interest. This organic legitimacy is also intended to be strengthened by the NGOs communicating European policies to their constituencies, so that the latter become more aware and, therefore, supportive of the process and the Commission's role. Finally, functional representation increases procedural legitimacy because it is part of 'good governance'. 'Good governance' refers to the DG's open-door policy towards functional representatives ('participation'), their responsible conduct in their practices of involving the latter, and the cooperative style of 'working together' with them ('partnership'). All in all, then, democracy is conceptualised as 'working together', representation as based on trust, and functional representatives' involvement in policy making as 'partnership'.

Functional representation is thus first and foremost intended to make policy making in the social OMC more *rational*, in the sense of joining forces with all relevant actors and of producing better outcomes as a result of this, rather than increasing the people's self-governance (in the direction of the ideas of G.D.H.

Cole) or improving the control of executives (as in David Mitrany's vision). Inputs are to a large extent instrumental to achieving preferred outcomes, in addition to being limited by conditional funding and structural barriers related to the high level of aggregation. They are not meant to determine what sorts of outputs are to be sought. In accordance with this, political accountability is largely missing, replaced by 'good governance' and a claim to organic legitimacy, i.e. DG Employment presents itself as knowing the goal and as responsibly organising the common effort to achieve it.

Yet, although DG Employment's concept is distinctly one of governing *for* the people, the rationality of this model is not exclusively geared towards output legitimacy, but also builds on input legitimacy, particularly in the sense of broadening the representative basis and making it more equal. The strong emphasis on involving all affected (together with the support given to some of them), the inclusion of descriptive representation of the poor, and the stress on the right to be listened to all advance a concept of political representation that is more socially equal and diverse than is often the case. The continual development of the European Meetings of People Experiencing Poverty, such as the recent efforts to provide delegates with feedback about the sequels to their conferences, show that there is a sincere commitment to establishing this form of representation as an integral part of European social policy making, which also sends a message to the Member States as to the importance and value of descriptive representation. Funding EU-wide umbrella organisations (thus promoting the formation of national networks) and urging to involve social NGOs on the national and subnational levels, too, also serves to propagate the idea of representing weak social groups in policies that affect them in countries where this does not have a strong tradition.

However, this conception has a severe catch, *viz.* the firm insertion of all these arguments in a framework of *partnership*. By conceptualising functional representation as a process of 'working together', much of the democratic potential it could otherwise have is lost due to three main problems: First, in presenting the involvement of functional representatives as partnership, the DG implies that their role is to provide beneficial contributions. Second, related to this, governance is conceived of as a cooperative joint effort without conflicts between the participants. Third, the partnership framework also involves funding functional organisations to promote DG Employment's objectives in the social OMC. All this together undermines the argument that functional representation generates democratic legitimacy, and at the same time also calls into question the representative claims the DG makes about the organisations it involves (and, by implication, about itself).

DG Employment's text defines participating in OMC governance as partnership, built on the commonsensical topos that by 'working together' better results will be achieved for the benefit of all participants. In line with this topos, the DG does not answer the question of who is a relevant functional actor with respect to some policy area on the basis of the support basis of an organisation (however defined), but on the basis of the *contribution* it can make to solving a given problem – *see* Chapter Six. In the chapters following this, the issue was restated in terms of a gap, in the DG's text, between the representation of constituencies (depicted as based on 'closeness' to them) and the capacity to make the expected contributions at the EU level. The observation of such a gap is of course based on the extratextual notion that these two do not self-evidently go together but may well have trade-offs. In contrast to this understanding, the DG amalgamates representation and contributing, to form one whole: '[V]oluntary and non governmental organisations serve to bring the needs of people closer to the decision-makers. *In this way, they can be partners* in delivering vital services and information' (European Commission 2000a; emphasis added). In general, the inputs functional representatives can provide are presented as instrumental to output legitimacy, in the sense of efficient policy making. In the DG's expectations of the NGOs they work with, the mediation of views is only a starting point, albeit an important one, and making useful contributions is decisive:

> [T]he role of civil society organisations goes beyond advocacy or influence; they should also build partnerships with other NGOs involved in different areas and commit themselves to delivering concrete results – for instance in the framework of the European strategy against exclusion. (European Commission 2003b)

'[D]elivering concrete results' in the framework of the social OMC requires highly professional and well-resourced organisations. The formulation also suggests that the expected contributions are useful from DG Employment's point of view. In other words, functional representation is not presented as mediating whatever inputs the most affected support, but something fitting the DG's political agenda.

This latter quotation also shows that being partners in the OMC not only has implications for what is contributed, but for the ways of working too. The 'partnership' topos not only refers to how the DG would like to see its own relationships with functional representatives, but also constitutes a wider framework for policy making in the social OMC in general. Ultimately, the whole society should 'work together' in order to achieve the OMC's objectives, including NGOs among each other. 'Partnership' is presented by the DG as the characteristic way of doing things in the OMC; to be part of this process, actors therefore also have to adapt themselves to this culture. As well as that, being partners of the DG means entering a relationship with benefits and responsibilities for both parties (cf. Chapter Seven); the DG can thus make requirements of would-be partners. Incidentally, stronger coordination among the NGOs not only reduces the DG's workload, but can also make the European social NGO lobby stronger on the whole. Actively shaping the functional representation field by giving NGOs incentives to collaborate thus also makes the latter better partners from the perspective of DG Employment.

The relationship between the capacity to contribute effectively to the OMC in partnership with DG Employment and other actors in the sector, on the one hand, and the mediation of views 'from the ground', on the other hand, deserves further investigation. It is clear that in order to meaningfully participate in complex political processes, functional organisations need a considerable level of professionalism. At the same time, there is evidence that supporters of functional associations mostly do not wish to actively engage with or even closely follow the activities of their chosen representatives (Warleigh 2001: 633–4; Clarence *et al.* 2005; Maloney 2008: 75–7). Yet, this does not necessarily mean that the activities of these representatives do not matter to them, or that an association's European level is automatically unrepresentative of the local level. More research is needed regarding how legitimate and democratic functional representation can be conceptualised in settings with high aggregation and changing patterns of support, and what conditions it has to fulfil. We need to know more about the relationships of the Brussels-based NGO community with their constituencies, and about the repercussions of DG Employment's incentives for professionalisation – along with structural factors of representing at the EU – for the functioning of these organisations. So far, little attention has been paid to the possibility that extending functional representation to the European level might entail similar problems and questions for democratic representation as has been the case with territorial representation.

The presentation of functional representation as contributing to efficient policy making directly leads to the second concern related to the partnership approach, *viz.* the assumption of *conflictlessness* underlying the text. The DG presumes that the more 'stakeholders' are involved, the more effective policy making will be, and the better the resulting outputs. In line with this, inputs are treated as information, 'needs', 'views', and more rarely 'opinions', but never as interests. There is no allusion to the possibility that the 'stakeholders' could have opposed or incompatible interests perhaps exactly because they have stakes in the matter discussed. In particular, social policy is nowhere openly conceptualised in terms of redistribution, but rather as a matter of political will to tackle poverty.[1] In short, the DG presents a highly rationalistic view of governance, in which 'working better' is by definition a matter of 'working together'. This depoliticisation is logically necessary to plausibly characterise policy making as partnership. At the same time, however, presenting things in this way makes the social OMC much less prone to causing public debate, which is generally provoked by the public opposition of interests. Paired with the general lack of publicity in this area, this poses problems for the political accountability of the DG as well as the involved functional organisations. Describing policy making as conflictless 'working together' for shared goals obfuscates political responsibilities and existing differences between different actors' interests, as well as political alternatives to the choices made. Furthermore, making partnership a condition of access to the circle of actors who can influence OMC polices raises serious concerns about the role of those groups who disagree with the DG's basic orientations. This concern pertains not only to functional associations with deviant views (e.g. opposing the

---

1. Cf. Føllesdal (2003: 78), who makes a similar point about the White Paper on European governance (European Commission Communication COM(2001)428 of 25 July 2001).

Europeanisation of social policies, or their framing in economic terms), but also to the internal mediation of different views within the networks involved by the DG. Favouring the representation of large functional groups through a limited number of Europe-wide umbrella organisations means that diversity must to an important extent be managed *within* these networks (rather than in the governance processes coordinated by DG Employment), while at the same time influence at the EU level depends significantly on the capacity to express a coherent message.

It is remarkable that even the descriptive representation of people living in poverty is inserted into this framework of conflictless cooperation, albeit with slightly different emphases. Although this form of representation is also strongly justified on the grounds of changing the political agency of the affected as well as their image in the perception of the better-off, the descriptive representatives' messages are treated as 'expertise' about 'what it is like to be poor', i.e. about the reality on the ground. Through this, they are made unpolitical pieces of information that do have a special value, but are one contribution among others without any visible friction. This contradicts a part of the DG's own justifications for this practice and serves to obscure the radical potential inherent in this form of representation. Considering that descriptive representation in general has been researched mainly in relation to gender and ethnic minorities, practices such as this one of people living in poverty representing their fellow sufferers are worth being researched more, and offer a lot of different perspectives for enquiry.

Ultimately, then, in the DG's text the only possible way of representing functional groups in the social OMC is the participation in a joint project. This master frame not only defines more principled opposition as non-existent, it also presents DG Employment as the actor who knows how things should be done. Based on the Commission's organic legitimacy as the authoritative interpreter of the European interest, the DG coordinates the joint project to which everyone is encouraged to contribute – i.e. to become part of a scheme that is already outlined.

Also, their model of 'participative democracy' is conceived within this same conceptual frame of 'working together'. First of all, 'participation' is here defined as charitable engagement (particularly voluntary work) in local grassroots associations aimed at reducing poverty. This form of 'active citizenship' is conceptualised as activities that are already part of the common European project to 'combat poverty and social exclusion', whether or not the concerned are aware of this. Through the emphasis on the grassroots fundaments of European social NGOs, these activities are then linked to the social OMC. By these equations, the joint project is demonstrated to be real and firmly rooted in society:

Many Europeans engage in social NGOs to reduce poverty.

DG Employment works to reduce poverty in Europe.

→ *We* work for shared objectives.

DG Employment cooperates with social NGOs to reduce poverty.

→ We are working *together* for shared objectives.

By conceptualising European social policy as cooperative 'working together', the text overcomes the dichotomy of self-government and rule, a traditional puzzle for theorists of political representation. In the vision outlined by the DG, the Commission as the promoter of the European general interest works for goals that are important to the citizens, and by involving organisations through which the latter actively advance these goals themselves, 'we all' 'work together' in a joint endeavour. Although the DG has a coordinating role, it does not impose anything on the people, but rather acts out what needs to be done (as agreed by the national executives too), and helps to extend the citizens' engagement to the European level. In this arrangement, there is no clear-cut division of principals and agents or governing and governed, but the main actor is 'we', embodied by the Commission. At the same time, by claiming to represent this 'we', the DG constructs this constituency, i.e. engages in the building of a European 'we', characterised as a participative civil society where social exclusion is a major concern that unifies people. This claim not only makes plausible the description of functional representation as partnership and contributing to a European project, but also sheds light on the absence of political accountability to the citizens. The concept of accountability rests on the dichotomy of account givers and account holders, and on their potential disagreement. If, however, the representative is defined as embodying the represented rather than governing them, and mainly helping to execute their wishes, this relationship of control can be seen as less important, and it is enough to ensure responsible conduct ('good governance'), i.e. that things are done properly and fairly. The frame of 'working together' does not evoke the possibility that some groups could have opposed views; instead, there are only those aware of the common project and those not yet aware.

Accordingly, 'awareness-raising' is important in order to ensure broad support and to reach all those who could potentially contribute to the joint project. Raising awareness is one of the main tasks of the Key Networks. Their contributions in the partnership with the DG are thus not only inputs, but also the communication of the social OMC to the citizens, which leads to the third problem of the partnership approach, *viz.* the *use* of functional representation to advance DG Employment's specific goals within the OMC. The aim of 'awareness-raising' is to create legitimacy – i.e. 'a more supportive environment' – by educating 'policy makers and the general public'.[2] Especially concerning 'policy- and decision-makers and stakeholders', this awareness is intended to make them 'take ownership of EU objectives and priorities', because '[p]ositively changing the understanding of these parties will enable national policies to converge further towards those of the EU' (European Commission 2008j). Although the representation of the affected to the DG (input legitimacy) is the main justification for involving functional representatives in general, the promotion of 'EU objectives and priorities' is a central argument presented to support the core funding of the Key Networks. It is based on the premise that these 'EU objectives and priorities' represent the

---

2. DG Employment (2010) 'European Year for Active Ageing 2012: questions & answers'. Online. Available http://ec.europa.eu/social/BlobServlet?docId=5702&langId=en, accessed 21 June 2011.

European general interest embodied by DG Employment: 'You [the citizens] will ultimately benefit from PROGRESS as Member States will promote laws, policies and practices in line with EU and national social goals'.[3] Hence, in the case of the Key Networks, partnership is taken so far as to form a *joint lobby* for the Europeanisation of social policies, i.e. for dealing with more social issues at the EU level, and for strengthening the influence of the European process on national policies. How this 'lobby sponsoring' (Bauer 2002: 388–90) works is evident in DG publications like the following:

Events

COFACE European Family Conference

The event will look at *the importance of an EU focus* on the family, and the EU's role in combating family poverty and social exclusion.[4]

From the Ground

EAPN's campaign on minimum income

'Everyone deserves a decent life.' That is the slogan of the new campaign for adequate minimum income schemes launched last December by the European Anti-Poverty Network. 'Most of the EU Member States have minimum income schemes in place, but there are serious flaws in their accessibility and their adequacy,' explains the campaign. The ongoing 'Active Inclusion' process is an opportunity to make progress.

Last October, the European Commission published a Communication on modernising social protection for greater social justice and economic cohesion. The Communication is open to public consultation until February and will lead to concrete proposals on how to move forward. *However, it will only be implemented if it is widely supported by the Member States.* The Commission is also working to assess the possible impact of acting to establish common basic requirements and guiding principles at the EU level for minimum income support schemes. '*EU-level willingness to go further on the issue is hindered by a lack of political commitment,*' says the campaign. '*It is the right time to put pressure on political leaders,*' the NGO network adds. *Its website provides model letters to send to officials at national and European level.*[5]

---

3. European Commission (2008) 'What social Europe can do for you'. Online. Available http://ec.europa.eu/employment_social/publications/booklets/general/pdf/ke0008001_en.pdf, accessed 23 September 2008.

4. DG Employment (2010) 'COFACE European Family Conference'. Online. Available http://ec.europa.eu/social/main.jsp?catId=88&langId=en&eventsId=276&furtherEvents=yes, accessed 14 December 2010. Emphasis added.

5. European Commission 2008b. Emphasis added. Note how EAPN's campaign and the DG's initiative are interlaced, on the textual level as well as in terms of their activities' timing.

As becomes clear in these examples, the partnership with the funded NGOs decisively differs from the general 'working together' topos in that it is directed towards a third group of actors: the Member States. In other words, cooperating with these organisations is not only meant to increase the legitimacy of the DG's policies by contributing resources and thus making those policies better, but the Key Networks are also supposed to convince others of these policies' qualities. This concerns particularly the promotion of doing things on the EU level. In return, the Key Networks' campaign messages are then cited in DG publications in order to underpin their own position, a practice which works on the premise (supported by DG Employment's discourse) that these messages represent the organisations' constituencies.

In addition to national policy makers, 'awareness-raising' is also directed towards the citizens at large – with whom NGOs are said to have better and closer connections than the DG itself – so that they can ensure that they 'are informed about' 'EU policies'.[6] Contrarily to the Member States, whose 'lack of political commitment' hinders 'EU-level willingness to go further' (European Commission 2008b), the citizens are (re)presented as being supportive of the DG's objectives but unaware of the European process. Making them aware and ensuring their support are therefore two sides of the same coin. Yet, experience of the Commission's pedagogic efforts to convince citizens of their views raises doubts about the prospects of this scheme. Apart from this need for a reality check, it is of course highly dubious to finance organisations to promote particular political aims, and then present these organisations' messages as inputs in order to benefit from their legitimacy as representatives of the affected.

Furthermore, defining functional representatives as partners whose helpful contributions improve problem solving in a harmonious political process, and especially using them also as funded agents to advocate the Europeanisation of social policies, not only poses serious problems for the concept of democracy advanced by DG Employment, but it also conflicts with the way in which the DG itself conceptualises representation to work within functional associations and thereby undermines the legitimacy of the latter.

Concerning democracy, the most obvious issue is the fact that depicting functional representation as 'working together' in partnership presumes that the participants *already agree* on the basic orientations. Social NGOs in particular are presented as naturally supporting the OMC objectives. This raises the question of whether such functional organisations in the social policy sector who are disagreeing with the DG's political orientations have the same chances of being involved as those who agree, or whether the partnership paradigm defines dissenters from the outset as being outside the OMC framework and thus not coming into consideration as 'partners'. Put differently, can NGOs collectively be presented as natural partners of the DG because those organisations or subgroups that are

---

6. DG Employment (no date) 'Relations with civil society'. Online. Available http://ec.europa.eu/employment_social/fundamental_rights/civil/civ_en.htm, accessed 18 September 2008.

not interested in such a partnership are simply not visible in the OMC discourse? Notwithstanding the DG's text's emphasis on 'working together', it is not very concrete what it is that should be done together. What is more, there is no allusion to how disagreements should be dealt with. Instead, political choices are presented as without alternative, and reaching them as a question of political will and getting everybody involved. This is especially problematic in view of the fact that the Commission is not a neutral arbitrator, but has its own institutional interest, *viz.* the Europeanisation of social policies, both in the sense of broadening the issues dealt with on the EU level and in the sense of deepening the cooperation. If they conceptualise functional representatives one-dimensionally as their partners, this implies that different inputs from different functional groups are not treated in the same way. In short, the starting point of DG Employment's concept of democracy is not representing the views of the affected and the interaction of different views, but the European general interest (as interpreted by them), and acting according to this in a cooperative and efficient way. Rather than being about participating in a procedure to determine what to do, it is about participating in a project that needs to be done.

However, the problem is not only one of the Commission, which of course pursues its own interests just as any other political actor. If European social policy were discussed in public debates, possible disagreeing actors would oppose their own narratives to the DG's, so that the latter would need to address diverging views in its own discourse.

Treating functional organisations as partners also creates internal contradictions within DG Employment's discourse about governance in the social OMC, which reveal a key dilemma of this discourse, namely the *incompatibility* of available arguments about the legitimacy of functional representatives of socially disadvantaged groups and the DG's model of involving them in policy making. Social NGOs are claimed to represent those especially affected by social policies gyroscopically, based on their reputation as intrinsically motivated by empathy with socially weak groups and their local and psychological closeness to the common people. They are depicted as rooted in ordinary citizens' charitable engagement for the benefit of the poor, and thus essentially different from politicians and executive officers ('bureaucrats'). Importantly, the legitimacy claimed for them as representatives rests essentially on this 'untaintedness' (Saward 2009: 19) by electoral politics; they are trusted to be committed to their cause and their values (which they share with their constituents) and independent from political or economic ties, just as gyroscopes rotate around their axes, maintaining their own orientation (Mansbridge 2003: 520–2). This representative claim builds on widely held perceptions that identify (particularly social) NGOs with 'soft' values of caring for the weak rather than 'hard' ones of competition and monetary profit. If these associations are simultaneously presented as partners of a political institution, and even as lobbying for particular policies hand in hand with that institution, this gyroscopic legitimacy is undermined. NGOs become part of a camp with certain political objectives.

That said, where is the limit between naturally developing epistemic communities among functional representatives, civil servants, politicians, academics, etc. (cf. Haas 1989: esp. 384–7; 1992: esp. 3), and a situation where functional representatives are no longer external actors in relation to political institutions? In the case of the Key Networks, the state of affairs is rather unambiguous: these organisations advance the Europeanisation of social policies in return for funding that ensures their existence at the European level. They are to an important extent agents of the unit that hosts them. If this principal–agent relationship is not always plainly visible, this is because the Key Network status is only accessible for associations who share the Inclusion Unit's orientations, some of them godfathered by DG Employment. For other NGOs, the distinction is blurred and depends on the intensity of cooperation, which is an empirical question. My main concerns here are the conceptual implications of combining gyroscopic representation and the 'working together' topos in one frame of legitimisation. The particular form of legitimacy assigned to NGOs here is of course no invention of DG Employment, but based on common concepts of how public interest associations represent. Argumentation claiming legitimacy has to build on existing notions of what constitutes legitimacy, in order to apply these to the particular case. However, the commonness of the notions drawn on here also means that these cannot be inserted in whatever context or interpreted in whatever way without falling foul of established meanings. Exactly this happens when the DG emphasises their close ties with social NGOs and justifies their financing with these associations' support and contribution to the OMC. The contradictions arising from this are best observed in relation to accountability.

A constituent having chosen (accepted) a representative along the gyroscopic rationale need not continually follow the activities of that representative, but relies on her to remain true to her principles. It is enough that information is available when desired, and that support can easily be maintained or withdrawn (Mansbridge 2003: 520–2). In addition to their own values, gyroscopic representatives are often accountable to networks of peers working in the same sector and having similar values (Goodin 2003b: 373–9; cf. Ch. 11), which also plays a role in keeping them on track. Finally, organisations entrenched in grassroots engagement can be expected to have a stable orientation on the basis of their local activities. Concretely and regularly working for the values one advocates will strengthen one's determination, not only because the experiences in this work confirm the need for such engagement, but also to avoid cognitive dissonance. This is not to say that social NGOs represent *only* gyroscopically, or that gyroscopic representation is automatically legitimate or democratic; it merely implies that the gyroscopic logic forms an important part of how social NGOs represent their constituencies, and how they are perceived. Political actors of the electoral system, by contrast, are not normally trusted to be reliably accountable to their own consciousness, at least not primarily. Consequently, their motivations and intentions are less important for their accountability, and they are principally judged on the basis of their actions. Because these actions imply binding consequences for the represented, and because they are not believed to be significantly and reliably motivated by a commitment to values shared with the represented, accountability is hierarchical and formal, with the citizenry at large as the ultimate principal (Goodin 2003b: 368–70, 372–3). Executive administrations such as the DG, whose staff cannot be changed by the represented, are expected to adapt their comportment to the preferences of the people, via the leadership of their Commissioner, via the legislative (the EP and the Council), or via public deliberation. This also involves strategic action in response to what kinds of choices seem promising in a given political constellation. Such adaptations of political positions in response to power are much less accepted for gyroscopic representatives.

Now, if a functional association with a strong civil society identity and largely perceived to act gyroscopically closely cooperates with a political institution that is seen as part of a formal principal–agent chain and under the control of the electorate, it inevitably has to adapt its logic of action to this environment, at least to some extent. It becomes less independent in its political choices, its leadership level will no longer necessarily stem from voluntary activists on the grassroots level but tend to adopt the language of conventional policy makers, and it achieves privileged influence on generally binding rules, i.e. power. Consequently, it will be less trusted to act firmly and reliably according to certain principles and values without much need for oversight. In other words, it loses part of the very capital on which its representative claim was built, and will be seen as more in need of control. Moreover, if public administrators come to play an important role in the networks of peers around functional representatives, and especially if their weight as account holders is increased through the funds they provide, the accountability realised through these networks changes from strengthening the representatives' inner conviction to overseeing their activities. It is quite a different thing to be accountable to colleagues from like-minded functional associations rather than to civil servants (Goodin 2003b: 385). On the basis of similar considerations, Robert E. Goodin cautions against mixing different logics of accountability. These logics being the core of different rationales of representations, the same can be said about mixing different modes of representation:

> Different sectors being accountable, each in their own complimentary way, can yield greater accountability across social institutions overall. But arrangements that straddle sectors (whether through partnership or competition) inherently blur the distinctions between the sectors. In so doing, those arrangements undermine the accountability of each sector in its own terms and, hence, the interlocking system of social accountability overall. (Goodin 2003b: 360)

Treating functional representatives as partners reduces their credibility as gyroscopic representatives rooted in charitable engagement and creates demands for a legitimacy based more strongly on continuous justification and control, which is difficult for functional associations to fulfil and often does not fit the way they are organised. Hence, their legitimacy as political partners inevitably becomes insufficient. On the other hand, adapting to these demands would change their very character as representatives, which would also result in a loss of legitimacy. Additionally, this would alter the whole rationale of involving them in governance processes. In brief, legitimacy from involving functional representatives can only be claimed if the legitimacy of these representatives themselves is not compromised, which presupposes careful attention to their specific ways of building their legitimacy.

Concerning the DG itself, treating social NGOs as 'partners' who are provided with conditional funding and visibly instrumentalised, while at the same time presenting the latter as authentic representatives with deep commitment to and roots in civic engagement is self-contradictory and therefore undermines their proper argumentation. The text attempts to circumvent this trade-off by depicting the involved NGOs as *naturally* having compatible objectives, and by depicting the civil society they represent as intrinsically engaged for similar aims as the DG. In other words, the NGOs' and the DG's goals are presented as matching, so that it seems natural to work together. However, such unanimity across a functional sector appears suspicious. Hence, the *depoliticisation* of the social OMC and the portrayal of functional representation as a harmonious joint effort for shared goals are necessary to hold up the concepts of democratic legitimacy advanced in DG Employment's text. The DG's model can only be maintained as long as European social policy does not become subject to public debate, i.e. as long as there is a lack of political accountability and public input. This is hardly a sustainable basis for democratic governance.

The functional representation of socially marginalised groups, such as the poor, is difficult to realise in other ways than with strong gyroscopic and charitable elements. Associations building on these rationales can have considerable legitimacy in the eyes of their constituents and supporters. The problem of DG Employment's argumentation is thus not so much the modes of representation they claim for social NGOs, but their insertion in the specific frame of partnership as conflictless cooperation for joint objectives. Under the liberty of association, NGOs can organise their representative structures as they prefer, as long as they remain within the limits of legality. It is the right of institutions within the territorial system of representation to decide under which conditions they grant which kind of access to which kinds of organisations, and it is their responsibility to design this process as a whole in democratically legitimate ways. In other words, the Commission, which has developed a hallmark of involving NGOs as a means to legitimise the EU, could seek to develop a model of democracy that allows European policy making to *benefit* from the particular legitimacy that gyroscopic and symbolic functional representatives can have, in such a way as to make the political process as a whole more democratic. The principle whereby affectedness leads to a right to be listened to and the development of descriptive representation as one pillar of the poor's functional representation are promising advances in this respect. However, the partnership framework is not a felicitous choice. The 'working together' discourse makes it easy to instrumentalise or exclude functional representatives and undermines the specific legitimacy that social NGOs could provide. Therefore, an arrangement where different modes of representation complement each other to make the system on the whole more representative can hardly be founded on such a concept of 'working together, working better' as advanced by DG Employment. Instead of forming a symmetric 'partnership' with joint responsibilities for achieving certain results, functional and territorial representatives should be *separated* and have a clear division of labour. It has to be clear that functional representatives represent only a part of those bound by policies, while territorial representatives are authorised by and accountable to the whole citizenry. Representing their respective constituencies should unambiguously take priority over possible responsibilities towards each other. The ultimate responsibility of the territorially representative institutions for public policies also means that the solutions for the democratic legitimacy of functional representation in the social OMC have to be sought first and foremost in the relationships between functional and territorial representation.

Embedding functional representation in territorial representation as a solution?

The contradictions in DG Employment's argumentation show that functional representation does not automatically or necessarily increase democratic legitimacy, but depends on how it is envisaged to work and how it relates to the rest of the political setting. The question of how it might be conceptualised to better contribute to democratic legitimacy in the social OMC thus sends us back to its relations with the institutions of the *territorial system of representation*. It is these institutions that are ultimately responsible for democratic policy making and that set the framework in which functional representatives act. For the present case, this means not only the social NGOs' relationship with DG Employment, but also with the EU's system of territorial representation at large and the set-up of the OMC.

To start with the former, the main issue is obviously that of the core funding provided to the Key Networks. This financing is clearly necessary if one wants socially marginalised groups to be functionally represented at the European level at all. There are good reasons to want this: concerning the social OMC specifically, they are those most affected by policy making; more generally, supporting their representation makes functional representation at the EU on the whole more equal with regards to different social groups and different interests. The problem is that DG Employment, which has a vested interest in Europeanising social policies, determines the conditions for receiving such funding and decides which organisations are chosen. This arrangement opens possibilities for instrumentalisation and creates incentives to prioritise cooperation, professionalisation, and aggregation in umbrella organisations over questions of how the views of the represented are mediated. The obvious solution, then, would be to shift the allocation of core funding for social NGOs either to the European Parliament (EP) or the Member States, which in the social OMC are represented in the Social Protection Committee (SPC). Certainly, these have their own institutional interests too, but they are collective bodies composed of representatives with different views. Both alternatives would therefore entail a debate about what kinds of organisations should be supported, under what conditions, for what tasks, and why; both alternatives would also entail finding a compromise between different views regarding these questions. In either case, the financing of functional associations could no longer be framed as unproblematic 'partnership', but a different narrative would have to be found to legitimise the practice. Thus, the input of the affected, which is now mainly conceptualised as helpful contributions to a joint project, would possibly be presented more as an intrinsic democratic value. Such a conceptualisation widens the circle of potential functional associations to be involved and has repercussions for how this involvement would need to be organised. In the case of the EP, the debate would in principle be public, while the SPC's work is not very transparent. However, from the judicial point of view, the SPC is a more realistic alternative.

The relationship between functional and territorial representation is not only important in order to prevent symbiotic partnerships between particular actors and a restricted circle of functional representatives – it also has to be seen in the context of which constituency is the ultimate fundament of democratic representative policy making. As argued in Chapter Two, all public policies must go back to the citizenry as a whole. Functional representation is necessarily more informal and changeable than territorial institutions, and it can inevitably involve only a part of all groups that arguably could be involved, although the outcomes of the process can be binding on the citizenry as a whole. Moreover, these circumstances tend to replicate existing social inequalities. Therefore, political goal setting, the weighing of different groups' interests, conflict solving, and final decision making have to be done in institutions that are accountable to the territorial constituency through formal (formally equal and formally binding) and deliberative processes. In other words, governance processes involving functional representation should be 'nested' in democratic institutions of the territorial representation system (Føllesdal 2011: 97).[7] In the social OMC, where policies remain national legislation, this primarily concerns the European-level agenda setting and means giving a greater role to political institutions that in the chain of delegation are closer to the electorate than the Commission. Also in this regard, transferring the Key Networks' funding decisions to the Member States' executives or the European Parliament would be advisable, since it would give these actors a greater say regarding the participants in the process, and by implication also its overall direction.

Embedding governance processes in institutions representing territorial constituencies not only ties them more strongly to the political will formed in public arenas, but also raises the potential for politicisation, which advances public deliberation and thereby strengthens communication between the represented and the representing. One way to achieve this 'is to have elected officials participate' in governance forums, which 'are likely to bring contested and politicised issues

---

7. Cf. Héritier and Lehmkuhl 2011: 139–43; Greven 2007: 244; Benz and Papadopoulos 2006: 2; Wälti et al. 2004: 108; Peters and Pierre 2004: 78, 88; Pierre 2000b: 242–4; Goodin 2003b: 382.

to the public's attention, thus enhancing public accountability of decisions' (Wälti et al. 2004: 95). Therefore, a stronger role for the EP would be preferable to strengthening the SPC as a decision maker in the social OMC. Moreover, it would be necessary for the national governments – individually and through the Council – to get more engaged in the social OMC, especially concerning its agenda setting, so that these policies are debated in the national public spheres. This would also make European social policy making more visible to the people, i.e. it would be seen to be taking place in the first place. In short, making citizens aware of the social OMC is much more promising through bringing up the European dimension of social policies in national debates about respective issues than through NGOs alone. Raising awareness without politicising, by contrast, comes down to mere public relations, the results of which remain modest. If national governments are reluctant to put OMC policies on their public agenda, while DG Employment seeks to 'make more visible the positive role played by good social protection and inclusion policies',[8] this is in itself revealing about the legitimacy of the social OMC as a whole.

As Føllesdal remarks, nesting governance processes in institutions of territorial representation makes new modes of government less 'new' (Føllesdal 2011: 97). Conversely, therefore, it is precisely the 'newness' of these methods, namely the location of policy making outside the traditional arenas of parliament and the public sphere, that makes them less democratic. Put differently, the lack of democratic legitimacy is inbuilt in the OMC, and cannot be made up for simply by involving functional representatives in this architecture. Again, involving functional representation cannot as such render policy making more democratic, but democracy depends on how the different elements of a political system work together.

This insight also concerns the specific challenges of policy making at the European level in general. Scholars of European integration have generally avoided the consideration that some democratic deficits of the EU might precisely be due to the fact that issues are dealt with at such a high level of aggregation. However, the contradictions in DG Employment's argumentation for the legitimacy of functional representation suggest that at least for social NGOs this may be the case. If the legitimacy of such organisations to represent the socially weak is indeed based on their 'closeness' to these constituencies, it is difficult to stretch this legitimacy to the European level. In particular, it becomes all the more difficult if NGOs are required to organise in highly aggregated umbrella networks that gather them in pyramid-like structures reducing diversity towards the top. The management of diversity is here outsourced to the functional networks' decision-making arenas – which are rarely very transparent – rather than being dealt with in public deliberation or weighed by accountable politicians. On the other hand, it would push the Commission's boundaries to involve even national-

---

8.   DG Employment (2008) 'Awareness-raising projects'. Online. Available http://ec.europa.eu/ employment_social/spsi/awareness_raising_projects_en.htm, accessed 18 September 2008.

level NGOs from all Member States, and engaging in European policies would also be impossible for most national associations. Granted that the representatives in the Brussels secretariats of functional networks are just as committed to their organisations' missions as local voluntary workers, the mediation of views from the local up to the European level still remains a question mark. In this perspective, the EU level of social NGOs can be legitimate as representatives of their general *cause* – i.e. the broad concern for the socially marginalised (which is a great part of their work in the social OMC, also in the DG's conception) – rather than as representatives of the *views* of the poor or of the knowledge of their organisations' local workers. However, it is highly questionable how far the two can be divided, given that there may well be different views about how to properly understand 'the cause'. To be democratic, a claim to represent a group's 'cause' has to be accepted by that group (or at least made repeatedly in sufficiently accessible forums without encountering objection), i.e. it must resonate with views in that group about what their 'cause' is. However, the notorious problems of connecting EU policies to the public sphere(s) also apply to European NGOs. It seems reasonable to assume that the publications of the social NGOs involved in the OMC mainly reach those working with European social policies in one way or another, and do not even reach all their national member networks (Interview no. 2). Hence, the gap in DG Employment's text between the NGOs' local 'closeness' and their EU-level activities is symptomatic of real-life difficulties in linking the two. In light of the enormous number of functional representatives working in Brussels and the hopes set on them to make EU policy making more democratic, this issue deserves much more critical research.

Rationalisation: representation without democracy

DG Employment's 'working together' discourse is part of a general tendency to *rationalise* concepts of democracy. 'Participation' no longer primarily refers to the collective self-determination of a political community, but has become a method to generate rational outcomes, which are now the main criterion for the normative evaluation of political processes (Buchstein and Jörke 2007: 186; cf. Greven 1993; 2009; Bellamy and Castiglione 2000: 73–4). In the late sixties and early seventies of the twentieth century, 'participation' still referred mainly to the participation of individuals (rather than collective actors), and was conceptualised in terms of emancipation and the democratisation (and politicisation) of the society as a whole. The related debates centred not least on 'the preferred structures and general aims of democracy from the individual citizen's perspective' (Greven 2007: 236; cf. pp. 235–7). Just as in the earlier conceptual roots of functional representation, political participation in these earlier discourses was a means to give each citizen greater influence on collective decisions, and thereby on her environment. This understanding is directly based on the core values of modern democracy, whereby equal citizens have the 'right to participate in establishing and running the system of law and government' (Greven 2009: 87) that they live in.

In DG Employment's argumentation, by contrast, the participation of functional associations (and, according to the text's line of reasoning, their constituents) is not primarily geared to increasing people's self-determination, but to improving problem-solving capacity and 'stakeholders'' acceptance. Although the intrinsic value of citizens' participation is still present in the text, this argument is clearly subordinate to the dominant paradigm of rationalising the political process, in which inputs from functional groups are contributions that help make policies more efficient and effective. 'Participation' is thus a means to enhance governability and makes policy making 'better', not least from the *executive's* point of view. Governance is presented as a process with an inbuilt direction, which is justified with the need to reduce poverty and secure welfare. This conception implies a division between rational, controllable, productive input, and uncontrolled input, which is potentially unproductive and irrational. The DG's definition of 'relevant actors' as those capable of making useful contributions (from the DG's point of view) is a way to filter inputs for this purpose. In the same vein, functional representatives are not meant to represent their constituencies' views, but information about their factual needs. As such, this is nothing radically new; from any individual's or institution's perspective there are presumably always inputs that are preferable to others. What is new is that this division has entered publicly advanced concepts of democracy.

Now, one might ask whether the distinction between technocratic problem solving and the citizens' genuine 'co-authorship' (cf. Habermas 1994: 153) of public law is not an artificial one, and whether solving collective 'problems' is not the immanent purpose of democratic participation. In this vein, Paul Magnette enquires (in a comment on Michael T. Greven's article, cited above (Greven 2007)):

> One would like to know why democratic principles should be put first. After all, what the citizens actually call for, if we can trust Eurobarometer surveys, are efficient policies ensuring their security and defending their socioeconomic interests. (Magnette 2007: 252)

However, this question constructs a wrong dichotomy. The point is that it is not evident how security and socioeconomic interests are to be defined, what are efficient policies to ensure them, whether 'efficiency' is the main criterion for choosing between different policy options, and how conflicting interests should be dealt with. There is no reason to assume that some citizens are more enlightened than others to answer these questions (Dahl 1989: esp. Ch. 7 and 5), but equal democratic input is needed to arrive at an understanding that is supported by a majority and to weigh divergent interests, and political accountability is needed to ensure that representatives pursue outputs that are supported by the represented (cf. Føllesdal 2011: 99). In fact, Magnette himself in a different context criticises the Commission for having 'long argued that the Union would be legitimate if it produced good policies, and that, "at the end of the day, what interests them (the citizens) is not who solves these problems, but the fact that they are solved" (Prodi, 21 July 1999)' (Magnette 2003: 147–8).

The primacy of democratic principles – the equal opportunity of all affected to influence the outcomes – does not mean that all citizens have to be politically active all the time, or that all issues have to be politicised. Rather, it means that all citizens can engage themselves politically when they wish, so that any issue can potentially become politicised, and that in this case collective engagement can have an effective influence on it (cf. Habermas 1994: 434). As well as that, taking everybody's possibility to influence political processes as an intrinsic value is not incompatible with the fact that decisions will ultimately be taken by elites. Policy making is always dominated by elites, including democratic policy making (cf. Manin 1997: Ch. 4). What is decisive in a democracy is, firstly, that these elites are sufficiently permeable; secondly, that the represented can replace those elites holding power at a given time with others; and thirdly, quantitatively and qualitatively sufficient communication (Durkheim 1958: 85) between the elites and the rest of the people. The latter condition is necessary for the first two to be fulfilled, and it is the precondition for citizens' political engagement.

Such communication also advances other prerequisites for political engagement, *viz.* that citizens feel that they understand the issues at stake and that their participation can have an impact, and that these issues are morally important to them. They are more likely to perceive things in this way if the political system's institutional structure is clear, and if there are clearly distinct political actors with clearly different positions (Magnette 2003: 152–3). In other words, political participation – and thus the representation of citizens through a variety of associations and institutions – depends considerably on the potential for *politicisation* in a political system. This potential is not only a question of institutional design, but also a question of how the political process in general is perceived to work. Issues are more likely to become politicised if politics is commonly perceived as an open-ended process in which inputs via representatives may visibly influence the outcomes.

This brings me back to DG Employment's rationalistic concept of democracy. In their account of the social OMC, the frame for policies is already determined, and functional representation mainly functions to optimise the outputs to be achieved within this frame, rather than as potential influences on the frame itself. Moreover, the text remains on a very general level as to how individual engagement links to EU-level action. The main way in which the DG's argumentation depoliticises the political process is the consistent characterisation of the political process as a joint undertaking of 'working together' without significant conflicts between the collaborators. This does not imply that conflicts were in fact absent from OMC policy making, but is part of a strategy of dealing with them and of presenting the policy-making process. The Commission typically seeks to resolve conflicts in informal negotiations behind the scenes and by breaking issues down into smaller questions that can be discussed as technical matters. The political initiative eventually worked out in this way is then presented in public as an established consensus of all 'stakeholders' (Magnette 2003: 152–3). This practice, as well as the way it is presented, not only discourages political debate, but also prevents it from taking place, because political processes become invisible to the public.

What is more, introducing political proposals as the necessary and already agreed way forward in the name of the European interest alienates people from politics, because it creates the image that detached European elites arrange things among themselves without leaving alternatives for the actual political process (Magnette 2003: 157). This perception further discourages interest and engagement.

The consensual concept of democracy as 'working together' is closely related to the division of political inputs into controlled, rational or productive input, and uncontrolled, potentially unproductive or irrational input. Concretely, the negotiation of compromises in intransparent networks means that only insiders with exceptional capacities have access to the decisive phase of policy making. For one thing, this raises the question of who the presented consensus is a consensus of. For another thing, introducing initiatives as agreed projects in which everybody now has to 'work together' implies that those who have no access to the actual negotiating process and who disagree with significant parts of the policy proposal can be closed away from the political debate. Conceptualising policies as a matter of 'working together' 'presupposes a common perception of political and social problems, as well as the belief that cooperation leads to consensus and more rational policy outputs' (Greven 2007: 236). In other words, such an argument builds on the implicit premise that 'everybody' agrees, so that things merely have to be implemented. This rhetorical strategy implicitly disqualifies those disagreeing as not being part of 'everybody', so that their views are irrelevant for the discussion (Perelman and Olbrechts-Tyteca 1969: 33). Not only does this argumentation give no room for political debate, but it can also be used to label opposition as disturbing the efficient problem solving that the reasonable, productive community of 'all relevant actors' is undertaking. Hence, opposition appears as 'the "irrational" rejection of "inevitable"' (Blühdorn and Welsh 2007: 191) schemes, as counterproductive inputs, by contrast to the rational, constructive inputs of those participating in the 'working together' and contributing their resources to the attainment of a common goal that is in the common interest. Presenting things in this way depoliticises the political process as a whole, the activities of DG Employment, and functional associations in the sector. It also strips the poor's descriptive representation of much of its political potential.

In the same vein, the blending of 'raising awareness' and rallying support for the DG's objectives in the social OMC does not encourage genuine political debate – i.e. the representation of citizens' political views – but is primarily aimed at educating citizens. The way things are framed when DG Employment presents its plans to the public does not leave much room for different opinions: 'Who, apart from purely anti-European citizens, could disagree with such a vague and encompassing set of objectives? And if nobody disagrees, why should there be public debate?' (Magnette 2003: 153). The Commission's communication with the citizens is essentially pedagogy; instead of encouraging engagement, this renders people passive – however, in particular circumstances, it may also provoke destructive opposition directed against the 'system' as such,[9] because such educative discourse does not treat people as politically mature sovereigns but counts only very narrowly defined activities (charity) as 'participation' and takes only a limited range of views into account as 'relevant contributions'. As noted before, the effect of this approach is much aggravated by the very lack of public debate advanced by it, which is also due to many structural factors and which means that the DG's discourse is not challenged by other narratives and therefore makes up a great share of all public text about the social OMC.

The absence of any stronger notion of political accountability in the DG's text is in line with this context. If politics is conceptualised as doing together what is reasonable, and if the Commission embodies the European interest, its legitimacy can be based on 'good governance', which is mainly geared towards increasing the citizens' trust. It thus envisages *responsible* rather than *democratically representative* policy making (cf. Blühdorn and Welsh 2007: 191). On this note, the DG's concept of democracy in relation to functional representation in the social OMC can be condensed as the *primacy of representation over democracy*, i.e. representation as such is essential for their claim to legitimacy, but it does not need to be democratic representation. Representative claims need not be built on authorisation by and accountability to a majority of the (affected) citizens, and representatives need not mediate the views of the affected on European social policies, but are rather expected to speak *for* them. Functional representation is not meant to change anything substantive about the orientation of the DG's policies. The input received from representatives does thus not have much intrinsic value as the voice of the sovereign people, but is mainly seen as instrumental to achieving the DG's preferred outcomes – in other words, representation is not primarily meant to make the process democratic, but it is a tool of policy makers, which is used within a global strategy of depoliticisation.

The European Commission is not the only actor who advances a rationalistic concept of democracy at the expense of the sovereignty of the people. The alarming thing is that such concepts go hand in hand with institutional developments that effectively reduce the citizens' equal opportunities to influence the outcomes of political processes that affect them. At the Commission, these developments are particularly visible, and also favoured by structural factors, such as the general lack of public debate over European policies as well as the level of aggregation and complexity. Narratives such as DG Employment's, which assign the citizens the role of taking their place in a political project designed somewhere else, legitimise these tendencies.

The enlarged scope and increasingly technical nature of issues dealt with by public policy, together with globalisation and international as well as intersectional interdependency, have made politics complex to the degree that it has become impossible to understand for most people. What is more, this complexity often makes it de facto impossible to hold anyone accountable for policies (cf. Blühdorn

---

9. For an example of how a 'rhetoric of unanimity' can lead to opposition as a matter of principle, *see* Rozenberg 2011.

and Welsh 2007: 191). Furthermore, shifting policy making to international arenas (in order to deal with this complexity) not only creates the 'democratic dilemma' (Dahl 1994; cf. Mitrany 1966a: 122, 126) that the single citizen's influence is minimised, but also leads to problems of transparency and belonging (Greven 2009: 96–8). Hence, it is not surprising that the citizens less and less perceive themselves as the 'co-authors' of political regulation, although this is still a diffuse feeling, for example in the form of widespread aversion to 'Brussels'. However, the recent financial crisis has not only made the diminished possibilities for popular influence much more visible, but its consequences may also perceptibly reduce European welfare levels. Taken together, these effects might lead to more disruptive reactions. DG Employment's concept of democracy as 'working together' works to legitimate these developments. Instead of conceptualising functional representation as a measure to *compensate* for the loss of the people's influence on the political process, it is made a tool that essentially supports this tendency.

In this, the DG's text differs decisively from modern concepts of functional representation that all see it as a means to strengthen the people's effective authorship of public policies. The two theories presented in the Introduction, G.D.H. Cole's guild socialism and David Mitrany's functionalism, both conceptualised functional representation as a remedy against the centralisation of power in remote executives and as a way to make policies more representative of the people's views. DG Employment's references to voluntary grassroots organisations are only a shadow of Cole's ideas about functional representation as personal self-determination in mostly local associations; from Mitrany's model, only the technocratic output orientation remains. The text builds on – and profits from – the topoi of these earlier conceptions, *viz.* civil society as the building blocks of democracy, the closeness of functional associations to the citizens, their unique knowledge about people's everyday lives and conditions on the ground, the role of voluntary engagement for the functioning of society, associations' role as representative structures, etc. Yet, these topoi are redefined so as to make functional representatives partners of the executive.

To conclude, contrarily to most official and academic discourses, functional representation cannot be seen as a solution to the 'erosion of democracy' (Greven 2009). Not only do governance processes involving functional representatives pose a range of practical as well as conceptual democratic problems (*see* Chapter Four), but as this study has shown, functional representation can also be used in manipulative ways that further obscure political processes and responsibilities, create new inequalities, and undermine the legitimacy of the involved organisations in addition to that of the public institutions involving them. In other words, there is nothing democratic about functional representation per se, but its effect on democracy depends on the way it is implemented within the entire political system. Therefore, democracy in the EU needs to be looked at in a wider context that examines the territorial and the functional system; formal and informal processes; and local, national, and European levels within one framework, rather than offering one element of the political process to compensate for problems in others.

Now, if democratic principles are opposed to the Commission's institutional interests, it does not come as a surprise that the DG seeks to redefine these principles in a way that suits them. Somewhat more worrying is the fact that this effort does not meet with more opposition, and that similar 'redescriptions' (Buchstein and Jörke 2007) of democracy can also be observed in political science:

> These [current democratic] theories use a concept of 'democracy' that admits a deep chasm between participation in the political process and the 'rational' results of that process. Forced to take a stand on this dilemma, current democratic theories opt against political participation.

> We call this transformation the 'rationalisation' of democracy. According to this term, the focus of modern theories of democracy has shifted to the evaluation of the quality of the results of politics. Democratic theory is output-orientated and its theoretical efforts aim mainly at enhancing the rationality of this output. Significant differences within this paradigm only arise with respect to the criteria of rationality, such as effectiveness, feasibility, fair representation of interests, gender, justice or the public good. Despite these differences, political participation is no longer regarded as the goal, but as one of several possible ways of enhancing the rationality of collectively binding decisions. (Buchstein and Jörke 2007: 186)[10]

The EU governance literature in particular has generally been more interested in problem-solving capacity than in effective democratic control, and the OMC branch especially has for a long time looked at the process through the lenses provided by the official discourse, rather than asking what all this means in terms of the people's possibilities to influence the directions policies take. One reason may be that we do not have any easy solutions to offer. The consideration that European integration may as such be detrimental to democracy is an inconvenient one, as is the result of the present study that functional representation may not be able to improve the situation. As well as that, it seems difficult to give up the linear-progressivist narrative whereby the EU is destined to become ever more integrated and more democratic (cf. Gilbert 2008: esp. 658n3). However, the concepts of democratic legitimacy advanced by both practitioners and scholars of politics serve to normalise or challenge the citizens' diminished possibilities for effective influence and control, and they are thereby themselves part of how democracy works and evolves.

---

10. Cf. Greven 1993; 2007: 238–9; 2009: 95; Bellamy and Castiglione 2000: 73–4.

Appendix: Primary Sources

European Commission publications 2000–10

Source	Number of documents
DG Employment internet pages	79
–June 2008	
http://ec.europa.eu/employment_social/index_en.html	
June 2008–	
http://ec.europa.eu/social/home.jsp?langId=en	
Press releases (IP and MEMO)	45
http://europa.eu/rapid/	
Documents	
COM, SEC, and D documents	39
http://ec.europa.eu/transparency/regdoc/recherche.cfm?CL=en	
Social Exclusion Programme-related documents and publications (including internet pages)	18
DG Employment internet pages	
PROGRESS-related documents and publications (including internet pages)	45
DG Employment internet pages	
DG papers	18
DG Employment internet pages	
Conference materials	11
DG Employment internet pages	
Printed publications	
Social Agenda: The European Commission's magazine on employment and social affairs	28
Brussels: European Commission, DG Employment.	
Exchange: Social protection & inclusion in the EU	42
Brussels: European Commission, DG Employment, Unit Inclusion, Social Policy Aspects of Migration, Streamlining of Social Policies.	

Source	Number of documents
Others (brochures, leaflets, etc.) http://ec.europa.eu/social/main.jsp?catId=738&langId=en	17
Speeches, homepages, articles, and published interviews	
Commissioner László Andor (2010–) *http://europa.eu/rapid/* *http://ec.europa.eu/commission_2010-2014/andor/index_en.htm*	8
Commissioner Vladímir Špidla (2004–9) *http://europa.eu/rapid/* http://ec.europa.eu/employment_social/emplweb/speeches/index_en.cfm# *http://ec.europa.eu/commission_barroso/spidla/index_en.cfm*	63
Commissioner Dimas (2004) *http://europa.eu/rapid/* http://ec.europa.eu/employment_social/emplweb/speeches/index_en.cfm# http://ec.europa.eu/archives/commission_1999_2004/dimas/index_en.html	1
Commissioner Anna Diamantopoulou (1999–2004) *http://europa.eu/rapid/* http://ec.europa.eu/employment_social/emplweb/speeches/index_en.cfm# http://ec.europa.eu/archives/commission_1999_2004/diamantopoulou/index_en.htm	38
President José Manuel Barroso (2004–) *http://europa.eu/rapid/* http://ec.europa.eu/archives/commission_2004-2009/president/index_en.htm http://ec.europa.eu/commission_2010-2014/president/index_en.htm	9
President Romano Prodi (1999–2004) *http://europa.eu/rapid/* http://europa.eu.int/comm/commissioners/prodi/index_en.htm http://ec.europa.eu/archives/commission_1999_2004/prodi/index_en.htm	0
Speeches of DG Employment officials http://ec.europa.eu/employment_social/emplweb/speeches/index_en.cfm#	83
Total	**544**

Bibliography

Primary Sources

European Commission documents

European Commission (2000a) Commissioner Anna Diamantopoulou, 'The national and European role of social welfare organisations', speech given in Athens, 19 May 2000. Online. Available http://ec.europa. eu/employment_social/speeches/2000/000519ad_en.pdf (accessed 9 October 2008).

European Commission (2001a) Commissioner Anna Diamantopoulou, 'New forms of European governance and the role of civil society', speech at a Greek Trade Union Conference, Tripoli, 29 September 2001. Online. Available http://ec.europa.eu/employment_social/speeches/2001/010929ad_en.pdf (accessed 8 October 2008).

— (2001b) Director-General Odile Quintin, speech at a conference organised by the Commission's 'Governance' Task Force, 27 June 2001. Online. Available http://ec.europa.eu/employment_social/speeches/2001/270601oq_fr.pdf (accessed 17 October 2008).

— (2002a) Call for Proposals VP/2002/008, no date. 'For the support to European networks involved in the fight against poverty and social exclusion'.

— (2003a) Commissioner Anna Diamantopoulou, address at the General Assembly of the National Confederation of Disabled People, Athens, 14 February 2003. Online. Available http://ec.europa.eu/employment_social/speeches/2003/ad140203_en.pdf (accessed 8 October 2008).

— (2003b) Director-General Odile Quintin, speech at the conference Civil Dialogue and Enlargement, Budapest, 23 June 2003. Online. Available http://ec.europa.eu/employment_social/speeches/2003/oq230603_en.pdf (accessed 16 October 2008).

— (2003c) Commissioner Anna Diamantopoulou, speech at a charity event organised by the Society of Friends of the Macedonia-Thrace branch of the Hellenic Society against Cancer, Thessaloniki, 24 October 2003. Online. Available http://ec.europa.eu/employment_social/speeches/2003/ad241003_en.pdf (accessed 8 October 2008).

— (2005a) Call for Proposals VP/2005/007, no date. 'For the support to European networks involved in the fight against poverty and social exclusion'.

— (2005b) 'Income poverty and social exclusion in the EU25', *Statistics in Focus: Population and social conditions* (13), Eurostat.

—   (2006a) Call for Proposals VP/2006/009, no date. 'For the support to European networks involved in the fight against poverty and social exclusion'. Online. Available http://ec.europa.eu/social/main.jsp?catId=6 31&langId=en&callId=30&furtherCalls=yes (accessed 19 March 2013).

—   (2007a) 'Editorial: Giving a voice to people experiencing poverty', *Exchange: Social protection & inclusion in the EU*, 2.

—   (2007b) Call for Proposals VP/2007/013, no date. 'Establishment of 3-year partnerships with Eu-level [sic] networks active in the field of combating social exclusion and discrimination, promoting gender equality and the integration of disabled people and representing roma [sic] people'. Online. Available http://ec.europa.eu/social/main.jsp?cat Id=631&langId=en&callId=92&furtherCalls=yes (accessed 19 March 2013).

—   (2007c) 'Editorial', *Exchange: Social protection & inclusion in the EU*, 4.

—   (2007d) 'Giving a voice to people experiencing poverty', *Exchange: Social protection & inclusion in the EU*, 2.

—   (2007e) 'Better understanding of poverty comes from talking face to face', *Exchange: Social protection & inclusion in the EU*, 2.

—   (2007f) 'A toolkit for developing integrated homeless strategies', *Exchange: Social protection & inclusion in the EU*, 2.

—   (2008a) PROGRESS/009/2007-revised of 18 March 2008. 'Draft Strategic Framework for the Implementation of the Community programme for employment and social solidarity – PROGRESS' (adopted by the Progress Committee 17 April 2008). Online. Available http://ec.europa.eu/employment_social/progress/docs/progress_015_08_ en.pdf (accessed 27 November 2008).

—   (2008b) 'EAPN's campaign on minimum income', *Exchange: Social protection & inclusion in the EU*, 1.

—   (2008c) 'Conference in Brussels tackles "new social realities"', *Social Agenda*, 18.

—   (2008d) 'Ending homelessness: local European actors brainstorm', Exchange: Social protection & inclusion in the EU, 3.

—   (2008e) 'The four pillars in the fight against poverty', *Exchange: Social protection & inclusion in the EU*, 2.

—   (2008f) 'News in brief', *Social Agenda*, 18.

—   (2008g) 'Editorial', *Exchange: Social protection & inclusion in the EU*, 1.

—   (2008h) 'Institutional care – the only option? The EU is looking at ways to make it possible for people with disabilities to live independently in the community', *Social Agenda*, 17.

—   (2008i) Remarks of Commissioner Vladímir Špidla, draft speech for the launching event of the 'Awareness raising campaign on the role of civil society and the importance of active citizenship', Nicosia, 21 November 2008. Online. Available http://ec.europa.eu/employment_social/speeches/2008/ sp_081125_10_49_10_en.pdf (accessed 10 December 2008).

—   (2008j) *Ensuring Progress Delivers Results: Strategic framework for implementation of Progress, the EU programme for employment and social solidarity (2007–2013)*, Luxembourg: Office for Official Publications of the European Communities.

—   (2009a) *Progress Annual Performance Monitoring Report 2008: The community programme for employment and social solidarity – PROGRESS (2007–2013)*, Luxembourg: Office for Official Publications of the European Communities.

—   (2009b) 'News in brief', *Social Agenda*, 21.

—   (2010a) *Annual Performance Monitoring Report 2009: Monitoring the performance of the European Union programme for employment and social solidarity – PROGRESS (2007–2013)*, Luxembourg: Publications Office of the European Union.

—   (2010b) Call for Proposals VP/2010/012, no date. 'Establishment of 3-year framework partnership agreements with EU-level NGO networks in the areas of social inclusion, non-discrimination, gender equality, the integration of persons with disabilities and the representation of the Roma'. Online. Available http://ec.europa.eu/social/main.jsp?catId=631&langId=en&callId=252&furtherCalls=yes (accessed 19 March 2013).

—   (2010c) 'Making the most of EY2010', *Exchange: Social protection & inclusion in the EU*, 1.

—   (2010d) '17 % of EU citizens were at-risk-of-poverty in 2008', *Statistics in Focus: Population and social conditions* (9), Eurostat.

—   (2010e) *Income and Living Conditions in Europe*, A. B. Atkinson and E. Marlier (eds). Eurostat. Luxembourg: Publications Office of the European Union.

European Union documents

European Communities (2003) *Draft Treaty Establishing a Constitution for Europe*. Submitted to the European Council meeting in Thessaloniki, 20 June 2003, Luxembourg: Publications Office of the European Union.

—   (2007a) *A More Cohesive Society for a Stronger Europe*, Brussels: Publications Office of the European Union.

—   (2007b) *Progress: The EU programme for employment and social solidarity 2007–2013. Ensuring the Community can play its part to support Member States' commitments to create more and better jobs and offer equal opportunities for all*, Luxembourg: Office for Official Publications of the European Communities.

Interviews

1	Policy Officer, DG Employment	Brussels, 3 November 2009
2	EAPN Europe	Brussels, 11 October 2010
3	EAPN Europe	e-mail interview, 15 and 20 January 2009
4	Cabinet Member, European Commission	Brussels, 5 November 2009
5	Policy Coordinator, DG Employment	Brussels, 6 November 2009
6	Policy Officer, DG Employment	Brussels, 6 November 2009
7	Policy Officer, DG Employment	Brussels, 6 November 2009
8	Policy Officer, DG Employment	Brussels, 9 February 2010

References

Abromeit, H. (1998) 'How to democratise a multi-level, multi-dimensional polity', in A. Weale and M. Nentwich (eds) *Political Theory and the European Union*, London: Routledge.

Adams, J. ([1776] 1851) 'Letter to John Penn', in C. F. Adams (ed.) *The Works of John Adams, Second President of the United States: With a life of the author, notes and illustrations, by his grandson Charles Francis Adams*, vol. IV, Boston: Charles Little and James Brown. Online. Available http://files.libertyfund.org/files/2102/Adams_1431-04_Bk.pdf (accessed 21 March 2013).

Alcoff, L. (1991) 'The problem of speaking for others', *Cultural Critique*, 20: 5–32.

Andersen, S. S. and Burns, T. R. (1996) 'The European Union and the erosion of parliamentary democracy: a study of post-parliamentary governance', in S. S. Andersen and K. A. Eliassen (eds) *The European Union: How democratic is it?*, London: Sage Publications.

Anderson, B. (1991) *Imagined Communities: Reflections on the origin and spread of nationalism*, London: Verso.

Ankersmit, F. R. (1996) *Aesthetic Politics: Political philosophy beyond fact and value*, Stanford: Stanford University Press.

— (2002) *Political Representation*, Stanford: Stanford University Press.

Aristotle (1991) *The Art of Rhetoric*, translated with an introduction and notes by H. C. Lawson-Tancred, London: Penguin.

Armstrong, K. A. (2003) 'Tackling social exclusion through OMC: reshaping the boundaries of governance', in T. Börzel and R. Cichowski (eds) *State of the Union: Law, politics and society*, vol. 6, Oxford: Oxford University Press. Online. Available http://eucenter.wisc.edu/omc/Papers/Protection/Armstrong.pdf (accessed 21 March 2013).

Austin, J. L. (1975) *How to Do Things with Words*, edited by J. O. Urmson and M. Sbisà, Harvard: Harvard University Press.

Barnett, M. N. and Finnemore, M. (1999) 'The politics, power, and pathologies of international organizations', *International Organization*, 53(4): 699–732.

Bauer, M. W. (2002) 'Limitations to agency control in European Union policy-making: the Commission and the Poverty Programmes', *Journal of Common Market Studies*, 40(3): 381–400.

Baumgartner, F. R. and Jones, B. D. (1991) 'Agenda dynamics and policy subsystems', *The Journal of Politics*, 53(4): 1044–74.

Beck, U. and Grande, E. (2004) *Das kosmopolitische Europa: Gesellschaft und Politik in der zweiten Moderne*, Frankfurt am Main: Suhrkamp.

Bellamy, R. (2010) 'Democracy without democracy? Can the EU's democratic "outputs" be separated from the democratic "inputs" provided by competitive parties and majority rule?', *Journal of European Public Policy*, 17(1): 2–19.

Bellamy, R. and Castiglione, D. (2000) 'The uses of democracy: reflections on the European democratic deficit', in E. O. Eriksen and J. E. Fossum (eds) *Democracy in the European Union: Integration through deliberation?*, London: Routledge.

— (2011) 'Democracy by delegation? Who represents whom and how in European governance', *Government and Opposition*, 46(1): 101–25.

Bellamy, R., Castiglione, D., Føllesdal, A. and Weale, A. (2011) 'Evaluating trustworthiness, representation and political accountability in new modes of governance', in A. Héritier and M. Rhodes (eds) *New Modes of Governance in Europe: Governing in the shadow of hierarchy*, Basingstoke: Palgrave Macmillan.

Bellamy, R. and Kröger, S. (2011) 'The (re)configuration of political representation in the EU', outline for workshop 27 at the European Consortium for Political Research Joint Sessions, Antwerp, April 2012.

Benner, T., Reinicke, W. H. and Witte, J. M. (2004) 'Multisectoral networks in global governance: towards a pluralistic system of accountability', *Government and Opposition*, 39(2): 191–210.

Benz, A. (1998) 'Ansatzpunkte für ein europafähiges Demokratiekonzept', in B. Kohler-Koch (ed.) *Regieren in entgrenzten Räumen*. Politische Vierteljahresschrift, Sonderheft 29, Opladen: Westdeutscher Verlag.

— (2007) 'Accountable multilevel governance by the open method of cooperation?', *European Law Journal*, 13(4): 505–22.

Benz, A. and Papadopoulos, Y. (2006) 'Introduction. Governance and democracy: concepts and key issues', in A. Benz and Y. Papadopoulos (eds) *Governance and Democracy: Comparing national, European and international experiences*, London: Routledge.

Blühdorn, I. and Welsh, I. (2007) 'Eco-politics beyond the paradigm of sustainability: a conceptual framework and research agenda', *Environmental Politics*, 16(2): 185–205.

Bohman, J. (2000) *Public Deliberation: Pluralism, complexity, and democracy*, Cambridge, Mass.: MIT Press.

Borges, J. L. (1998) *Collected Fictions*, trans. A. Hurley. New York: Penguin.

Borrás, S. (2007) 'The European Commission as a network broker', *European Integration online Papers* (EIoP), 11(1). Online. Available http://eiop. or.at/eiop/index.php/eiop/article/view/2007_001a (accessed 21 March 2013).

— (2008) 'The legitimacy of new modes of governance in the EU: a descriptive-analytical approach', in R. Dehousse and L. Boussaguet (eds) *The Transformation of EU Policies: EU Governance at Work*, Mannheim: CONNEX. Online. Available http://www.mzes.uni-mannheim.de/ projekte/typo3/site/fileadmin/BookSeries/Volume_eight/Chapter%204. pdf (accessed 21 March 2013).

Borrás, S. and Conzelmann, T. (2007) 'Democracy, legitimacy and soft modes of governance in the EU: the empirical turn', *Journal of European Integration*, 29(5): 531–48.

Borrás, S. and Greve, B. (2004) 'Concluding remarks: new method or just cheap talk?', *Journal of European Public Policy*, 11(2): 329–36.

Borrás, S. and Jacobsson, K. (2004) 'The open method of co-ordination and new governance patterns in the EU', *Journal of European Public Policy*, 11(2): 185–208.

Bovens, M. (2007) 'Analysing and assessing accountability: a conceptual framework', *European Law Journal*, 13(4): 447–68.

Bovens, M., Schillermans, T. and 't Hart, P. (2008) 'Does public accountability work? An assessment tool', *Public Administration*, 86(1): 225–42.

Büchs, M. (2008) 'How legitimate is the open method of co-ordination?', *Journal of Common Market Studies*, 46(4): 765–86.

— (2009) 'The open method of coordination – effectively preventing welfare state retrenchment?', *European Integration online Papers (EIoP)*, 13(1). Online. Available http://eiop.or.at/eiop/index.php/eiop/ article/view/2009_011a (accessed 21 March 2013).

Buchstein, H. and Jörke, D. (2007) 'Redescribing democracy', *Redescriptions: Yearbook of political thought and conceptual history*, 11: 178–200.

Burke, E. ([1792] 1999) 'A letter to Sir Hercules Langrishe on the Catholics of Ireland', in E. Burke (1999) *Select Works of Edmund Burke: A new imprint of the Payne edition*, vol. 4, Indianapolis: Liberty Fund. Online. Available http://oll.libertyfund.org/title/659/20404 (accessed 21 March 2013).

Bussemer, T. (2011) *Die erregte Republik: Wutbürger und die Macht der Medien*, Stuttgart: Klett-Cotta.

Carpenter, L. P. (1973) *G. D. H. Cole: An intellectual biography*, Cambridge: Cambridge University Press.

Carroll, L. ([1872] 2008) *Through the Looking-Glass*, Project Gutenberg. Online. Available http://www.gutenberg.org/files/12/12-h/12-h.htm (accessed 21 March 2013).

Castiglione, D. and Warren, M. E. (2006) 'Rethinking democratic representation: eight theoretical issues', paper prepared for the conference Rethinking Democratic Representation, Centre for Study of Democratic Institutions,

University of British Columbia, May 2006. Online. Available http://
www.politics.ubc.ca/fileadmin/user_upload/poli_sci/Faculty/warren/
Rethinking_Democratic_Representation_May_2006.pdf (accessed 21
March 2013).

Christiansen, T., Føllesdal, A. and Piattoni, S. (2003) 'Informal governance in the
European Union: an introduction', in T. Christiansen and S. Piattoni (eds)
Informal Governance in the European Union, Cheltenham: Edward Elgar.

Clarence, E. L., Jordan, G. and Maloney, W. A. (2005) 'Activating participation:
generating support for campaign groups', in S. Roßteutscher (ed.)
*Democracy and the Role of Associations: Political, organisational and
social contexts*, London: Routledge.

Claude, I. L. Jr. ([1956] 1965) *Swords into Ploughshares: The problem and
progress of international organization*, 3rd rev. edn, London: University
of London Press.

Cohen, J. and Rogers, J. (eds) (1995) *Associations and Democracy: The real
utopias project*, vol. I, London: Verso.

Cole, G. D. H. (1917) *Self-Government in Industry*, London: Bell and Sons.

— (1920) *Social Theory*, London: Methuen & Co.

— (1950) *Essays in Social Theory*, London: Macmillan.

— ([1920] 1980) *Guild Socialism Restated*, with a new introduction by R.
Vernon, New Brunswick: Transaction Books.

Coleman, S. (2005) 'The lonely citizen: indirect representation in an age of
networks', *Political Communication*, 22(2): 197–214.

— (2009) 'The representation of representation: the future of political
communication', lecture at the XLI Annual Conference of Finnish
Political Scientists, Tampere, 13 March 2009. Author's notes.

Cram, L. (1997) *Policy-Making in the EU: Conceptual lenses and the integration
process*, London: Routledge.

Dahl, R. A. (1989) *Democracy and its Critics*, New Haven and London: Yale
University Press.

— (1994) 'A democratic dilemma: system effectiveness versus citizen
participation', *Political Science Quarterly*, 109(1): 23–34.

— ([1998] 2000) *On Democracy*, New Haven: Yale University Press.

Dawson, M. (2009) 'EU law "transformed"? Evaluating accountability and
subsidiarity in the "streamlined" OMC for Social Inclusion and Social
Protection', *European Integration online Papers (EIoP)*, 13(1). Online.
Available http://eiop.or.at/eiop/texte/2009-008a.htm (accessed 21 March
2013).

de la Porte, C. and Nanz, P. (2004) 'The OMC – a deliberative-democratic mode
of governance? The cases of employment and pensions', *Journal of
European Public Policy*, 11(2): 267–88.

de la Porte, C. and Pochet, P. (2005) 'Participation in the open method of coordination: the cases of employment and social inclusion', in J. Zeitlin and
P. Pochet (eds) with L. Magnusson, *The Open Method of Co-ordination*

in Action: The European employment and social inclusion strategies, Brussels: Peter Lang.

Dierckx, D. and Van Herck, N. (2010) *Impact study on the European Meetings of People Experiencing Poverty*, Brussels: EAPN. Online. Available http://www.eapn.eu/images/stories/docs/EAPN-position-papers-and-reports/report20sep_final.pdf (accessed 21 March 2013).

DiMaggio, P. J. and Powell, W. W. (1991) 'The iron cage revisited: institutional isomorphism and collective rationality in organisational fields', in W. W. Powell and P. J. DiMaggio (eds) *The New Institutionalism in Organizational Analysis*, Chicago: The University of Chicago Press.

Dovi, S. (2002) 'Preferable descriptive representatives: will just any woman, black, or Latino do?', *American Political Science Review*, 96(4): 729–43.

Dryzek, J. S. (1997) *The Politics of the Earth: Environmental discourses*, Oxford: Oxford University Press.

—— (2000) *Deliberative Democracy and Beyond: Liberals, critics, contestations*, Oxford: Oxford University Press.

Dunn, J. (1999) 'Situating democratic political accountability', in A. Przeworski, S. C. Stokes and B. Manin (eds) *Democracy, Accountability, and Representation*, Cambridge: Cambridge University Press.

Durkheim, E. (1958) *Professional Ethics and Civic Morals*, trans. C. Brookfield, Glencoe, IL: The Free Press.

EAPN (2005) *The EU We Want: Views from those fighting poverty and social exclusion on the future development of the EU*, Brussels: EAPN.

—— (2009) *Small Steps – Big Changes: Building participation of people experiencing poverty*, Brussels: EAPN. Online. Available http://eapn.eu/index.php?option=com_content&view=article&id=856%3Aeapn-book-small-steps-big-changes&catid=40%3Aeapn-books&Itemid=84&lang=en (accessed 11 March 2011).

Easton, D. (1965) *A Systems Analysis of Political Life*, New York: John Wiley & Sons.

Eberlein, B. and Kerwer, D. (2002) 'Theorising the new modes of governance', *European Integration online Papers (EIoP)*, 6(5). Online. Available http://eiop.or.at/eiop/texte/2002-005a.htm (accessed 21 March 2013).

Ehrenberg, J. (1999) *Civil Society: The critical history of an idea*, New York: New York University Press.

Elster, J. (1998) 'Deliberation and constitution making', in J. Elster (ed.) *Deliberative Democracy*, Cambridge: Cambridge University Press.

Erhel, C., Mandin, L. and Palier, B. (2005) 'The leverage effect: the open method of co-ordination in France', in J. Zeitlin and P. Pochet (eds) with L. Magnusson, *The Open Method of Co-ordination in Action: The European employment and social inclusion strategies*, Brussels: Peter Lang.

Farrell, F. (2008) 'The role of "third sector" at EU level', *Revista Española del Tercer Sector*, special issue (9): 127–30.

Fearon, J. D. (1999) 'Electoral accountability and the control of politicians: selecting good types versus sanctioning poor performance', in A. Przeworsky, S. C. Stokes and B. Manin (eds) *Democracy, Accountability, and Representation*, Cambridge: Cambridge University Press.

Ferrera, M., Matsaganis, M. and Sacchi, S. (2002) 'Open coordination against poverty: the new EU "social inclusion process"', *Journal of European Social Policy*, 12(3): 227–39.

Føllesdal, A. (2003) 'The political theory of the White Paper on Governance: hidden and fascinating', *European Public Law*, 9(1): 73–86.

— (2011) 'The legitimacy challenges for new modes of governance: trustworthy responsiveness', *Government and Opposition*, 46(1): 81–100.

Føllesdal, A. and Hix, S. (2006) 'Why there is a democratic deficit in the EU: a response to Majone and Moravcsik', *Journal of Common Market Studies*, 44(3): 533–62.

Fouilleux, E. (2004) 'CAP reforms and multilateral trade negotiations: another view on discourse efficiency', *West European Politics*, 27(2): 235–55.

Gargarella, R. (1998) 'Full representation, deliberation, and impartiality', in J. Elster (ed.) *Deliberative Democracy*, Cambridge: Cambridge University Press.

Geyer, R. (2001) 'Can European Union (EU) social NGOs co-operate to promote EU social policy?', *Journal of Social Policy*, 30(3): 477–93.

Gide, C. (1904) *Les Sociétés coopératives de consommation*, Paris: Armand Colin. Online. Available http://gallica.bnf.fr/ark:/12148/bpt6k5540842d/f1.image.r=Gide+sociétés+coopératives.langFR and http://gallica.bnf.fr/ark:/12148/bpt6k5540842d.r=les+sociétés+cooperatives+de+consommation.langFR.swf (accessed 21 March 2013).

Gilbert, M. (2008) 'Narrating the process: questioning the progressive story of European integration', *Journal of Common Market Studies*, 46(3): 641–62.

Goodin, R. E. (2003a) *Reflective Democracy*, Oxford: Oxford University Press.

— (2003b) 'Democratic accountability: the distinctiveness of the third sector', *European Journal of Sociology*, 40(3): 359–96.

Greenwood, J. (1997) *Representing Interests in the European Union*, Basingstoke: Palgrave Macmillan.

— (2003) *Interest Representation in the European Union*, Basingstoke: Palgrave Macmillan.

— (2007a) 'Organised civil society and input legitimacy in the EU', in J. DeBardeleben and A. Hurrelmann (eds) *Democratic Dilemmas of Multilevel Governance*, Basingstoke: Palgrave Macmillan.

— (2007b) 'Review article: organized civil society and democratic legitimacy in the European Union', *British Journal of Political Science*, 37(2): 333–57.

Greven, M. T. (1993) 'Ist die Demokratie modern? Zur Rationalitätskrise der politischen Gesellschaft', *Politische Vierteljahresschrift*, 34(3): 399–413.

—   (2007) 'Some considerations on participation in participatory governance', in B. Kohler-Koch and B. Rittberger (eds) *Debating the Democratic Legitimacy of the European Union*, Lanham: Rowman & Littlefield.

—   (2009) 'The erosion of democracy – the beginning of the end?' *Redescriptions*, 13: 83–102.

—   Grimm, D. (2009) *Souveränität: Herkunft und Zukunft Eines Schlüsselbegriffs*, Berlin: Berlin University Press.

Gutmann, A. and Thompson, D. (1996) *Democracy and Disagreement: Why moral conflict cannot be avoided in politics, and what should be done about it*, Cambridge, MA: Harvard University Press.

—   (2004) *Why Deliberative Democracy?*, Princeton: Princeton University Press.

Haas, P. M. (1989) 'Do regimes matter? Epistemic communities and Mediterranean pollution control', *International Organization*, 43(3): 377–403.

—   (1992) 'Introduction: epistemic communities and international policy coordination', *International Organization*, 46(1): 1–35.

Habermas, J. (1994) *Faktizität und Geltung: Beiträge zur Diskurstheorie des Rechts und des demokratischen Rechtsstaats*, 4th edn, Frankfurt am Main: Suhrkamp.

Hajer, M. A. (1995) *The Politics of Environmental Discourse: Ecological modernization and the policy process*, Oxford: Oxford University Press.

Halpin, D. (2001) 'Integrating conceptions of interest groups: towards a conceptual framework of sectional interest group imperatives', paper prepared for the European Consortium of Political Research General Conference, Kent, September 2001.

Halpin, D. R. (2006) 'The participatory and democratic potential and practice of interest groups: between solidarity and representation', *Public Administration*, 84(4): 919–40.

Hamilton, A. (1788) 'The federalist no. 78: the judiciary department', in A. Hamilton, J. Madison and J. Jay (2003) *The Federalist with Letters of 'Brutus'*, T. Ball (ed.), Cambridge: Cambridge University Press.

Hantrais, L. (2000) *Social Policy in the European Union*, 2nd edn, Basingstoke: Macmillan.

Hay, C. (2007) *Why We Hate Politics*, Cambridge: Polity Press.

Heidenreich, M. and Bischoff, G. (2008) 'The open method of co-ordination: a way to the Europeanization of social and employment policies?', *Journal of Common Market Studies*, 46(3): 497–532.

Heinelt, H. and Meinke-Brandmaier, B. (2006) 'Comparing civil society participation in European environmental policy and consumer protection', in S. Smismans (ed.) *Civil Society and Legitimate European Governance*, Cheltenham: Edward Elgar.

Héritier, A. and Lehmkuhl, D. (2011) 'New modes of governance and democratic accountability', *Government and Opposition*, 46(1): 126–44.

Hilson, C. (2006) 'EU citizenship and the principle of affectedness', in R. Bellamy, D. Castiglione and J. Shaw (eds) *Making European Citizens: Civic inclusion in a transnational context*, Basingstoke: Palgrave Macmillan.

Hintikka, K. A. (2009) 'Kansalaiset, liikehdinnät, puolueet ja internet', in R. Mickelsson (ed.) *Puolueiden tulevaisuus*, Helsinki: Suomen Oikeusministeriö. Online. Available http://www.om.fi/Etusivu/ Julkaisut/1247667717444 (accessed 21 March 2013).

Hirst, P. Q. (1993) 'Introduction', in P. Q. Hirst (ed.) *The Pluralist Theory of the State: Selected writings of G. D. H. Cole, J. N. Figgis, and H. J. Laski*, London: Routledge.

— (1994) *Associative Democracy: New forms of economic and social governance*, Amherst: Massachusetts University Press.

— (2000) 'Democracy and governance', in J. Pierre (ed.) *Debating Governance*, Oxford: Oxford University Press.

Hix, S. (2005) *The Political System of the European Union*, 2nd edn, Basingstoke: Palgrave Macmillan.

Holzinger, K. (2004) 'Bargaining through arguing: an empirical analysis based on speech act theory', *Political Communication*, 21(2): 195–222.

Houseman, G. L. (1979) *G. D. H. Cole*, Boston: Twayne.

Hüller, T. and Kohler-Koch, B. (2008) 'Assessing the democratic value of civil society engagement in the European Union', in B. Kohler-Koch, D. de Bièvre and W. Maloney (eds) *Opening EU-Governance to Civil Society: Gains and challenges*, Mannheim: CONNEX. Online. Available http:// www.mzes.uni-mannheim.de/projekte/typo3/site/fileadmin/BookSeries/ Volume_Five/Chapter07_H%FCller_BKK.pdf (accessed 21 March 2013).

Imber, M. F. (1984) 'Re-reading Mitrany: a pragmatic assessment of sovereignty', *Review of International Studies*, 10(2): 103–23.

Immergut, E. M. (1995) 'An institutional critique of associative democracy', in J. Cohen and J. Rogers (eds) *Associations and Democracy: The real utopias project*, vol. I, London: Verso.

Jachtenfuchs, M., Diez, T. and Jung, S. (1998) 'Which Europe? Conflicting models of a legitimate European political order', *European Journal of International Relations*, 4(4): 409–45.

Jacobsson, K. (2004) 'Soft regulation and the subtle transformation of states: the case of EU employment policy', *Journal of European Social Policy*, 14(4): 355–70.

Johansson, H. (2012) 'Whom do they represent? Mixed modes of representation in EU-based CSOs', in S. Kröger and D. Friedrich (eds) *The Challenge of Democratic Representation in the European Union*, Basingstoke: Palgrave Macmillan.

Kangas, A. (2007) *The Knight, the Beast and the Treasure: A semeiotic inquiry into the Finnish political imaginary on Russia, 1918–1930s*, Tampere: Tampere University Press.

Kant, I. (1795) *Zum ewigen Frieden: ein philosophischer Entwurf*, textlog.de. Online. Available http://www.textlog.de/kant_frieden.html (accessed 21 March 2013).
— ([1781] 2008) *The Critique of Pure Reason*, trans. J. M. D. Meiklejohn. Forgotten Books. Online. Available http://www.forgottenbooks. org/info/Critique_Pure_Reason_Trlxslatxd_from_the_German_ Reason_1000144859.php (accessed 21 March 2013).
Keane, J. (2003) *Global Civil Society?*, Cambridge: Cambridge University Press.
Klatt, J. (2010) '"Mehr Demokratie" nur für Einige?', Göttinger Institut für Demokratieforschung. Online. Available http://www.demokratie-goettingen. de/blog/„mehr-demokratie"-nur-fur-einige/ (accessed 21 March 2013).
Klein, R. and O'Higgins, M. (1985) 'Social policy after incrementalism', in R. Klein and M. O'Higgins (eds) *The Future of Welfare*, Oxford: Basil Blackwell.
Kohler-Koch, B. (1999) 'The evolution and transformation of European governance', in B. Kohler-Koch and R. Eising (eds) *The Transformation of Governance in the European Union*, London: Routledge.
— (2000) 'Framing: the bottleneck of constructing legitimate institutions', *Journal of European Public Policy*, 7(4): 513–31.
— (2006) 'Research on EU governance: insight from a stock-taking exercise', *Connex Newsletter* 3: 4–6. Online. Available http://www. mzes.uni-mannheim.de/projekte/typo3/site/fileadmin/newsletter/3nd-Newsletter.pdf (accessed 21 March 2013).
— (2007) 'The organization of interests and democracy in the European Union', in B. Kohler-Koch and B. Rittberger (eds) *Debating the Democratic Legitimacy of the European Union*, Lanham: Rowman & Littlefield.
— (2008) 'Civil society contribution to democratic governance: a critical assessment', in B. Kohler-Koch, D. de Bièvre and W. Maloney (eds) *Opening EU-Governance to Civil Society: Gains and challenges*, Mannheim: CONNEX. Online. Available http://www.mzes.uni-mannheim.de/projekte/typo3/site/fileadmin/BookSeries/Volume_Five/ Introduction_II_BKK.pdf (accessed 21 March 2013).
— (2010a) 'Civil society and EU democracy: "astroturf" representation?', *Journal of European Public Policy*, 17(1): 100–16.
— (2010b) 'How to put matters right? Assessing the role of civil society in EU accountability', *West European Politics*, 33(5): 1117–41.
Kohler-Koch, B. and Rittberger, B. (2006) 'Review article: the "governance turn" in EU studies', *Journal of Common Market Studies*, 44(1): 27–49.
Kooiman, J. (2000) 'Societal governance: levels, modes, and orders of social-political interaction', in J. Pierre (ed.) *Debating Governance: Authority, steering, and democracy*, Oxford: Oxford University Press.
Kröger, S. (2007) 'The end of democracy as we know it? The legitimacy deficits of bureaucratic social policy governance', *Journal of European Integration*, 29(5): 565–82.

— (2008) 'Nothing but consultation: the place of organised civil society in EU policy-making across policies', *European Governance Papers*, No. C-08–03. Online. Available http://ceses.cuni.cz/CESES-136-version1-7B_NMG_civil_society_nothing_but_consultation_kroger.pdf (accessed 21 March 2013).

— (2009) 'The open method of coordination: underconceptualisation, overdetermination, de-politisation and beyond', *European Integration online Papers (EIoP)*, 13(5). Online. Available http://eiop.or.at/eiop/texte/2009-005a.htm (accessed 21 March 2013).

Kröger, S. and Friedrich, D. (2012) 'Political representation in the EU: a second transformation?', in S. Kröger and D. Friedrich (eds) *The Challenge of Democratic Representation in the European Union*, Basingstoke: Palgrave Macmillan.

— (eds) (2012) *The Challenge of Democratic Representation in the European Union*, Basingstoke: Palgrave Macmillan.

Laffan, B. (2002) 'The European Commission: promoting EU governance', in J. R. Grote and B. Gbikpi (eds) *Participatory Governance: Political and societal implications*, Opladen: Leske & Budrich.

Laffan, B. and Shaw, C. (2005) 'Classifying and mapping OMC in different policy areas', *NewGov: New Modes of Governance Project*, ref. 02/D09. Online. Available http://www.eu-newgov.org/database/DELIV/D02D09_Classifying_and_Mapping_OMC.pdf (accessed 21 March 2013).

Lascoumes, P. and Le Galès, P. (2007) 'Introduction: understanding public policy through its instruments – from the nature of instruments to the sociology of public policy instrumentation', *Governance*, 20(1): 1–21.

Lefort, C. (1988) *Democracy and Political Theory*, Cambridge: Polity Press.

Leo XIII (1891) *Rerum novarum*, encyclical of Pope Leo XIII on capital and labour. Online. Available http://www.vatican.va/holy_father/leo_xiii/encyclicals/documents/hf_l-xiii_enc_15051891_rerum-novarum_en.html (accessed 21 March 2013).

Lipset, S. M. (1960) *Political Man: The social bases of politics*, Garden City, NY: Doubleday & Company.

Lord, C. and Pollak, J. (2010) 'The EU's many representative modes: colliding? cohering?', *Journal of European Public Policy*, 17(1): 117–36.

Luban, D. (1996) 'The publicity principle', in R. E. Goodin (ed.) *The Theory of Institutional Design*, Cambridge: Cambridge University Press.

Magnette, P. (2003) 'European governance and civic participation: beyond elitist citizenship?', *Political Studies*, 51(1): 144–60.

— (2007) 'A comment on Heinelt and Greven', in B. Kohler-Koch and B. Rittberger (eds) *Debating the Democratic Legitimacy of the European Union*, Lanham: Rowman & Littlefield.

Majone, G. (1998) 'Europe's "democratic deficit": the question of standards', *European Law Journal*, 4(1): 5–28.

Maloney, W. A. (2008) 'The professionalization of representation: biasing participation', in B. Kohler-Koch, D. de Bièvre and W. Maloney (eds) *Opening
EU-Governance to Civil Society: Gains and challenges*, Mannheim:
CONNEX. Online. Available http://www.mzes.uni-mannheim.de/pro-
jekte/typo3/site/fileadmin/BookSeries/Volume_Five/Chapter03_Malo-
ney.pdf (accessed 21 March 2013).

Maloney, W. A., Jordan, G. and McLaughlin, A. M. (1994) 'Insider groups and
public policy: the insider/outsider model revisited', *Journal of Public
Policy*, 14(1): 17–38.

Manin, B. (1985) 'Volonté générale ou délibération: esquisse d'une théorie
générale de la délibération politique', *Le Débat*, 33: 72–93. Translated by
E. Stein and J. Mansbridge as 'On legitimacy and political deliberation',
Political Theory, 15(3): 338–68 (1987).

—   (1997) *The Principles of Representative Government*, Cambridge:
Cambridge University Press.

Manin, B., Przeworski, A. and Stokes, S. C. (1999) 'Introduction', in A. Przeworski, S. C. Stokes and B. Manin (eds) *Democracy, Accountability, and
Representation*, Cambridge: Cambridge University Press.

Mansbridge, J. (1999) 'Should blacks represent blacks and women represent
women? A contingent "yes"', *The Journal of Politics*, 61(3): 628–57.

—   (2003) 'Rethinking representation', *American Political Science Review*,
97(4): 515–28.

March, J. G. and Olsen, J. P. (1995) *Democratic Governance*, New York: The Free
Press.

Matsaganis, M. and Tsakloglou, P. (2001) 'Social exclusion and social policy
in Greece', in D. G. Mayes, J. Berghman and R. Salais (eds) *Social
Exclusion and European Policy*, Cheltenham: Edward Elgar.

Mayes, D. G. (2001) 'Introduction', in D. G. Mayes, J. Berghman and R. Salais
(eds) *Social Exclusion and European Policy*, Cheltenham: Edward
Elgar.

Mazey, S. and Richardson, J. (1994) 'The Commission and the lobby', in G.
Edwards and D. Spence (eds) *The European Commission*, London:
Cartermill.

Mill, J. S. (1991) *On Liberty and other Essays*, Oxford: Oxford University Press.

Mitrany, D. ([1954] 1966a) 'An advance in democratic representation', in D.
Mitrany, *A Working Peace System*, Chicago: Quadrangle Books.

—   (1966b) 'The prospect of European integration: federal or functional', in
D. Mitrany, *A Working Peace System*, Chicago: Quadrangle Books.

—   (1966c) 'A working peace system', in D. Mitrany *A Working Peace
System*, Chicago: Quadrangle Books.

—   (1975a) 'A political theory for the new society', in A. J. R. Groom and
P. Taylor (eds) *Functionalism: Theory and practice in international
relations*, London: University of London Press.

— (1975b) 'Retrospect and prospect', in D. Mitrany *The Functional Theory of Politics*, London: Robertson.

Navari, C. (1995) 'David Mitrany and international functionalism', in D. Long and P. Wilson (eds) *Thinkers of the Twenty Years' Crisis: Inter-war idealism reassessed*, Oxford: Oxford University Press.

Nicol, D. (2010) *The Constitutional Protection of Capitalism*, Oxford: Hart Publishing.

Offe, C. (2003) 'The European model of "social" capitalism: can it survive European integration?', *Journal of Political Philosophy*, 11(4): 437–69.

Olson, M. Jr. (1965) *The Logic of Collective Action: Public goods and the theory of groups*, Harvard Economic Studies, vol. CXXIV, Cambridge, MA: Harvard University Press.

O'Neill, J. (2001) 'Representing people, representing nature, representing the world', *Environment and Planning C: Government and Policy*, 19(4): 483–500.

Orwell, G. (1946) *Politics and the English Language*. Online. Available http://www.mtholyoke.edu/acad/intrel/orwell46.htm (accessed 22 March 2013).

Page, E. C. (2010) 'Accountability as a bureaucratic minefield: lessons from a comparative study', *West European Politics*, 33(5): 1010–29.

Palier, B. (2008) 'The EU as a cognitive and normative entrepreneur: the Europeanization of welfare reforms', in R. Dehousse and L. Boussaguet (eds) *The Transformation of EU Policies: EU governance at work*, Mannheim: CONNEX. Online. Available http://www.mzes.uni-mannheim.de/projekte/typo3/site/fileadmin/BookSeries/Volume_eight/Chapter%202.pdf (accessed 22 March 2013).

Palola, E. (2006) 'Sosiaalipolitiikka muutosprojektina: analyysi Euroopan komission tiedonantojen modernisaatiodiskurssista', *Janus*, 14(4): 372–88.

— (2007) *Näkökulmia Eurooppalaiseen sosiaalipolitiikkaan: malli, väestö, resurssit ja kommunikaatio*, Helsinki: Stakes.

Palonen, K. (2009) '"Demokratiapolitiikka": demokratian epäpolitisointia: reunahuomautuksia oikeusministeriön keskusteluasiakirjaan "Demokratiapolitiikan suuntaviivat"', *Politiikka*, 51(2): 146–50.

Papadopoulos, Y. (2007) 'Problems of democratic accountability in network and multilevel governance', *European Law Journal*, 13(4): 469–86.

— (2010) 'Accountability and multi-level governance: more accountability, less democracy?', *West European Politics*, 33(5): 1030–49.

Perelman, C. (1982) *The Realm of Rhetoric*, Notre Dame, IN: University of Notre Dame Press.

Perelman, C. and Olbrechts-Tyteca, L. ([1958] 1969) *The New Rhetoric: A treatise on argumentation*, trans. J. Wilkinson and P. Weaver: Notre Dame, IN: University of Notre Dame Press.

Peters, B. G. and Pierre, J. (2004) 'Multi-level governance and democracy: A Faustian bargain?', in I. Bache and M. Flinders (eds) *Multi-Level Governance*, Oxford: Oxford University Press.

— (2006) 'Governance, accountability and democratic legitimacy', in A. Benz and Y. Papadopoulos (eds) *Governance and Democracy: Comparing national, European and international experiences*, London: Routledge.

Pfister, T. (2009) 'Governing the knowledge society: studying Lisbon as epistemic setting', *European Integration online Papers (EIoP)*, 13(6). Online. Available http://eiop.or.at/eiop/texte/2009-006a.htm (accessed 22 March 2013).

Phillips, A. (1995) *The Politics of Presence*, Oxford: Oxford University Press.

— 1998) 'Democracy and representation: or, why should it matter who our representatives are?', in A. Phillips (ed.) *Feminism and Politics*, Oxford: Oxford University Press.

— (2004) 'Defending equality of outcome', *The Journal of Political Philosophy*, 12(1): 1–19.

Pierre, J. (2000a) 'Introduction: understanding governance', in J. Pierre (ed.) *Debating Governance: Authority, steering, and democracy*, Oxford: Oxford University Press.

— (2000b) 'Conclusions: governance beyond state strength', in J. Pierre (ed.) *Debating Governance: Authority, steering, and democracy*, Oxford: Oxford University Press.

— (ed.) (2000) *Debating Governance: Authority, steering, and democracy*, Oxford: Oxford University Press.

Pitkin, H. F. (1967) *The Concept of Representation*, Berkeley: University of California Press.

Pius XI (1931) *Quadragesimo anno*, encyclical of Pope Pius XI on reconstruction of the social order. Online. Available http://www.vatican.va/holy_father/pius_xi/encyclicals/documents/hf_p-xi_enc_19310515_quadragesimo-anno_en.html (accessed 22 March 2013).

Plotke, D. (1997) 'Representation is democracy', *Constellations*, 4(1): 19–34.

Pollak, J., Bátora, J., Mokre, M., Sigalas, E. and Slominski, P. (2009) 'On political representation: myths and challenges', RECON *Online Working Paper*. Online. Available http://www.reconproject.eu/main.php/RECON_wp_0903.pdf?fileitem=16662583 (accessed 22 March 2013).

Przeworski, A. (1999) 'Minimalist conception of democracy: a defense', in I. Shapiro and C. Hacker-Cordón (eds) *Democracy's Value*, Cambridge: Cambridge University Press.

Przeworski, A., Stokes, S. C. and Manin, B. (eds) (1999) *Democracy, Accountability, and Representation*, Cambridge: Cambridge University Press.

Quota Project (2013) 'Global database of quotas for women'. Online. Available http://www.quotaproject.org (accessed 8 February 2013).

Radaelli, C. M. (2000) 'Whither Europeanization? Concept stretching and substantive change', *European Integration online Papers (EIoP)*, 4(8). Online. Available http://eiop.or.at/eiop/texte/2000-008a.htm (accessed 22 March 2013).

—   (2003) *The Open Method of Coordination: A new governance architecture for the European Union?*, Rapport No. 1, Stockholm: Sieps. Online. Available http://www.sieps.se/sites/default/files/3-20031.pdf (accessed 22 March 2013).

Radaelli, C. M. and Schmidt, V. A. (2004) 'Conclusions', *West European Politics*, 27: 364–79.

Radulova, E. (2007) 'The OMC: an opaque method of consideration or deliberative governance in action?', *European Integration*, 29(3): 363–80.

—   (2009) 'The construction of EU's childcare policy through the open method of coordination', *European Integration online Papers (EIoP)*, 13(1). Online. Available http://eiop.or.at/eiop/index.php/eiop/article/view/2009_013a (accessed 22 March 2013).

Raunio, T. (2007) 'National parliaments and the future of European integration: learning to play the multilevel game', in J. DeBardeleben and A. Hurrelmann (eds) *Democratic Dilemmas of Multilevel Governance*, Basingstoke: Palgrave Macmillan.

Rawls, J. (1999) *A Theory of Justice*, Cambridge, MA: Belknap Press of Harvard University Press.

Rehfeld, A. (2006) 'Toward a general theory of political representation', *The Journal of Politics*, 68(1): 1–21.

Rein, M. and Schön, D. (1991) 'Frame-reflective policy discourse', in P. Wagner (ed.) *Social Sciences and Modern States: National experiences and theoretical crossroads*, Cambridge: Cambridge University Press.

Rhodes, R. A. W. (2000) 'Governance and public administration', in J. Pierre (ed.) *Debating Governance: Authority, steering, and democracy*, Oxford: Oxford University Press.

Richardson, J. (2007) 'A comment on Kohler-Koch', in B. Kohler-Koch and B. Rittberger (eds) *Debating the Democratic Legitimacy of the European Union*, Lanham: Rowman & Littlefield.

Rosanvallon, P. ([2006] 2008) *La contre-démocratie: la politique à l'age de la défiance*, Paris: Seuil. Translated by A. Goldhammer as *Counter-Democracy: Politics in an age of distrust*, Cambridge: Cambridge University Press (2008).

—   ([2008] 2010) *La légitimité démocratique: impartialité, réflexivité, proximité*. Paris: Seuil. Translated by A. Goldhammer as *Democratic Legitimacy: Impartiality, reflexivity, proximity*, Princeton: Princeton University Press (2011).

Rozenberg, O. (2011) 'Debating about Europe at the French National Assembly: the failure of the rhetoric of unanimity', in C. Wiesner, T. Turkka and K. Palonen (eds) *Parliament and Europe: Rhetorical and conceptual studies on their contemporary connections*, Baden-Baden: Nomos.

Ruggie, J. G. (1993) 'Territoriality and beyond: problematizing modernity in international relations', *International Organization*, 47(1): 139–74.

Ruzza, C. (2002) '"Frame bridging" and the new politics of persuasion, advocacy and influence', in A. Warleigh and J. Fairbrass (eds) *Influence and Interests in the European Union: The new politics of persuasion and advocacy*, London: Europa Publications.

— (2004) *Europe and Civil Society: Movement coalitions and European governance*, Manchester: Manchester University Press.

— (2006) 'European institutions and the policy discourse of organised civil society', in S. Smismans (ed.) *Civil Society and Legitimate European Governance*, Cheltenham: Edward Elgar.

Sabel, C. F. and Zeitlin, J. (2008) 'Learning from difference: the new architecture of experimentalist governance in the EU', *European Law Journal*, 14(3): 271–327.

Sanders, L. M. (1997) 'Against deliberation', *Political Theory*, 25(3): 347–76.

Sapiro, V. (1981) 'When are interests interesting? The problem of political representation of women', *American Political Science Review*, 75(3): 701–16.

Sartori, G. (1987) *The Theory of Democracy Revisited. Pt. 1, The Contemporary Debate*, Chatham, N J: Chatham House.

Saurugger, S. (2006) 'The professionalisation of interest representation: a legitimacy problem for civil society in the EU?', in S. Smismans (ed.) *Civil Society and Legitimate European Governance*, Cheltenham: Edward Elgar.

— (2007) 'Democratic "misfit"? Conceptions of civil society participation in France and in the European Union', *Political Studies*, 55(2): 384–404.

— (2008) 'The social construction of the "participatory turn": the European Union and "organised civil society"', in R. Dehousse and L. Boussaguet (eds) *The Transformation of EU Policies – EU Governance at Work*, Mannheim: CONNEX. Online. Available http://www.mzes.uni-mannheim.de/projekte/typo3/site/fileadmin/BookSeries/Volume_eight/Chapter%206.pdf (accessed 22 March 2013).

Saward, M. (2000) 'A critique of Held', in B. Holden (ed.) *Global Democracy: Key debates*, London: Routledge.

— (2005) 'Governance and the transformation of political representation', in J. Newman (ed.) *Remaking Governance: Peoples, politics and the public sphere*, Bristol: Policy Press. Online. Available http://oro.open.ac.uk/16392/1/GovernanceAndThe.pdf (accessed 22 March 2013).

— (2006) 'The representative claim', *Contemporary Political Theory*, 5(3): 297–318.

— (2009) 'Authorisation and authenticity: representation and the unelected', *The Journal of Political Philosophy*, 17(1): 1–22.

— (2010) *The Representative Claim*, Oxford: Oxford University Press.

— (2011) 'Slow theory: taking time over transnational democratic representation', *Ethics & Global Politics*, 4(1): 1–18.

Sbragia, A. (2000) 'The European Union as coxswain: governance by steering', in J. Pierre (ed.) *Debating Governance*, Oxford: Oxford University Press.

Schäfer, A. (2006) 'Resolving deadlock: why international organisations introduce soft law', *European Law Journal*, 12(2): 194–208.

Scharpf, F. W. ([1970] 1975) *Demokratietheorie zwischen Utopie und Anpassung*, Kronberg/Ts.: Scriptor.

—   (1999) *Governing in Europe: Effective and democratic?*, Oxford: Oxford University Press.

Schimmelfennig, F. (2001) 'The community trap: liberal norms, rhetorical action, and the eastern enlargement of the European Union', *International Organization*, 55(1): 47–80.

Schmidt, V. A. (2006) *Democracy in Europe: The EU and national polities*, Oxford: Oxford University Press.

—   (2008) 'Discursive institutionalism: the explanatory power of ideas and discourse', *Annual Review of Political Science*, 11(1): 303–26.

Schmidt, V. A. and Radaelli, C. M. (2002) 'Europeanisation, discourse and policy change: mapping the new research agenda', paper presented at the European Consortium of Political Research Joint Sessions, Turin, March 2002.

—   (2004) 'Policy change and discourse in Europe: conceptual and methodological issues', *West European Politics*, 27(2): 183–210.

Schmitter, P. C. (1979) 'Still the century of corporatism?', in P. Schmitter and G. Lehmbruch (eds) *Trends Toward Corporatist Intermediation*, Beverly Hills: Sage.

—   2001) 'Parties are not what they once were', in L. Diamond and R. Gunther (eds) *Political Parties and Democracy*, Baltimore: The John Hopkins University Press.

—   (2002) 'Participation in governance arrangements: is there any reason to expect it will achieve "sustainable and innovative policies in a multi-level context"?', in J. R. Grote and B. Gbikpi (eds) *Participatory Governance: Political and societal implications*, Opladen: Leske & Budrich.

—   (2007) *Political Accountability in "Real-Existing" Democracies: Meaning and mechanisms*, European University Institute. Online. Available http://www.eui.eu/Documents/DepartmentsCentres/SPS/Profiles/Schmitter/PCSPoliticalAccountabilityJan07.pdf (accessed 22 March 2013).

Schmitter, P. C. and Streeck, W. (1999) 'The organisation of business interests: studying the associative action of business in advanced industrial societies', MPIfG discussion paper, No. 99/1, Köln: Max-Planck-Institut für Gesellschaftsforschung.

Schwarzmantel, J. (2008) *Ideology and Politics*, Los Angeles: Sage.

Scott, J. and Trubek, D. M. (2002) 'Mind the gap: law and new approaches to governance in the European Union', *European Law Journal*, 8(1): 1–18.

Seitz, B. (1995) *The Trace of Political Representation*, Albany: State University of New York Press.

Setälä, M. (2003) *Demokratian arvo: teoriat, käytännöt ja mahdollisuudet*, Helsinki: Gaudeamus.

— (2009) 'Rhetoric and deliberative democracy', *Redescriptions*, 13: 61–82.

Sieyès, E. -J. (1789) *Qu'est-ce que le Tiers-Etat?*, S.l.: s.n. Online. Available http:// gallica.bnf.fr/ark:/12148/bpt6k47521t/f1.image.r=.langFR (accessed 22 March 2013).

Skinner, Q. (2002) *Visions of Politic, Vol. I: Regarding Method*, Cambridge: Cambridge University Press.

Smismans, S. (2003) 'European civil society: shaped by discourses and institutional interests', *European Law Journal*, 9(4): 473–95.

— (2004) *Law, Legitimacy, and European Governance: Functional participation in social regulation*, Oxford: Oxford University Press.

— (2006) 'Civil society and European governance: from concepts to research agenda', in S. Smismans (ed.) *Civil Society and Legitimate European Governance*, Cheltenham: Edward Elgar.

— (2007) 'New Governance – the solution for active European citizenship, or the end of citizenship?', *Columbia Journal of European Law*, 13(3): 1–28.

Sørensen, E. (2002) 'Democratic theory and network governance', *Administrative Theory & Praxis*, 24(4): 693–720.

Sudbery, I. (2003) 'Bridging the legitimacy gap in the EU: can civil society help to bring the Union closer to its citizens?', *Collegium*, 26: 75–95.

Summa, H. (1996) 'Kolme näkökulmaa uuteen retoriikkaan', in K. Palonen and H. Summa (eds) *Pelkkää retoriikkaa*, Tampere: Vastapaino.

Sunstein, C. R. (1991) 'Preferences and politics', *Philosophy and Public Affairs*, 20(1): 3–34.

Tanasescu, I. (2009) *The European Commission and Interest Groups: Towards a deliberative interpretation of stakeholder involvement in EU policy-making*, Brussels: Brussels University Press.

Taylor, C. (1992) 'The politics of recognition', in A. Gutmann (ed.) *Multiculturalism and 'The Politics of Recognition'*, Princeton: Princeton University Press.

Taylor, P. (1990) 'Functionalism: the approach of David Mitrany', in A. J. R. Groom and P. Taylor (eds) *Frameworks for International Co-operation*, London: Pinter.

Thiery, P. (2005) 'Zivilgesellschaft', in D. Nohlen and R.-O. Schulze (eds) *Lexikon der Politikwissenschaft: Theorien, Methoden, Begriffe*, München: C. H. Beck.

Thompson, D. F. (1980) 'Moral responsibility of public officials: the problem of many hands', *American Political Science Review*, 74(5): 905–16.

Trenz, H. -J. (2009) 'European civil society: between participation, representation and discourse', *Policy and Society*, 28(1): 35–46.

Trubek, D. M. and Trubek, L. G. (2005) 'The open method of coordination and the debate over "hard" and "soft" law', in J. Zeitlin and P. Pochet (eds) with L. Magnusson, *The Open Method of Co-ordination in Action: The European employment and social inclusion strategies*, Brussels: Peter Lang.

Tsakatika, M. (2007) 'A parliamentary dimension for EU soft governance', *Journal of European Integration*, 29(5): 549–64.

Urbinati, N. (2000) 'Representation as advocacy: a study of democratic deliberation', *Political Theory*, 28(6): 758–86.

— (2006) *Representative Democracy: Principles and genealogy*, Chicago: The University of Chicago Press.

Urbinati, N. and Warren, M. E. (2008) 'The concept of representation in contemporary democratic theory', *Annual Review of Political Science*, 11(1): 387–412.

Usui, Y. (2007) 'The democratic quality of soft governance in the EU Sustainable Development Strategy: a deliberative deficit', *Journal of European Integration*, 29(5): 619–33.

Vickers, B. (1989) *In Defence of Rhetoric*, Oxford: Clarendon Press.

Vleminckx, K. and Berghman, J. (2001) 'Social exclusion and the welfare state: an overview of conceptual issues and policy implications', in D. G. Mayes, J. Berghman and R. Salais (eds) *Social Exclusion and European Policy*, Cheltenham: Edward Elgar.

Wälti, S. and Kübler, D. (2003) '"New governance" and associative pluralism: the case of drug policy in Swiss cities', *The Policy Studies Journal*, 31(4): 499–525.

Wälti, S., Kübler, D. and Papadopoulos, Y. (2004) 'How democratic is "governance"? Lessons from Swiss drug policy', *Governance: An International Journal of Policy, Administration, and Institutions*, 17(1): 83–113.

Warleigh, A. (2001) '"Europeanizing" civil society: NGOs as agents of political socialization', *Journal of Common Market Studies*, 39(4): 619–39.

Warren, M. E. (2009) 'Governance-driven democratization', *Critical Policy Studies*, 3(1): 3–13.

Weale, A. (2011) 'New modes of governance, political accountability and public reason', *Government and Opposition*, 46(1): 58–80.

Whelan, F. G. (1983) 'Prologue: democratic theory and the boundary problem', in R. J. Pennock and J. W. Chapman (eds) *Liberal Democracy: Nomos XXV*, New York: New York University Press.

Williams, M. S. (1998) *Voice, Trust, and Memory: Marginalized groups and the failings of liberal representation*, Princeton: Princeton University Press.

Wittgenstein, L. ([1953] 2001) *Philosophical Investigations: The German text, with a revised English translation*, trans. G. E. M. Anscombe. Malden: Blackwell Publishing.

van Deth, J. W. (2008) 'European Civil Society: The empirical reality on the multi-level system of the EU', in B. Kohler-Koch, D. de Bièvre and W. Maloney (eds) *Opening EU-Governance to Civil Society: Gains and challenges*, Mannheim: CONNEX. Online. Available http://www.mzes. uni-mannheim.de/projekte/typo3/site/fileadmin/BookSeries/Volume_ Five/Chapter14_van%20Deth.pdf (accessed 21 March 2013).

van Deth, J. W. and Maloney, W. (2008) 'Is local civil society conductive [sic] to European participatory engineering?', in B. Kohler-Koch, D. de Bièvre and W. Maloney (eds) *Opening EU-Governance to Civil Society: Gains and challenges*, Mannheim: CONNEX. Online. Available http://www.mzes.uni-mannheim.de/projekte/typo3/site/fileadmin/BookSeries/Volume_Five/Chapter10_van%20Deth-Maloney.pdf (accessed 21 March 2013).

von Gierke, O. ([1868/1873] 1990) *Community in Historical Perspective*, A. Black (ed.) , Cambridge: Cambridge University Press.

von Wright, G. H. (1963) 'Practical inference', *The Philosophical Review*, 72(2): 159–79.

Young, I. M. (1990) *Justice and the Politics of Difference*, Princeton: Princeton University Press.

—— (1997) 'Deferring group representation', in I. Shapiro and W. Kymlicka (eds) *Nomos XXXIX: Ethnicity and Group Rights*, New York: New York University Press.

—— (2000) *Inclusion and Democracy*, Oxford: Oxford University Press.

Zeitlin, J. and Pochet, P. (eds) with Magnusson, L. (2005) *The Open Method of Co-ordination in Action: The European employment and social inclusion strategies*, Brussels: Peter Lang.

Index

Lightning Source UK Ltd.
Milton Keynes UK
UKOW07f1914201114

241927UK00003B/100/P